New Monasticism
and the Transformation
of American Evangelicalism

New Monasticism and the Transformation of American Evangelicalism

WES MARKOFSKI

OXFORD
UNIVERSITY PRESS

OXFORD
UNIVERSITY PRESS

Oxford University Press is a department of the University of Oxford.
It furthers the University's objective of excellence in research, scholarship,
and education by publishing worldwide. Oxford is a registered trade mark
of Oxford University Press in the UK and in certain other countries.

Published in the United States of America by
Oxford University Press
198 Madison Avenue, New York, NY 10016,
United States of America

© Oxford University Press 2015

Cataloging-in-Publication Data is on file at the Library of Congress.

9780190236496 (hbk.)
9780190258016 (pbk.)

1 3 5 7 9 8 6 4 2

Printed in the United States of America on acid free paper

*For Neel—my ideal partner and best friend
in the big adventure—with all my love.*

Contents

Acknowledgments   ix

1. Introduction: A New Evangelicalism?   I

PART I: *Neo-Monasticism and American Evangelicalism*

2. Evangelical Religion and Politics in the Twentieth Century   31
3. Neo-Monasticism and the Field of American Evangelicalism   70

PART II: *The Urban Monastery*

4. Belief and Meaning in an Urban Monastery   161
5. Politics and Religion in an Urban Monastery   194
6. Organizing Community for Holistic Mission: An Urban
    Monastery in Action   225

7. Conclusion: The Transformation of American Evangelicalism   275

Appendix   289
Notes   297
References   339
Index   359

Acknowledgments

I WOULD FIRST like to thank the leaders and participants of the Urban Monastery and other neo-monastic communities for sharing their lives, time, passion, insight, and experiences with me throughout the research process. This book could not have been written without you. Many thanks as well to the gentlemen at North Downs for their hospitality and good humor while hosting our nomadic family during an extended season of manuscript writing.

I owe an enormous debt to Mustafa Emirbayer, my mentor at the University of Wisconsin—Madison, for his guidance and enthusiasm for this project from the very beginning. If, as Bourdieu famously observed, the discipline of sociology may be best likened to a craft, then Mustafa's excellence as a master craftsman is surpassed only by his skill in passing on the craft to those of us who have had the good fortune to spend time as his apprentices.

In addition to Mustafa, I would also like to thank Phil Gorski, Pam Oliver, Matt Desmond, Chad Goldberg, Christian Smith, and the three anonymous reviewers at Oxford University Press for reading and offering invaluable comments on the manuscript in its various stages. Whatever problems remain, this book has benefitted enormously from their expertise and critical engagement. Thanks to Felix Elwert for reminding me to "make sure it's interesting to read!"—a charge I have tried my best to live up to. Thanks also to Erik Wright and the fine participants of the 2008 Conference on Envisioning Real Utopias for their enthusiasm and comments on an early version of this research.

Many thanks as well to Jake Myszka, Tim Collier, Jeremy Kroening, Justin Markofski, Hans Obma, Halena Ernst, and Josh Thurow for their friendship and feedback throughout the long writing process. Wayne Becker, Matyas Sandor, Rick Richardson, Camille Banks, and the Guthrie clan of Nopiming deserve special thanks for their great encouragement and irreplaceable contributions to my personal and intellectual development over the years.

I am incredibly grateful to my editor at Oxford University Press, Cynthia Read, for her enthusiasm and expertise in guiding this project toward completion. Thanks for deciding to take a chance on a first-time author. Thanks as well to Gina Chung and Cherline Daniel for their gracious and diligent work in helping prepare the manuscript for publication, and to all of the other fine individuals at Oxford whose work has contributed to this book's publication.

Last, but certainly not least, I would like to thank my mom, Abby Witter, for her incredible strength, love, and belief in me for as long as I can remember. I owe you my life. Thanks also to my father, Daniel Markofski, for his love and encouragement in this endeavor, and to Rita Malhotra for her longstanding generosity and support. Words cannot express how grateful I am to share this journey with Neel Malhotra Markofski, my wife and best friend, whose love and creativity fills my life with beauty; and with our two daughters, Kaia Eliana and Natasha Dochás, whose presence and personalities are an endless fount of joy and delight. You are my great loves.

Soli Deo gloria.

New Monasticism
and the Transformation
of American Evangelicalism

Chapter 1

Introduction
A New Evangelicalism?

DEVON IS A former Manhattan party promoter and international model who became serious about following Christ while on a photo shoot in Milan, Italy. Lilith is a critically acclaimed fine artist with an Ivy League MFA and a working studio in the Urban Monastery. Elle is a former homecoming queen, medical student, and second-generation civil rights activist. Manuel is a Brazilian soccer player with long black dreads whose mother grew up in a socialist commune. Jason is a former analyst for the Federal Reserve on his way to an MBA program at Harvard's Kennedy School of Government, hoping to devote his professional life to fighting global poverty and inequality as a policy advisor in developing countries. Two women in their late twenties travel the world as leaders in a national Christian organization—frequently facing resistance from the white male-dominated world of evangelical leadership—while also serving local victims of human sex trafficking and mobilizing university students to become anti-trafficking activists. Jessica is a Cuban-Russian-Jewish art school graduate and urban gallery manager who "loathed George Bush" and had an "easy" time voting for Obama in the 2008 presidential election. All are under the age of 35, all are leaders or active participants in the Urban Monastery, and all are evangelical Christians.

As unlikely as the personal profiles of these and many of the other 150 participants in the Urban Monastery appear compared to typical representations of American evangelicals, the place they meet on Sunday for worship seems equally unlikely. Located in the urban core of a major Midwestern city, the Urban Monastery occupies three floors of an old industrial building that sits next to a porn shop, directly across the street from a popular nightclub with a predominately African American clientele, on a block dominated by three payday loan offices, a pawn shop, and vacant buildings covered in graffiti, broken windows, and boarded doors. Foot traffic in the neighborhood surrounding the Urban Monastery, which is located two blocks west of the street that unofficially divides black from white in this highly segregated city,

is racially diverse. A local pharmacy that sits kitty-corner to the Urban Monastery has vigilant on-site security officers guarding the door. As I return to the
Urban Monastery on Friday evening after an interview over a pint at the local
craft brew pub, I watch a pack of twenty young adults from the nearby art institute prance around a busy intersection, trying to attract passersby to an art
show in a gallery across the street. There is a good chance several of them
have spent time at the Urban Monastery, which hosts a large community of
artists and art students. They are dressed head-to-toe in bright pastel colors,
tight-fitting spandex body suits, and a wild assortment of hats, masks, wings,
glitter, and exotic make-up. Their movements are indecipherable. Sitting at
the corner bus stop across the street, six middle-aged African American men
watch them with what looks like a mixture of incredulity, bemusement, and
boredom.

Later that night, a line forms outside the nightclub across the street from
Urban Monastery, waiting to pass through a metal detector and be patted
down by security before disappearing into the bass-thumping darkness. As
night passes, small bands of revelers wander down the center of the largely
deserted street, apparently high or intoxicated. When morning arrives, a short
ten-minute walk leads to a trendy café, restaurant, and bar district frequented
by university students and young professionals. An indie coffee shop is packed
at 11:00 a.m. with skinny, tattooed, fashionable young adults sipping coffee
over conversations and laptops. On the walk back, I notice the door of a tiny
local public library branch, bristling with window bars and a large "No fire-
arms or weapons allowed" sign.

The Urban Monastery's geographic location exemplifies neo-monastic
evangelicals' commitment to combine the "inward breath of prayer with the
outward breath of social engagement" by establishing spiritual communities
that are "situated in 'the thick of the action,' wherever we can find the poor
and the lost."[1] Rather than remaining isolated in safe, suburban pockets of
evangelical subculture, neo-monastic communities like the Urban Monastery intentionally establish themselves in places where social needs are evident and the practice of Christian spirituality less common. The Justice
Monastery is located in a neighborhood notoriously known as "the poorest
postal code in North America," where the median income is less than 30 percent of the mean in its metropolitan area, 5,000 injection drug users reside
in a ten-block radius, HIV-positive and Hepatitis A rates are among the highest in the Western world, and the leading causes of death are drug overdoses
and suicides. The Arts and Homeless Youth Monastery runs a music venue,
art co-op, homeless outreach center, and transitional housing program with
vocational skills training in a diverse inner-city neighborhood in one of the
Midwest's largest cities. The Recovery Monastery provides mentoring and

housing for middle-aged men coming out of addiction in another poor urban neighborhood in the Midwest.

"Inhaling the breath of God" through prayer is central to the communal life of the Urban Monastery and other neo-monastic communities, where there is a spacious room available for people to pray 24 hours a day, 7 days a week.[2] Twenty or so sofas and chairs are scattered around the prayer room. Light bulbs hang from wires on the ceiling, white lights wrap around exposed silver water pipes, and overhead track lighting illuminates the drawings, pictures, and written prayers that cover all four walls of the prayer room. Numerous prayer stations around the perimeter of the room encourage guests to practice self-examination, confess sin, pray for the city, and write any words, images, or scripture that comes to mind while praying. A massive floor to ceiling world map occupies one wall of the prayer room, with pictures and information about short- and long-term mission projects connected to the Urban Monastery. A quote attributed to noted African American Harvard professor Cornel West—"Justice is what love looks like in public"—is written on the map near information about an upcoming trip to Thailand, where three Urban Monastery leaders are traveling to participate in anti-human trafficking work. A placard taped on the map explains the purpose of the trip and invites people to pray:

> *How we got involved in human trafficking in our city:*
> Over the last two years, some of us have become increasingly involved with an anti-trafficking coalition under the Department of Justice here in our city. Through our participation in this coalition, we have been able to serve a number of women after their rescue from trafficking situations, particularly from forced prostitution. Being able to see first-hand the devastating effects of trafficking on the lives of these victims is something that has compelled us to pursue the abolition of modern day slavery in all its forms, not only here in our city, but in other cities and nations as well.

> *Purpose: Why do we go?*
> 1. To get on-the-ground experience with what human trafficking looks like overseas, to be ones who not only talk about the suffering of others but who are willing to engage in it.
> 2. To minister to long-term missionaries who have given their lives to the enormous task of loving and serving women and children who are victims of human trafficking.
> 3. To explore what it would look like to help college students in the United States participate in the modern-day abolition movement.

Every six weeks the Urban Monastery holds a week of nonstop prayer, during which time members of the community sign up to pray in hourly shifts so that at least one person is praying in the prayer room every minute of that week.

Prayer is central to the common life of neo-monastic communities in general. They often have a permanent prayer room where community participants and others can go for personal spiritual reflection, as well as regular rhythms of nonstop, night-and-day prayer for periods ranging from one day to a week or more. The Justice Monastery began their first 24–7 prayer room with individual community members taking turns praying nonstop over the course of an entire year. From the windows of their prayer room in one of the many "slum hotels" in their inner-city neighborhood, Justice Monastery participants pray for the drug dealers and junkies working the streets, many of whom have become their friends. During their regular rhythms of nonstop prayer, the Recovery Monastery invites neighbors, community members, monastic interns, and neighborhood partners into their converted "prayer garage" in the backyard of a neighborhood home. As exemplified by these diverse expressions of personal and communal prayer, neo-monastic evangelicals expect the "inward breath" of prayer and communion with God to "exhale" or express itself in acts of hospitality, justice, creativity, and mission in both local and global contexts.

Ten young adults live in the central Urban Monastery building—five women and five men. Each of the two floors that they occupy has a large commercial-style kitchen and walk-in pantry with food and food supplies that suggest frequent cooking for large gatherings. The Urban Monastery's five male residents live on the fourth floor of the building, accessible via either a large industrial elevator or a narrow, rugged brick-enclosed metal stairway. On the men's flat, the rule for eating is "you find it, you eat it." The Urban Monastery hosts hundreds of visitors throughout the year. Devon—hospitality director for the Urban Monastery—takes pride in welcoming guests with an open, collectivist approach to sharing food and material resources. While inviting me to help myself to whatever food or drink I see in the pantry, he assures me that Urban Monastery residents "don't think of their stuff as *theirs,* but *ours.*"

I am one of four visitors sleeping at the Urban Monastery on this visit. One is a leader in another urban neo-monastic community a few hours away who is here on personal retreat. Two tall, tattooed young men are sprawled out on couches in the main living area. Both wear dark skinny jeans and grungy T-shirts—the informal uniform of the urban hipster-traveler set. Devon tells me their story: they are graffiti artists roaming the country, no permanent home, not Christians. While traveling through the city two years prior they found the Facebook profile of an Urban Monastery resident who shared similar tastes in music and art. They connected, were invited to sleep at the Urban Monastery while passing through and have done so numerous times since. Devon happily tells me that the last time they visited he saw one of them flipping through Devon's Bible, and that upon leaving they told him, "We love coming to this city because we love this place." They are conscientious of the communal spirit, washing their own dishes and having easy interactions with the many community members who flow in and out of the flat throughout the day.

Such visitors are common at the Urban Monastery, where local homeless men, university students, artists, visitors from other neo-monastic communities around the world, dumpster diving homeless youth who spend much of their time hitchhiking across the country on trains and automobiles, and curious Christians looking for alternative expressions of Christian spirituality are all regular guests. Providing hospitality to neighbors, travelers, and people in need is a common practice of neo-monastic communities. The Arts and Homeless Youth Monastery runs two transitional houses for young adults just released from the juvenile justice system, trying to get off the street, or recovering from drug or alcohol addictions; and who have sought help in finding employment, developing life skills, and growing in Christian spirituality. The Recovery Monastery hosts middle-aged men battling addictions in a gritty working-class neighborhood. The Justice Monastery runs a recovery house for young women, cleans rooms and connects with residents in the slum hotels where many of their poor neighbors live, and engages in public advocacy for clean affordable housing in the neighborhood at local government meetings. Neo-monastic communities engage their neighbors in multiple ways throughout the week, ranging from after-school programs and volunteer-staffed cafés to free community meals, events, and simple friendship.

The Urban Monastery's five female residents share the third floor of the building with the community prayer room and offices for the leaders of local and national ministry projects. A third floor bookshelf holds the following titles:

The End of Poverty
Freakonomics
The Purpose-Driven Life
Boundaries (Christian counseling)
Captivating (Christian inspiration)
Poverty of Welfare
Shaping History through Prayer and Fasting

Slaves to Fashion
3 old Bibles
2 copies of Shane Claiborne's *The Irresistible Revolution*
East Africa travel book
My Utmost for His Highest (a classic Christian text by Oswald
    Chambers)
Dress and Identity (two volumes)
2 Anne Lamont books
Memoirs of a Geisha
The Poisonwood Bible
The Vision and the Vow
The New Friars
Amazing Grace (Jonathon Kozol)
Mere Christianity, Chronicles of Narnia (C. S. Lewis)

Like the Urban Monastery itself, the bookshelf displays a rather odd and unexpected mixture of ideas and values regarding global poverty and economic inequality, fashion and identity, classic Christian literature, counseling and spiritual formation, megachurch and neo-monastic evangelicalism, and travel: with some acclaimed anti-colonialist literature that levels a withering critique of white Christian missionaries in Africa sprinkled in for good measure. Urban Monastery participants are not unaware of evangelical Christianity's poor reputation among America's creative and intellectual classes.

The Urban Monastery building feels gritty, spacious, industrial, urban, and effortlessly creative. Massive cylindrical concrete pillars speckled with green, black, burgundy, and beige paint flecks support high ceilings and offset antique red brick walls and dark, scuffed concrete floor. In addition to housing the Urban Monastery's male residents, the fourth floor is also where Lilith's art studio is located. A series of 8 x 10 foot canvases display her colorful, dynamic abstract paintings throughout the Urban Monastery, while massive white blank canvases lean against the wall outside her studio, awaiting transformation. Large black windows frame the downtown skyline forty blocks away. Community members visit throughout the day to talk, pray with, and observe the artist working in her fourth floor studio, and she occasionally emerges to make a cup of tea in the men's kitchen while stopping to chat with whoever happens to be around.

In addition to holding community worship gatherings, the ground floor of the Urban Monastery building doubles as a high-quality art gallery for local artists and art students. Just as the practice of prayer, hospitality, and living in poor urban neighborhoods are typical of neo-monastic communities, providing resources for the arts and creativity is also common practice. The Arts and Homeless Youth Monastery owns and runs an arts co-op that provides gallery space for both Christian and non-Christian working artists. They also host a yearly art festival and block party attended annually by over a thousand people, along with week-long training seminars for local and national folk artists, as well as other gallery nights and special events throughout the year. The Recovery Monastery participates regularly in their city's annual public art festival as a means of raising awareness and increasing access to the arts for residents in their disadvantaged neighborhood. Through these practices and others, neo-monastic communities attempt to make the arts accessible to residents of disadvantaged communities, use the arts for community empowerment, and overcome the mutual antagonism and hostility that often characterizes interactions between American evangelicals and the secular arts community.

The physical location and structure of the Urban Monastery building are a near perfect embodiment of Urban Monastery participants' distinctive theological, social, and political points of view; a *holistic communitarianism* that stands in stark contrast to the theological individualism, political conservatism, and traditional religious practices of dominant expressions of American evangelicalism. The organization of physical space in the Urban Monastery itself speaks to a different perspective on how to think about and practice Christian spirituality than is typical of dominant expressions of American evangelicalism. As Roland—a fashionable young musician, composer, and leader in the Urban Monastery Arts Collective—told me during a frequently interrupted conversation in one of the Urban Monastery' community livings spaces, this is not an accident:

ROLAND: The space that we're sitting in right now is a space that is unique I think, not just in evangelical culture, but in culture in general. It's a space where someone has a bedroom fifty yards away; there's an art studio; we're sitting in a communal living room space next to an open kitchen; there's a prayer room and art gallery downstairs; and about a dozen people have walked through the door since we started this conversation ten minutes ago. It's this crazy mix of relational living space, public space that you get in a café—though cafes tend to be more insular—and then you also have studio work space for creative types, all set in an urban context. It's a very unique splicing together of how people live the different dimensions of their lives.

It reminds of a book about how monasteries used to be built. Architecturally they were built around courtyards—public spaces—which was also a part how they understood their missiology, in that the first interactions that new people would have with the community would happen on these public square levels in the marketplace. And then there were public living rooms where there would be meals shared and more intimate connections, then you would have the work spaces of the monasteries, and then at the furthest level in you would have private quarters, which are the most intimate spaces.

That architecture describes a different progression of how social interactions are built and strengthened that cannot happen in a suburb, where there is no middle space between the road and personal living space. In a suburb, either you are a stranger passing through the street, or you are welcome into the most intimate space of the family. I enjoy how Urban Monasteries organize their life to create that sort of gray, middle social space, which creates room for strengthening relationships and a different kind of social progression.

I think that also fits how we in Urban Monasteries tend to think more in terms of relationships over the course of history rather than in terms of insular cases of spiritual revelation—which do happen—but not counting on that for being the only or sole experience of conversions, as compared to more traditional evangelical churches I've been in where the goal is to create enough emotional turmoil or ecstasy in the audience so that when the pastor makes his altar call, you get hands up in the air.

The bringing together of public/private and sacred/secular space, of art studios and prayer rooms, galleries and worship gatherings, private living quarters and public gathering spaces—set in an urban location that bisects black and white, rich and poor, young artists and homeless street people—is an intentional incarnation of the holistic communitarian vision of the neo-monastic evangelicals in the Urban Monastery. This vision aims to overcome various religious, social, and political antinomies and antagonisms, and to replace dominant expressions of American evangelicalism with a more communitarian and progressive approach to evangelical religion and politics in America.

Conservative Culture Warriors: The Common-Sense View of American Evangelicals

When citizens of the United States hear conservative Christians talk religion and politics, they are accustomed to hearing something about America's moral decline, the erosion of the family, God's judgment, and the betrayal of America's heritage as a Christian nation founded on biblical principles:

> The Bible is absolutely infallible, without error in all matters pertaining to faith and practice, as well as in areas such as geography, science, history, etc. The disintegration of our social order can be easily explained. Men and women are disobeying the clear instructions God gave in His Word.
>
> —Rev. Jerry Falwell in *Listen America*[3]

> [After the terrorist attacks on America on 9/11]: I really believe that the pagans, and the abortionists, and the feminists, and the gays and the lesbians who are actively trying to make that an alternative lifestyle, the ACLU, People For the American Way, all of them who have tried to secularize America. I point the finger in their face and say "you helped this happen" . . . [by] throwing God out of the public square.
>
> —Rev. Jerry Falwell, during 700 Club interview with Pat Robertson[4]

Although Falwell—the late conservative megachurch pastor and cofounder of the Moral Majority—quickly apologized for his remarks after 9/11, these comments are similar in tone and content to many other political statements made by conservative Christian leaders in recent decades. While announcing the successful lobbying of President Bush to declare a "Marriage Protection Week" in 2003, conservative Christian leaders had this to say about the prospect of legalizing gay marriage in America:

> What you're doing is undermining the whole legal definition, the underpinnings of the institution of the family, and when that goes, everything goes with it, including the stability of the country . . . and the future of Western civilization.
>
> —Dr. James Dobson, Founding President of Focus on the Family[5]

> It is the poster issue for the titanic struggle that is going on in our society between those who believe in a Judeo-Christian basis for our culture and those who believe in a neo-pagan, relativist base for our culture.
>
> —Dr. Richard Land, President of the Ethics and Religious Liberty
> Commission of the Southern Baptist Convention[6]

Such statements became commonplace among conservative Christian activists addressing abortion, gay marriage, and aspects of public school education involving school prayer, evolutionary science, and sex education since the late 1970s. As a result of this upsurge in political activism among conservative Christians, politicians, scholars, activists, and media outlets publicized the outbreak of a "culture war" in America pitting religious conservatives against secular liberals.[7]

The rhetoric of these conservative Christian leaders is striking for its intensity, sectarianism, and continuity with another cultural conflict in America almost one hundred years ago. While the origins of the current wave of political activism among conservative Christians stem from the rise of the religious Right in the late 1970s, it was an earlier conflict between theologically conservative and theologically liberal Protestants (who came to be known as *fundamentalists* and *modernists*, respectively) that established conservative Protestantism as a distinct religious movement in the United States. Originally a theological conflict among religious elites concerning how to interpret the Bible in light of modern scientific and philosophical thought, the fundamentalist–modernist controversy in the early 1920s was transformed into a national political struggle centered on the teaching of evolution in public schools. Like today, commentators used culture war language to describe the conflict: "Two worlds have clashed . . . the world of tradition and the world of modernism. One [fundamentalism] is static, authoritarian, and individualistic; the other [modernism] is dynamic, free, and social."[8] Like today, conservative Christian leaders warned that neglecting America's Christian heritage and biblical foundation would lead to moral collapse and national disaster. They sought to "save American civilization from the dangers of evolutionism," warning that "corrupt Biblical scholarship was at the root of the astounding moral collapse of German civilization" that resulted in World War I.[9] They formed "Christian America" foundations and warned that America must "return to the Bible or collapse" in the wake of declining morals and belief in God.[10] At first glance, the issues and rhetoric that have energized conservative Christian activism in America at the beginning of the twenty-first century look remarkably similar to those that energized it at the beginning of the twentieth century.[11] Has nothing changed?

Given these similarities, it is tempting to view conservative Christianity in the United States as a static, monolithic, ultraconservative religious-political movement engaged in a century-long struggle against science, secularism, and left-liberal politics. In the words of James Davison Hunter, the leading scholar of the "culture war" perspective on contemporary American politics:

Protestants long ago conceded control over the affairs of state and economy, education, and other institutional areas, but the family, sexuality, and the private sphere generally—the well-spring of moral discipline in society—have remained heavily under their influence. The private sphere, and the family in particular, may prove to be the final battleground in conservative Protestantism's century-long battle with modernity.[12]

If one could take the politics of the early fundamentalist movement and to-day's Christian Right as representative of conservative Protestantism in general, one would have some justification for accepting this common-sense view of America's religious and political landscape, a view that equates religious conservatism with across-the-board cultural, economic, and political conservatism.[13]

This common-sense view of Christian conservatism is often explained by scholars and journalists as stemming from the status or class resentment of conservative Christians. One such prominent explanation of conservative Christian politics is the "status politics" model.[14] According to this view, conservative Protestants have mobilized politically in response to their increasingly marginalized social status and class position in modern America. Fundamentalist and evangelical Christians are said to be disproportionately poor, rural, southern, and less educated than mainline Protestants, religious and secular liberals, and the general population—which explains their traditionalist religious and cultural beliefs and their desire to "reclaim America for Christ" against an onslaught of religious and cultural pluralism, scientific naturalism, and changing moral perspectives on sexuality and the family.[15]

The status resentment argument has been applied to both early and late twentieth-century conservative Christian politics. Writing about fundamentalism's national political mobilization against the teaching of evolution in public schools in the 1920s, historian George Marsden observes: "The central theme was, inescapably, the clash of two worlds, the rural and the urban . . . [On the one side] fundamentalism, the South, crackpot hawkers of religion, obscurantism . . . and on the other side intellectuals, lawyers, journalists, sophisticates, modernists."[16] Conservative Christian politics was about poor, rural, uneducated people combating science and modernity; and about preserving a fading Protestant cultural hegemony in the face of rapid urbanization, secularization, and immigration in the early twentieth century.

Similarly, status resentment theory explains the rise of the Christian Right in the early 1980s in terms of its ability to "attract groups who resent their cultural, political and moral devaluation by the dominant society."[17] And just as the culture wars thesis was popularized by politicians such as James Buchanan, status resentment theory has become part of the common-sense view of contemporary conservative Christian politics. As President Barack Obama said while speaking of rural, conservative, religious voters during a campaign swing through California:

> You go into some of these small towns in Pennsylvania, and like a lot of small towns in the Midwest, the jobs have been gone now for 25 years and nothing's replaced them. . . . [I]t's not surprising then they get bitter, they cling to guns or religion or antipathy to people who aren't like them or anti-immigrant sentiment or anti-trade sentiment as a way to explain their frustrations.[18]

The cultural politics of the religious Right are seen as expressions of the class and status resentment of conservative Christians marginalized by virtue of their loss of cultural hegemony, rural residence, and low education, income, and occupational status relative to other Americans.

This reading of the record of twentieth-century religion and politics in American has left us with a common-sense view of evangelical Christians as politically conservative culture warriors engaged in a permanent crusade against all things secular and progressive, whose politics are best explained as the bitter resentment (or *ressentiment*) of a culturally, economically, and geographically displaced people.[19] However, as is often the case for long-standing common-sense views of the natural and social world, the common-sense view of American evangelicalism now obscures more than it explains.

A New Evangelicalism?

If the common-sense view is inadequate for understanding twenty-first-century evangelical religion and politics, then what is the truth of the matter? How are we to understand American evangelicalism as it exists today? While the idea of a culture war in America between Christian conservatives and secular liberals is highly contested, it is true that evangelical Christianity has tended to favor conservative political and cultural positions throughout the twentieth century.[20] However, if a growing chorus of evangelical leaders and media pundits is to be believed, the era of uncontested evangelical conservatism is on the brink of collapse—if it has not collapsed already. According to these voices, American evangelical Christianity is in the midst of a political and cultural sea change that will dramatically transform both evangelicalism and the American cultural and political landscape in the years to come. If one believes the reports, it is largely a shift to the Left.[21] In his 2005 *New York Times* best-selling book *God's Politics*, progressive evangelical leader Rev. Jim Wallis writes:

> The Religious Right no longer controls the agenda. Global and domestic poverty, the environment, HIV/AIDS, and the ethics of war are all now clearly on the agenda of the faith community, alongside the critical issues of family values and the sacredness of life. . . . A new movement of moderate and progressive religious voices [is] challenging the monologue of the Religious Right. An extremely narrow and aggressively partisan expression of right-wing Republican religion has controlled the debate on faith and politics in the public square for years. But that is no longer true.[22]

As if to prove the point, a spate of *New York Times* articles have highlighted recent evangelical mobilizations to combat global warming, poverty, and HIV/AIDS—along with global human rights issues including the conflict in Darfur, debt cancellation for developing countries, and human trafficking. These are not culture war issues. Articles such as, "Evangelical Leaders Join Global Warming Initiative," "Emphasis Shifts for New Breed of Evangelicals," "The Evangelical Crackup," and "Evangelicals a Liberal Can Love," signaled the emergence of new issues and a new rhetoric of political action among many evangelical Christians.[23] As prominent *New York Times* journalist and self-described liberal Nicholas D. Kristof remarks, "Today, conservative Christian churches do superb work on poverty, AIDS, sex trafficking, climate change, prison abuses, malaria and genocide in Darfur."[24] In "The Evangelical Crackup," David D. Kirkpatrick argues that while the Christian Right is certainly not dead, its hegemony over evangelical political discourse is being eroded by challenges from progressive evangelical leaders like Jim Wallis, "the lonely voice of the tiny evangelical left."[25] If these and many other reports from evangelical leaders and outside observers alike are to be believed, the days of a "tiny evangelical left" dwarfed by a hegemonic conservative Christian Right are numbered.

And it is not just a handful of voices from the "tiny evangelical left" who think so. A new generation of national evangelical leaders, such as influential megachurch pastors Bill Hybels and Rick Warren, has become increasingly critical of the Christian Right's view of religion and politics in America:

> I am an evangelical. I'm not a member of the religious right and I'm not a fundamentalist. . . . I am an American; I believe in pluralism, and I don't think we need a God party.
> —Rick Warren, Senior Pastor and Founder of Saddleback Church, during a 2005 conference hosted by the Pew Forum on Religion and Public Life[26]

> [Rev. Bill Hybels speaking on the Iraq war and the Christian Right]: The quickness to arms, the quickness to invade, I think that caused a kind of desertion of what has been known as the Christian right. . . . [Evangelicals are saying] "We are interested in more than your two or three issues. We are interested in the poor, in racial reconciliation, in global poverty and AIDS, in the plight of women in the developing world."
> —Bill Hybels, Senior Pastor and Founder of Willow Creek Community Church in a 2007 New York Times Magazine article[27]

In light of these developments, the common-sense view of evangelical religion and politics is increasingly problematic. One cannot simply assume that the religious conservatism of white evangelicals entails an overarching cultural, economic, and political conservatism.[28]

Just like the common-sense view of evangelical politics, old demographic assumptions about evangelicals as marginalized outsiders have likewise become problematic. It becomes harder to argue a group is marginalized when one of its most recognizable figures gives the inaugural invocation for the highest political office in the land, as Rev. Rick Warren did for President Barack Obama on January 20, 2009. Five months earlier, Warren hosted an unprecedented hour-long interview with both presidential candidates during the nationally televised Saddleback Civil Forum on the Presidency at his famous church in Orange County, California. Warren introduced the forum by saying, "I have to tell you up front, both of these guys are my friends. They both care deeply about America. They are both patriots."[29] An admission of friendship with a Democratic presidential candidate by an evangelical pastor such as Warren would have been deeply problematic only a decade earlier, as fellow evangelical megachurch pastor Bill Hybels discovered after scandalously inviting then President Bill Clinton to speak at a leadership conference hosted by Hybels's Willow Creek Association.[30] Apart from highlighting a changing political landscape within the evangelical movement, events like the Saddleback forum are symbolic of the resurgent influence and status of evangelicals in American public life. As sociologist D. Michael Lindsay notes in his 2007 book *Faith in the Halls of Power*, over the last thirty years evangelicals have joined the American elite in politics and academia; in Hollywood and on Wall Street. They have become influential insiders in state and national electoral politics.[31] Their rapidly growing megachurches are located in affluent suburban and exurban communities from which they draw their highly educated members.[32] And white evangelicals are increasingly indistinguishable from the general population in terms of their average income, education, and likelihood to live in rural communities or the South.[33]

While megachurch evangelical leaders such as Hybels and Warren are increasingly critical of the Christian Right, willing to be associated with Democratic Party politicians, and more likely to support certain left-liberal political causes, dominant expressions of evangelicalism in America remain rooted in theological individualism and conservative politics.[34] However, a small—but visible and growing—movement of neo-monastic evangelicals is trying to take American evangelicalism in more radical directions. These young evangelical neo-monastics protested the war in Iraq and went on peacekeeping missions to Iraq and Palestine. They have moved into disadvantaged urban neighborhoods to establish intentional communities across race and class lines in "the abandoned places of Empire."[35] They meet in pubs, paint nudes, and perform hip-hop in urban bars and schools to build interracial community networks and empower racially marginalized youth. They establish decentralized churches and spiritual communities that divert resources from church buildings and professional ministers to food pantries and social justice projects. They mobilize private and public resources to protect immigrant rights, support education, and fund the arts in diverse low-income neighborhoods. In each of these activities, neo-monastic evangelicals see themselves as embodying the "true" Christian gospel while offering a prophetic critique of dominant expressions of religion and politics in America.[36]

And their numbers are growing. The number of new monastic communities has more than tripled in size since 2010, which now include over 200 communities in 34 US states and 12 foreign nations.[37] The actual number of communities that identify with the new monasticism is likely much larger, and, similar to the "Emerging Church" movement, the high national profile of several new monastic movement leaders in the evangelical world means that a significant majority of American evangelicals have been exposed to the movement.[38] New monastic leaders and communities have captured national media attention from a wide range of secular and religious outlets, including CNN, *The Boston Globe*, *SPIN*, *Esquire*, Fox News, Al Jazeera, and NPR; and have inspired several lead articles in evangelicalism's flagship periodical *Christianity Today* about how new monastic leaders are "dominating the Christian best-seller lists" with their "radical" critique of evangelical politics and religious culture.[39]

From 2006 to 2011, I immersed myself in the fascinating world of evangelical neo-monasticism—and in the Urban Monastery, in particular—an influential neo-monastic community located in a gritty, racially diverse urban neighborhood in a major Midwestern city. Through in-depth interviews and ethnographic participant-observation, I spent thousands of hours getting an on-the-ground experiential education in neo-monastic evangelicalism. I attended their art galleries, exhibition openings, and album release parties. I studied the Bible, went to church, and prayed through the night with them. I witnessed them sharing the gospel through music, art, and conversation. I smoked clove cigars and drank single malt scotch with them. I attended leadership meetings, worship gatherings, and conferences with them. I walked the streets and talked to homeless people with them. I sat with them in pubs and on front porches discussing theology and politics deep into the night. I read their books and listened to their music. I watered gardens, washed dishes, and ate countless community meals with them. For seven months, I lived with them. This book is about these neo-monastic evangelicals, their relation to traditional evangelicalism, and about the social and historical processes through which American evangelicalism is reproduced and transformed.

Neo-Monasticism and American Evangelicalism

As a surprising new development that has been increasing in visibility and influence within American evangelicalism, the new monasticism is interesting in its own right, despite having remained largely invisible to mainstream academe.[40] However, while conducting interviews and site visits and analyzing the books and literature being produced by emerging neo-monastic leaders, it quickly became apparent that the theological and political standpoints being developed by neo-monastic evangelicals were of great theoretical and historical significance with respect to American evangelicalism as a whole. Most notably perhaps, neo-monastic evangelicals are highly critical of conservative evangelicalism and its deep connections to the Christian Right and conservative Republican Party politics. Their holistic communitarian approach to Christian spirituality is a significant break with dominant expressions of twentieth-century American evangelicalism—which have been marked strong tendencies toward theological individualism and political conservatism—and requires special attention and explanation. Apart from wondering at its existence or explaining it away as the unfortunate accommodation of orthodox evangelicalism to modernity among well-educated evangelicals,[41] the evangelical left and its allies have been largely ignored by scholars of evangelical religion in America.[42] This book joins a small but growing list of studies that provide some remedy for that neglect.

If there is indeed an "evangelical crackup" fragmenting evangelicalism into increasingly oppositional political and religious camps, then the most sociologically interesting and politically significant question about evangelicals today concerns relations among emerging positions within evangelicalism, not what the "average" or "typical" evangelical thinks about religion and politics in America. Fortunately, some recent work has begun to address these questions. Over a decade ago, Christian Smith's landmark studies *American Evangelicalism: Embattled and Thriving* and *Christian America? What Evangelicals Really Want* reminded us that contemporary American evangelicalism is far more theologically and politically diverse than the common-sense view suggests.[43] The point is reinforced in Greeley and Hout's *The Truth about Conservative Christians* and in moral cosmology theory's arguments about the importance of *theological individualism* and *theological communitarianism* in shaping the socioeconomic standpoints of religious individuals, about which we will have much more to say in chapter 2.[44] However, while Smith's work, in particular, provides an excellent portrait of "ordinary evangelicals," these studies focus on explaining the religious vitality and general religious and political orientations of evangelicals as a group, rather than on explaining particular positions within evangelicalism and how they relate to one another.[45] Smith acknowledges that it is a mistake to view evangelicals as a "monolithic religious bloc," but his analyses nevertheless focus on evangelicalism as a single categorical unit, rather than on exploring the distinctive religious and political standpoints of different streams within American evangelicalism.[46] Other recent studies of post-boomer religiosity in America take a similar approach.[47]

Several recent books have helpfully moved beyond prior scholarship's narrow focus on conservative evangelicalism in order to explore different streams within the evangelical movement. Historian David R. Swartz's monograph *Moral Minority: The Evangelical Left in an Age of Conservatism* traces the origins and development of the evangelical left in the late twentieth century.[48] Almost two decades after its arrival on the American religious scene, the "Emerging Church" has become the subject of rising interest and several recent books.[49] Recent work in the new anthropology of Christianity has emphasized the internal differentiation and complexity of evangelical beliefs, practices, and uses of scripture in everyday life.[50] Of particular note are James S. Bielo's *Emerging Evangelicals: Faith, Modernity, and the Desire for Authenticity* and Omri Elisha's *Moral Ambition: Mobilization and Social Outreach in Evangelical Megachurches*, which offer excellent nuanced ethnographic accounts of emerging church and megachurch evangelical faith communities, respectively. Each of these books acknowledges the multiplicity of theological, social, and political perspectives within American evangelicalism, emphasizing the "plasticity of lived religion" among different streams within the movement.[51] Where Bielo's *Emerging Evangelicals* examines the emerging church and its relation to the American evangelical establishment, Elisha's *Moral Ambition* explores the struggles of a small group of evangelical social activists trying to mobilize fellow megachurch members around a variety of social outreach ministries across race, place, and class lines.[52] Along with Brian Steensland and Philip Goff's edited volume on *The New Evangelical Social Engagement*, these studies attest to growing scholarly awareness and interest in the evangelical left and its allies, and in the multiple expressions of the "new evangelicalism" in the United States.[53]

Still, this work remains a drop in the ocean compared to the enormous literature that continues to treat the Christian Right and conservative evangelicalism as if they were the only game in town. Thus, many questions about the "new evangelicalism" remain—both empirical and theoretical. For example, in their introductory chapter to *The New Evangelical Social Engagement*, Steensland and Goff make several suggestive gestures toward explaining the rising tide of left-leaning social activism among American evangelicals, focusing on three broad trends in particular: (1) changing sociodemographics and young evangelical reactions against the Christian Right; (2) a broader (generational) cultural shift in America toward more left-liberal attitudes on environmental protection, homosexuality, and war; and (3) the declining influence of mainline Protestantism relative to evangelicalism in the United States, resulting in less need for evangelicals to patrol the boundary between themselves and the Protestant mainline.[54] As Part I of this book will attest, these gestures have merit. However, they do not answer the question of how or why exactly these "broader cultural trends" are having the effects that they are within contemporary evangelicalism.[55] In other words, they do not specify the actual social processes or mechanisms through which these trends are generating new religious and political standpoints among evangelicals, or why these standpoints take the specific shape that they do across different movements within American evangelicalism.[56] One of this book's primary tasks, then, is to develop a robust theoretical account of the religious and political standpoints of neo-monastic evangelicals; and in so doing, to address the more general question of how religious and political standpoints within the field of American evangelicalism are reproduced and transformed.[57]

In describing American evangelicalism as a *field*, I am deliberately invoking the theoretical language of French social theorist Pierre Bourdieu. There are a number of compelling arguments for adopting a field-analytic approach to the study of contemporary American evangelicalism. First, it provides a conceptual apparatus for systematically examining multiple positions within the field of American evangelicalism and their relation to one another other—such as neo-monastic evangelicalism, megachurch evangelicalism, and the Christian Right—a requirement for any serious study of the multiple faces of American evangelicalism in the twenty-first century. Second and related, field theory offers us a theoretical language appropriate to the empirical reality of the open, dynamic, and decentralized institutional structure of evangelical religion in America.[58] Third, it avoids the two classic forms of reductionism common to theorizing about the sources of evangelical standpoints and strategies of action: the "downwards conflation," which reduces religious and political standpoints to social location (as in status resentment theory); or, alternatively, the "upwards conflation," which denies the role of social and historical influences on evangelical religious and political standpoints (as in many evangelical self-descriptions and idealist interpretations of evangelicalism).[59] As sociologist Craig Calhoun aptly notes: "One of the advantages of Bourdieu's notion of field is that with it we can see both the largely successful efforts to create a quasi-autonomous religious field and the limits of its independence from the larger field of struggle which is society."[60] Fourth, the field-theoretic approach helps us resolve a number of long-standing sociological debates concerning American evangelicals, such as whether evangelicals are essentially dogmatic religious traditionalists or innovative religious pragmatists.[61] It also illuminates and extends previous theoretical arguments about the causes of evangelical vitality in America.[62] Finally, in giving attention to both social structure and social change, or sociology and history, it enables us to elucidate some of the complex social-historical processes through which the field of American evangelicalism is reproduced and transformed.

Building on the central insights of field theory, this book develops a *practical social hermeneutic* approach to the study of evangelical culture and agency.[63] To say that we need a practical social *hermeneutics* of American evangelicalism is to argue that the meaning-content of religious culture and its interpretation is a causally relevant factor in evangelical agency. In other words, this book supports the "strong program in culture" that views religious culture—and culture more generally—as a relatively autonomous causal factor in human agency (as I argue at length in Part II).[64] To say that we need a practical *social* hermeneutics of American evangelicalism is to argue that the process of biblical interpretation and theological meaning construction is inextricably bound up with social and historical processes, and that the religious and political standpoints of evangelicals are causally influenced by social forces. I will argue that Bourdieusian field theory provides the best analytical framework for understanding how social and historical forces influence the standpoints and strategies of action of different movements within American evangelicalism, and I will develop a field-theoretic analysis of neo-monasticism's relation to other theoretically and substantively relevant movements within American evangelicalism.[65] Finally, to say that we need a *practical* social hermeneutic of evangelical agency is to affirm that culture influences action not through the "logician's logic" of the scholar or academic theologian but through the "fuzzy" logic of practice, in which a minimalist set of symbolic elements can be used to generate meaningful interpretations of a near-infinite range of actions and social objects.[66]

Looking Ahead

To this end, Part I examines the historical and contemporary American evangelical context in relation to which neo-monastic evangelicals have constructed their distinctive religious and political standpoints. One of the central arguments of Part I is that historical struggles—particularly the fundamentalist–modernist struggles of the early twentieth century—remain institutionalized in the boundaries, classification schemes, standpoints, and *doxa* of the contemporary field of American evangelicalism. It is these historical struggles, I argue in chapter 2, which explain American *evangelical exceptionalism* with respect to moral cosmology theory. Moral cosmology theory correctly identifies *theological individualism* and *theological communitarianism* as key indicators of evangelical social and economic standpoints,[67] but runs aground by ignoring how specific historical struggles within the field of American Protestantism moved dominant expressions of twentieth-century American evangelicalism toward a thoroughgoing political conservatism that was neither logically nor theologically necessary.[68] Whereas dominant expressions of American evangelicalism have practiced a specific type of theological individualism, neo-monastic evangelicals are theological communitarians.[69] This has significant consequences for the distinctive political and religious standpoints and strategies of action of neo-monastic evangelicals, as I demonstrate in Part II.

Having introduced the dominant (and dominated) twentieth-century religious and political standpoints in relation to which evangelical neo-monasticism is constructed in chapter 2, chapter 3 proceeds with a field-theoretic examination of neo-monasticism's relation to contemporary American evangelicalism. Building on the seminal work of French social theorist Pierre Bourdieu, I argue that American evangelicalism is best understood as a relatively autonomous field of historical struggle among agents holding competing visions of the legitimate representation of biblical Christianity in America. After briefly explaining field theory and defining its key analytic concepts, chapter 3 uses original ethnographic and textual analysis to map out neo-monasticism's relation to four theoretically significant positions in the contemporary evangelical field: the Christian Right/conservative evangelicalism, megachurch evangelicalism, the evangelical left, and the emerging church. I argue that the Urban Monastery's holistic communitarian theological system—while derived from biblical sources and symbols—is also derived from neo-monasticism's struggle against dominant representations of evangelical Christianity in America and from its avant-garde position in the evangelical field. Against simplistic popular and scholarly (mis) representations of American evangelicalism as monolithically conservative, chapter 3 demonstrates how field analysis gives us eyes to see the dynamic diversity of religious and political perspectives within American evangelicalism, and how they systematically relate to one another. After having mapped out the structure of the American evangelical field as it relates to neo-monasticism, chapter 3 proceeds with a detailed relational analysis of the field in the form of seven propositions, thereby specifying some of the dynamic social processes that drive continuity and change in the field of American evangelicalism. By analyzing neo-monasticism as a particular case of how American evangelicalism is reproduced and transformed, chapter 3 demonstrates how the field-theoretic approach opens the way for a more comprehensive, dynamic, and historically situated understanding of the multiple faces of evangelical Christianity in America.

After setting the historical and theoretical stage in Part I, Part II of the book raises the curtain on the Urban Monastery.[70] Chapter 4 traces the origins of evangelical neo-monasticism and some of its key leaders and institutions, including the Urban Monastery. Against the theological individualism of dominant positions in American evangelicalism, neo-monastic evangelicals have developed their distinctive theological meaning system—which I call *holistic communitarianism*—by rearranging relationships of priority among core symbolic elements of traditional evangelical theology.[71] Whereas historic American evangelicalism has prioritized evangelism, personal salvation, individual moral transformation, and one's personal relationship with God as the hallmarks of faithful religion and the solution to social problems, Urban Monastery participants emphasize God's relational and communal nature as the pattern for human interaction and believe that working for social justice is no less important than sharing the gospel with individuals.

Urban Monastery participants are *holistic* in their refusal to prioritize evangelism over social justice activism, their support for structural as well as personal solutions to social problems, their refusal of single-issue voting, their efforts to deconstruct the boundaries between the "sacred" and the "secular," and their understanding of Christian mission in the world. They are *communitarian* in placing relationships and communal practices, rather than the isolated individual, at the center of religious life. Neo-monastic evangelicals are also theological communitarians as defined by moral cosmology theory, supporting government-based interventions in both the social and economic arenas as discussed in chapter 5.

While chapter 4 focuses on the development of holistic communitarianism as a distinctive theological meaning system in the Urban Monastery, chapter 5 examines its expression in the political standpoints of Urban Monastery participants. As holistic communitarians, Urban Monastery participants believe that poverty, economic inequality, and militarism are moral issues that Christians need to consider when deciding who to vote for—no less than other "moral values" issues such as the traditional Christian Right shibboleths of abortion or gay marriage. Urban Monastery participants tend toward left-liberal political standpoints with the exception of abortion, where they remain strongly pro-life. Nevertheless, they preferred Barack Obama to John McCain in the 2008 presidential elections. While the mere fact that a group of predominantly white evangelicals preferred Obama to McCain is significant in itself, the process that Urban Monastery participants went through in deciding who to vote for is even more interesting. Most Urban Monastery participants had an extremely difficult time deciding who to vote for. Through tears and anger, Urban Monastery participants expressed deep frustration at the way in which many American evangelicals have come to associate Republican Party voting with religious faithfulness. Urban Monastery participants, on the other hand, are deeply torn between the conservative and liberal polarities of American electoral politics, occupying a *contradictory cultural location* with respect to the Christian Right and the progressive Left. Chapter 5 explores the objective and subjective dimensions of the Urban Monastery's contradictory cultural location and offers an up-close look at the political standpoints of a group of neo-monastic evangelicals.

After examining how holistic communitarianism is expressed in the theological and political standpoints of Urban Monastery participants in chapters 4 and 5, respectively, Chapter 6 explores how it is put to work in the Urban Monastery's social organization and strategies of action. Here we see how neo-monasticism's break with the individualistic theology of traditional evangelicals finds expression in new ways of *organizing community* and practicing *holistic mission* in the world. Although religious and cultural meanings are often more fragmented, incomplete, and contradictory than they are coherent and comprehensive, the beliefs and practices of Urban Monastery participants show a remarkable degree of integration. Chapter 6 examines how Urban Monastery participants explicitly draw on core symbolic elements of their distinctive holistic communitarian meaning system to construct lines of individual and collective action in the world, practicing holistic communitarianism as a relatively comprehensive and coherent strategy of action.[72] Just as the vigilant application of a religious ethic enabled early ascetic Protestant sects of Europe to organize private and public life according to a distinctive religious *Weltanschauung* (or worldview), Urban Monastery participants' practice of holistic communitarianism is an example of how the vigilant application of a system of cultural meaning can become a unifying principle of action of remarkable strength and scope. Like Max Weber's depiction of ascetic Protestantism in *The Protestant Ethic and the Spirit of Capitalism* and other works, Urban Monastery participants practice a form of "inner-worldly asceticism" that seeks the "methodical penetration of conduct with religion" in everyday life.[73] Unlike Weber's ascetic Protestants, however, the Urban Monastery practices a type of *celebratory asceticism* that is communitarian rather than individualistic in emphasis.

Finally, chapter 7 pulls Parts I and II back together into an original *practical social hermeneutic* model of evangelical religious and political standpoints and strategies of action. Standing against the cultural and social reductionisms which have dominated much thinking about evangelicals, I summarize how a practical social hermeneutic approach centered on field theory is able to account for the historical, cultural, and social determinants of diverse evangelical position-takings and transformations. Chapter 7 also explores some implications of the transformation of American evangelicalism for the future of religion and politics in the United States. If neo-monastic evangelicals and their allies have anything to say about the matter, it will be a future dominated by a more communitarian and progressive representation of biblical Christianity than Americans have grown accustomed to.

Notes on Method

Between 2006 and 2011, I engaged in participant observation with four neo-monastic communities, conducted thirty-one in-depth interviews, and had thousands of conversations with neo-monastic leaders and community members from six different communities across North America. I began with eleven preliminary in-depth interviews of individual participants and leaders of five separate neo-monastic communities across North America, along with site visits to four of these communities as a participant observer over the course of a two-year period (2006–2008). Each of the four neo-monastic communities I visited is located in a low-income, racially diverse urban neighborhood, in US cities with populations ranging from 200,000 to 2,000,000 people. Three of these eleven interviews were with founding leaders of three different evangelical neo-monastic communities: one on the West coast, one in the Northeast, and one in the Midwest. Along with these initial interviews, I observed and took ethnographic field notes across a number of group settings, including public art openings hosted by neo-monastic evangelical communities, hip hop concerts performed by community members at local bars and other music venues, worship services, Bible studies, community meals, leadership meetings, and national and international gatherings of neo-monastic communities. During this time I became immersed in the world of neo-monastic evangelicalism, gained access to movement leaders and communities, and began clarifying the theoretical and methodological approach developed in this book.

On the basis of these exploratory interviews and site visits, I selected the Urban Monastery for further analysis.[74] The Urban Monastery is a leading evangelical neo-monastic community located in a large Midwestern city (metro population two million). While some neo-monastic communities are composed of a mixture of evangelical, Catholic, mainline Protestant, and even non-religious members, the Urban Monastery is thoroughly evangelical—an important characteristic given this book's focus on neo-monasticism's relation to American evangelicalism. The Urban Monastery is also one of the largest neo-monastic communities in the country and houses national offices for a national network of communities related to neo-monasticism. Urban Monastery leaders teach at national and international conferences, have developed learning materials that are used by other religious communities around the world, and serve on leadership teams for various national projects and governance structures within their network. The Urban Monastery is therefore a critical, intense case of neo-monastic evangelicalism,[75] whose relatively large size and influence is methodologically advantageous given the lack of prior research on this population. While it is larger, more established, and more evangelical than many other neo-monastic communities, the Urban Monastery is an otherwise typical neo-monastic evangelical community with respect to its geographic location and the demographic characteristics of its participants. This is, of course, not to say that there is no variation among different evangelical neo-monastic communities across these characteristics, just that the Urban Monastery does not stand out as an outlier.

Building on my exploratory interviews and ethnographic observations, I conducted twenty more in-depth interviews with leaders and participants in the Urban Monastery, as well as site visits and a demographic survey of community participants between May 2008 and June 2009, then spent another seven months living with Urban Monastery participants while working on this manuscript between January and August of 2011.[76] I selected interview subjects based on my own knowledge of the community (developed in the early phases of the project) along with the help of informants in the group to ensure that my interview subjects varied across potentially relevant demographic and organizational categories.[77] Just under one-third of my interview subjects were core community leaders, most of whom received small salaries or stipends for their work with the Urban Monastery. Another one-third of respondents were core members who served in various secondary leadership roles on a voluntary basis, and one-third were newcomers. Although my sample included a large percentage of people involved in some kind of leadership role in the Urban Monastery (60 percent), this represents only a slight oversampling of Urban Monastery leaders, given that just under half of all Urban Monastery participants have significant leadership responsibilities and are formally recognized as leaders in the community. Eighty-five percent of interview subjects were white (compared to 93 percent of whole community), 50 percent were female (compared to 58 percent of whole community), and all were between the ages of 20 and 34 (compared to 94 percent in whole community). Exactly half of interview subjects held bachelor's degrees (compared to 53 percent of the whole community), 25 percent were undergraduate college students (compared to 23 percent of whole community), and 15 percent had some graduate-level education (compared to 16 percent of whole community). Fifty-five percent of interview subjects were single (compared to 63 percent of all Urban Monastery participants).

I conducted in-depth interviews with each respondent lasting between one and three hours,[78] then transcribed and coded each interview following a standard grounded theory approach; beginning with open coding to discover emergent categories from the full complexity of the interview and observational data, followed by focused coding as core theoretical and empirical themes emerged.[79] In-depth interviews, transcription, coding, and analytic memo writing were done simultaneously in an iterative process, allowing for maximum flexibility and precision in data collection.[80] For example, I did not begin my investigation of evangelical neo-monasticism with field theory in mind. Rather, I started noticing how field theory could explain the ways that neo-monastic evangelicals were constructing their distinctive religious and political standpoints and strategies of action in relation to other evangelicals while I was in the field.[81] As I continued my investigation, the efficacy of a field-theoretic approach moved from a tentative hypothesis to a firm conclusion as ongoing observation and analysis repeatedly confirmed its extraordinary utility for explaining what was happening in the new monastic movement, the "new evangelicalism," and in the field of American evangelicalism more generally.

One of the primary advantages of qualitative research as a method of social enquiry is that it allows us to observe in detail how real people understand themselves and the world they live in, recognizing that "people's own knowledge and ways of knowing are crucial elements of social action and thus of social analysis."[82] Thanks to the growth of reflexive and critical perspectives in the social sciences in recent decades, sociologists have become increasingly sensitive to the ways in which existing academic theories of social groups or social relations can ignore, repress, and infantilize the human subjects of social research.[83] As Max Weber recognized, the temptation for social scientists and intellectuals to "explain away" the beliefs, attitudes, and motivations of religious individuals and groups is particularly acute in light of modern Western scientific and philosophical assumptions.[84] To use Weber's words: "The modern man is in general, even with the best will, unable to give religious ideas the significance for culture . . . which they deserve."[85] Regardless of one's position on the veracity of particular religious accounts of the world or the nature of religion's social contributions—whether good or ill—consistently explaining away religious believers' accounts of themselves leads to distorted theories of religion. Rather, as Christian Smith reminds us, studying religion "requires that we pay close attention not only to religious groups' organizational structures and promotional techniques, but also to the actual substance of the subcultural beliefs and practices of distinct religious traditions."[86] In other words, "the *meaning-content* of theologies, customs, worldviews, and rituals actually matter."[87] One way to do this is to observe, read, and listen to religious people as they explain themselves. At a substantive and stylistic level, hearing respondents speak of their beliefs and experiences in their own voice allows for a different sort of understanding of how they see the world than is possible when a sociologist speaks for them.[88] It also makes for more interesting reading. For these theoretical, ethical, and stylistic reasons, this book aims to allow the reader to hear interview subjects and religious leaders explain themselves, in their own words, whenever possible.

In highlighting the importance of listening to religious subjects explain themselves and taking their explanations seriously (if, not always, at face value), I am not, however, arguing for a strictly phenomenological or "person-centered ethnography" that denies the causal efficacy or analytic relevance of social and cultural structures.[89] It is true—in a certain sense—that "only people act."[90] However, whether one is a realist or instrumentalist with respect to the objects of social theory, it is difficult to construct accounts of the infinitely complex yet patterned social world without the aid of transpersonal sociological concepts such as *race, ideology, culture, bureaucratization,* and the like.[91] Within the discipline of sociology, even staunch methodological individualists, who are in principle committed to the possibility of reducing all social structural explanations to individual behavior, acknowledge that it is useful—indeed, sometimes necessary—to treat theoretical concepts such as *class, culture, field,* and so on as if the social entities or processes they refer to had real causal powers that influence the beliefs and behaviors of people.[92] We must indeed be careful not to ignore or explain away the self-understanding of religious individuals and communities. At the same time, we must remember that we are not always transparent to ourselves, nor are the forces which organize the social world always transparent to us.[93] For this reason, as sociologists have long argued, we need to construct conceptual tools that help us to "see" what is not readily apparent to the naked eye—or to the perceptions and apperceptions of common sense and practical experience—just as the natural sciences have taught us that we need special instruments to see, for example, that what we call a solid is in fact composed of a great deal of empty space.

Finally, much like Bourdieu's study of the French intellectual field of which he was a part in *Homo Academicus*, researching this book has been an exercise in intensive personal and intellectual reflexivity.[94] Having grown up in the evangelical world, I have extensive practical and personal experience with each of the five movements discussed in this book, along with many others. I attended conservative evangelical churches in my childhood and early youth, was involved in megachurch and emerging church groups while at university and immediately thereafter, and have volunteered alongside organizations on the evangelical left. I attended a predominantly African American Protestant church and then an evangelical Anglican church for several years. And from May 2008 to May 2010, I helped lead a small experiment in neo-monastic living that has since disbanded. I currently attend a small, theologically and politically diverse, non-denominational campus church. In writing this book, I have found the ubiquitous scholarly practice of decomposing, interrogating, and reincorporating the practical knowledge of experience into "objectified" social-scientific knowledge to be both immensely challenging and immensely rewarding. I have also found myself at times resisting my own conclusions and being tempted to throw this manuscript into a hot fire. In the end, however, I managed to complete the difficult task of subjecting one's own social world to the sociological gaze: the success of which I leave the discerning reader to judge.

PART I

Neo-Monasticism and American Evangelicalism

Suffice it to say that the separation of sociology and history is a disastrous division, and one totally devoid of epistemological justification: all sociology should be historical and all history sociological. In point of fact, one of the functions of the theory of fields is to make the opposition between reproduction and transformation, statics and dynamics, or structure and history, vanish.[1]

—PIERRE BOURDIEU

One of the central arguments of this book is that the religious and political standpoints of neo-monastic evangelicals—and of other movements within American evangelicalism—are constructed in relation to one another and to the historic field of American evangelicalism. Making this argument requires an examination of the historical development of evangelical Christianity in America, which is the subject of chapter 2. In addition to providing a summary of the dominant twentieth-century evangelical standpoints in relation to which neo-monastic evangelicalism is constructed, the key point of chapter 2 is that historical struggles—particularly founding struggles between fundamentalist and modernist Christians in the early twentieth century—remain institutionalized in the boundaries, classification schemes, and *doxa* of contemporary evangelicalism. It is these historical struggles which explain American evangelical exceptionalism with respect to moral cosmology theory. Moral cosmology theory correctly identifies *theological individualism* and *theological communitarianism* as key indicators of evangelical social and economic standpoints, but runs aground by ignoring how specific historical struggles within the field of American Protestantism—specifically, the fundamentalist–modernist struggle in the early 1900s—moved dominant expressions of twentieth-century conservative Protestantism toward a thoroughgoing political conservatism that was neither logically nor theologically necessary.

Having introduced the dominant (and dominated) twentieth-century religious and political standpoints in relation to which evangelical neo-monasticism is constructed in chapter 2, chapter 3 proceeds with a field-analytic examination of neo-monasticism's relation to contemporary American evangelicalism. After briefly explaining field theory and defining its key analytic concepts, chapter 3 maps out the objective positions and subjective position-takings of neo-monasticism in relation to four theoretically significant positions in the contemporary evangelical field: the Christian Right/conservative evangelicalism, megachurch evangelicalism, the evangelical left, and the emerging church. Against simplistic popular and scholarly (mis)representations of American evangelicalism as monolithically conservative, chapter 3 appropriates Bourdieusian field theory to explore the dynamic diversity of competing religious and political standpoints within American evangelicalism, and how they systematically relate to one another. By analyzing neo-monasticism as a particular case of how American evangelicalism is reproduced and transformed, chapter 3 demonstrates how the field-theoretic approach opens the way for a more comprehensive, dynamic, and historically situated understanding of the multiple faces of evangelical Christianity in America.

Chapter 2

Evangelical Religion and Politics in the Twentieth Century

IT IS IMPOSSIBLE to grasp the new monasticism's significance as a specific case of how American evangelicalism transforms and reproduces itself without first examining the historical context from which it arose. The Urban Monastery's *holistic communitarian* perspective on religion and politics, for example, is in many ways a direct reversal of the theological individualism and political conservatism that have dominated the American evangelical landscape since the early 1900s. The social processes that drive transformations in the American evangelical field are inextricably historically bound. No matter how "new" or "radical" a religious innovation or political reversal in the field may appear to be, even the most avant-garde positions bear the mark of the entire history of the American evangelical field and are constructed in relation to it.[2] Furthermore, given the power of dueling common-sense views of evangelical religion and politics being peddled by both conservative and liberal activists today, it is worth taking some time to separate historical reality from politically fueled myth and legend.

For most of the last century, popular and scholarly common sense has presumed that being a religious conservative automatically makes one a social, economic, and political conservative. Indeed, as proponents of religious consistency theory have argued, this equation of religious conservatism with across-the-board political conservatism is so obvious and sound that "it nearly goes without saying."[3] However, the common-sense view of the relationship between religious and political conservatism is increasingly problematic. While a growing chorus of young evangelical activists argue that "Evangelical Does Not Equal Republican,"[4] a growing collection of sociological studies have likewise challenged the "obvious" notion that the structure of conservative religious belief strongly predisposes evangelicals toward conservative social, economic, and political attitudes.[5] Moral cosmology theory, in particular, argues that religiously orthodox believers (including American evangelicals) are in fact predisposed toward left-liberal economic attitudes because of their theological communitarianism:

> Because the religiously orthodox are theologically communitarian in viewing individuals as subsumed by a larger community of believers subject to timeless laws and God's greater plan, they are disposed toward economic communitarianism, whereby the state should provide for the poor, reduce inequality, and meet community needs via economic intervention.[6]

Theologically liberal modernists, on the other hand, "are inclined to economic individualism, whereby the poor are responsible for their fates, wider income differences promote individual initiative, and government should not interfere in the economy."[7]

Over the last fifteen years, moral cosmology theorists have accumulated an impressive body of evidence from Christian, Jewish, and Muslim contexts around the world that lends support to their counterintuitive theory.[8] In this chapter, I argue that moral cosmology theory correctly identifies *theological individualism* and *theological communitarianism* as key indicators of evangelical social, economic, and political standpoints. [9] I also argue, however, that moral cosmology theory runs aground by ignoring how specific historical struggles within the field of American Protestantism—specifically, the fundamentalist–modernist struggle in the early 1900s—pushed dominant expressions of twentieth-century conservative Protestantism toward a thoroughgoing economic and political conservatism that was neither logically nor theologically necessary. Key to my argument, and consistent with Bourdieusian field theory, is the importance of historical struggle in shaping the religious and political standpoints of American evangelicals over time. While white conservative Protestants tended toward a moderate social and political conservatism in the nineteenth century, it was not until the early twentieth-century fundamentalist–modernist struggles that white conservative Protestantism became an overwhelmingly conservative political force.

The first part of this chapter traces out a narrative analytic history of dominant expressions of twentieth-century conservative Protestantism in America, which were characterized by: (1) theological individualism and the prioritization of evangelism over other forms of social engagement; (2) conservative economic views and affinity with the American business sector; (3) conservative social views on race, gender, sexuality, and the family; and (4) patriotic efforts to consolidate and advance America's identity and heritage as a Christian nation. We will see these themes echoed in the religious and political position-takings of dominant expressions of contemporary American evangelicalism in the following chapter: positions that neo-monastic evangelicalism is largely constructed against. The second part of the chapter introduces two dominant expressions of American evangelicalism since the 1970s that have played a significant role in the development of evangelical neo-monasticism—the Christian Right and megachurch evangelicalism—as well as two historic predecessors to evangelical neo-monasticism; namely, the Jesus People movement and the evangelical left. The third part of the chapter considers moral cosmology theory's claims regarding the relation between American evangelicals' theological and political standpoints, with a specific focus on the significance of *theological individualism* and *theological communitarianism* for understanding the social and economic standpoints of American evangelicals. As we will see in Part II, this distinction is crucial for understanding the distinctive *holistic communitarian* standpoints and strategies of action which organize meaning and action within the Urban Monastery. The chapter concludes its argument by examining the role of the fundamentalist–modernist struggle in mediating the relationship between neo-monasticism and the settlement house movement made famous by Jane Addams and Hull House.

American Evangelicalism (pre-1920): Racial and Religious Roots of the Fundamentalist–Modernist Struggle

The 1800s were the "golden years" of evangelical influence in America.[10] "In 1870 almost all American Protestants thought of America as a Christian nation. . . . Viewed from their dominant perspective, the nineteenth century had been marked by successive advances of evangelicalism, the American nation, and hence the kingdom of God."[11] This taken for granted synthesis of the advance of God's kingdom with the advance of the American nation was made possible by the widespread cultural dominance of Protestant Christianity in the late nineteenth century. Public schoolchildren read the Bible and other texts—such as McGuffey's reader—that emphasized moral virtue, hard work, obeying scripture, and keeping the Sabbath. American Protestants shared a "deep concern for morality, respectability, and order" and "believed that they had a mission among the poor at home and among the heathen abroad to, (in the words of President McKinley), 'uplift and Christianize.'"[12] Conservative Protestant Christianity was the moderate, respectable religion of nineteenth-century America's white Protestant majority.[13]

Politically, this majority demonstrated concern for the poor and some sympathy with the labor movement, but from a generally conservative, "middle-class Victorian" perspective—a perspective that emphasized religion, temperance, hard work, education, and personal responsibility as the solutions to the problems of the poor. Social order and respect for authority were prioritized over labor concerns or social justice activism. Free enterprise capitalism and the individual pursuit of wealth were seen as supported by biblical morality.[14] In other words, late nineteenth-century conservative Protestants tended to be politically moderate: while holding generally conservative positions, they were in step with the cultural mainstream and did not push an aggressive conservative Christian agenda in the political arena. As the nation's dominant cultural bloc, they did not need to.

Dwight L. Moody, the leading figure of late nineteenth-century evangelical revivalism, represents an ideal typical form of the premillennialist strain of late nineteenth-century conservative Protestantism.[15] Moody was by far America's most visible and influential religious leader of the 1880s and 1890s, despite the fact that he was not an ordained minister and had no formal theological training.[16] Like many other evangelical leaders who preceded and followed him, Moody was well-connected to prominent business leaders—many of whom were also evangelical Protestants—and viewed hard work, self-mastery, decisiveness, activism, careful financial stewardship, and mass-market entrepreneurialism as Christian virtues as much as they were practical aids to success in business.[17]

In his revivals, his theology, and the religious institutions he helped establish, Moody defined the character of the nascent fundamentalist movement that would emerge in full force in the early twentieth century. His revivals drew massive crowds in urban centers across the country and were particularly popular in the Northeast and Midwest. His sermons were delivered in a sober, earnest, folksy, and decisive style that focused on the love of God, the need for personal salvation, and the possibility of forgiveness of sins through faith in Jesus. His preaching was accompanied by simple hymns set to catchy popular folk music.[18] The primary goal of Moody's revival meetings was always the conversion of individuals to faith in Christ. In other words, Moody's revival meetings looked a lot like the late nineteenth-century version of the modern evangelical megachurch. Moody believed that "salvation is instantaneous" for any individual who went through the three steps of conversion, holding a theology of spiritual conversion that was well-suited to the social technology of revival in its immediacy, clarity, totality, and appeal to decisive action.[19]

During the pinnacle of his career as a revivalist, Moody eschewed both politics and social reform to focus exclusively on the evangelistic work of saving individual souls. He avoided politics as too controversial and avoided social reform because evangelism and revival were seen as the best way to meet social needs and effect social transformation.[20] It was personal faith in Christ that led to the personal responsibility, moral uplift, and civic virtue that would guarantee the health of American society. As Moody put it, "revival is the only hope for our republic; for I don't believe that a republican form of government can last without righteousness."[21] This individualist and conversionist approach to politics and social change was rooted in a long-standing tradition of American evangelical revivalism that continues to influence evangelicalism to this day.[22] In a classic statement of theological individualism, Moody captures a perspective that has remained alive and well among American conservative Protestants to the present day: "I look upon this world as a wrecked vessel. . . . God has given me a lifeboat and said to me, 'Moody, save all you can.'"[23]

American Evangelicalism's Original Sin: Racial Roots of the Fundamentalist–Modernist Struggle

One can make a strong historical argument for the view that evangelicalism's otherworldly theological individualism and prioritization of evangelism arose in part from early efforts by white American and British clergy to interpret the Christian gospel in such a way as to make it consistent with the institution of slavery.[24] Conservative Protestant views on race have also played a significant role in the consolidation of conservative religion and politics through the twentieth century, beginning with the fundamentalist–modernist struggle in the early 1900s. While authoritative studies of contemporary evangelicalism argue against the notion that white conservative Protestants hold more racial prejudice than other white Americans,[25] support for racial inequality is nevertheless an important part of the historical development of the theological and political standpoints of white American evangelicals. If the institution of slavery and racial oppression is "America's original sin,"[26] American evangelicalism must bear its burden for helping to legitimize America's system of racial inequality, accomplished through a devastating combination affirmation and silent assent.

George Whitefield, the legendary eighteenth-century revivalist and oft-designated "founder" of American evangelicalism, energetically preached on the religious equality of whites and blacks and, unlike other revivalists of the era, preached to both groups at his revival meetings. He also actively supported and defended the institution of slavery in America and owned slaves himself.[27] While early American slaveholders resisted attempts to Christianize slaves because of the gospel's emancipatory and egalitarian implications, by Whitefield's time white American and British Christian leaders had successfully managed to separate the idea of spiritual emancipation from the idea of social emancipation in their preaching and practice of the gospel.[28] Converting to Christianity might set a slave free from sin, but not from slavery. A Christian slave was equal to his master "in the Spirit," but not in the flesh. Otherworldly spiritual equality had nothing to do with inner-worldly social equality. Indeed, it was commonplace for white Christian preachers such as Whitefield to argue that slavery was a gift to blacks because it afforded them the opportunity to hear whites preach the gospel to them and thereby save their souls.[29] One does not have to strain the eyes to see how this separation of the spiritual and social implications of the gospel gave religious sanction to slavery and racial oppression in colonial America; nor is it difficult to trace the outline of this view in the otherworldly theological individualism of dominant expressions of twentieth-century American evangelicalism.

This is not to say that white evangelicals consistently backed the existing order of racial domination in the United States. However—as they themselves acknowledge—the occasionally energetic efforts of progressive elements within white evangelicalism to challenge slavery and racial inequality were partial and deeply flawed.[30] By the late eighteenth century, the emancipatory rhetoric of the Revolutionary War inspired an early abolitionist movement in the northern states whose economies were largely independent of slave labor and whose African American populations were small.[31] While they opposed slavery, these early abolitionists—almost all of whom were Christians—did not view blacks as social equals, nor did they demand the immediate end of slavery. Rather, believing in the priority and power of evangelism to transform individuals and society, they argued that "a direct and immediate assault on slavery was unnecessary" because slavery "would be abolished gradually by the diffusion of the gospel."[32] It was not until the 1830s that the abolitionist movement began demanding the immediate end of slavery and began incorporating free blacks (such as Fredrick Douglas and Sojourner Truth) into their abolitionist societies.

Charles Finney, America's leading evangelical revivalist of the period, was a major figure in the abolitionist movement, mentoring young abolitionist leaders and claiming that one could not be both a slaveholder and a Christian.[33] However, as the abolitionist movement he helped establish became increasingly strident in its demands for racial equality, he came to view the abolitionist movement as a hindrance to the gospel: "Finney considered slavery a sin, but asserted that there should be no 'diversion of the public mind' from the task of converting people and inculcating their minds with 'the gospel.'"[34] Finney's concern for the priority of evangelism eventually led him to part ways with non-evangelical abolitionists, such as William Garrison, whose demands for racial equality grew increasingly fervent and whose focus on evangelism waned. Moreover, while Finney staunchly opposed slavery, like most northern whites he did not oppose racial segregation itself, as his own church's practice of racial segregation made clear.[35]

At this point we can make two immediate observations concerning the racial roots of the fundamentalist–modernist struggle and of dominant expressions of evangelical theology more generally. First, Charles Finney's split with the non-evangelical abolitionist movement foreshadowed the twentieth-century split between theologically conservative Protestants and their "spiritual" gospel and theologically liberal Protestants and their "social" gospel. In his prioritization of evangelism over issues of social or racial justice, Finney represented the views of both northern and southern evangelicals of the period, although his spirited advocacy of the abolitionist cause positively distinguished him from his evangelical contemporaries who were largely silent on the matter of racial oppression.[36]

Second, while the theological beliefs of white evangelicals influenced their perspectives on racial equality, the historical record suggests that their views tended to reflect and reproduce—rather than challenge—the existing order of racial inequality in their immediate local contexts.[37] Dependent on slave labor and surrounded by a large African American population, white southern Christians developed biblical arguments in favor slavery and segregation, while white Christians in the industrialized north opposed slavery but not racial segregation. The record of American evangelical position-takings on racial equality strikes a decisive blow against the "upwards conflation" that would deny the influence of social location and material interests on the theological and political standpoints of evangelicals.[38]

Theological Roots of the Fundamentalist–Modernist Struggle

Notwithstanding conventional wisdom, the early twentieth-century fundamentalist movement originated as an intellectual, urban, and northern phenomenon focused on combating theological liberalism in the Protestant denominations; not the anti-intellectual, rural, and southern caricature it became after the late 1920s political mobilization against evolution.[39] The groundwork for the categories of conflict between theologically conservative fundamentalists and secular and religious modernists originated among divinity school theologians and church leaders of the northern Protestant denominations (in particular, the Baptist and Presbyterian denominations).[40]

In the face of growing intellectual challenges from theological modernists who were in the process of reinterpreting traditional Christian beliefs—such as the divinity and resurrection of Christ—in light of modern scientific and philosophical developments, leaders in these broadly evangelical denominations began developing a rigorous defense of the traditional Christian faith.[41] It was an intellectual defense, rooted in Scottish Common Sense Realism that defended both the "perspicuity of nature" and the Bible.[42] As the leading Presbyterian seminary in America, Princeton became the center of the conservative Protestant defense of biblical authority and inerrancy within the denominations. They eventually joined forces with Moody and the premillennialist leaders of the late nineteenth-century Bible and Prophecy Conferences to defend the common sense, literal interpretation of the Bible against modernist challenges.[43]

The disputes between theological conservatives and liberals in the Protestant denominations were centered directly on the "authority of scripture, its scientific accuracy, and supernatural elements of Christ's person and work."[44] It was during these battles that the Presbyterian "famous five points" of conservative Protestant orthodoxy were constructed, consisting of, "1) inerrancy of scripture, 2) the Virgin Birth of Christ, 3) his substitutionary atonement, 4) his bodily resurrection, 5) the authenticity of the miracles."[45] These five points became the litmus test of fundamentalist belief in the 1920s and remain part of evangelical *doxa* to the present day.[46] Beginning in 1910, evangelical oil magnate Lyman Stewart funded a massive defense, spanning five years and twelve volumes, of the conservative Protestant position called *The Fundamentals*. Though mostly ignored by leading theologians of the day, *The Fundamentals* were very widely disseminated, with three million free copies being distributed to Protestant clergy and religious leaders throughout the English-speaking world. The texts gave expression to conservative Protestantism's burgeoning "broad united front" against modernism and theological liberalism in the early twentieth century.[47]

The content of *The Fundamentals* clearly demonstrates the theological, rather than political, focus of the fundamentalist movement prior to World War I. It avoided political issues and focused on promoting evangelism and mission while vigorously defending the scientific and historical accuracy of the Bible. Of the ninety articles published in its twelve volumes, fully one-third were devoted to defending the divine inspiration, inerrancy, and historical accuracy of the Bible.[48] One-third defended other traditional Christian doctrines such as the divinity and resurrection of Jesus. An entire volume was dedicated to articles about evangelism and foreign mission. Fifteen articles focused on personal salvation, personal piety, and premillennial eschatology.[49] Only three

articles addressed the topic of evolution, which became the focus of fundamentalist political activism in the 1920s. While *The Fundamentals* came to be
viewed retrospectively as an early fundamentalist battle cry against modernism, its contents and tone were far more moderate than the extreme anti-
modernist sentiments that developed in the 1920s, when the fundamentalist's
political battle against the teaching of evolution in public schools and their
theological battle against liberalism in the Protestant denominations came to
a climax.

The groups that coalesced around the anti-modernist position did so to
defend the divine origins and content of the Bible, its literal interpretation,
and traditional Christian doctrines like the divinity and resurrection of
Christ for the forgiveness of sins. Three streams in particular—D. L. Moody
and his followers, the premillennialist movement, and conservative Presbyte-
rians led by the Princeton theologians—set the pattern for possible position-
takings in the field of conservative Protestantism for decades to come. From
Moody came theological individualism and the "miracle motif" approach to
politics,[50] mass-market evangelism and the prioritization of evangelism over
social reform, moral pietism, belief in religious and business entrepreneurialism, and a pessimistic view of the world and the possibility of social transformation. From the premillennialist's came a preoccupation with "end
times" eschatology and a corresponding emphasis on evangelism over social
reform, biblical literalism, and a tendency toward separatism. From conservative Presbyterianism came crystallized doctrines of biblical inspiration and
inerrancy, biblical literalism, and a Puritan reformist heritage that actively
sought to exert Christian influence in American political and public life. As
these distinct but related movements within conservative Protestantism
joined forces against modernism in the early twentieth century, they set the
pattern for the types of standpoints and struggles that would dominate the
field of American evangelicalism throughout the twentieth century and into
the present day. It was the concrete historical struggle against modernism—
not abstract theological reflection or systematic biblical interpretation—that
established the founding *doxa* of the newly emerging field of fundamentalist
Protestantism in America.[51]

These turn of the century disputes in the American Protestant field were
fierce battles to be sure, but they were largely confined to denominational leaders, clergy, and seminary faculties during this period. Fundamentalism's original preoccupation was with preserving traditional Christian theology inside
the church, not pursuing a Christian cultural or political agenda outside of it.
Just as the social-material roots of white evangelical perspectives on racial inequality warn against the "upwards conflation" which reduces evangelical

position-takings to religious culture, the specifically theological-religious roots of the fundamentalist–modernist controversy strikes a blow against the "downwards conflation" that would crudely reduce religious standpoints to mere expressions of political or economic interest. The specifically *religious* nature of the fundamentalist–modernist struggle within American Protestantism also speaks to the relative autonomy of the Protestant religious field with respect to the larger American political and social fields.[52] It was only in the context of heightened anxieties surrounding World War I and turn-of-the-century challenges to white Protestant hegemony that theological conservatives began to be sufficiently concerned about the "modernist threat" in America to shift their attention from intra-denominational theological skirmishes to the public cultural and political arena.

American Evangelicalism (1917–1929): The Fundamentalist–Modernist Struggle

The years between 1917 and 1920 saw theologically conservative Protestants move from a moderate to a staunchly conservative politics.[53] Of course, things were not always so. William Jennings Bryan—the 1920s most infamous fundamentalist—was a peace activist, economic populist, and leader in the Progressive Movement.[54] Prior to 1917, one could find many progressive elements among theologically conservative Protestants, including significant commitments to pacifism and economic populism. By the 1920s, however, economic and political progressivism had almost completely disappeared, replaced by a strident political conservatism. This dramatic polarization and consolidation of religious and political conservatism was largely the result of the battle against the theological modernists and the liberal Social Gospel. Christian social activism as emphasized by the Social Gospel became associated with other theologically liberal positions, such as the acceptance of evolutionary theory and the denial of Jesus's divinity and resurrection. The intensity of the conflict between conservatives and liberals in the Protestant denominations hardened symbolic boundaries such that it became increasingly impossible to hold a moderate or mixed position on certain theological and social issues. One was either anti-evolution, anti-Social Gospel, anti-liberal, and believed in the inerrancy and authority of the Bible and its literal interpretation (a *fundamentalist*), or one supported the reinterpretation of the Bible in light of scientific and philosophical modernism and advocated a this-worldly social gospel as the true meaning of Christian spiritual and ethical life (a *modernist*). The primary responsibility of Christians in the world became crystallized as either evangelism—spreading the gospel of salvation, spiritual renewal, and moral regeneration to individuals for the next world—or social action, the reduction of poverty and human suffering, and the expansion of social justice and equality in this world. The fundamentalist–modernist struggle transformed the face of conservative Protestantism in America to lasting effect.

World War I played a significant role in increasing the popularity of fundamentalism's premillennialist theology and heightening polarization of the growing fundamentalist–modernist divide. The war seemed to validate premillennialist predictions of decline and disintegration, rather than peace and progress, for "Christian civilization" in the West. At the beginning of the war, it was ironically theological liberals who questioned the patriotic zeal of these premillennialist conservative Protestants, arguing that the conservatives' gloomy view of the world was a betrayal of faith in Christian America. These pro-war theological liberals worried that conservative Protestants' premillennial theology dampened their zeal for America's Christian calling to "make the world safe for democracy" against German aggression.[55] Skeptical theological conservatives countered, "Who will make [American] democracy safe for the world?"[56] However, as the war dragged on, most conservative Protestants—along with most of America—increasingly sounded the bell of patriotic religious nationalism. As celebrity revivalist Billy Sunday succinctly put the matter: "Christianity and Patriotism are synonymous terms and hell and traitors are synonymous."[57] Within the rapidly growing fundamentalist movement, German war-mongering came to be viewed as a direct result of Germany's lapse into theological liberalism and secularism, which further intensified and politicized fundamentalists' arguments against theological modernism in their own American contexts.

The war thus sharpened the focus of conservative Protestants on "dangers" at home as well as the German danger abroad. From the fundamentalist perspective, these dangers were legion. The period between 1880 and World War I saw massive demographic changes in the United States as a result of rapidly rising industrialization, urbanization, and immigration.[58] The secularization of American universities was well under way, eroding religious authority in favor of scientific authority and academic freedom. Accustomed to thinking of America as a Christian (i.e., Protestant) nation,[59] conservative Protestants became increasingly alarmed about these challenges to white Protestant hegemony, believing as they did that American security and prosperity was directly linked to the preservation of its Christian values and heritage.[60] They saw in Germany a warning about the consequences facing America if it abandoned this heritage in favor of theological liberalism and modernity in general. The fundamentalist–modernist controversy was about to break out into the open.

The first explicitly fundamentalist organization—the World's Christian Fundamentals Association—was formed in 1919, as the focus of conservative Protestants shifted from evangelism and "end times" speculation to concern over the identity and future of America.[61] Its goal was to defend traditional Christian doctrines against religious and secular modernism, and to call the nation to return to the Bible and its Christian heritage to avoid the otherwise inevitable collapse of American society. Other like-minded organizations proliferated in the burgeoning fundamentalist movement, sounding a "return to Christian roots" theme focused on spiritual revival, a return to Christian morality, the defense of conservative Protestant theology, and eventually anti-evolutionism.[62]

Anti-evolutionism did not become a primary fundamentalist concern until the 1920s.[63] It was in the aftermath of World War I that the "'might is right,' Bible-denying philosophy of evolution" became the focus of fundamentalist efforts to save "Christian America" from succumbing to the forces of philosophical, scientific, and theological modernism.[64] The battle against evolution marked a significant shift in fundamentalism's primary focus on religious activities such as evangelism, foreign missions, and defense of biblical literalism, to a more public and political focus on stemming America's "moral decline" brought on by religious and secular modernism. It transformed fundamentalism from its roots as an urban, northern, religious movement to preserve conservative Protestant theology against modernist influences into an increasingly politicized, rural, and southern movement focused on preserving traditional Christian values in American society. "What modernism is to the church," fundamentalists argued, "evolution is to the culture."[65] Evolutionism, it was argued, led to atheism, to communism, to militarism (just look at Germany!), and to the erosion of traditional morality.[66] Allowing evolution to be taught in public schools would inevitably lead to moral corruption, social disintegration, and divine judgment for America. Fundamentalists viewed the battle against evolution as a battle for the soul of America as a Christian nation, which, from the fundamentalist point of view, was the very foundation of American identity, security, and prosperity.[67]

The struggle against evolution came to a head in the summer of 1925, when former Democratic presidential candidate William Jennings Bryan volunteered to represent the State of Tennessee in its case against public school teacher John Scopes, who was accused of teaching evolution in a public school.[68] Partly because of Bryan's status as a major political figure, the trial was overwhelmed with national media attention. While Scopes was convicted, the trial was a devastating defeat for Bryan and the fundamentalist cause in the court of public opinion. According to published accounts, Bryan was embarrassed by the ACLU's top trial lawyers, making the anti-evolutionist position look generally ignorant and ridiculous. H. L. Mencken, one of America's most influential journalists at the time, ridiculed Bryan and the fundamentalists, explaining their position as expressions of rural, southern, anti-intellectualist rage against urbanism, modernism, and change in general.[69] On the heels of the Scopes trial, fundamentalism was (mistakenly, as it turned out) left for dead as a political and religious movement in the United States.[70] However, the oppositional theological and political standpoints and boundaries constructed during the fundamentalist struggle against modernism set the pattern for dominant expressions of conservative Protestantism in America through the rest of the century.

American Evangelicalism (1930–1970): Individualism and Conservatism Consolidated

The struggle against theological and secular modernism reinforced conservative Protestants' theological individualism in defeat as it did in the heat of the battle. During the active phase of the fundamentalist–modernist conflict, conservative Protestants fought against the social gospel of theological liberals by emphasizing the personal, spiritual, and otherworldly aspects of biblical faith. The very public failure of their anti-evolution campaign, along with their failed struggle to purge the Protestant denominations of theological liberalism, reinforced conservative Protestants' belief in the corruption of social institutions and their skepticism about the possibility of social transformation without spiritual revival.[71] In the midst of partial withdrawal from the Protestant denominations and national politics, conservative Protestants refocused their energies on evangelism—preaching the gospel of personal salvation from sin and God's judgment through faith in Jesus Christ. Like the late nineteenth-century revivalist D. L. Moody before them, a new generation of conservative Protestant leaders emerged whose singular focus was the salvation of souls.[72] Like Moody, they did their best to avoid politically or theologically controversial issues in order to focus solely on the task of evangelism, which was the most important duty of every Christian. In the words of a typical new evangelical leader: "The function of the church is to evangelize the world . . . before the return of the Lord."[73] All other individual, social, or political activity was meaningless in comparison to this essential pursuit. Referring to Charles Fuller and Harold Ockenga—cofounders of Fuller Theological

Seminary and leaders of 1950s new evangelicalism—historian George Marsden writes:

> Each focused his ministry on the urgency of massive efforts to win sinners to Jesus. The world was in crisis, the ultimate root of which was unbelief. The best way to combat the modernists and secularists who had undermined the civilization was to preach the gospel message simply and effectively. The message was found in the Bible alone. The certainty of the truth of the Bible, that every word was the word of God, was the only hope for a world in turmoil and uncertainty.[74]

The struggle against modernism thus reinforced conservative Protestants' theological individualism and prioritization of evangelism over other forms of social engagement both during and after the conflict, creating the unique historical conditions that help explain *evangelical exceptionalism* with respect to moral cosmology theory.

While this focus on evangelism was the defining characteristic of the fundamentalist/evangelical movement in the 1930s and 1940s, it continued to advocate fundamentalist perspectives on the divine inspiration and authority of the Bible, the modernist threat to America, and suspicion toward theological and political left-liberalism.[75] Throughout the 1930s and into the early 1950s, conservative Protestant leaders—including the young Billy Graham—continued to sound the classic fundamentalist theme that "a return to Christian theism was America's only hope for avoiding destructive judgment."[76] They vigorously defended the divine inspiration of the Bible and vigorously attacked both liberal theology and liberal politics. Conservative evangelical colleges advertised their "conservative social and economic views" and assured parents that they were places where communism and modernism were "conclusively disproven."[77] Standing against the "northern liberal philosophies" of the modernist establishment, conservative religious entrepreneurs in the Sunbelt launched new private colleges around a "comprehensive doctrine that blended Christ and capitalism":[78]

> WE BELIEVE: In the Book, the Blood, and the Blessed Hope . . . That soul-winning evangelism and training in discipleship are the primary responsibilities of the church . . . In basic, old-fashioned Americanism and the free enterprise system; In an uncompromising stand against Modernism, Socialism, Communism and every form of "One Worldism!"[79]

"Plain-folk" conservative evangelicals learned to view New Deal social and economic programs skeptically as harbingers of atheistic communism,[80] as leading conservative evangelical preachers and institutions such as the American Council of Christian Churches attacked mainline Protestant churches and ecumenical groups as communist sympathizers.[81]

Although mid-century evangelicalism did not feature the sort of mass-based political mobilization that characterized the early and late twentieth century, its leaders remained active in promoting conservative economic and political perspectives, while also receiving widespread financial support from America's conservative business elite.[82] Led by evangelical oil executive J. Howard Pew and other prominent corporate leaders, many of the nation's largest corporations provided substantial funding to a wide range of conservative Protestant religious organizations, from popular periodicals and youth ministries to Christian colleges and evangelistic crusades.[83] Through the religious organizations that they supported, conservative business leaders trumpeted the alarm that "New Dealism, Socialism, and Communism are substantially the same thing—and all of them are the very antithesis of Christianity."[84]

Dominant expressions of mid-century conservative Protestantism were bulwarks of theological and economic individualism, defending "private enterprise and traditional Protestant values" as the foundation of American identity and prosperity.[85] "The business of business pervaded white Protestant culture in the 1920s," when American pastors and presidents alike agreed that "material prosperity and godliness go hand in hand."[86] The theological individualism inherent in evangelicalism's revivalist tradition fit nicely alongside libertarian free market ideology of twentieth-century American conservatism post-1920.[87] Premillennialist theology's pessimistic view of social institutions and the human heart mirrored conservative pessimism toward solving economic or social problems through "social engineering," while white evangelicals' commitment to "accountable freewill individualism" supported the laissez-faire economic principles favored by free market advocates and conservative businessmen.[88] "Although fundamentalism was a spiritual movement," evangelical historians agree, "conservative theology correlated, if not perfectly, with conservative politics."[89]

Compared to pre-1920s conservative Protestantism, mid-century fundamentalism was increasingly combative and sectarian.[90] By the late 1940s a growing number of "new evangelical" leaders had become increasingly frustrated with the heightened separatism, anti-intellectualism, and combativeness of the fundamentalist movement.[91] New evangelical leaders such as Billy Graham, Charles Fuller (popular radio evangelist and Fuller Seminary cofounder), Harold Ockenga (founding president of the National Association of Evangelicals), and Carl F. H. Henry began to stake out *evangelicalism* as a new position in the field of conservative Protestantism that would eventually overtake fundamentalism as the dominant expression of conservative Protestantism in America. In an influential book titled *The Uneasy Conscience of Modern Fundamentalism*, Carl F. H. Henry—Fuller Seminary cofounder and the first editor of *Christianity Today*—argued that while evangelism and revival were the primary ways that the church should engage with the world, Christians could not ignore the broader cultural and social problems facing America.[92] Speaking for the new evangelicals, Henry criticized fundamentalists' "religious escapism" and their neglect of public engagement and social reform. He criticized aggressive militarism, racial prejudice, and the unjust exploitation of workers, and was eventually forced to leave his role as editor of *Christianity Today* because the magazine's financial backer—wealthy evangelical oil magnate J. Howard Pew—insisted that Henry refrain from criticizing capitalism in any way. Henry was an economic conservative, yet even his mild critiques of the free-enterprise system proved too progressive for Pew, who demanded that *Christianity Today* maintain a staunch conservative economic stance.[93]

The leaders of the "new evangelicalism" were economic and political conservatives who held firmly to "traditional Protestant American values of hard work and self-help":

> They believed that freedom from external control was a chief social virtue and that rugged individualism was the key to success. Not surprisingly, these respectable fundamentalists got along especially well with a number of pious members of the conservative business community.[94]

Though less extreme than their fundamentalist brethren, the new evangelicals shared the fundamentalists' generally conservative politics and theology, their high view of biblical authority and inspiration, and their prioritization of evangelism over other forms of social engagement. This focus on evangelism and social order over social justice activism is nowhere more apparent than in white evangelical responses to the civil rights movement, which ranged from silent acceptance of Jim Crow segregation to outright opposition to Martin Luther King Jr. and the movement he helped to lead. Many white evangelicals viewed the civil rights movement as a misguided attempt by "communist agitators" and godless liberals to impose a racially integrated social order that was either impractical or unbiblical, depending on one's point of view.[95]

After the embarrassment of the Scopes trial and fundamentalism's descent into an increasingly separatist and alarmist style of anti-intellectualism, new evangelical leaders were highly motivated to restore theologically conservative Protestantism to a place of greater public respectability and influence.[96] Increasingly, they found success. Mainstream media coverage of Billy Graham's evangelism crusades made him a national figure by 1950, granting him access to the nation's political and economic elites while serving as a spiritual advisor to American presidents beginning with Eisenhower in 1953.[97] Partly as a result of Graham's early evangelistic crusades in Los Angeles, Henrietta Mears and others established an evangelical presence among Hollywood elites. These new evangelicals sought dialogue with intellectually respectable theologians from mainline Protestant denominations, took more moderate positions on biblical inerrancy, and worked to train a new generation of legitimate evangelical scholars who would have the capacity to reestablish evangelicalism as an intellectually respectable religious position in America.[98] The new evangelicalism would eventually give rise to a reinvigorated mass-based political mobilization of conservative Christians in the 1980s, an affluent megachurch evangelicalism rooted in the middle-class suburbs, and a growing evangelical elite increasingly comfortable operating in the nation's "halls of power."[99]

American Evangelicalism (1970s–): From Jesus Freaks and Culture Warriors to Megachurches and the Moral Minority[100]

In consolidating conservative Protestant opposition to the social gospel movement, to secular and religious modernism, and to left-liberal political standpoints more generally, the fundamentalist–modernist struggle and its aftermath set the stage for new positions in the American evangelical field that would reproduce dominant twentieth-century evangelical points of view concerning the prioritization of evangelism, theological individualism, social and economic conservatism, and religious nationalism. As the 1980s approached, Christian Right activists mobilized conservative evangelicals into a New Right coalition that wed social traditionalism, economic conservatism, and anti-communist religious nationalism together, while a new model of megachurch evangelicalism began to take off in the suburbs which eschewed politics in order to focus on energetic and innovative efforts to reach individuals for Christ. We cannot understand evangelical neo-monasticism without understanding its (largely oppositional) relation to these two movements, which came to occupy dominant positions in the American evangelical field.[101] In addition to the Christian Right and megachurch evangelicalism, this period also gave rise to the Jesus People movement and the evangelical left, movements whose communitarian and left-leaning political standpoints are historic predecessors to contemporary evangelical neo-monasticism.

Rise of the Christian Right

In the aftermath of fundamentalism's vigorous political mobilization and defeat in the 1920s, conservative Protestants redoubled their focus on evangelism, missions, church growth, and Christian education.[102] "As far as the relationship of the church and the world," preached pre-Moral Majority Jerry Falwell in 1965, "it can be expressed as simply as the three words which Paul gave Timothy: 'preach the Word.'"[103] Returning to the revivalist dispensationalism of D. L. Moody's evangelistic crusades and Bible and Prophecy conferences, dominant mid-century conservative evangelical leaders such as Falwell, Tim LaHaye, and Hal Lindsey told American Christians "that they had nothing else to do with their lives on this earth but pray, live right, and save souls."[104] While they did not abandon politics completely, mid-century evangelicals were more likely to express their conservative political views in religious broadcasts, colleges, and periodicals than they were to engage in direct political action.[105] Between 1953 and 1974, every major study of American religion showed that evangelicals were less likely to be politically active than other groups.[106] By 1981, the opposite was true: evangelicals had rather suddenly become the most politically active religious group in America.[107] While evangelism and mission remained their primary concern, ordinary conservative Protestants increasingly viewed direct political activism as part of Christian social responsibility, and their involvement in politics was driven primarily by concern about the decline of conservative Christian influence and traditional morality in America's families, schools, and popular culture.

The return of the conservative Protestant grassroots to the political arena en masse was largely the work of the new Christian Right's emergence in the late 1970s, foreshadowed by the rising political clout of conservative evangelicals in the Sunbelt and Southern California in particular.[108] Its primary focus was to pursue legislation and elect candidates committed to "social traditionalism" to combat "the breakdown of family, community, religion, and traditional morality in American life" caused by "liberals operating through the federal government":

> In this view, the government had undermined family, religion, and morality through such diverse actions (and inactions) as Internal

Revenue Service cases against Christian private schools, the failure to crack down on pornography, support for abortion and the ERA [Equal Rights Amendment], advocacy of lenient drug laws, opposition to prayer in public school, and by generally encouraging a secular humanist outlook.[109]

The public leaders of the new Christian Right were ministers of the country's largest conservative Protestant churches and television evangelists with huge national followings. They were integrated into the broader New Right conservative coalition by longtime conservative political activists from outside the world of evangelical religion.[110] They were highly successful entrepreneurs who built enormous and lucrative religious organizations that included megachurches, private schools and colleges, mission organizations, and media empires.[111] And their advent sparked a new era of conservative Protestant political activism that has had a significant impact on American religion and politics over the last thirty years. While experiencing the usual ebbs and flows of electoral failure and success at both state and national levels, by 2000 Christian Right organizations and activists were firmly established as Republican Party insiders with significant clout over the party's platform, candidates, and ability to mobilize support in electoral campaigns.[112] Beginning with its emergence in the late 1970s, the Christian Right had gone "from an outsider social movement to a conventional interest group to a durable faction within a major party,"[113] with conservative Protestants constituting the majority of its core constituency.[114]

The cast of characters is now largely familiar. Republican political organizers Paul Weyrich and Richard Viguerie—both conservative Catholics—encouraged Rev. Jerry Falwell to establish the Moral Majority in 1979, helping to link the emerging religious Right with the wider constellation of conservative interests and political organizations. Beginning in 1976, Falwell had been organizing "I Love America" rallies in state capitols across the country to advocate a return to traditional morality in America alongside local pastors and politicians.[115] He aligned himself with other emerging conservative leaders such as Phyllis Schlafly's Eagle Forum to oppose gay rights and the Equal Rights Amendment (ERA) for women.[116] The Moral Majority was joined by two other prominent conservative Protestant political organizations in 1979, the Religious Roundtable and Christian Voice. The Christian Voice was formed by two California ministers to pursue a pro-family, anti-pornography, and anti-gay rights platform, and got its message out through Pat Robertson's Christian Broadcasting Network.[117] The Religious Roundtable—in which all of the leading television evangelists of the 1970s participated—was formed to promote the political education and mobilization of Southern

Baptist, Presbyterian, and Methodist ministers and congregations toward conservative political causes.[118] After a failed presidential bid in 1988, Pat Robertson founded the Christian Coalition in an attempt to unite conservative Christians in a "pro-family" platform whose goals included electing a "pro-family Congress by 1994 and pro-family president by 2000," goals that were essentially met during the 1994 congressional and 2000 presidential elections.[119] The late 1970s also witnessed the founding of several other organizations that would rise to increasingly prominent roles within the Christian Right in later years, including Beverly LaHaye's Concerned Women for America—founded by the wife of *Left Behind* series coauthor and Moral Majority cofounder Tim LaHaye—Donald E. Wildimon's American Family Association, James Dobson's Focus on the Family, and D. James Kennedy's Coral Ridge Ministries.[120]

The strength of the new Christian Right lay in its ability to organize mass-based political mobilization in favor of Republican "pro-family" candidates, a strength that is well-suited for winning elections and exerting legislative pressure but not always effective in accomplishing substantive policy change. Like the broader "New Right" conservative coalition of which it was a part, the Christian Right quickly learned that electing conservative politicians was a necessary but not sufficient stepping stone on the road to successful conservative policy implementation.[121] To enact their "pro-family" political agenda, they would have to deal with the courts. In particular, they would have to deal with an ascendant "liberal legal network" that enraged religious and nonreligious conservatives alike by forcing public school desegregation, challenging the tax-exempt status of certain conservative religious organizations and schools (many of which maintained racial segregation), legalizing abortion, and limiting prayer and religious expression in public schools.[122] To meet this challenge, a handful of conservative public interest law firms emerged to help the Christian Right fight the "civil war for values . . . in our nation's courts," most notably the American Center for Law and Justice and the Alliance Defending Freedom (formerly the Alliance Defense Fund).[123] The Alliance Defending Freedom was founded by high-profile leaders from thirty-five conservative Christian ministries—including James Dobson, and the late D. James Kennedy and Bill Bright—in order to combat the "dramatic loss of religious freedom in America's courts and the resulting challenges to people of faith to live and proclaim the Gospel."[124] Founded by Pat Robertson in 1990 and led by prominent CEO and Chief Counsel Jay Sekulow, the American Center for Law and Justice (ACLJ) is the largest and most visible firm involved in litigating religious freedom and other cases of interest to religious conservatives.[125] While these organizations have had significant success in safeguarding religious expression as a type of free speech protected under the First Amendment, the tacit acceptance of pluralism inherent in their most successful legal strategies belies the aggressive "Christian America" rhetoric sounded by Christian Right leaders for the purposes of grassroots mobilization.[126]

There is much evidence of the Christian Right's success at mobilizing white conservative Protestant voters in support of conservative Republican Party politics. From the 1970s to the present, evangelicals went from being apolitical Democrats to politically active Republicans.[127] The most politically active pastors in major conservative Protestant denominations believe that free market capitalism is the only economic system compatible with Christian belief, are motivated by social (not economic or other) issues, and believe that it is hard to be a political liberal and a true Christian.[128] They are also overwhelmingly conservative and Republican. National Election Study data from 1980 to 2004 shows a steady convergence of evangelicalism and Republican Party identification, with white evangelicals supporting Republican presidential candidates by more than a 2:1 margin.[129] Evangelical views on health care, defense spending, and government aid also became increasingly conservative between 1980 and 2004—reflecting the increasing number of evangelicals identifying with conservatism and the Republican Party in general over this period.[130] In the 2000 presidential election, 76 percent of white evangelicals and 87 percent of clergy from five evangelical denominations voted for George W. Bush, and white evangelicals were even more likely to vote for Bush in 2004 than they were in 2000.[131] If the fundamentalist-modernist struggles of the 1920s set the foundations for a thoroughgoing political conservatism among dominant expressions of conservative Protestantism in America, the rise of the Christian Right since the late 1970s reinforced these foundations; building up a new—yet familiar—popular political movement of conservative evangelicals, still fiercely opposed to the secular and religious Left, who sought to restore America's faith in its Christian identity and calling in the world, in the traditional family and biblical morality, and in the virtues of free market entrepreneurialism and capitalism.[132]

Megachurch Evangelicalism

Alongside the rise of the Christian Right, perhaps the most significant development in American evangelicalism since the mid-1970s has been the rise of the megachurch. While evangelicalism has been the fastest growing segment of American Christianity since the 1970s, megachurches are the fastest growing evangelical churches.[133] In 1970, there were 50 Protestant churches in the

United States with 2,000 members or more: by 2005 there were over 1,200—
almost all of which were started after 1970.[134] The rapid rise of the evangelical
megachurch through the 1980s moved in lockstep with the rapid expansion
of the suburban Sunbelt, as in the case of one of America's most famous
evangelical megachurches, Rick Warren's Saddleback Church in Orange
County, CA.[135] As a newly ordained, Texas-trained Southern Baptist pastor
supported by the denomination's leading lights, Warren sold a major southern California real estate developer on a plan to incorporate room for a new
Southern Baptist church plant and private school into its Laguna Hills' development plans, to great success.[136] Following in the entrepreneurial footsteps
of predecessors such as D. L. Moody and Charles Fuller, Warren's quintes-
sentially evangelical combination of folksy communication, evangelistic zeal,
and business savvy turned his "purpose-driven life" trademark into one of
America's most recognizable religious brands.

Like Saddleback Church, the vast majority of megachurches are located
in the Sunbelt regions of the south and southwestern United States. Texas
and California have the most, while the Atlanta, Houston, Los Angeles, and
Orlando have the heaviest concentration of megachurches among urban
areas.[137] Over 80 percent of megachurches have a significant white-majority
membership base, and most are located in suburban neighborhoods composed of relatively wealthy, well-educated, professional families with young
children:[138]

> [Evangelical megachurches] combine orthodox theological orienta-
> tions with the therapeutic personalism that marks Baby-Boomer reli-
> giosity. Megachurches are often described as innovators in church
> architecture and worship practices. The prototypical megachurch—
> Willow Creek Community Church in Illinois—looks more like a cor-
> porate office park or community college than a church. It seats several
> thousands in its theater-style worship space, minimizes overt displays
> of Christian symbols (e.g., there is no cross in the sanctuary), and
> offers a wide range of services and activities.[139]

These activities include things like pre-schools and primary schools, age- and
interest-based small groups, sports leagues and recreational outings, social
services and outreach programs, and multiple worship services catering to
different subcultures throughout the week: activities that offer diverse music
and teaching formats designed to appeal to different demographic subgroups
(e.g. twenty-somethings, teens, parents, older adults, etc.).[140]

The churches they influence have similar characteristics. The pastors of Willow Creek Association (WCA) churches are overwhelmingly white, male, educated, and middle-aged.[141] They lead churches that are overwhelmingly white, middle class, and located in the South and Midwest. Much like the megachurch they seek to emulate, WCA churches are more likely than other evangelical churches to support social service programs ranging from food pantries to parenting support programs.[142] These programs tend to be understood as a type of evangelistic "organized benevolence,"[143] a way to "help individuals in the larger community solve their own problems"; demonstrating the individualist and relational style of social outreach favored by the typical megachurch evangelical.[144] Unlike neo-monastic leaders, these megachurch pastors tend to be both theologically and politically conservative: 83 percent voted for Bush in the 2000 presidential election, while 60 percent identified as Republicans.[145] While megachurch evangelicals tend to be more socially engaged and politically moderate than other evangelical churches, they remain overwhelmingly conservative on the whole.[146]

The seeker-sensitive megachurch tries to attract nonbelievers by minimizing the cultural gap between the language and experience of going to church and everyday middle-class activities like going to work or going shopping:

> Seeker churches have a strong, explicit mission to evangelize or reach the "unchurched" and are willing to experiment with worship styles, architecture, and religious ideas in order to make Christianity appealing and authentic to a boomer and post-boomer population alienated or indifferent to organized religion . . . [they] intentionally minimize the distance between the outside world and the church by showing how Christianity is relevant and applicable to the world of middle-class suburbanites. More specifically, many "Seeker" megachurches tend to emphasize the personalistic aspects of faith—a believer's personal relationship with Jesus and the ways in which faith can help individuals address numerous domestic or personal issues in order to demonstrate that Christianity is relevant.[147]

While seeker-sensitive and purpose-driven evangelical megachurches are architecturally, technologically, and organizationally innovative, their prioritization of evangelism and theological individualism reproduces one of twentieth-century American evangelicalism's dominant religious points of view.[148]

The Evangelical Left

While the increasing visibility and prominence of the evangelical left is new, its existence is not. Jim Wallis was an antiwar student activist at Michigan State in the 1960s and attended Trinity Evangelical Divinity School (a prominent evangelical seminary outside Chicago), where he and fellow seminary students established *Sojourners* as a faith-based magazine committed to peace and social justice (originally called *The Post-American*), along with an egalitarian Christian community which relocated to inner-city Washington, DC, in the early 1970s: a community that bore striking resemblance to many contemporary neo-monastic communities in its emphases on racial and economic justice and the practice of community and holistic mission in poor, marginalized urban neighborhoods.[149] Today, *Sojourners* is an ecumenical evangelical organization articulating "the biblical call to social justice" to a media subscription list of over 250,000 readers.[150]

Besides Sojourners, a number of other organizations are involved in mobilizing evangelicals around social justice issues traditionally associated with left-liberal political orientations. Dr. Tony Campolo, popular international author and speaker and emeritus Professor of Sociology at Eastern University, founded the Evangelical Association for the Promotion of Education (EAPE) in 1971. EAPE has supported the establishment of universities, elementary and secondary schools, AIDS hospices, orphanages, and literacy programs in Haiti, the Dominican Republic, and inner cities throughout North America. EAPE also partners with other evangelical left, emerging church, ecumenical, and neo-monastic communities and organizations. Campolo's son Bart established Mission Year in 1996, mobilizing over 1,000 young adults to spend a year living in urban intentional communities to "pursue Beloved Community" and "fight injustice in their cities."[151]

Dr. Ronald J. Sider—a leading evangelical author, professor, and founder of Evangelicals for Social Action and its flagship magazine *PRISM*—traces the origins of the evangelical left to a gathering of key evangelical intellectuals and leaders in Chicago in 1973, where he coauthored *The Chicago Declaration of Evangelical Social Concern* with Jim Wallis and others.[152] The declaration was an early attempt to "reverse the 'Great Reversal'" in American evangelicalism, a reversal that had divorced the personal and spiritual work of the church from its social and political responsibility to uphold justice and mercy.[153] The Chicago Declaration was a public confession and condemnation of American evangelicalism's complicity with global and domestic economic inequality, racism, militarism, and gender inequality:

> We acknowledge that God requires justice. But we have not proclaimed or demonstrated his justice to an unjust American society. Although the Lord calls us to defend the social and economic rights of the poor and oppressed, we have mostly remained silent. We deplore the historic involvement of the church in America with racism and the conspicuous responsibility of the evangelical community for perpetuating the personal attitudes and institutional structures that have divided the body of Christ along color lines. Further, we have failed to condemn the exploitation of racism at home and abroad by our economic system.
>
> We affirm that God abounds in mercy and that he forgives all who repent and turn from their sins. So we call our fellow evangelical Christians to demonstrate repentance in a Christian discipleship that confronts the social and political injustice of our nation.
>
> We must attack the materialism of our culture and the maldistribution of the nation's wealth and services. We recognize that as a nation we play a crucial role in the imbalance and injustice of international trade and development. Before God and a billion hungry neighbors, we must rethink our values regarding our present standard of living and promote a more just acquisition and distribution of the world's resources.
>
> We acknowledge our Christian responsibilities of citizenship. Therefore, we must challenge the misplaced trust of the nation in economic and military might—a proud trust that promotes a national pathology of war and violence which victimizes our neighbors at home and abroad. We must resist the temptation to make the nation and its institutions objects of near-religious loyalty.
>
> We acknowledge that we have encouraged men to prideful domination and women to irresponsible passivity. So we call both men and women to mutual submission and active discipleship.
>
> We proclaim no new gospel, but the Gospel of our Lord Jesus Christ who, through the power of the Holy Spirit, frees people from sin so that they might praise God through works of righteousness.[154]

The declaration is typical of the "confessional protest" style of social engagement that nineteenth-century evangelicals used to build the abolitionist and temperance movements into the first integrated national social movements in the United States.[155] Instead of blaming others for the nation's social problems, the Chicago Declaration followed these earlier nineteenth-century confessional protest movements in acknowledging the church's own responsibility for the "sins of the nation" and appealing to religious principles to mobilize popular support for broad-based social reform.[156]

Many of the Chicago Declaration's signers were or became prominent leaders in evangelical left and mainstream evangelical institutions: including Jim Wallis, Ron Sider, Sharon Gallagher (early leader in the Jesus People and evangelical feminist movements), Richard Mouw (president of Fuller Theological Seminary), John Howard Yoder (author of *The Politics of Jesus*), Dr. Samuel Escobar (influential Peruvian missiologist and senior IFES and FTL leader), and Dr. John Perkins (influential African American author and founder of the Christian Community Development Association).[157] Brought together by Ron Sider and his Evangelicals for McGovern political campaign, participants in the Thanksgiving Workshop for Evangelical Social Action (where the Chicago Declaration was written) made national headlines for their efforts to organize evangelicals for progressive political reform.[158] Against conservative evangelicalism's prioritization of evangelism and theological individualism, they criticized the church growth movement's neglect of social justice activism as "demonic,"[159] arguing, "It is wrong to think that our social and political problems will be solved simply by changing individual lives."[160] Thanksgiving Workshop participants criticized conservative evangelical leaders who "fail to preach about the sins of institutionalized racism, unjust economic structures, and militaristic institutions which destroy people as much as do . . . 'personal' sins."[161] Black evangelical leaders such as John Perkins, Tom Skinner, and William Pannell wrote books, articles, and sermons arguing that America's "conservative brand of Christianity perpetuates the myth of white supremacy. It also tends to associate Christianity with American patriotism, free enterprise, and the Republican Party."[162] Standing against American militarism and religious nationalism, the young Jim Wallis and his *Post-American* community maintained regular public protests against "the United States of Babylon" and its economic and military interventionism.[163] However, despite its early momentum, by the late 1970s this nascent coalition of diverse left-leaning evangelicals found itself fractured and floundering in the face of internecine theological and political disagreements and an ascendant Christian Right.[164] Nevertheless, the evangelical left managed to carve out a distinctive position in the evangelical field as oppositional gadfly to an increasingly dominant conservative evangelical right—and along another oppositional evangelical movement born in the 1970s—would impact the development of a new evangelical monasticism a generation later.

Jesus People

The Jesus People movement was charismatic evangelicalism's answer to the 1960s youth counterculture, complete with its own "religious Woodstock" (as keynote speaker Billy Graham named a week-long 1972 camp meeting in Dallas attended by 75,000 young adults), rock concerts, communes, street demonstrations, (non-chemical) ways to "turn on" (to Jesus!), experimentalism, peace and love slogans, and long-haired men wearing hippie clothes.[165] It had its own newspapers (the *Hollywood Free Paper*, with a circulation of 450,000 in 1972), best-selling books (Hal Lindsey's apocalyptic *The Late Great Planet Earth* had over 9 million copies in print by 1979), rock stars, and coffee houses (the *Salt Company Coffee House* in Hollywood and *The Living Room* in San Francisco's Haight-Ashbury district, where the Jesus People movement was born). The "One Way" sign—a hand with index finger pointed straight up in the air, in contrast to the two-fingered peace sign or defiant raised fist of other movements in the counterculture—became the Jesus People movement's omnipresent symbolic gesture, reproduced on T-shirts, signs, and bumper stickers.[166] In the midst of 1960s experimentalism with drugs, sexuality, social roles, and eastern and alternative spirituality, the One Way symbol reaffirmed the traditional evangelical belief that following Jesus was the only true path to happiness, truth, right living, and eternal salvation.[167]

The Jesus People movement's origins and center of gravity lay in California, but it also developed a national network of communes, coffee houses, alternative media outlets, traveling music bands, and churches across the country which served as the movement's organizational infrastructure. Shiloh Youth Revival Centers, for example, established over 75 communes with approximately 5,000 core members and over 100,000 visitors across the country during the 1970s.[168] Typical members of Jesus People communities such as Shiloh were young (18–21), single, white (over 95 percent), male high school graduates from middle-income families and nominal religious backgrounds.[169] Many but not all were converts from the 1960s counterculture. Many Jesus People communes practiced a radical economic egalitarianism where members shared 100 percent of their income, assets, and debt in a "common purse." Upon becoming a member of a Shiloh center, an individual would turn over his money and assets and commit to working to support the community (often in a commune-run business enterprise), while the commune would pay of all of the individual's debts.[170] In contrast to their economic egalitarianism, many communes also exhibited an authoritarian leadership style and denied major leadership roles to women. There were, however, important exceptions to this rule, such as Berkeley's Christian World Liberation Front, which helped launch the evangelical feminist movement behind Sharon Gallagher and others.[171]

With regard to their internal organizational structure, Jesus People communes thus tended to be economically progressive but socially conservative. How did this translate to Jesus People perspectives on politics and social change? Here, like most conservative evangelicals, they tended toward unremittingly spiritual and individualistic analyses of social and political problems.[172] The Jesus People movement was intensely apocalyptic, and therefore intensely apolitical. Since the world was soon coming to an end, it was no use wasting time trying to improve this world's political or economic structures: what mattered was the eternal destiny of individual souls.[173] While most Jesus People participants maintained a deep cynicism and indifference to politics, those that did vote tended to be more left-liberal than conservative during the movement's heyday (they were antiwar, supported racial integration, voted for McGovern in 1972, etc.), but became increasingly conservative through the late 1970s and 1980s with the rise of the Christian Right.[174]

Theologically, the Jesus People practiced a type of conservative, charismatic evangelicalism aptly described as "experiential fundamentalism."[175] Like other conservative evangelicals, they believed in the literal interpretation of the Bible; the divinity, crucifixion, and resurrection of a historical Jesus; and humanity's need for forgiveness and salvation through faith in Christ. Most Jesus People also believed that the return of Jesus and the end of the world as we know it was close at hand, thanks largely to Hal Lindsay's wildly popular book, *The Late Great Planet Earth*.[176] While controversial in some circles, the Jesus People movement was embraced by many mainstream evangelical leaders. As Billy Graham remarked in a 1971 *Time* magazine article on the Jesus People: "If it is a fad, I welcome it!"[177] In Graham's own book on the Jesus People, he affirmed the movement as "Jesus centered," "Bible-based," "committed to Christian discipleship," having a "great zeal for evangelism," and "re-emphasizing the Second Coming of Jesus Christ."[178] He also noted the movement's strong emphasis on "experiencing Jesus" through the Holy Spirit, which included belief in supernatural encounters with God (and demons), healing, and speaking in tongues. Jesus People tended to privilege a simple, experiential, and emotional—rather than intellectual or formal—approach to God in teaching and worship. This combination of emphases on the experiential, evangelistic, and apocalyptic aspects of American evangelicalism—along with its youthful demographics and countercultural roots—fueled the movement's characteristic intensity and evangelistic fervor. As such, the Jesus People movement shared many religious and political standpoints with dominant expressions of twentieth-century conservative Protestantism.[179]

However, while holding *doxic* positions on core evangelical theological standpoints, the Jesus People movement was at the same time a radical break with the way those beliefs were embodied and communicated. The movement used popular rock and folk music to carry its message to the world, attempting to bridge a significant cultural gap between standard evangelical music and hymnology and popular culture.[180] Rock concerts and touring bands performed original Christian rock music for the first time, providing the movement with one of its primary vehicles for communicating the gospel and igniting increased devotion to God among the faithful. While many twentieth-century conservative evangelicals cultivated a strong sense of separation and distinctiveness from the wider culture, Jesus People marked their distinctiveness by wearing their faith on their bodies in the form of Jesus slogans, t-shirts, pins, and the like, or displaying bumper stickers on their vehicles. Their music, vocabulary, slogans, symbols, clothing, and physical appearance—not to mention their street preaching—loudly and visibly proclaimed their distinctive identity to the world. Rather than getting high on drugs, Jesus People experienced spiritual highs through the Holy Spirit. Rather than singing nineteenth-century church hymns or songs to protest the war in Vietnam, Jesus People created modern rock music that glorified Jesus. Rather than dressing up for church on Sunday or joining a hippie commune, Jesus People created economically egalitarian Christian communes and worshipped God barefoot on the beach. While the secular counterculture wore long hair and weird clothing as a sign of rebellion against conservative gender and social norms, Jesus People wore long hair, sandals, and robes because Jesus was the "original hippie."[181] While other religious folks judged the experimental and experience-craving counterculture from inside thick religious walls, Jesus People started coffee shops in radical neighborhoods and embraced experiential religion. Although their core religious standpoints had much in common with dominant expressions of twentieth-century American evangelicalism, the Jesus People movement embodied and communicated those beliefs in radically different ways, simultaneously reproducing and transforming American evangelicalism along the way.[182]

After its dramatic emergence into national consciousness in the early 1970s, by 1980 the Jesus People movement had largely dissipated, with many of its core organizations disbanded (the Shiloh Youth Revival Centers in 1978), disowned (the Children of God sect), or mainstreamed into new nondenominational church networks like Calvary Chapel or Vineyard Christian Fellowship.[183] As members of Jesus People communes got older, married,

and had children, many relocated to the suburbs, which prompted their rein-
tegration into mainstream middle-class jobs, economic practices (individual
household versus communal finances), physical appearances, and suburban
evangelical churches.[184] The Jesus People's early antiwar, communitarian,
left-leaning (but largely apolitical) impulses were replaced by a growing political conservatism. Nevertheless, the movement had a significant and lasting
impact on American evangelicalism, laying the groundwork for the emergence of the massive contemporary Christian music industry, Christian
bookstores and films, and aiding the development of a distinctive commercial
evangelical subculture.[185] It also became an inspiration (and caution, depending on the topic of conversation) for many neo-monastic leaders and communities, as we will see in Part II.

Theological Individualism, Evangelism Priority, and Moral Cosmology Theory

The Jesus People movement is a strong empirical example of the direct relationship between theological and economic communitarianism. Combining
a communally oriented economic egalitarianism with conservative views on
gender, sexuality, and the family, the Jesus People movement is a confirming
case for moral cosmology theory. However, the Jesus People were not typical
American evangelicals.

Moral cosmology theory is logically persuasive. Theological individualists (*religious modernists*), for whom religious standards change over time,
tend to assert the right of individuals to live and interpret religious tradition
as they please, leading to social and economic individualism and a consistent laissez-faire approach to both social and economic issues. Alternatively,
theological communitarians (the *religiously orthodox*) believe in enduring,
transcendent moral standards that impose themselves on the individual and
govern all aspects of a community's economic and social order.[186] Theological communitarians thus tend to be socially conservative because they believe in unchanging moral standards regarding sexuality and the family, but
tend to be economically left-liberal because they affirm "society's responsibility to provide for those in need, reduce inequality, and intervene in the
economy to meet community needs."[187] Moral cosmology theorists argue
that the tendency for the religiously orthodox to be economic and social
communitarians "applies to all of the Abrahamic faith traditions, regardless
of their specific theological tenets."[188] Moral cosmology theory thus deduces
economic and social attitudes from religious believers' abstract theological

orientations toward communitarianism (the orthodox) or individualism (modernists), regardless of variations in the specific content of theological beliefs among the Abrahamic faith traditions.[189]

Moral cosmology theory anticipates that American evangelicals, as religiously orthodox believers who hold to the existence of timeless moral standards regarding the family and sexuality, should tend toward social conservatism (table 2.1).[190] On this count, moral cosmology theory is correct. On social issues relating to abortion, sexuality, and the family, evangelicals are indeed social conservatives: and overwhelmingly so.[191] While the actual practices of evangelicals with respect to sexuality and divorce are more similar to other Americans than might be expected in light of these attitudes, evangelicals are significantly more conservative than other Americans and far more likely to consider such issues when making voting decisions.[192] Moral cosmology theory also anticipates that evangelicals—as orthodox religious believers—will tend to have left-liberal economic views which support government interventions and policies aimed at reducing poverty and economic inequality.[193] However, the historical and social scientific record overwhelmingly suggests that American evangelicals tend to be both social and economic conservatives, and that moral cosmology theory's expectations regarding the economic attitudes of American evangelicals are mistaken (table 2.2).[194] Historical studies of twentieth-century evangelicals,[195] studies of pastors and movement leaders,[196] and studies of rank-and-file evangelicals all agree that the vast majority of evangelicals are either economic conservatives or disinterested in the potentially progressive economic implications of their faith.[197] From a religious perspective, it is perhaps surprising that American evangelicals have been economic conservatives for most of the twentieth century, given the Bible's strong prophetic condemnations of economic oppression, injustice, and inequality.[198] From a sociological perspective, it is even more surprising given that evangelicals have tended to be less educated and less affluent than the general population throughout most of the twentieth century, and whose own economic interests would thus seem to align with more left-liberal standpoints on economic issues.[199] How then are we to explain evangelical exceptionalism with respect to moral cosmology theory?

Table 2.1 Moral Cosmology Theory

	Theology	Social attitudes	Economic attitudes
Orthodox believers	communitarian	conservative	left-liberal
Modernist believers	individualist	left-liberal	conservative

Table 2.2 Evangelical Exceptionalism

Evangelicals (Orthodox)	Theology	Social attitudes	Economic attitudes
Predicted	communitarian	conservative	left-liberal
Actual	*individualist**	conservative	*conservative*

*American evangelicals tend to be theological individualists, but not in exactly the sense that Davis and Robinson (2006) use the term.

While moral cosmology theory argues that religiously orthodox believers tend to be consistent theological, social, and economic communitarians, American evangelicals are in fact *theological individualists* with respect to their prioritization of evangelism and strong preference for interpersonal, rather than structural, solutions to social problems.[200] American evangelicals, like the majority of white Americans, tend to view social inequality as the result of individual differences in talent or diligence, believe in the individual's right to self-determination, and believe social problems are best solved by changing individual behavior rather than by changing social structures of inequality.[201] According to most twentieth-century American evangelicals, the best way to change individual behavior—and by extension change society—is through personal relationships, spiritual conversion, and the moral regeneration of individuals through faith in Christ.[202] This "miracle motif" approach to social problems is profoundly individualistic, reducing social problems such racism, poverty, and good government to problems of individual beliefs and behavior.[203]

Throughout this chapter, we have seen that the prioritization of evangelism over other forms of social engagement is a major feature of historic American evangelicalism. From Charles Finney's break with non-evangelical abolitionists in the early 1800s, to D. L. Moody's revivalist premillennialism in the late 1800s, to Billy Graham's prioritization of evangelism in the mid-1900s, American evangelicals and their leaders have viewed evangelism as the most important social responsibility of Christian individuals and churches, regularly and explicitly subordinating other types of engagement to the work of preaching the gospel and seeking the conversion of individuals to faith in Christ. Twentieth-century white evangelical views on race are particularly instructive here. Thus, for example, although Billy Graham and fellow new evangelical leaders in the 1940s and 1950s viewed racism as sin, Graham's southern evangelistic crusades remained segregated until the 1954 Supreme Court decision against school segregation so as not to hinder his evangelistic work among white southerners.[204] Like Moody and the early abolitionists before him, Graham believed that social problems such as racism could only be solved through the conversion and moral regeneration of individuals, rather than through direct social protest or political activism.[205] He also shared Moody's premillennialist pessimism regarding the possibility of positive social change in human culture and institutions prior to the return of the Lord, and suspected the civil rights movement of being the work of communist sympathizers and agitators.[206]

Billy Graham's prioritization of evangelism over the active pursuit of racial justice was typical of the white evangelical attitude during the civil rights era—although Graham's views on racial equality were arguably more progressive than many other white evangelicals during the period.[207] When white southern evangelicals were not actively, and sometimes violently, fighting for the preservation of Jim Crow segregation and racial division "in the name of Jesus," they were preaching a spiritualized "gospel of individual salvation and personal orderliness" that bifurcated evangelistic proclamation from the gospel's material embodiment in racial justice and Martin Luther King Jr.'s "beloved community."[208] Expressing the theological individualism and "anti-modernist fundamentalism" of the period, southern evangelical leaders proclaimed, "Now is the time to move the emphasis from the material to the spiritual,"[209] publicly denounced the civil rights movement, and argued that "the cross has nothing to do with the civil rights of black Mississippians."[210] In general, "White Christian conservatives . . . remained largely indifferent to black suffering, preoccupied instead with evangelism and church growth; and with personal vices like drinking, dancing, and 'heavy petting.'"[211] When American evangelicals did sincerely seek to address the "race problem," they did so through the lens of a "color-blind gospel" that sought to "fight economic and racial injustice in the same manner as did Billy Graham: one individual soul at a time."[212] The prioritization of evangelism and theological individualism of white American evangelicals has served as both cause and effect of their broader social conservatism, resulting in a tendency for Americans evangelicals to reflect and reproduce—rather than challenge and transform—the existing social and economic order of American society and their local social-historical context.[213]

Christian Smith and Michael O. Emerson's study of contemporary evangelical approaches to racial inequality in America in *Divided by Faith* further illustrates the point.[214] The vast majority of white evangelicals think of racial problems and solutions in individualist terms. Even more than other Americans, evangelicals tend to attribute the socioeconomic gap between whites and blacks to differences in individual motivation, rather than explaining it in terms of educational inequality or discrimination.[215] They believe that "getting to know people of another race" is the best way to address racial problems.[216] In their preference for individualist rather than social or structural explanations of racial and economic inequality, evangelicals are like the majority of white Americans, only more so:

> White Americans favor individualistic explanations over structural ones. White American evangelicals are even more inclined to this pattern. None of the white evangelicals we interviewed, with the exception of a few non-isolated whites . . . spoke of inequality in other ways available to them from the Bible and Christian tradition. For example, they did not mention biblical principles and references calling for economic justice and equality. . . . Contemporary evangelicals' explanations for racial inequality, then, are essentially unchanged from nearly a century ago. . . . Now, as then, the racial gap is not explained by unequal opportunity or discrimination or shortcomings of the society as a whole, but rather by the shortcomings of blacks. . . . This helps us understand why our respondents, apart from being irritated at the racial inequality question, were not at all bothered by the racial inequality itself. Except for a few people, inequality in no way troubled, moved, or animated our respondents.[217]

Likewise, just as the vast majority of white American evangelicals explain racial inequality in individualist terms, they tend to view economic inequality through the same individualist lens that resonates with libertarian economic principles:

> The contemporary evangelical perspective, like that of its ancestors, is one that strongly supports laissez-faire capitalism. Individuals should be free to pursue their own ends, and rewards should be distributed based on effort. A meritocracy is both a goal and what America already is.[218]

According to dominant expressions of twentieth-century American evangelicalism, social problems such as economic or racial inequality are best solved through person-to-person relationships that transform individual beliefs and behavior, not through structural changes such affirmative action or anti-discrimination laws.

Partially anticipating moral cosmology theory in a book titled, *What Does the Lord Require? How American Christins Think about Economic Justice*, sociologist

Stephen Hart argues that Christians who have a communitarian view of their faith tend to have moderately left-liberal economic views, while those who have an individualistic view of their faith tend to be economic conservatives.[219] However, despite its many strengths, moral cosmology theory's emphasis on the abstract, formal features of moral-religious meaning systems obscures how twentieth-century American evangelicalism's specific, historically conditioned form of theological individualism has in fact pushed evangelicals toward economic individualism and conservatism. Although this theological individualism confounds moral cosmology theory's expectation of left-liberal economic views among evangelicals, the general observation that theological communitarians tend to hold more left-liberal economic views is strongly confirmed by Urban Monastery participants and other neo-monastic evangelicals, as we will see below.

Conclusion: Evangelical Exceptionalism and the Enduring Effects of History

While moral cosmology theory has had considerable success at predicting the social and economic standpoints of Christian, Jewish, and Islamic religious believers globally, the theory acknowledges that "unique historical circumstances may affect whether moral cosmology theory holds in a specific context."[220] According culture theorist Ann Swidler, in "unsettled" contexts of significant political or religious struggle, "cultural positions crystallize into clearly opposed cultural systems" which "generate clear ideological disagreements that force people to choose sides."[221] As such, "social formulas that mediate ongoing negotiations of antagonistic interests may be particularly enduring."[222] This is particularly true when historical struggles result in the genesis of new religious or political cleavages—as was the case during the fundamentalist–modernist struggle in the early twentieth century. The struggle split American Protestantism into two clearly demarcated cultural and institutional camps, each with its own oppositional perspective on what the legitimate expression of Christianity in America ought to look like. The cultural meanings and classification schemes generated during the fundamentalist–modernist struggle shaped the "founding point of view" of the field of twentieth-century conservative Protestantism, a point of view that continues to define orthodoxy and influence the theological and political standpoints of contemporary evangelicalism in profound ways.[223]

Moral cosmology theory fails to account for the conservative economic views of American evangelicals because of their theological individualism,

Table 2.3 Positions and Oppositions: Fundamentalism and Modernism
circa 1920s

Fundamentalist/theologically conservative Protestantism	Modernist/theologically liberal Protestantism
Divinely inspired/inerrant Bible	Human/historical/imperfect Bible
Jesus: resurrected Savior/Divine Son of God	Jesus: human moral exemplar
"Literalist" hermeneutic	"Critical" (non-literalist) hermeneutic
Creationism	Evolutionary theory
Evangelism priority	Social justice priority
Individualism	Social/communitarianism
Conservative politics	Left-liberal politics
Otherworldly/Spiritual Gospel	This-worldly/Social Gospel

and because the fundamentalist–modernist conflict established an enduring cultural pattern that identified left-liberal economic views with "the enemy": theologically liberal modernists and their secular cousins. As summarized in table 2.3, the fundamentalist–modernist struggle hardened symbolic boundaries in such a way that it became nearly impossible to hold left-liberal economic and political standpoints while also holding conservative theological views. Prior to the fundamentalist–modernist conflict, most American Protestants affirmed the importance of both the otherworldly and this-worldly aspects of Christian faith and practice.[224] After the conflict, however, conservative Protestants increasingly viewed social justice activism as a marker of the theological liberalism that, in their view, was undermining traditional Christian faith.

Evangelical antagonism toward left-liberal politics and economic policy was powerfully reinforced with the rise of the Christian Right and its largely successful political mobilization of religious conservatives into Republican Party supporters since the 1970s. Conservative evangelicals were key cogs in the emergent New Right coalition that combined small government, free-market economics, and meritocratic individualism with anti-communist patriotism and a conservative moral agenda at home.[225] The New Right's heated anti-government rhetoric reinforced conservative Protestants' already considerable distrust of government-based solutions to economic problems.[226] Thus, while moral cosmology theory is correct to argue that there is no necessary logical relationship between evangelicals' theological and economic conservatism, a century's worth of struggle against left-liberal religion and politics in the United States resulted in a historically contingent, yet durable, pattern of social and economic conservatism among dominant expressions of twentieth-century evangelicalism in the United States.

We may conclude this chapter by considering a puzzle concerning the communitarian neo-monastic movement's historical precursors. While drawing on various streams of historic Christian monasticism,[227] the new monasticism's emphasis on the practice of communitarian spirituality amidst the "abandoned places of empire" also evokes several, more contemporary, Christian social movements in the United States.[228] Participants in neo-monastic communities point to the twentieth-century Catholic Worker, Anabaptist, and Jesus People movements as inspiration for their communitarian style of spiritual and social engagement. Several contemporary Mennonite and Catholic Worker communities identify explicitly with the new monasticism.[229] In many respects, however, the communitarian movement that bears most resemblance to evangelical neo-monasticism is the turn-of-the-century settlement house movement made famous by Jane Addams and the Hull House in Chicago.[230] Like contemporary neo-monastic communities, settlement houses were "typically located in poor urban neighborhoods" and "were home to young men and women called 'residents'" who lived and worked together in community "right alongside the poor."[231] Like the typical participant of a neo-monastic community, settlement house residents were predominantly young, white, educated, middle- and upper-middle-class Protestants who intentionally relocated to poor, ethnically diverse urban neighborhoods as an expression of Christian social teaching and practice. Although varied in their exact type and intensity of religious expression, settlement houses in the United States "had a strong religious foundation":

> The settlement house was a church of sorts, allowing residents to worship God through acts in the real world. . . . Some [social settlements] operated more as religious convents, particularly in smaller cities, while others were closer to the Hull-House "model" (if we can speak of such a thing), pursuing social morality in the spirit of the Gospels.[232]

Like many participants of neo-monastic communities, settlement house residents intentionally relocated from middle-class residential locations to the poor, urban, immigrant zones of cities like Chicago and New York, where the Dickensian nightmare of unregulated industrial capitalism was more lived reality than literary fiction. Settlement house practitioners were highly critical of the bureaucratic economism of "professional charity" workers and organizations, and worked hard to build "reciprocal relationships" of mutual empowerment and exchange with their disadvantaged neighbors—a stance that we will hear echoed in the writings, words, and practices of Urban Monastery participants and other neo-monastic evangelicals in the following chapters.[233] And just like Urban Monastery participants, practitioners of the settlement house movement held a holistic view of social and spiritual transformation that viewed hospitality, education, the arts, community, and social justice activism as essential elements of good civic and religious practice.[234]

Given these many similarities, it is more than a little surprising that—after reading thousands of pages of neo-monastic writings, interviewing scores of neo-monastic community leaders and participants, and spending countless hours with members of neo-monastic communities around the country for over five years—I did not encounter one single mention of the settlement house movement as an inspiration or model for contemporary neo-monasticism. Neo-monastic evangelicals are willing to draw inspiration from fourth-century Eastern Orthodox desert monks, from medieval Catholic monastic orders, from charismatic eighteenth-century German Brethren communities, and from twentieth-century Catholic socialists; yet a relatively recent Anglo-American Protestant movement bearing remarkable resemblance to the new monasticism is completely ignored. How can this be?

As with several other puzzles concerning American evangelicalism that will be addressed in the next chapter, this odd neglect of the settlement house movement within the new monasticism requires a Bourdieusian sensitivity to the role of historical struggle in shaping religious culture. Indeed, the absence of any reference to the settlement house movement strengthens one of this chapter's main arguments: namely, that the dominant theological and political standpoints of twentieth-century American evangelicals were significantly influenced—some would say distorted—by the fundamentalist struggle against modernists and the social gospel in the early twentieth century. Like a sibling rivalry or a struggle between former business partners competing for clients after a falling out, it is theologically liberal Protestants—not medieval or modern Catholics or other religious groups—against whom American conservative Protestants have had to define and defend themselves in their struggle over the legitimate expression of Christianity in the United States. The fundamentalist–modernist struggle hardened symbolic boundaries between liberal and conservative (evangelical) Protestants so completely that any ideas, individuals, or movements associated with the "liberal social gospel"—as Jane Addams and Hull House clearly were—were largely expunged from evangelical thought and historical consciousness. The fact that many evangelicals today—particularly those who identify with neo-monasticism, the emerging church, and the evangelical left—no longer view left-liberal Protestantism as "the enemy" is beside the point.[235] Historical struggles—particularly founding struggles between fundamentalist and modernist Christians in the early twentieth century—remain institutionalized in the boundaries, classification schemes, and *doxa* of contemporary American evangelicalism, even where the original definitions and disputes that gave rise to those struggles no longer hold sway. Because the settlement house movement, Jane Addams, and Hull House were associated with the illegitimate "liberal social gospel" tradition of modernist Protestantism (that is, with "the enemy"), they have no place in American evangelicalism's historical community of discourse.[236]

In evoking the concepts of field, *doxa*, struggle, and the like, we have begun using the theoretical language of Bourdieusian field analysis. Having introduced the dominant (and dominated) twentieth-century positions and position-takings in relation to which evangelical neo-monasticism is constructed in this chapter, we are now prepared to dive headlong into a field-theoretic examination of neo-monasticism's relation to the contemporary field of American evangelicalism.

Chapter 3

Neo-Monasticism and the Field
of American Evangelicalism

AS A SYMBOL of religious practice, *monasticism* evokes images of intense devotion, otherworldliness, and utopian religious community: a pure alternative society organized according to the highest principles of divine and brotherly love. Monasticism is also a symbol of protest against the dominant religious and social powers of the day, of radical reform, even "revolution":

> Nearly every major monastic movement began as a violent reaction to compromised religion.[1] Monasticism, at its best, has always been a cry for change—in our own hearts, in an over-accommodating Church and in society at large. This is the form of radical faith that first drew me to Jesus—not the Constantinian, top-down religion associated with high status and political power, but the faith of the underdog. Angry faith. Twenty-four-hour-a-day, radical, subversive, all-or-nothing allegiance to Jesus Christ, friend of the poor.[2]

Neo-monastic evangelicals have appropriated historical models of Christian monasticism and infused the symbol of monasticism with their own meanings of radical hospitality, community, and holistic spirituality. For those who enter in, the call to a new monasticism is a call to a radically new way of seeing the world and living within it, a vision that challenges existing forms of religious, social, and political life. Not least, it is a direct challenge to dominant expressions of evangelical Christianity in the United States.

Neo-monastic evangelicalism is indeed radical in many ways, particularly in relation to dominant expressions of twentieth-century American evangelicalism. The call to geographic relocation to disadvantaged urban neighborhoods, to radical hospitality and intentional community, and to various forms of egalitarianism stand out against the popular image of evangelicals as a bastion of suburban individualism and conservatism. At the same time, neo-monastic evangelicals reproduce many elements of traditional evangelical faith. Just as the symbol of monasticism carries both radical and traditional elements, so the neo-monastic movement simultaneously challenges and preserves, subverts and upholds, traditional American evangelicalism in ways that will be demonstrated throughout this chapter.[3] This dualistic feature of American evangelical life has puzzled observers of evangelicalism for years. While scholars such as James Davison Hunter and John C. Green view traditionalism and resistance to change as a defining feature of the movement,[4] others view evangelicals as pragmatic innovators who are perpetually reinventing the faith in an attempt to appeal to religious consumers in America's rapidly changing society and religious marketplace.[5]

A simple explanation for these disagreements is that scholars who focus their attention on the *religious beliefs* of evangelicals—as Hunter and Green do—tend to view evangelicals as traditionalists due to their refusal to abandon traditional Christian beliefs like the divinity of Jesus or the existence of universal moral standards. Alternatively, scholars who focus their attention on the *religious practices* of evangelicals—as Alan Wolfe does—tend to see evangelicals as innovators because they are constantly tinkering with new ways to get the gospel message out:[6] from their early adoption of new communication technologies like radio, television, and the Internet to their continual appropriation of new musical and cultural forms;[7] to new techniques of revivalism and public meetings;[8] to the construction of new "seeker-friendly" religious buildings, services, and preaching styles;[9] to the appropriation and incorporation of dominant discursive idioms from popular culture (such as "therapeutic personalism")[10] into Christian spirituality. Indeed, evangelicals themselves often use this distinction between the *message* of the Christian gospel and the *methods* used to communicate it to describe which elements of their faith they believe are open to innovation (the methods) and which ones are not (the message).[11]

There is some truth to this view. Evangelical history is littered with examples of openness to innovation in how the gospel is publicly proclaimed, alongside sharp resistance to innovation in doctrinal beliefs such as the inerrancy of scripture or the virgin birth of Christ.[12] However, historical and social processes do not simply change the methods of Christian expression: they also affect the message itself. To be sure, there are some core theological commitments one must hold in order to call oneself an evangelical. But a simple *message/methods* or *beliefs/practices* distinction between evangelical traditionalism and evangelical innovation is inadequate. Both the message and the methods of evangelical spirituality are influenced by the social and historical contexts in which they are developed, and both can serve as stakes in the struggle between different visions of the evangelical faith; that is, between the multiple, competing versions of the *legitimate representation of biblical Christianity* that exist *within the field of evangelical religion itself.*

Introducing Bourdieusian Field Theory

In describing evangelicalism as a field in which different agents struggle to gain influence over specific stakes and meanings of value to evangelicals, I am invoking the theoretical language of Pierre Bourdieu. It will be helpful to provide a brief overview of some basic concepts from field theory here as a preface to this chapter's subsequent substantive analysis of neo-monasticism's relation to other theoretically relevant positions in the field of American evangelicalism.

Complex, differentiated societies like the United States are composed of multiple relatively autonomous social spaces or *fields* that are neither completely independent nor completely reducible to one another.[13] Each field— political, artistic, religious, scientific, and so on—has its own particular stakes or rewards and its own specific principles of vision and division according to which different positions in a given field are defined and differentiated. For example, the academic field is organized by a "permanent rivalry for truth" about the social and natural world, while the economic field is organized by competition over economic capital. These distinctive principles of vision and division form the "fundamental laws" or *nomos* of a given field, which are also themselves the object of struggles between agents occupying different positions in a field.[14] Participation in a field requires that one adopt the *nomos* of the field, invest in its stakes, believe in the value of the rewards it offers, and adopt its view of the world while paying heed to the particular "rules and regularities" that govern participation in the field or subfield in which one is invested.[15]

The structure of any social field is determined by the distribution of diverse forms of *capital* (cultural, economic, social, symbolic, etc.) possessed by individual or collective agents occupying different positions in the field.[16] Economic and social capital are familiar concepts, while cultural capital includes academic credentials such as professional degrees as well as varying abilities to consume different types of cultural goods such as classical music or fine art.[17] Symbolic capital confers a widespread recognition of the value of specific forms of capital and legitimacy to the honors and profits given to those who possess it.[18] As a simple if somewhat dated example, a person with a medical degree in the United States not only receives the specific rights and profits guaranteed those who hold this specific form of institutionalized cultural capital (such as the right to practice medicine and to make a relatively high salary), but she also is the beneficiary of the exalted occupational prestige of the medical profession that grants her special recognition in the community, widespread acknowledgment of her intelligence, and the acceptance of legitimacy of her relatively high compensation and social position. While many complain about the high salaries of corporate lawyers, CEOs, star athletes, and certain entertainment figures who are "famous for being famous," the legitimacy of high salaries for physicians is almost universally recognized as legitimate. This is an example of symbolic capital.

One of the fundamental insights of Bourdieusian field theory is that the points of view that different actors take on religious, cultural, or political matters are systematically related to their objective positions within a field. An agent's point of view on political, cultural, or religious matters is always just that: a particular "view from a point" in social space:[19]

> The field of positions is methodologically inseparable from the field of stances or position-takings, i.e. the structured system of practices and expressions of agents. Both spaces, that of the objective positions and that of stances must be analyzed together, treated as "two translations of the same sentence" as Spinoza put it.[20]

In other words, political, cultural, or religious points of view do not float freely from social structure; rather, they are constructed by actors whose points of view differ in relation to the particular positions they occupy in social space. This means that actors occupying different objective positions in a field tend to have different subjective views of that field influenced by their positions, and vice versa. To give one example that will be developed further below, agents who occupy dominant positions in a field tend to adopt *conservation strategies* that attempt to preserve the existing structure of the field (and therefore also preserve their own dominant position within it).[21] On the other hand, agents who occupy dominated positions are more likely to adopt *challenger strategies* that oppose and subvert the existing structure of the field in various ways (and therefore also advance their own position within it).[22]

A second fundamental insight of the field-analytic approach is that the distinctive points of view held by agents occupying different positions in the social structure are not developed in isolation but rather are constructed in relation to one another. To borrow Bourdieu's succinct formulation: "To think in terms of field is to *think relationally*."[23] This means, for instance, that in order to fully grasp the origins and significance of neo-monastic evangelicalism's distinctive religious and political points of view, we must examine its relation to other positions and position-takings in the American evangelical field. Although it is beyond the scope of this study to develop a comprehensive comparative analysis of the American evangelical field, it is still possible to analyze the relations between neo-monasticism and other theoretically significant evangelical position-takings through a combination of ethnographic and textual analysis. A sociological analysis of texts in the relational mode must proceed according to a "principle of intertextuality" which analyzes both the internal structure of the text and also the social context (the field of religious or cultural production) in which it is produced.[24] The field-analytic approach thus avoids both forms of reductionism common to textual analysis (and cultural analysis more generally): analyzing isolated texts independently according their internal structure (while ignoring the relational social context in which they are produced and used), and the opposite mistake of analyzing texts in deterministic terms as mere reflections of social conditions.

Textual analysis is a particularly appropriate method for studying evangelical standpoints on religious and political matters. American evangelicals are "people of the book" in more ways than one. While the Bible functions as the inspirational and authoritative bedrock of evangelical spirituality, the evangelical subculture is also home to a well-documented and dynamic popular book culture.[25] Whereas Catholic and mainline Protestant denominations are more likely to make important theological and political statements through encyclicals and other official pronouncements, evangelical leaders take their arguments directly to the people in popular books.[26] Furthermore, American evangelicalism is a notoriously celebrity-driven subculture in which charismatic leaders build massive followings and religious organizations and thereby gain recognition and influence in the evangelical field, which is perhaps not surprising given evangelicalism's status as the popular religion of America, a nation with its own notoriously celebrity-driven culture.[27] Indeed, it is hard to find an evangelical leader of any influence who has not published a book (or, more commonly, many books). For evangelicals, publishing best-selling books serves either as confirmation of a leader or movement's existing status in the evangelical field, or as a gateway to increased prominence for up-and-coming leaders and movements: it is an important form of field-specific cultural capital among evangelicals. It is in these books that one can find the most comprehensive statements of influential and competing religious and political position-takings in the evangelical field.

Ethnographic studies of American evangelicals confirm the widespread influence of books authored by prominent evangelical leaders among ordinary grassroots evangelicals.[28] Just as Urban Monastery participants frequently cited ideas and texts authored by nationally recognized neo-monastic, emerging church, megachurch, and conservative evangelical leaders to me while I was in the field conducting research for this book; anthropologist James S. Bielo's monograph *Emerging Evangelicals* is shot through with examples of ordinary evangelicals citing specific books and authors to describe their religious and political standpoints, their sense of religious identity, and their "deconversion" from the dominant megachurch and conservative expressions of American evangelicalism.[29] Bielo concludes, "Anyone paying attention will affirm that books are important in Evangelical culture . . . the book publishing industry is a significant mode of knowledge circulation for Emerging Evangelicals."[30] And as James Davison Hunter reminds us, movement leaders and elites have an inordinate influence on the religious, cultural, and political position-takings of American evangelicals, as well as on public discourse concerning politics, culture, and religion in the United States more generally.[31] While it is true that books written by evangelical movement leaders do not fully represent the views of all evangelicals, textual analysis of books by influential leaders is the best way to get at the public religious and political standpoints of evangelical elites which structure the field.

Of course, an analysis involving texts written by evangelical movement leaders runs the risk of naively reproducing what Christian Smith refers to as the "representative elite fallacy," where scholars and popular observers of American evangelicalism blithely assume that the religious and political standpoints of high-profile leaders accurately represents the views of ordinary evangelicals on the ground.[32] The representative elite fallacy involves several interrelated problems: it tends to obscure the diversity, tension, and conflict between competing points of view within the evangelical field; it conflates knowledge production with knowledge consumption and elite standpoints with the standpoints of "ordinary evangelicals"; and it lacks empirical grounding in the practice of everyday lived religion.[33] My decision to use textual analysis to help trace out the relationship between neo-monasticism and other significant positions in the evangelical field, however, was born out of on-the-ground ethnographic observations of the processes through which Urban Monastery participants and leaders constructed their distinctive theological and political standpoints in relation to other positions in the evangelical field. Moreover, the strength of a field-theoretic approach to textual analysis is precisely that it systematically illuminates, acknowledges, and accounts for the internal diversity, complexity, and tension within any given social field or position. Finally, my focus in this chapter is to examine processes of *cultural or religious knowledge production* in the evangelical field (i.e., how the distinctive theological and political standpoints of neo-monastic evangelicals and other significant movements within American evangelicalism are constructed in relation to one another and to the evangelical field as a whole). I do not claim that the texts analyzed here represent the full range of views among ordinary evangelicals on the ground or that they capture the full range of internal diversity within each of the five positions analyzed below.[34] Readers interested in thick, on-the-ground depictions of ordinary conservative, megachurch, or emerging evangelicals may look to other ethnographic and historical studies of these movements already in existence.[35] Rather, I use the analysis of texts written by evangelical movement leaders here as a tool to summarize those positions in the evangelical field in relation to which neo-monastic evangelicalism is constructed, and to examine the social processes through which distinctive theological and political standpoints within the evangelical field are constructed, reproduced, and transformed.

If the representative elite fallacy can lead to the production of distorted images of American evangelicalism, an exclusive focus on ordinary evangelicals' practice of "lived religion" that is cut off from movement elites risks distortions of its own variety.[36] For example, it is commonplace for scholars of the emerging church to treat the new monasticism as a mere subset of the larger emerging church movement.[37] But from a field-theoretic perspective, this is problematic. As we will see below, evangelical neo-monasticism and the emerging church have distinctive origins, movement leaders, institutional networks, position-takings, and trajectories as it relates to the evangelical field. They emerged in different social-political contexts, among different conversation partners, and represent distinctive *social generations*.[38] New monastic leaders do not typically think of themselves as a part of or descended from the emerging church.[39] It is true that emerging and neo-monastic evangelicals share a number of critiques of dominant expressions of American evangelicalism, and that it is common for grassroots evangelical individuals and communities to draw on both streams in constructing local religious identities and expressions.[40] This does not, however, mean that there is no distinction to be made between the neo-monastic and emerging church positions, just as the fact that the "lived religion" of some evangelical megachurches contains progressive elements usually associated with the evangelical left does not mean that there is no distinction between these varieties of American evangelicalism.[41] Focusing only on ordinary evangelicals' "lived religion" at the expense of movement elites obscures these differences, as evident in, for example, Bielo's *Emerging Evangelicals*. In principle, Bielo agrees that a relational or "dialogic" approach to the study of American evangelicalism must include both grassroots evangelicals and movement leaders in its analysis.[42] In practice, however, Bielo's near-exclusive reliance on the lived religion approach obscures the real relation between neo-monasticism, the emerging church, and the field of American evangelicalism. It seems that all of the neo-monastic evangelicals mentioned in *Emerging Evangelicals'* chapter on "everyday monastics" came directly out of emerging church contexts, which—along with some similarities between the emerging church and neo-monastic evangelicalism's critiques of conservative evangelicalism—leads the author to conclude that neo-monasticism represents a subset of the emerging church.[43] However, this view is both empirically and theoretically problematic, as will be made clear below.[44] Decoupling the study of everyday lived religion from the study of leaders and movement elites can obscure the relational structure and social processes through which different agents within the evangelical field construct their distinct-yet-related religious and political standpoints and strategies of action.[45]

In addition to evangelical neo-monasticism, then, this chapter examines the positions and position-takings of four other theoretically and substantively significant movements in American evangelicalism: megachurch evangelicalism, the Christian Right/conservative evangelicalism, the evangelical left, and the emerging church. One might ask: why these four movements rather than others? The answer lies in the data. I focus on neo-monasticism's relation to these four positions because neo-monastic evangelicals themselves reference the occupants of these positions in order to explain what was distinctive and significant about their own religious and political position-takings. As Jen—an artist, gallery manager, and new Urban Monastery participant—told me in response to a question about how her friends view her faith: "When I say I'm a Christian, I almost feel compelled to explain to people the type of church I go to, because it's better they think I'm going to a cult than going to a megachurch!" Jen, like every other Urban Monastery participant I talked to, went on to celebrate how participatory, "authentic," and "simple" the Urban Monastery was in contrast to the "programmatic," "impersonal," "bureaucratic," and "consumptive" expressions of church life they associated with megachurch evangelicalism. Likewise, when talking with Caleb—one of the Urban Monastery's founding leaders—about some of the biggest problems facing Christians in America, he responded:

CALEB: I see this big division in the church between evangelical America and—I guess for lack of a better word, emerging—I guess the church outside of evangelicalism. . . . I don't even know if I appropriately use that term.

INTERVIEWER: Who is evangelical America for you?

CALEB: I think I could almost say it more from a political standpoint, and say hardcore Republicans basically [laughs ruefully]. Did you see that movie Jesus Camp?

INTERVIEWER: Not yet.

CALEB: Ohhhhhhhhhh [drawn out, tortured tone]. We watched that movie in anthropology class, then I watched it at home, and I had to go take a shower afterwards. But I'm going—and this is basically the quandary— because I'm talking to the Lord in the shower and I'm like, "I do not want to be associated with that." . . . I think the bottom line of that movie is that these people are trying to raise up the next generation of die-hard Republicans. And that's definitely a harsh line to draw, but . . . yeah evangelical America has become very associated in my mind with a pretty rigid Republicanism. It's those conversations where I try and say something like, "Maybe . . . this is more difficult than, 'We vote Republicans because we're Christians,'" but there's *no* room for any of that. No room for questions.

Urban Monastery participants frequently lamented the widespread association of evangelicalism with Republican Party politics and framed discussions about political issues and religious identity in terms of their relation to the Christian Right/conservative evangelicalism. In their words and actions— sometimes consciously and sometimes not—I witnessed neo-monastic evangelicals constructing their distinctive religious and political standpoints in (often oppositional) relation to megachurch and conservative evangelicalism. The emerging church and evangelical left, on the other hand, share many of neo-monasticism's critiques of American evangelicalism while also differing from the neo-monastic point of view in important ways. In other words, the decision to focus on these particular positions was a theoretical one that arose logically from my ethnographic observations of neo-monastic communities and their participants.

To this end, I selected and coded three books each from the neo-monastic, emerging church, evangelical left, Christian Right/conservative evangelical, and megachurch point of view. Each book was selected using multidimensional criteria aimed at maximizing representativeness and commensurability.[46] In addition to coding three books from each position (fifteen books total), I also read and took extensive notes on forty-six additional books written by recognized leaders of each of these positions (see Appendix for the full list of these additional texts). While this approach does not allow us access to the full range of religious and political position-takings that are present among ordinary evangelicals, it does enable us to construct a reliable summary of the distinctive religious and political standpoints of influential and competing positions in the evangelical field in relation to which neo-monastic evangelicals are constructing their distinctive vision of legitimate biblical faith.

Before proceeding on to the substantive analysis of neo-monasticism's position within the evangelical field, some final clarifications are in order. The aim of this chapter is to demonstrate how the distinctive theological and political standpoints of neo-monastic evangelicals are constructed in relation to other theoretically significant positions in the evangelical field (and vice versa). In many ways, however, this analysis just scratches the surface of the internal diversity and complexity of American evangelicalism. A fully developed field analysis of American evangelicalism would pay more attention to the internal diversity within each of the five movements analyzed in this chapter,[47] as well as examining other positions such as the "New Calvinism" or David Gushee's emerging "evangelical center," for example.[48] Neo-monasticism itself encompasses a range of theological and political perspectives that, while unified in opposition to dominant positions, also contains internal diversity and oppositions within itself; oppositions that for sociological reasons will likely grow as neo-monasticism becomes more prominent in the field.[49] Similarly, there is significant theological and political diversity within megachurch evangelicalism that is not addressed in these pages.[50] Some leaders and institutions within megachurch evangelicalism have been moving toward more left-liberal political standpoints in recent years, while others are more entrenched in the theological individualism and political conservatism described below.[51] Likewise, conservative evangelicals range from the highly politicized culture warriors to apolitical conservatives who, while sharing the political attitudes of the Christian Right, have little use for politics themselves.

This relates to a second point. In the pages below I focus on the *founding* or *dominant* points of view of four significant movements in American evangelicalism in order to establish the basic structure of the evangelical field as it relates to neo-monasticism.[52] However, each of these positions has evolved in such a way that the "founding point of view" of megachurch evangelicalism, for instance, or of the emerging church, has itself been challenged and adapted over the years. As noted in chapter 1, some megachurch evangelicals are becoming increasingly holistic in their understanding of Christian mission in the world, and they are increasingly discontent with the founding point of view's singular focus on evangelism, church growth, and "therapeutic personalism."[53] And as we will see below, there is much diversity and contestation within the emerging church position that is only partially captured here. Many founders of the emerging church position do not even use the term anymore, and new fault lines and alliances between the emerging church, neo-monasticism, the New Calvinism, and other positions are constantly being formed.[54] In other words, the significant theological and political diversity within American evangelicalism that is represented by the five movements examined below is really just the tip of the iceberg.[55]

Third, a comprehensive field analysis of American evangelicalism would include a more detailed examination of the evangelical field's relation to other religious fields in the United States—such as mainline Protestantism, black Protestantism, Catholicism, and non-Christian religions—as well as to the field of international evangelicalism. While Part I lays the foundation for such an analysis, much work remains. For example, a comprehensive analysis of American evangelicalism would examine the relationship between evangelicalism and black Protestantism, which, while sharing many of the same theological convictions, are nevertheless treated as distinctive religious traditions by most scholars of religion (and for good reason).[56] Still, there is no bright red line separating black and white conservative Protestantism, just as there are no impermeable lines separating distinctive movements within American evangelicalism analyzed here.[57] A fully developed analysis of the American evangelical field would spend more time tracing the tortured and unequal relationship between the majority-white evangelical movement and theologically conservative black Protestantism in the United States than I have space to do here.[58]

Fourth and finally, it is important to be clear about the nature and limits of a field-theoretic explanation of social phenomena—and the nature and limits of sociological explanations more generally. Put simply, the human and social objects of sociological inquiry are of such infinite complexity that it is impossible for any sociological explanation to account for "everything" there is to know about one's object of study—no matter how comprehensive, complex, or competent a given attempt at sociological explanation may be. Here, once again, we see the wisdom of taking a Bourdieusian field-theoretic approach to our object of study:

> The Rules of Art helps us to see how Bourdieu understands sociological explanation in general and sociohistorical explanation in particular. For Bourdieu, there is no single, final, or even correct explanation of anything, only more complete, developed, adequate explanations. . . . Like Weber . . . Bourdieu sees the social world as an infinite manifold of causal interdependencies; thus . . . sociological explanation as Bourdieu conceives it consists in the effort to reconstruct a web of causal interdependence.[59]

Field theory was one of the primary analytic tools through which Bourdieu sought to reconstruct elements of the underlying "web[s] of causal interdependence" that gave rise to the observable social phenomena and processes which he sought to explain. And in the field of American evangelicalism—as in the social world more generally—there is always more going on than meets the eye—or the sociologist's gaze.

We are now finally in position to move forward; and given the complexity of the terrain in front of us, a map is in order. Our first task, accomplished in the next section, is to locate the social position of the neo-monastic movement in relation to other theoretically significant positions within the field of American evangelicalism. Our second task, accomplished in the section titled "Neo-Monasticism in the Field of Evangelical Position-Takings," is to locate the religious and political standpoints of neo-monastic evangelicals in relation to these same positions. After having mapped out the structure of relevant evangelical positions and position-takings in these next two sections, the third task is to shift our analytical attention from the *structure* of the contemporary evangelical field (as it relates to neo-monasticism) to the *processes* through which the field of American evangelicalism is reproduced and transformed. This third and final task is accomplished in the section titled "Some Properties of the Evangelical Field" in the form of seven propositions.

Locating Neo-Monasticism in the American Evangelical Field

In order to locate neo-monastic evangelicalism in the larger evangelical field, we must first delineate the specific types of capital that have force in the evangelical field and that structure the relations between different positions within it. The field of American evangelicalism is structured by five primary forms of capital. *Economic capital (CE)* refers to the economic resources belonging to churches and religious organizations of a given position. *Political capital (CP)* refers to a person or position's access to political power, including recognition by powerful political actors. Political action and special interest groups (such as the Family Research Council or the Christian Coalition), party caucuses and institutionalized influence within political parties (such as the Values Action Team in US Congress), and public relationships between high-profile political and religious leaders are all examples of political capital. *Cultural capital (CC)* refers to the specific forms of cultural capital that are recognized as significant among evangelicals: most notably, academic credentials and book authorship. Although other forms of cultural capital (such artistic recognition) have some influence among evangelicals, book authorship is a uniquely potent type of cultural capital in the evangelical field. While publishing scholarly books can enhance one's position in the evangelical field to some extent, popular books about evangelism, theology, politics, spirituality, or church growth are far more liable to increase one's position and standing in the field.[60] *Symbolic capital (CS)* refers to a person or group's *recognition* as a significant or influential agent in the field by mainstream media (such as *Time* magazine, *New York Times*, or PBS), Christian media (such as *Christianity Today*), or influential evangelical leaders.[61] Finally, the *number of people* associated with a church, organization, or movement within evangelicalism is a significant form of specific capital which I will refer to as *specific (people) capital (or CSp)*. *Specific (people) capital* goes beyond common notions of social capital in that building large churches, church networks, and religious organizations has a special religious and symbolic value among evangelicals by virtue of the value placed on evangelistic and entrepreneurial effectiveness in the field. This is the most widely recognized form of capital in the evangelical field, and it reflects American evangelicalism's populist and revivalist roots, its fundamental belief in the importance of winning people to Christ, and the free-market structure of the American religious field.[62]

Figure 3.1 locates neo-monasticism in relation to four significant movements in American evangelicalism with respect to their possession of cultural, economic, political, and specific (people) capital. Megachurch evangelicalism and the Christian Right occupy dominant positions in the field, while the evangelical left occupies a dominated but rising position. While their accumulation of cultural and symbolic capital has enabled neo-monasticism and the emerging church to emerge from the sea of evangelical anonymity as *recognized* positions in American evangelicalism, they nevertheless occupy dominated positions by virtue of their relatively small amounts of economic, political, and specific (people) capital. Figure 3.1's overlapping circles with porous, dashed boundary lines represent the dynamic and overlapping nature of these positions within the evangelical field.[63] For example, the emerging church and neo-monastic evangelicalism—while possessing distinct origins, leaders, institutional networks, and position-takings—also overlap with one another and with the position of the evangelical left.[64] The same is true of conservative and megachurch evangelicalism, the latter of which increasingly involves overlaps with the evangelical left as well as conservative evangelicalism.[65]

The Position of Megachurch Evangelicalism
(Csp+, Ce+, Cp+/–, Cc+/–)

Megachurch evangelicalism refers to the seeker-sensitive/purpose-driven megachurch movement, with Rick Warren's Saddleback Church and Bill

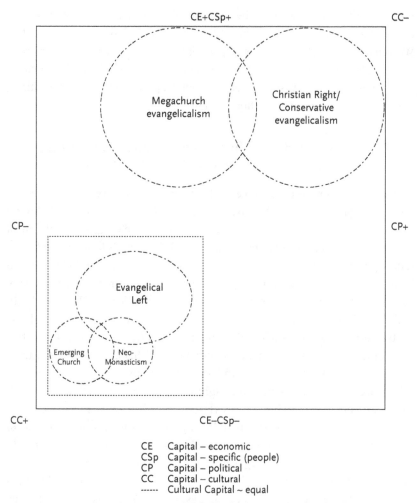

CE+CSp+   CC−

Megachurch
evangelicalism

Christian Right/
Conservative
evangelicalism

CP−

Evangelical
Left

Emerging
Church

Neo-
Monasticism

CP+

CC+   CE−CSp−

CE   Capital – economic
CSp Capital – specific (people)
CP   Capital – political
CC   Capital – cultural
------ Cultural Capital ~ equal

FIGURE 3.1 Neo-monasticism in the field of American evangelicalism

Hybels's Willow Creek Community Church being the prototypical examples.[66] Megachurch evangelicalism occupies a dominant position in the evangelical field by virtue of its possession of enormous economic and specific (people) capital. It has the largest and fastest-growing churches, the biggest budgets, the largest church associations, the top-selling books, the most affluent members, and the widest influence of any position in the evangelical field.[67] While megachurch evangelicalism is far more occupied with church growth and evangelism than with wielding political influence, it nevertheless possesses a significant amount of political capital by virtue of its significant resources and the national public profiles of its leaders—who often function as representative evangelicals in the national media—and their influence with millions of evangelical Christians. Much like Billy Graham before them, Rick Warren and Bill Hybels have developed high-profile public relationships with sitting US presidents. However, megachurch evangelicalism has neither sought nor gained the institutionalized political power of the Christian Right, which is reflected in their position in figure 3.1.

The Position of the Christian Right and Conservative Evangelicalism (Csp+, Ce+, Cp+, Cc–)

Between 5 percent and 10 percent of all Americans—over fifteen million people—explicitly identify themselves with the Christian Right.[68] Although this number falls short of both the fearful worries and exaggerated claims of the movement's opponents and champions, it is enough to place the Christian Right in a powerful position in the American evangelical field. A much larger number of evangelicals support Christian Right perspectives on core political issues, and thirty years of political mobilization by Christian Right and Republican Party activists have resulted in a significant evangelical majority that reliably supports Republican Party candidates and identifies with a wide range of conservative policy standpoints.[69] This accrual of significant political capital was built on a foundation of economic and specific (people) capital accrued by early Christian Right religious leaders such as Jerry Falwell, Pat Robertson, and Beverly LaHaye, who developed ministries with enormous budgets and national followings primarily through the use of broadcast media.[70] For example, former US presidential candidate Pat Robertson's Christian Broadcasting Network has an annual budget approaching $300 million and a viewership in the millions on over two hundred foreign and domestic television stations.[71] James Dobson's Focus on the Family boasts an active mailing list of over 2.5 million people, 1,300 employees, and a $130 million annual budget.[72] Dobson also helped grow the Family Research Council into one of conservative evangelicalism's largest advocacy organizations, with a staff of over one hundred people, a $14 million annual budget, and a 500,000 person mailing list.[73] The late D. James Kennedy's Coral Ridge Ministries broadcasting network reached a peak viewership of over 3 million and a $30+ million annual budget to go along with his 10,000+ member megachurch and Center for Reclaiming America.[74] As president of the political arm of the 16-million-member Southern Baptist Convention, Dr. Richard Land has become a leading figure on Capitol Hill while sitting on numerous government-appointed committees.[75] The Christian Right and conservative evangelicalism continue to occupy a dominant position in the evangelical field by virtue of its significant accumulation of political, economic, and specific (people) capital.[76]

The Position of the Evangelical Left (Csp−, Ce−, Cp+/−, Cc+)

In comparison to the enormous budgets, buildings, and followings of the Christian Right and megachurch evangelicalism, the *New York Times* profile of Jim Wallis as the "lonely voice of the tiny evangelical left" is not far off.[77] Wallis's *Sojourners* is by far the largest and most visible communications and advocacy organization of the evangelical left, but its subscription lists and $5 million budget are a fraction of the economic and specific (people) capital possessed by the Christian Right.[78] However, recent years have seen the evangelical left grow in both visibility and influence. *Sojourners* doubled its print readership between 2002 and 2006 while more than tripling its readership among evangelicals during that time, and Wallis's breakout book *God's Politics* spent fifteen weeks on the *New York Times* bestseller list.[79] Since the 2004 presidential election, Wallis has consulted with the Democratic Party in efforts to find more common ground between Democrats and evangelical Christians, and other prominent leaders such as Dr. Tony Campolo and Dr. Ronald J. Sider have joined Wallis in becoming regulars on national media platforms ranging from *Nightline* and *Larry King Live* to *The Daily Show* and *The Colbert Report*.[80] Like other influential evangelical ministers before him, Campolo served as spiritual advisor to a sitting US president (during the Clinton administration), a standard expression of symbolic political capital in the evangelical field. Roughly one-quarter of white evangelicals voted for Barack Obama in the 2008 presidential election and 20 percent self-identify as politically liberal.[81] The rising visibility, influence, and political capital of the evangelical left has resulted in more public declarations, campaigns, and policy initiatives similar in style and content to the 1973 Chicago Declaration to which the modern evangelical left traces its roots.[82] However, while the evangelical left is increasingly able to mobilize support from prominent mainstream evangelical leaders on an expanding list of environmental, immigration, poverty, and other social justice issues, the Christian Right's ability to severely curtail the influence of these mobilizations speaks to its still dominant influence in the evangelical field.[83] The evangelical left thus continues to occupy a dominated position in the evangelical field, though it is arguably moving in an upward and opposite trajectory through the field in relation to conservative evangelicalism and the Christian Right.

The Position of the Emerging Church (Csp–, Ce–, Cp–, Cc+)

The emerging church in the United States arose in the mid-1990s out of a series of evangelical conferences and leadership summits sponsored by the Leadership Network, which was founded by best-selling author and multi-millionaire cable television entrepreneur Bob Buford with the help of staff from *Christianity Today*.[84] These conferences focused on helping evangelicals reach the Gen X, post-boomer generation with the Christian gospel, were attended by thousands of evangelical pastors from around the country, and eventually became sponsored by Zondervan—a giant in the evangelical publishing industry—which enabled the emerging church movement to quickly gain recognition in the evangelical field. In 1995 the Leadership Network brought together a small group of young leaders from around the country who established a group called Emergent, which quickly spawned a series of book titles, websites, and conferences aimed at deconstructing modern evangelical church paradigms and practices in favor of a more historically rooted and culturally appropriate expression of biblical Christianity for postmodern culture.[85] While the early financial backing and recognition of these emerging church leaders by the Leadership Network and Zondervan paved the way for a few emerging churches to grow quite large, the vast majority of emerging churches are very small, often composed of a network of small cell churches that meet in homes, cafes, or pubs rather than large auditoriums. Similar to neo-monastic communities, their participants are overwhelmingly white, well-educated, "solidly middle class" young adults under the age of 40.[86] While there are no good estimates of the number of individuals involved in emerging churches, estimates of the number of churches or spiritual communities associated with the emerging church movement range from just over one hundred on the low end to over seven hundred on the high end.[87] The emerging church is also similar to neo-monasticism in that its visibility among evangelicals far surpasses its economic, political, and specific (people) capital. The emerging church has become a recognized position in the field because of its significant accrual of cultural and symbolic capital, but nevertheless occupies a dominated position in the evangelical field.[88]

The Position of Neo-Monasticism (Csp–, Ce–, Cp–, Cc+)

Since neo-monasticism is described at length below, we can be brief. Like the emerging church, neo-monastic evangelicalism occupies a dominated position in the evangelical field, possessing relatively little economic, political, or specific (people) capital in comparison to dominant positions in the field. While increasingly in-demand books and public appearances by new monastic leaders such as Shane Claiborne and Jonathon Wilson-Hartgrove reach millions of evangelicals, neo-monastic communities in the United States number around two hundred and have an average size of less than one hundred.[89] However, like the emerging church, the neo-monastic position has accrued significant amounts of cultural and symbolic capital by virtue of their leaders' best-selling books, in-demand speaking schedules, and regular appearances in prominent media outlets, both secular and evangelical, such as *SPIN, Esquire,* CNN, Fox News, Al Jazeera, NPR, and *Christianity Today.*[90] The number, size, and visibility of neo-monastic communities has grown rapidly over the last several years, and its growing popularity among young, educated, urban evangelicals likely points to an upward trajectory through the field. However, the neo-monastic movement is still in its nascent stage and occupies a dominated position in American evangelicalism similar to the emerging church.

Neo-Monasticism in the Field of Evangelical Position-Takings

Having sketched out the (objective) social position of neo-monasticism within the evangelical field, we may proceed to a textual and ethnographic investigation of the neo-monasticism's (subjective) religious and political position-takings in relation to dominant expressions of American evangelicalism, which, as we saw in chapter 2, have been characterized by four major themes: (1) theological individualism and the prioritization of evangelism over other forms of social engagement, (2) religious nationalism/promotion of "Christian America" perspective on foreign and domestic politics, (3) conservative social views on gender, sexuality, and the family, and (4) conservative economic views and affinity with the American business sector. These themes continue to play a major role in structuring the space of theological and political position-takings in the evangelical field today, as we will see below. Within each theme, I begin with dominant evangelical position-takings on the issue at hand, followed by the neo-monastic point of view and other main challengers to the dominant perspective from among the five evangelical movements under investigation: neo-monasticism, the emerging church, the evangelical left, conservative evangelicalism/the Christian Right, and megachurch evangelicalism. A summary of the analysis is presented in table 3.1.

Evangelism, Individualism, and Church Growth

Megachurch evangelicalism is relentlessly, energetically, and single-mindedly focused on reaching individuals with the Christian gospel and seeing churches grow as a result of "irreligious people [becoming] fully devoted followers of Jesus Christ."[91] There is perhaps no clearer example of the theological individualism and the prioritization of evangelism that runs so deeply through historic American evangelicalism than the seeker-sensitive/purpose-driven megachurch movement.[92] A quick survey of best-selling books by megachurch leaders emphatically makes the point, with titles such as: *Becoming a Contagious Christian, Building a Contagious Church: Revolutionizing the Way We View and Do Evangelism, Inside the Mind of Unchurched Harry and Mary: How to Reach Friends and Family Who Avoid God and the Church, The Purpose Driven Church: Growth without Compromising your Message and Mission, The Purpose Driven Life,* and *The Case for Christ: A Journalist's Personal Investigation of the Evidence for Jesus.* These books—all written by current or former leaders of Willow Creek Community or Saddleback Church—aim to motivate and train individual evangelicals how reach other individuals with the gospel, and to equip churches to grow through evangelism.[93] Willow Creek's *Becoming a Contagious Christian* series has trained over a million evangelicals to reach non-Christians with the gospel.[94] *Becoming a Contagious Church* expands on this curriculum in a monumental effort to equip churches to prioritize effective evangelism as their church's primary mission. What is missing from this 400+ page treatise on reaching individuals with the gospel is any mention of "reclaiming America for Christ" through politics. While "evangelism" appears over 250 times in the book, poverty is mentioned twice in passing and political issues are completely ignored. *Rediscovering Church* follows a similar pattern, with "evangelism," "the gospel," and "unchurched"/"irreligious"/"lost" people mentioned more than 75 separate times in the book while "social injustice," abortion, poverty, or environmental issues are mentioned 5 times combined. The point of view of Willow Creek church leaders is clear: "If we want to build a contagious church . . . evangelism needs to be our top priority," because "our greatest contribution to society is through helping to bring irreligious people into an authentic relationship with [Jesus Christ]."[95]

With over one million copies sold, Rick Warren's *The Purpose Driven Church* follows the megachurch script: more than 75 mentions of evangelism compared to just 2 mentions of poverty or social justice, a focus on practical strategies and proven principles for "conversion church growth,"[96] and the prioritization of evangelism and individual spiritual transformation as a method of social change:

> I believe that pastors are the most strategic change agents to deal with the problems society faces. Even many politicians are coming to the conclusion that spiritual revival is our only solution. Recently I read this statement from former Cabinet member William Bennett in *American Enterprise* magazine: "The most serious problems afflicting our society are manifestly moral, behavioral, and spiritual, and therefore are remarkably resistant to government cures." Does it seem ironic to you that at a time when politicians are saying we need a *spiritual* solution many Christians are acting like politics is the solution? While there is no doubt that the moral decline in our nation has produced a battlefield, it has also given us an incredible mission field! We must remember that Christ also died for the other side of the cultural war.[97]

This is the only substantial treatment of politics in the entire 400-page book. The message is clear and echoes the theological individualism and prioritization of evangelism shared by dominant expressions of historic evangelicalism: the spiritual transformation of the individual through faith in Christ is the only real hope for dealing with society's problems.[98] Evangelism and church growth, not politics or social reform, should be the focus of the church.

To that end, the book offers Warren's "proven five-part strategy that will enable your church to grow," including 50 pages devoted to the use of census data, surveys, and "psychographics" to develop evangelism strategies that target specific demographic groups, and 100 pages to help churches "bring in a crowd."[99] In all, *The Purpose Driven Church* contains over 110 mentions of church growth. All of these texts demonstrate a strong affinity for combining biblical principles with marketing strategies, business management models, and personal growth literatures: promising "field-proven blueprints" for increasing evangelistic effectiveness; "proven five-part strategies" for growing your church; a "forty-day spiritual journey" to discover your purpose; and "a formula for impacting your world" with the gospel.[100] Each offers dozens of pages of practical advice on creating professional-level programs and events; hiring, organizing, and motivating highly competent religious professionals; tailoring programs, music, marketing, and preaching to specific demographic targets; and designing church buildings and budgets strategically for maximum evangelistic effectiveness and church growth. Alongside biblical language, linguistic idioms and strategies from the business world are everywhere; a stark contrast to Urban Monastery participants and other neo-monastic and emerging evangelicals, who strongly prefer relational, familial, and organic linguistic metaphors and strategies of action to business and marketing ones.[101]

Thus, whereas the seeker-sensitive/purpose-driven megachurch point of view sees evangelism as the primary mission of the church, Urban Monastery participants argue that churches which preach evangelism while neglecting social justice are promoters of a "false gospel": "Both are core to who God is and who we as the Church are to be in the world. . . . Social justice is not the fullness, it needs to be coupled with evangelism; nor is evangelism the fullness, it needs to be coupled with acts of mercy and justice in the world" (Manuel, Anja). As we will explore at length in Part II, Urban Monastery participants organize community life around the practice of "holistic mission," which elevates the importance of social justice action to equal status with evangelism. Where megachurch texts promote marketing and business management models to train high-quality religious professionals, build complex organizational systems, and attract large crowds, Urban Monastery leaders and participants criticize the "formal," "attractional," and "consumptive form of church that's about receiving from professional ministers" (Mina), while using words like "fluid," "relational," "organic," "participatory," and "simple" to describe what Christian communities and churches ought to look like:

JESSICA: The Urban Monastery is like how the apostles in Acts used to have church: really small, intimate gatherings where the Holy Spirit—God—is the leader. It's simple church. Somehow it's so much more dynamic and deep because everything else is stripped away and you get to the core of why people go to church in the first place. It gets so buried by the organization of it all. And I wouldn't classify myself as someone who is anarchist or anything like that. But the rules have always bothered me.

In its prioritization of evangelism, theological individualism, professional-bureaucratic organizational structures, and geographic distribution, the megachurch and Urban Monastery points of view are worlds apart, despite sharing a common religious identity and heritage in American evangelicalism.

The Urban Monastic point of view is echoed in texts written by neo-monastic movement leaders. Urban Monastery participants' critique of individualism and promotion of communitarianism is also dominant in *School(s) for Conversion: 12 Marks of a New Monasticism*, a collection of essays written by people "trying to embody the gospel communally."[102] The book itself was edited not by an individual but by a community—The Rutba House—a "Christian community of hospitality, peacemaking, and discipleship" located in a poor, predominantly African American neighborhood in Durham, NC.

There are more than 150 references here to intentional community, communal living, or common life in only 170 pages of text. "Embodying the gospel communally" is the New Monasticism's primary response to the violence, inequality, and individualism it sees as corrupting American society and compromising the American church.

Alongside the ubiquitous discussion of community, *School(s) for Conversion* contains more than 70 references concerning hospitality to the "stranger" or "other." New Monastic communities promote and practice an expansive understanding of "hospitality to the stranger," championing "the pursuit of a healthy reciprocity of receiving as well as giving [as] a practice of humility, respect, and justice . . . with marginal cultures and poor populations."[103] However, "in order to welcome the stranger," they argue, "one must be near and available to the stranger. Thus we may be called to radical relocation."[104] Because of New Monastic communities' belief in the importance of hospitality and community across race and class lines, "relocation [from the suburbs] to the abandoned places of Empire" stands as the first of the "12 Marks of New Monasticism."[105] *Punk Monk: New Monasticism and the Ancient Art of Breathing* is also deeply communitarian, criticizing individualism and containing more than 100 references and multiple chapters explaining the urgent need for "counter-cultural communities of prayer, mission, and justice" among the poor.[106] It also contains 30+ references to hospitality and 50+ references to creativity and the arts. Compared to other neo-monastic texts, *Punk Monk* is distinctive for its heavy emphasis on prayer (150+ mentions) and on evangelism, mission, or sharing the gospel (120+ mentions).

Finally, in his best-selling book *The Irresistible Revolution: Living as an Ordinary Radical*, neo-monastic leader Shane Claiborne leaves no doubt about his point of view concerning dominant expressions of evangelical Christianity in America: "The Church is a whore," he writes, lifting a famous aphorism attributed to St. Augustine, "but she's my mother."[107] Or, quoting his "old mentor" and evangelical left leader Tony Campolo: "If we were to set out to establish a religion in polar opposition to the Beatitudes Jesus taught, it would look strikingly similar to the pop Christianity that has taken over the airwaves of North America."[108] Claiborne refers to his New Monastic community (called The Simple Way) as "missionaries to the church" on escape from a "Christian industrial complex" that cultivates "spiritual bulimia . . . marked by an over-consumptive but malnourished spirituality, suffocated by Christianity but thirsty for God."[109] Claiborne takes frequent rhetorical shots at Willow Creek Community Church, Wheaton College, and the evangelical consumer subculture, along with many other prominent evangelical institutions and practices.[110] His primary target is the Christian Right and the conservative politicization of American evangelicalism, but *The Irresistible Revolution* also includes much playful and qualified—yet stinging—criticism of his white, middle-class, culturally isolated, suburban megachurch depiction of American "pop evangelicalism":

> There is much noise in evangelical Christianity. There are many false prophets (and false profits) out there, and all kinds of embarrassing things being done in the name of God. But there is another movement stirring, a little revolution of sorts. . . . There are those of us who, rather than simply reject pop evangelicalism, want to spread another kind of Christianity, a faith that has as much to say about this world as it does the next.[111]

Standing against the dominant expressions of evangelical Christianity in America, *The Irresistible Revolution* is a manifesto for neo-monastic communities and their sympathizers who want to "begin to be Christians again."[112]

Similar to their neo-monastic brethren, the emerging church movement was born in part out of engagement and disenchantment with megachurch evangelism.[113] The emerging church's extensive engagement with megachurch evangelicalism is reflected in books such as Dan Kimball's *The Emerging Church*, which differs from neo-monasticism in sharing megachurch evangelicalism's laser focus on reaching people with the gospel, along with its relative neglect of social and political issues. Just as megachurch evangelicals' commitment to evangelism makes them "willing to experiment with worship styles, architecture, and religious ideas in order to . . . show how Christianity is relevant and applicable to the world of middle-class suburbanites,"[114] *The Emerging Church* explores "how the church can reach out to emerging generations" in a "postmodern or post-Christian context."[115] Indeed, Kimball's book sustains a fascinating debate with Rick Warren about the seeker-sensitive/purpose-driven megachurch position in relation to the emerging church position, with Warren describing Kimball's book as an example of "what a purpose-driven church can look like in a postmodern world."[116] *The Emerging Church* contains more than 95 references to evangelism, mission, or sharing the gospel in a post-Christian/postmodern context, highlighting a primary focus on evangelism and mission which the emerging church's founding point of view shares with megachurch evangelicalism.[117]

However, *The Emerging Church* also contains much qualified criticism and opposition to megachurch evangelicalism, with five chapters specifically devoted to developing a "post-seeker-sensitive" approach to mission and the church.[118] The book contains 40+ critical mentions of "seeker-sensitive" evangelicalism and more than 80 critical references to the "modern" church's obsessive preoccupation with "the three B's (buildings, budgets, and bodies [i.e., church size])."[119] Similar to Urban Monastery participants and other neo-monastic evangelicals, Kimball advocates a shift from individualistic to communal expressions of faith, from modern program-driven "consumer church" to "raw," participatory and experiential (50+ mentions) "missional church," and from a "hierarchical, goal-driven, CEO/manager" approach to leadership, to more team-based and relational approaches.[120] There are also 65+ positive mentions of creativity and the arts.

Kimball's entire book is structured around a deconstruction/reconstruction polemic,[121] arguing for a radical reconstruction American evangelicalism while also taking care to honor the evangelistic values and effectiveness of megachurch evangelicalism in past generations.[122] At the same time, *The Emerging Church* argues that the shift from modernity to postmodernity is "more than a generation gap."[123] Rather, America and the Western world are in a "major period of cultural transition" akin to the Enlightenment (!), which requires a radical deconstruction and reconstruction of dominant expressions of evangelical theology, ecclesiology, and mission.[124] In Kimball's words, "Rethinking the emerging church involves rethinking almost *everything* we do."[125] *The Emerging Church* contains no less than fifteen graphs and charts comparing modern culture and the (old, outdated) megachurch standpoint with postmodern culture and the (new, cutting-edge) emerging church standpoint.[126] The list of evangelical beliefs and practices which need to be "deconstructed" is immense, containing 100+ examples of how the nature and meaning of truth, communication and worship styles, understandings of leadership and authority, the gospel, evangelistic strategies, and the process of spiritual formation all need to be radically altered in order to embody and communicate the gospel effectively in America's emerging postmodern, post-Christian culture.

Most of the religious and cultural analysis contained in *The Emerging Church* is drawn from the early theological musings of emerging church guru Brian McLaren, the cofounder of Emergent Village, former pastor, and prolific author whose book *A New Kind of Christian* is widely recognized as the text that helped put the emerging church on the American evangelical map.[127] A quick survey of some of McLaren's book titles—*A New Kind of Christian, A New Kind of Christianity, Adventures in Missing the Point: How the Culture-Controlled Church Neutered the Gospel, What Would Jesus Deconstruct?, The Secret Message of Jesus, Finding our Way Again,* and *Everything Must Change*—aptly communicates his oppositional stance to dominant expressions of contemporary American evangelicalism. In *A New Kind of Christian,* McLaren playfully yet mercilessly goes after evangelical shibboleths such as the nature of biblical authority,[128] the practice of evangelism,[129] the true meaning of the gospel,[130] heaven and hell,[131] and the possibility of salvation for people belonging to other religions.[132] Regarding evangelism, McLaren writes that "our whole approach to conversion is so . . . mechanistic and consumeristic and individualistic and controlling" and that conservative Christians' "preoccupation with being saved sometimes strikes me as strangely selfish. . . . I think our definition of 'saved' is shrunken and freeze-dried by modernity."[133] Regarding the gospel, evangelicals must "escape from the narrowing of the gospel to an individualistic story only about saving souls to a missional, communal, and global story about changing the world."[134] Evangelism, salvation, and the gospel receive more than 70 mentions of a mixed variety—ranging from support to criticism to various attempts at redefinition.

A New Kind of Christian embodies the emerging church's appropriation of postmodernism in its literary style, as well as its content, carrying out a critical deconstruction of traditional evangelicalism in the form of a fictional narrative. Ever the provocateur, McLaren makes the character "Neo"—a divorced, Episcopalian, Jamaican-born public schoolteacher with a doctorate in the philosophy of science—the sage and hero of his book. Through a series of fictional conversations and email exchanges, Neo patiently guides a disillusioned white evangelical pastor through a crisis of faith while explaining to him the need for a new kind of Christianity in the postmodern West. Like other emerging church texts, A New Kind of Christian makes much of the transition from modernism to postmodernism in Western culture, with more than 150 references to the modern/postmodern trope and its implications for Christianity.

Just as Brian McLaren's A New Kind of Christian communicates its message in literary style, as well as content, so too does Doug Pagitt's Church Re-Imagined. Pagitt—cofounder of Emergent Village and founding pastor of an influential emerging church in Minneapolis called Solomon's Porch—champions the practice of "participatory" and "interactive" spiritual community (25 mentions) and decentralized team leadership, while opposing passive religious consumerism and hierarchical managerial leadership: his book thus includes running "journal entries" from six members of Pagitt's emerging church. Pagitt champions female leadership in the church (10+ mentions): the journal entries are written by three women and three men. Pagitt champions the practice of Christianity as an "integrated, whole Kingdom life" in community rather than attendance at a Sunday event: the book's seven core chapters highlight seven theological values practiced throughout the week at

Solomon's Porch: Worship on Sunday; Physicality (yoga and alternative medicine!) on Monday; Dialogue (Bible discussion) on Tuesday; Hospitality on Wednesday; Belief (Bible study) on Thursday; Creativity on Friday; and Service on Saturday.[135] The emphasis on practicing holistic Christian spirituality in community runs strong throughout the book, which contains more than 60 nontrivial references to "community" or "communal." Throughout, *Church Re-Imagined* argues that the postmodern world calls for an understanding of Christian spirituality that is "holistic" and "communal" rather than narrowly spiritual and individualistic,[136] lamenting that "the marks of 'successful' church have been reduced to tangible evidence such as size, market share, political influence, healthy budgets, and the creation of model citizens of the American Dream."[137] From Pagitt's point of view, the church should be a "holistic missional Christian community,"[138] not a market-driven, program-based, demographic-targeting "provider of religious goods and services" that treats Christianity like "a product that can be marketed, sold, and consumed to meet needs."[139] In each of these perspectives, Pagitt sounds very much like Urban Monastery participants and other neo-monastic evangelicals in their opposition to religious individualism, consumerism, professionalism, bureaucratization, and business-marketplace models of religious organization and church growth.

Christian America, American Imperialism, and War

In his book *The Ten Offenses: Reclaim the Blessings of the Ten Commandments*, Christian Coalition founder Pat Robertson argues that the "war between the spiritual and secular vision for America" constitutes an "alarmingly serious threat to our nation's foundation and Christian heritage."[140] The book's first 40 pages argue that America was founded as a Christian nation and thus has been blessed by God with great wealth and power—a view that Urban Monastery participants find deeply problematic. Urban Monastery participants describe the idea of a "Christian America" uniquely blessed by God among the nations as a result of its Christian heritage as "arrogant," "colonialist," and "disgusting."[141] The next 20 pages of *The Ten Offenses* argue that elite "secular humanists" are undermining this foundation to America's great peril, and subsequent chapters outline a litany of moral decline stemming from the abandonment of the Ten Commandments as the foundation of American law and culture.[142] *The Ten Offenses* contains more than 70 positive mentions of America's "Christian heritage," "Christian foundations," or identity as a "Christian nation." From Robertson's point of view, Marxists, socialists, and "every Democratic presidential candidate" who "beats the drum of class warfare" belong to the network of institutions and "liberal elites" who are ruining America:

> Knowingly or unknowingly, the ACLU, the National Abortion Rights League, Planned Parenthood, the National Organization of Women, the Gay-Lesbian Alliance, the American Atheists, Marxists, People for the American Way, Americans United for Separation of Church and State, advocates of political correctness in education, and all of their allies across the land in Congress, the state legislatures, and the media are hastening the destruction of the United States of America and the freedoms and lifestyle we all enjoy.[143]

The Ten Offenses is a clear and forceful statement of the Christian Right perspective on America's religious foundations, moral decline, and the terrible consequences of losing the culture war. Robertson's deep nostalgia for America's past and alarm for its future is shared by Dr. Richard Land—author of the infamous "Land Letter" to George W. Bush in support of war in Iraq—in his book *For Faith and Family: Changing America by Strengthening the Family.* Like Robertson, Land argues that American wealth and power is the result of its founding as a Christian nation based on biblical principles:

> The leaders responsible for founding America and guiding it through the past two and a half centuries—leaders responsible for crafting the freest, richest, most powerful nation in the history of the world—were almost all operating from a Judeo-Christian worldview. . . . Since the Pilgrims, Judeo-Christian values and morality have been absolutely essential to America's health and success.[144]

Land's book contains more than 25 references that advocate "legislating morality" and argue against the separation of church and state.[145]

While sharing the concerns of other conservative evangelical leaders regarding America's "cultural rot" and "widespread acceptance of immorality";[146] the late Dr. D. James Kennedy's final book (*How Would Jesus Vote?*) is less harshly polemical and somewhat more careful about the relationship between religion and politics than either *The Ten Offenses* or *For Faith and Family*:

> It is not up to Christians to try to bring in [Christ's] kingdom by force. . . . God created only one country in the history of the world: ancient Israel. He did not create America. The United States is not the new Israel. The United States is not now nor ever was a theocracy. . . . We

do not claim that God is on the side of the United States. What we do claim is that as many people as possible in the United States should strive to be on God's side.[147]

However, *How Would Jesus Vote?* also advocates for a strong Christian influence in education, government, and the public sphere while frequently denying (25+ mentions) any constitutional intention to build a "wall of separation" between church and state.[148] One chapter and more than 15+ pages defend increased military spending for the war on terror against the "Islamic threat," while chapter 11 takes a hard line against "illegal aliens who are taking advantage of our way of life":

> We must secure the borders to prevent criminals and potential terrorists from entering our country. These are serious threats. Acting in a Christian way includes concern for self-defense. It is astounding how many crimes are committed by illegal immigrants.[149]

How Would Jesus Vote? contains more than 50 positive references and 15 pages devoted to America's founding and identity as a Christian nation, along with 25+ negative references to secular humanism—echoing Robertson and Land's arguments in *The Ten Offenses* and *For Faith and Family*, respectively.

Against the various forms of religious nationalism expressed in these and other Christian Right texts, the idea of "Christian America" is anathema to Urban Monastery participants:

LILITH: This nation, as much as it was sown in a desire for freedom, was also sown in violence. And that kind of sordid history is true of other nations as well. So I think it's reprehensible to have this high-minded view of ourselves. And just because we happen to have a lot of natural resources, to have this *pretension* of "manifest destiny" is *disgusting*. I can't handle it.

Urban Monastery participants are also highly critical of the "interventionist" and "pro-military" tendencies they attribute to the Christian Right:

RILEY: I don't believe in killing, and that's the most important thing I can say about my political standpoints in light of Christ. . . . I grew up around a lot of people who were mixing war and religion. And that's a problem.

Where Christian Right leaders worry about defending and preserving "Christian America" against foreign and domestic, cultural and military, symbolic and material threats such as secular humanism, Islam, terrorism, and the like, I found Urban Monastery participants opposing religious nationalism and American imperialism at every turn.

Texts written by neo-monastic leaders echo the on-the-ground perspectives of Urban Monastery participants. Shane Claiborne's deep "disaffection from America's cultural and patriotic Christianity"[150] is a torrent that runs throughout *The Irresistible Revolution*, which contains 60+ references to peacemaking, nonviolence, and anti-militarism. *The Irresistible Revolution* is relentless in its attacks on American militarism, nationalism, empire-building (30+ references), and the war in Iraq (and all war).[151] *School(s) for Conversion: 12 Marks of a New Monasticism* similarly criticizes American evangelicals for their failure to stand against the particularly pernicious problem of religious nationalism, lampooning "an age when 'Christian' America is the 'last remaining superpower' in an all-out 'war on terror.'"[152] Stories of Easter services on American battleships and American flags draped on crosses at religious gatherings are used to criticize the "unacknowledged alliance with Empire that plagues the church in North America":

> In this country the cross and the battleship, the Christian story and the American story, have become nearly inseparable. . . . Our tacit, even explicit support of America's militarism results in this unspoken-but-all-too-clear message: *we believe that Jesus is Lord, but we don't believe it enough to renounce our country's power and violence.*[153]

School(s) for Conversion contains more than 55 references to peacemaking, nonviolence, and anti-militarism and 20 critical references to "American empire."

In their critiques of Christian Right perspectives on American imperialism, militarism, and religious nationalism, neo-monastic evangelicals sound very much like their elders on the evangelical left. The first two parts of evangelical left leader Jim Wallis's book, *God's Politics: Why the Right Gets It Wrong and the Left Doesn't Get It*, defend a balanced Christian engagement in politics, one that respects pluralism while arguing that Christians need to "take back the faith" that has been "co-opted by the Right."[154] While the Christian Right extols America's founding as a Christian nation blessed by God with great wealth, power, and charitable goodness, Wallis grieves over "America's Original Sin": "The United States of America was established as a white society, founded upon the genocide of another race and then the enslavement of yet another."[155] The book contains 65+ negative references to the Christian Right. Parts III–V of *God's Politics* are organized around three provocative questions directly inspired by the Christian Right point of view, namely: "When Did Jesus Become Pro-War?" "When Did Jesus Become Pro-Rich?" and "When Did Jesus Become a Selective Moralist?"[156] In Part III, six chapters and more than 100 pages are devoted to peacemaking and arguments against American militarism and imperialism. In all, the book contains more than 125 mentions of peace, peacemaking, nonviolence, and opposition to war, including 30+ negative mentions of American and religious imperialism.

Dr. Tony Campolo—an evangelical Baptist minister and former professor of sociology at the University of Pennsylvania and Eastern University—shares Wallis's opposition to the Christian Right and penchant for asking provocative rhetorical questions. Campolo asks thirteen such questions as chapter titles in his book *Speaking My Mind*, including: "Are Evangelicals Too Militaristic?" [Answer: Yes], "Do We Understand Why So Many People Throughout the World Hate America?" [Answer: We should, and it's partly our fault that they do], "Is Islam Really an Evil Religion?" [Answer: No].[157] Campolo also shares Wallis's focus on peacemaking as a central component of authentically biblical Christianity. *Speaking My Mind* devotes three chapters to challenging the demonization of Islam,[158] self-serving American foreign policy,[159] and the "idolatrous patriotism" and militant religious nationalism fostered by segments of conservative evangelicalism.[160] Likewise, Dr. Ronald J. Sider's *I am not a Social Activist: Making Jesus the Agenda* contains 40+ references to nonviolence, pacifism, or peacemaking in its 211 pages.

Family, Sexuality, Republican Partisanship, and Single-Issue Voting

In addition to its purported desire to "reclaim America for Christ," the Christian Right is perhaps best known for its conservative politics of abortion, sexuality, and the family. According to Christian Right leader Dr. Richard Land in *For Faith and Family*, "America is facing the deepest moral and spiritual crisis in her history"[161] because secular humanism and relativism (15+ mentions), feminism, the "liberal establishment,"[162] and a "tiny cadre of radical homosexual activists" are "shaking the foundations of the American family," which is the "bedrock of society."[163] As a result—and in direct opposition to the holistic communitarian views of Urban Monastery participants we will encounter in Part II—Land argues that "the number-one battle line in our country today is the struggle over sexuality," in which "Christians, with their base in the Christian family unit, have the opportunity to reassert Judeo-Christian sexual values."[164] Land warns that if Christians don't exercise their "right and obligation . . . to ensure that the morality of [America's] laws reflects Judeo-Christian values,"[165] America will soon become "submerged in a polluted sea of pagan sexuality."[166] And since the traditional family is the bedrock of society (30+ mentions), "Consequently, today the very foundation of society is threatened."[167] In Land's dramatic formulation of what is at stake in political and cultural battles over sexuality and the family: "There is no middle ground between morality and meltdown."[168]

For Faith and Family uses strong language to defend "traditional Judeo-Christian, American moral values" against those responsible for promoting the "secular redefinition of the family away from biblical standards" and thereby accelerating America's "freefall into pagan sexuality."[169] The book devotes two chapters and more than 30 pages to defending the traditional heterosexual family, including defense of traditional gender roles and attacks on feminism.[170] One chapter and 20 pages attack the "homosexual agenda," using strong language to denounce homosexuality as a particularly "reprehensible, immoral,"[171] "vile," "unnatural," "deviant and abhorrent"[172] lifestyle which "God loathes and detests."[173] While encouraging the public mobilization of Christians against gays in the military, the Boy Scouts, and the Walt Disney Company for its "anti-family" programming, Land bluntly states: "We're going to deny, or do the best we can to deny, the normalization of a lifestyle that we believe is abnormal, deviant, [and] unhealthy."[174] Two chapters and more than 30 pages focus on arguments against pornography and "promiscuous sexual behavior."[175] Two chapters and 30+ pages decry abortion and embryonic stem cell research.[176] Similarly, Pat Robertson's *The Ten Offenses* devotes over three chapters to abortion, sexuality, and the breakdown of the family. In *How Would Jesus Vote?* Dr. D James Kennedy quotes Land while advocating single-issue voting against pro-choice politicians, arguing that opposition to abortion is the most morally unambiguous and important political issue for Christians.[177] Two chapters and just under 20 pages are devoted to "matters of life and death" such as abortion, stem cell research, suicide, euthanasia, and the death penalty—the latter being the only practice Kennedy supports.[178] One 10-page chapter focuses on how divorce, fatherlessness and illegitimacy, pornography, feminism, and homosexuality are promoting the breakdown of the family. Kennedy also voices his approval of Richard Land's and James Dobson's strident opposition to the "feminist" and "homosexual assault on marriage."[179]

In *Rediscovering Church*—Bill and Lynn Hybels' retelling of the Willow Creek story—Bill Hybels opens with a long litany of social problems facing America: the breakdown of marriage and the family, increasing crime rates and domestic violence, pornographic exploitation, rampant alcohol and drug abuse by teens and adults alike (fed in part by "entertainment media constantly pumping out an anti-morality message"), and worries about terrorism and environmental catastrophes caused by human irresponsibility.[180] Given the similarities between Hybels's remarks and Christian Right rhetoric about America's moral decline, one expects to find a call to "reclaim America for Christ" or "return to Judeo-Christian morality" upon further reading. Instead, one finds a classic statement of theological individualism:

> Social engineers, government programs, and increased funding for education are not going to eradicate the evils facing our society. . . . People need the church. . . . Nothing else is going to change the course of individual lives and the direction of this country. . . . Politicians can rearrange stuff on the surface of life, but they can't bring fundamental transformation into the life of one individual. And *this* is what our country desperately needs most.[181]

Astute readers will recognize echoes of the *miracle motif* view of social change that has dominated historic evangelical social thinking from D. L. Moody and Billy Graham to contemporary evangelical perspectives on racial inequality.[182] Indeed, rather than rallying evangelicals to politics, Hybels explains why megachurches like Willow Creek try to avoid political advocacy:

> We teach unapologetically on social topics that the Bible addresses, such as poverty, injustice, abortion, homosexuality, pornography, the environment, and so on. . . . As a church [however], we've been scrupulous about staying out of partisan politics, because there can be legitimate differences of opinion among Christians about how certain biblical values can be best translated into political policies in a pluralistic society. . . . We're committed to keeping a tight focus on what we feel we have been primarily called to do—reach lost people with the gospel and help them mature in their faith. We're convinced that, ultimately, a person's perspective on social issues won't fundamentally change until his or her heart is transformed by Jesus Christ.[183]

After implicitly distancing Willow Creek from the Christian Right's partisanship, narrow political focus, and tendency to ignore pluralism and the possibility of legitimate political differences among biblical Christians, Hybels returns to the priority of evangelism in a powerful restatement of theological individualism.

The advocacy of single-issue, Republican Party voting and incendiary rhetoric against religious outsiders found in these Christian Right texts are exactly the sorts of arguments that Urban Monastery participants oppose when asked about their own political viewpoints.[184] On single-issue voting, for example, here is what Jason, an original member of the Urban Monastery, had to say:

JASON: I'm definitely against abortion. . . . But what's the most important political issue? It's probably any policy that affects the human soul. I have to
look at other things like Nixon in Cambodia, and Bush in Iraq, and Clinton in Afghanistan, and all the times we've intervened—or Clinton *not*
intervening in Rwanda—look at *all* those things and ask, "Are those less
important than what's been on the forefront today [for conservative evan-
gelicals]? Than abortion?" . . . I don't know. I don't think so. Millions died
in Rwanda.

Jasper, a young musician and religious worker who grew up in a Southern Baptist megachurch in Texas, complained that "the church in the south defi-nitely glorifies one party over another and paints it like 'this is the Christian way to vote,' which I definitely disagree with. Even single-issue voting is dan-gerous." And when I asked Lilith, the Urban Monastery's artist in residence, about the idea of legislating morality, she responded vehemently: "Christians should *not* pass laws that require certain forms of morality from the outside in." The issue of single-issue voting for pro-life candidates is a complicated one for Urban Monastery participants: one that we will explore in detail in chapter 5. However, while Urban Monastery participants were almost unani-mously opposed to abortion, they were just as opposed to Christian Right claims that it is the responsibility of all Bible-believing Christians to vote for Republican Party candidates who opposed abortion. Nor did Urban Monas-tery participants share the Christian Right position on homosexuality or gay marriage, as we will see below.

Neo-monastic texts such as *The Irresistible Revolution* are largely silent on the issues of abortion and homosexuality, mentioning them in only in a few passing remarks against conservative evangelicalism.[185] Texts written by evangelical left leaders have more to say, although they too tend to focus far more attention on other issues such as poverty, inequality, and Christian peacemaking. Evangelical left texts, however, do have much to say about the Christian Right's association with conservative Republican Party politics. *God's Politics*, for example, is a direct broadside against the Christian Right and conservative evangelicalism's support for Republican Party politicians and policy positions.[186] Whereas Christian Right leaders argued that "it [was] the responsibility of every evangelical Christian" to "get serious about re-electing President Bush" in the 2004 presidential election, Jim Wallis's *Sojourners* took out a full-page ad in the *New York Times* which condemned the Christian Right for promoting "bad theology" and "dangerous religion" while arguing that "God is not a Republican . . . or a Democrat" and promoting an alternative Christian political vision:

> We will measure the candidates by whether they enhance human life, human dignity, and human rights; whether they strengthen family life and protect children; whether they promote racial reconciliation and support gender equality, whether they serve peace and social justice, and whether they advance the common good rather than only individual, national, and special interests.[187]

In a succinct overview of the evangelical left point of view, the ad names poverty, progressive tax policies, peacemaking, the environment, human rights, opposition to a "righteous empire" response to terrorism, and a "consistent ethic of life" as core political issues for biblical Christians, while condemning the Iraq war as an illegal "war of choice" justified by lies and deceit.[188]

In comparison to the enormous amount of text devoted to poverty, economic inequality, and peacemaking in *God's Politics*, the book's discussion of issues relating to sexuality and the family is miniscule. Gay marriage is addressed in a short 7-page section in the middle of one of the book's final chapters, while abortion shares a 13-page chapter with capital punishment and racial inequality gets its own 14-page chapter. On abortion, Wallis is "conservative" and "pro-life," while opposing "single-issue voting" and advocating "abortion reduction" policies (such as support for adoption and low-income single women) on which pro-life and pro-choice people can agree.[189] On gay marriage, Wallis condemns the Christian Right's "mean-spirited crusade" to blame the "breakdown of the heterosexual family" on gay and lesbian people while advocating a joint "pro-family" and "pro-gay civil rights" position.[190] He supports full civil rights for gays and lesbians—including civil unions—while considering but ultimately opposing gay marriage.[191] In all, *God's Politics* contains 25 mentions each of abortion and gay marriage/gay civil rights; this equals the number of mentions of gender equality and environmental issues and is slightly less than the 40+ references to racial reconciliation and racial justice. Taken together, these political standpoints mirror many Urban Monastery participants' political perspectives, with the exception that Urban Monastery participants tend to be more conflicted about voting decisions, more skeptical of the American political process, and more intensely opposed to abortion than Wallis appears to be.[192]

In *Speaking My Mind*, Tony Campolo follows Wallis in supporting civil unions and full civil rights for gays and lesbians. He chastises evangelicals for their harsh treatment of the LGBTQ community and argues that evangelical churches ought not to split over their views on the issue.[193] While Campolo acknowledges some signs of "moral degradation" in American society,[194] he also points to declining abortion rates, declining premarital pregnancies, and the largely monogamous American population to refute inflated Christian Right rhetoric concerning America's moral decline.[195] Furthermore, he reminds the Christian Right's "prophets of doom" that racial, gender, and economic inequality is significantly diminished compared to a century ago, noting wryly that these are signs of moral *progress* rather than moral decline.[196] Ron Sider's *I am not a Social Activist* pays more attention to gender equality and "Injustice Against Women"—the title of one of the book's chapters—than it does to the issues of abortion or homosexuality, which receive fewer than 5 mentions each.[197] Sider differs from Wallis and Campolo in his support for a constitutional amendment to ban gay marriage, though he otherwise supports gay civil rights.[198] However—as some of his other book titles such as *The Scandal of Evangelical Politics* and *The Scandal of the Evangelical Conscience* suggest—he joins other evangelical left leaders (and Urban Monastery participants) in distancing himself from the Christian Right and conservative evangelicalism:

> I'm an evangelical—but not the Jerry Falwell, Pat Robertson type . . . I'm the kind of evangelical who joined the civil-rights crusade, opposed the war in Vietnam, is a (biblical) feminist and environmentalist, and thinks government should help empower the poor.[199]

In all, Sider marshals 65+ scripture references in just over 200 pages of text to build his case for a "pro-life *and* pro-poor, pro-racial justice *and* pro-family" evangelical political philosophy, one that closely mirrors the *contradictory cultural location* of Urban Monastery participants that we will explore at length in chapter 5.[200]

Poverty and Economic Inequality

Poverty and economic inequality are barely mentioned in megachurch and Christian Right texts, in stark contrast to Urban Monastery participants and the neo-monastic point of view. When they are mentioned, Christian Right authors tend to give voice to conservative viewpoints on the subject. In *How Would Jesus Vote?* D. James Kennedy strongly opposes government involvement in caring for the poor, the welfare state, socialism, "social justice," and government-based health care, while celebrating capitalism and private property:[201]

> "I believe in capitalism. . . . I certainly do not believe in socialism, which is anything but Christian. The rise of capitalism and free enterprise derives historically, as do many positive aspects of our culture, from the influence of the gospel."[202]

How Would Jesus Vote? presents a "rising tide lifts all boats" theory of economic prosperity while arguing that "the poor in America would be much better off without welfare," since welfare destroys families and subsidizes indolence.[203] In all, the book contains two chapters, 40+ pages, and more than 45 negative references to socialism, communism, or the modern welfare state. Pat Robertson's *The Ten Offenses* contains only 9 separate mentions of poverty—the majority of which blame poverty on adultery, idolatry, and moral failure.[204] Despite lamenting the "disturbing disparity of wealth" in American society, Robertson vehemently opposes America's "steeply graduated" income tax and inheritance tax as "creations of Marxist communism" which violate the eighth commandment that "thou shalt not steal."[205] Robertson is appalled that "the top 25 percent of income earners pay 83 percent of all taxes" and "yet the politics of envy say that government should confiscate even more of the earning power of the productive sector of society so that there can be more money for the bureaucrats to spend."[206] Richard Land's *For Faith and Family* follows a similar line, lamenting poverty as an effect of family breakdown in more than 20 references.[207]

Urban Monastery participants have a decidedly different view of the importance of poverty and economic inequality as Christian political issues. While not univocal on the matter, many Urban Monastery participants joined Lilith in naming economic justice as their primary political concern:

LILITH: The economic system—what we do with our money—it's unjust. And I think [America] is going to pay. . . . I think it is greed. It's popular to talk about [economic inequality and predatory banking] now, but it's been going on for a long time. And politically, this country needs to *stop*. We need to stop enslaving other people with money. We need to stop enslaving ourselves, people in our own country. We need to stop being greedy. We have been given tremendous natural resources, but that's a *responsibility*. It's not an advantage to go to the races and beat everyone else. So I would say the greatest political issue is money.

Urban Monastery participants spoke in favor of policies that favored global and domestic economic redistribution, supported government efforts to help the poor, and—cutting against dominant, theologically individualist expressions of historic American evangelicalism—regularly referred to structural alongside individual or cultural explanations of poverty and economic inequality. Using the conceptual language of moral cosmology theory, Urban Monastery participants are theological and economic communitarians, rather than individualists, with respect to poverty and economic inequality.

This communitarian theme is also prevalent in the way that neo-monastic texts discuss issues of poverty and economic inequality. For example, in the book *School(s) for Conversion*, the New Monasticism's third mark—"sharing economic resources with fellow community members and the needy among us"—is a natural outgrowth of Christian community and hospitality: "Redistribution is not a prescription for community. Redistribution is a description of what happens when people fall in love with each other across class lines."[208] Each of the twelve marks expresses a strong communitarian perspective; including those marks that address racial divisions, economic redistribution, environmental care, and peace activism. *School(s) for Conversion* contains one chapter and 40+ mentions of economic inequality and poverty. While proclaiming the need for a "personalist and communal" response to global economic and political problems, *School(s) for Conversion* does not neglect to address the various national and global institutional structures it holds responsible for "systemic injustices" such as poverty, global inequality, and war.[209] *Punk Monk: New Monasticism and the Ancient Art of Breathing* also follows the neo-monastic script in demanding social and economic justice for the poor and oppressed and arguing that biblical Christianity requires an uncompromising commitment to justice for and solidarity with the poor (60+ mentions).

Meanwhile, Shane Claiborne's *The Irresistible Revolution* contains more than 120 references addressing poverty and economic injustice. Standing against a religious dualism that separates the spiritual from the material and the individual from the social, Claiborne argues for a holistic understanding of the gospel that connects spiritual conversion to economic redistribution:[210]

As we consider what it means to be "born again," as the evangelical jargon goes, we must ask what it means to be born again into a family in which our sisters and brothers are starving to death. Then we begin to see why rebirth and redistribution are inextricably bound up in one another, as a growing number of evangelicals have come to proclaim. It also becomes scandalous for the church to spend money on windows and buildings when some family members don't even have water.[211]

Spending money on bigger buildings rather than on the poor is one of many arguments against megachurch evangelicalism in *The Irresistible Revolution*, in which two chapters and over 50 pages are devoted to Claiborne's qualified yet critical perspective on the megachurch movement.[212] From Claiborne's point of view, megachurch evangelicalism produces economically and culturally homogeneous religious communities which reinforce the "layers of insulation" that "separate the rich and the poor from truly encountering one another."[213] Like other neo-monastics, Claiborne's preferred response to economic inequality is deeply communitarian, challenging both economic individualism and bureaucratized charity programs (both religious and secular) that fail to challenge existing hierarchies of power. In these charity programs,

> Rich and poor are kept in separate worlds, and inequality is carefully managed but not dismantled. When the church becomes a place of brokerage rather than an organic community . . . [it] becomes a distribution center, a place where the poor come to get stuff and the rich come to dump stuff. Both go away satisfied (the rich feel good, the poor get clothed and fed), but no one leaves transformed. No radical new community is formed.[214]

In making its case for a communitarian response to poverty and economic inequality, the book contains more than 130 references to the church as "community" or spiritual "family" in which rich and poor are called to share friendship, resources, and solidarity with one another "face to face."[215]

Texts written by evangelical left leaders similarly criticize dominant expressions of American evangelicalism for failing to recognize poverty and economic inequality as central religious and moral issues for Bible-believing Christians. Ron Sider became a household name among American evangelicals after publishing his provocative best-selling book, *Rich Christians in an Age of Hunger*, in 1977. The book has sold over 400,000 copies and been named "One of the Top 100 Religious Books of the Century" by *Christianity Today*.[216] *Rich Christians in an Age of Hunger* condemns the affluent lifestyles and relative stinginess of American Christians in the face of global hunger an affront to biblical justice. In *I am not a Social Activist*, Sider asks questions such as: "Are Evangelical Leaders on their Way to Hell?"

> There is a strong biblical reason for thinking that many evangelical leaders are idolatrous heretics. If that statement seems a bit strong, ask yourself these questions . . . is it not heresy to largely ignore the second most common theme in the Bible [i.e., economic injustice] and then pretend that one is offering biblical Christianity to one's people?[217]

I am not a Social Activist contains more than 100 references to poverty and economic injustice in its 211 pages. Similarly, for Jim Wallis, "The great crisis in American democracy today is the division of wealth."[218] In *God's Politics*, five chapters and almost 100 pages are devoted to poverty and economic justice. In all, the book contains more than 250 mentions of poverty or economic justice. Tony Campolo's *Speaking My Mind* also shares Wallis and Sider's focus on economic justice as a central component of authentically biblical Christianity, containing more than 125 mentions of poverty and economic justice.

Summary: Neo-Monasticism in the Field of Evangelical Position-Takings

Table 3.1 provides a visual summary of the key religious and political position-takings found in the preceding textual analysis of five related-but-distinct positions in the field of American evangelicalism. The neo-monastic point of view, like the other evangelical points of view described above, is constructed using symbolic elements drawn from Christian scriptures: but it is also constructed in relation to other positions in the field of American evangelicalism. There are many obvious examples of this claim in the pages above, such as Shane Claiborne's explicit and ongoing critiques of the Christian Right and megachurch evangelicalism in *The Irresistible Revolution*, or Urban Monastery participants' explicit attempts to distance themselves from conservative and megachurch evangelical perspectives. There are also more subtle and implicit examples of the relationally constructed nature of the neo-monastic point of view which are revealed by examining the structure of neo-monastic position-takings in comparison to the dominant standpoints of conservative and megachurch evangelicalism, as in table 3.1. Table 3.1 is not a comprehensive summary of the preceding textual analysis, but it does present a quick visual overview of some of the central agreements, oppositions, and distinctions that structure the space of position-takings among religious knowledge producers in the American evangelical field. For example, one can immediately observe that Christian Right and evangelical left are almost mirror opposites of one another in the relative attention they give to "social" issues such as the traditional family, sexuality, and abortion versus the attention they give to poverty and economic inequality (italicized text). And where evangelism overwhelmingly dominates the attention of megachurch evangelicals (row three, bold), the attention of neo-monastic evangelicals is balanced among evangelism, peacemaking, and justice issues, reflecting their *holistic communitarian* theology and opposition to theological individualism.[219] Similarly, the *absence* of neo-monastic attention to "family-values" issues in these texts also reflects their oppositional stance toward the dominant Christian Right point of view.

The dynamic diversity of evangelical standpoints described here ought to finally and decisively put to rest the tired old "monolithic bloc fallacy."[220] There is today no "evangelical point of view" concerning theological, social, or political matters. Rather, there are multiple, distinctive, often contradictory evangelical *points* of view in competition with one another to offer the *legitimate representation of biblical Christianity in the United States.* This is, of course, not to deny that some evangelical standpoints are more dominant and common than others. Nor is it to deny that there are common patterns and similarities that link evangelical points of view to one another other while distinguishing them from non-evangelical perspectives. For example, while there is radical variation in the attention these five evangelical movements give to each of the other standpoints listed in table 3.1, evangelism and sharing the gospel have a significant presence in all of them (row three)—albeit to varying degrees—demonstrating the *doxic* commitment to evangelism among participants the evangelical field. Despite the vast differences in religious, social, and political viewpoints taken by each of the five positions outlined in this chapter, there are also many underlying agreements concerning the sorts of things that can be argued about and those that are taken for granted because one is an evangelical. For example, each of the texts makes frequent appeals to the Bible to justify their particular viewpoint and argue that their point of view is the biblical point of view.[221] None argues that the Bible is irrelevant, immoral, or unnecessary for grasping spiritual truth. None argues that the crucifixion and resurrection of Jesus is a religious fairy tale invented by later followers. None denies the human need for salvation from sin and death or the possibility of resurrection through faith in Christ. None argue that it is unimportant or unethical to share the Christian gospel with others. And so on. These implicit agreements constitute the *doxa* of the

Table 3.1 Textual Analysis Summary (Approximated Number of Counts)

	Christian Right/ conservative evangelicalism	Megachurch evangelicalism	Emerging church	Evangelical left	Neo-monastic evangelicalism
Preserve/restore "Christian America"	300+	<10	<10	<10	<10
Traditional family/sexuality/abortion	500+	<10	<10	50*	<10
Evangelism/revival/spreading Gospel	50	330	150	100	130
Economic inequality/poverty	50*	<10	<10	480	220
Anti-militarism/anti-"American imperialism"	<10	<10	<10	250	130
Race/gender/environmental justice	20†	<10	<10	200	70

* Of the 50 mentions of poverty and economic inequality by Christian Right authors, less than 10 addressed poverty as a systemic problem, instead attributing poverty to family breakdown, drug and alcohol addiction, and bad personal habits. Similarly, of the 50 mentions of traditional family/sexuality/abortion by evangelical left authors, less than 10 expressed unequivocal support for the "conservative" position on these issues. Instead, they called for respect, tolerance, and civil rights for GLBTQ Americans and mutual understanding/compromise with those holding different perspectives on these moral issues.

† There were 20 positive mentions of racial justice in the Christian Right texts analyzed in this chapter. Where gender equality and environmental activism were addressed in these books, they were the subject of derision and opposition rather than support.

evangelical field: the "unthought thoughts," unquestioned assumptions, and taken-for-granted beliefs that define the central identity, character, and boundaries of what it means to be an evangelical Christian in America.[222] One cannot fully participate in the evangelical field without tacit (or, more often, explicit) agreement with this *doxa*.

Of course, in evangelicalism, as in any other religious or social field, what counts as *doxa* can and does change over time. But that is just to acknowledge that fields are human and therefore social and historical entities. All social fields, including religious ones, are the product of a particular and cumulative history of agreement and struggle between agents across time and changing social conditions. There was a time when abstaining from dance, alcohol consumption, and theater-going could be considered part of the *doxic* practice of conservative Protestantism, along with anti-evolutionism and a strictly literal account of the Genesis story of creation. That is no longer the case. These taken-for-granted boundary markers of early fundamentalism were challenged by actors in the early twentieth-century field of conservative Protestantism, eventually transforming them from *doxic* assumptions about "what it means to be a biblical Christian" into visible and contested position-takings within conservative Protestantism.[223] However, while the details of what counts as *doxa* in the evangelical field are not immutable, neither do they float unmoored on a sea without shores. What counts as *doxa* for American evangelicals today remains anchored in the genesis and development of the evangelical field in America throughout the late nineteenth and twentieth century. These points will be developed further in the next section, along with a more detailed exposition of the dynamic social processes that drive continuity and change in the evangelical field.

Some Properties of the American Evangelical Field

One measure of a social theory is the scope of its explanatory power. In other words, how wide a range of social phenomena is a theory capable of illuminating? It is hard to imagine more disparate social universes than the nineteenth-century French literary field and twenty-first-century American evangelicalism. Separated by centuries, continents, and national cultures, the former world was thoroughly secular, bohemian, anti-establishment, and anti-clerical; the latter religious and morally conservative. Yet many of the same social mechanisms that Pierre Bourdieu describes in his underappreciated socio-historical analysis of the French literary field in *The Rules of Art: Genesis and Structure of the Literary Field* are found at work in the field of American evangelicalism.[224] The rest of this chapter will examine some of these common social processes in the form of seven propositions, which provide the framework for an original field-theoretic analysis of American evangelicalism as it relates to evangelical neo-monasticism, as well as providing the "social" element for my practical social hermeneutic model of evangelical culture and agency.[225] In doing so, we will also see how a field-theoretic approach avoids fallacious reductionisms and helps us resolve various scholarly disputes concerning the nature of evangelicalism, thereby advancing our sociological understanding of this important, enigmatic, and frequently controversial segment of American society.

Proposition One: American evangelicalism is a field of agreement and struggle between agents holding competing visions of the legitimate representation of biblical Christianity in the United States.

To describe American evangelicalism in this way is to replace a number of alternative definitions and descriptions of evangelicalism: for example, that evangelicalism should be defined primarily in terms of religious doctrines or as a group of individuals who share a common set of religious beliefs, that the religious and political standpoints of evangelicals are monolithic, or that evangelical beliefs and practices are fundamentally static and conservative. Evangelicalism, rather, is best understood as a relatively autonomous social space in which agents are subject to a common yet differentially experienced set of social forces unique to the evangelical field, forces that impose themselves on all participants within it; that is, on those who share a common belief in the value of the field and of its specific stakes and rewards.[226] However, it is not just these agreements that define the field but also the struggles between agents who hold competing visions of the legitimate representation of biblical Christianity that in the end determine the structure of the evangelical field and hold it together:

> [The field] is a force-field acting on all those who enter it, and acting in a differential manner according to the position they occupy there . . . and at the same time it is a field of competitive struggles which tend to conserve or transform this force-field. And the position-takings (works, political manifestos or demonstrations, and so on), which one may and should treat for analytical purposes as a "system" of oppositions, are not the result of some kind of objective collusion, but rather the product and the stake of a permanent conflict. In other words, the generative and unifying principle of this "system" is the struggle itself.[227]

The act of engaging with occupants of other positions in the evangelical field—even when such engagement is antagonistic and oppositional in nature—is itself an act of commitment to the field, its stakes, its value, and its particular view of the world.[228] Only those who believe in the fundamental importance of biblical Christianity in America will struggle over its representation; and only those who demonstrate proper commitment to and investment (*illusio*) in its stakes will be taken seriously by others in the field.[229] For example, Jim Wallis's or Shane Claiborne's decisions to refer to themselves as evangelicals—even while challenging and opposing much of what they take to be the dominant point of view of American evangelicalism—are acts of engagement that commit them to certain beliefs (can't deny the divinity of Jesus) and styles of argument (can't ignore the Bible) which positively reinforce evangelicalism's existence and legitimacy. By struggling against dominant positions in the evangelical field, Wallis and Claiborne also strengthen and reproduce it.

Bourdieu wrote the aforementioned statement in the context of analyzing the field of nineteenth-century French literature. It shows Bourdieu at his creative and synthetic best: attempting to overcome the antinomy between conflict and consensualist schools of social theory by describing a social system whose unity lies in struggle.[230] While it is intended to be a universal statement about the nature and functioning of fields, it remains that fields vary with respect to the relative importance that struggle and agreement play in defining a field. Religious fields are more prone to emphasizing agreement—such as agreements over doctrinal statements, authority structures, or defining theological commitments—than many other social fields. Furthermore, these agreements are more likely to be explicit than they are in other fields, where the agreements between actors are more often tacit, implied, and invisible (even to actors themselves), sometimes consisting of nothing more than the "agreement" to struggle over financial or symbolic goods of a certain kind. While religious fields tend to contain more—and more explicit—agreements than many social fields, all fields (including the evangelical field) are comprised of struggle. Rather than destroying the evangelical field, however, struggles among evangelical agents who hold competing visions of biblical Christianity reproduce the field of American evangelicalism, while also continually transforming it. The specific mechanisms whereby this occurs will be explored in detail in the propositions below.

It is worth noting here how proposition one relates to two other dominant theories of evangelical vitality in the United States, namely, Christian Smith's subcultural identity theory and its rational choice cousin, "religious economies" theory.[231] Both religious economy and subcultural identity theory emphasize the positive effects of pluralism and religious competition on the vitality of evangelical religion in the United States. Subcultural identity theory, in particular, argues that American evangelicalism thrives precisely because it is embattled: "Evangelicalism," Smith argues, "flourishes on difference, engagement, tension, conflict, and threat":

> The evangelical tradition's entire history, theology, and self-identity presupposes and reflects strong cultural boundaries with nonevangelicals; a zealous burden to convert and transform the world outside itself; and a keen perception of external threats and crises seen as menacing what it views to be true, good, and valuable. These, we maintain, go a long way toward explaining evangelicalism's thriving.[232]

According to Smith, the growth and vitality of evangelical religion in America is largely due to its ability to construct a distinctive religious subculture that has successfully set itself apart from both Christian and secular "others" while simultaneously engaging the ever-changing modern world with the gospel.[233] Both religious economy and subcultural identity theory, then, agree with proposition one in affirming the central role of competition and struggle in sustaining evangelical religious vitality. However, whereas Smith and others have demonstrated how evangelicalism's external struggles with competing religious and secular "others" contributes to its strength, I am arguing that internal struggles within the field of American evangelicalism itself likewise strengthens the evangelical field, while simultaneously also transforming it.[234]

Proposition one also highlights the kinship between a field-theoretic approach to American evangelicalism and the "dialogic" approach posited by scholars associated with the new anthropology of Christianity (or, better, "Christianities").[235] Both approaches highlight the internal differentiation of evangelicalism and the ways in which evangelical agents construct their religious and political points of view in relation to (or "dialogue with") other movements and positions in American Christianity. For example, in *Emerging Evangelicals: Faith, Modernity, and the Desire for Authenticity*, anthropologist James S. Bielo argues—consistent with my argument in this chapter—that the emerging church "was born out of opposition":

> Emerging Evangelicalism is a movement defined by a deeply felt disenchantment toward America's conservative Christian subculture. My consultants assigned a wide range of problems to their Evangelical brethren: suburban largesse, faulty biblical exegesis, poor theologies of worship, misguided evangelistic practices, and megachurch consumerism . . . to name just a few.[236]

Despite their oppositional stance toward conservative evangelicalism, however, Bielo notes that "their cultural critique did not result in a loss of faith"; rather, it led emerging evangelicals toward efforts to return to an "authentic faith" that better reflected what "real Christianity" ought to look like.[237] This "return to origins" trope is common among avant-garde challengers to dominant positions within a social field, as we will see in proposition four below. The larger point, however, is that—consistent with proposition one—Bielo finds emerging evangelicals constructing their distinctive religious identity through a dynamic process of "accepting and rejecting the categories, narratives, and vocabulary of Evangelicalism."[238] In other words, as proposition one asserts, the emerging church's oppositional stance toward conservative evangelicalism does not destroy or negate the field of American evangelicalism; rather, it is a natural and generative expression of it.[239]

Both the dialogic and field-theoretic approaches to American evangelicalism challenge the common practice of defining evangelicalism primarily in terms of individuals who share a common set of religious beliefs, religious practices, or who are regular participants/consumers of evangelical subculture.[240] Evangelicalism, rather, ought to be understood in relational terms as a space where multiple evangelical "Christianities" constitute themselves "via a series of relationships" through "dynamic interaction" with other one another and with other Christian and non-Christian positions or fields, such as mainline Protestantism, Catholicism, "secular humanism," and the like.[241] As Bielo notes, the dialogic approach to American evangelicalism "only requires that religious subjects share a dialogue, through which they may agree, argue vehemently, work cooperatively, or many other variations."[242] Thus, for example, from both the dialogic and field-theoretic perspectives, it makes good sociological sense to include fundamentalist Protestants such as Jerry Falwell in one's analysis of American evangelicalism, given that it is practically impossible for contemporary American evangelicals of whatever variety to explain their religious and political points of view without reference to conservative evangelicalism and the Christian Right.[243]

Despite these shared dispositions concerning the relational nature, definition, and study of American evangelicalism, field theory parts company with the dialogic approach in several important ways, and in so doing improves upon it. First of all, the dialogic approach conceptualizes relations in strictly phenomenological and interactionist terms, such that religious agents' influence on one another depends on the extent to which concrete religious subjects "share a dialogue" about religious matters.[244] This is made explicit in Bielo's discussion of "person-centered ethnography," which flatly denies the causal efficacy of "extrahuman forces" such as culture, habitus, or social structure, while restricting causal agency to human "individuals and communities" alone.[245] As I argue chapter 1, this view is untenable. Where the dialogic approach defines "relationships" in concrete interactionist terms, field theory recognizes that social relations are "not [merely] interactions between agents or intersubjective ties between individuals, but objective relations which exist 'independently of individual consciousness and will,' as Marx said."[246] Field theory illuminates social mechanisms whereby evangelical agents may influence and be influenced by one another without directly interacting or sharing a dialogue, but rather as the result of the differential distribution of diverse forms of capital which objectively structure the field of American evangelicalism and an agent's position within it.

This relates to a second point. The dialogic and field-theoretic approaches share a common conviction concerning the "dynamic borders" of American evangelicalism: that no single set of religious or sociological boundary markers can neatly tie up which people, communities, or institutions constitute the category "American evangelicalism" into a discrete, transhistorical, substantialist bundle.[247] However, the dialogic approach goes too far in posing the "discrete definitional" and "dialogical" approaches to evangelicalism as an either-or proposition, and in so doing, it unhelpfully dissolves the real, meaningful, and theoretically substantial (collective) subject that we refer to as "American evangelicalism."[248] This is highly problematic from an analytical standpoint. "American evangelicalism" exists as a practical and theoretical category of American religion because it serves as a robust referent to a distinctive social-historical religious field, marked by certain characteristics that set it apart from other American "Christianities" and the larger society.[249] The category "evangelicalism" does not impose an "artificial" or "arbitrary" designation onto the field of American religion;[250] rather, it is a meaningful, empirically robust, and theoretically useful designation for an internally diverse but distinctive variety of Christianity. As proposition one asserts, there are "binding element[s], mutual ground, feature[s] in common" which constitute American evangelicalism as a distinctive religious movement compared to other varieties of Christianity, pace Bielo's critique of the "definitional" approach.[251] American evangelicalism is a field of both struggle and agreement concerning legitimate representation of biblical Christianity in America.

In dissolving the subject of "evangelicalism," the dialogic approach makes it impossible to make meaningful distinctions between the kinds of "dialogue" that evangelicals maintain with one another—for example, about the meaning of the gospel or the relationship between evangelism and social justice, which occur under certain social-historical conditions and according to certain institutionalized rules of discourse which apply only to those within the evangelical field (such as the necessity of grounding one's perspective in biblical authority)—and those they have with other varieties of Christianity or with non-Christians. However, Catholics who "share a dialogue" with evangelicals concerning the nature of justification or the sanctity of life do not thereby become part of the evangelical field; they remain Catholics. Atheists who "share a dialogue" with evangelicals about the existence of God do not thereby become part of the evangelical field; they remain atheists. There are real distinctions to be made between these "dialogues" and those which take place among agents within the evangelical field. They are subject to different kinds of social forces, different rules of argument, and different tacit (and explicit) agreements and assumptions. However, from the dialogic perspective, these dialogues are all analytically indistinguishable. Unlike the dialogic approach, then, the field-theoretic approach to American evangelicalism recognizes the internal diversity and differentiation of the evangelical field without thereby annihilating "evangelicalism" as a meaningful religious category or flattening dialogical religious discourse into a single, undifferentiated type. The knowledge-extending fruit of the field-theoretic approach for illuminating what goes on within "American evangelicalism" should be clear throughout this chapter.

Perhaps most important, the person-centered dialogic approach ignores the fact that dialogic interactions or relations among evangelical agents do not happen in an unstructured, willy-nilly, ad hoc fashion. Rather, as field theory recognizes, relations and dialogues among evangelical agents occur within an objectively structured social space which has profound implications and influence on the manner in which agents relate to one another within the evangelical field. The dialogic approach focuses us on the right (relational) questions—i.e., "What happens when Christianities interact?"[252]—but offers little in the way of guidance toward answering those questions. The field-theoretic approach, on the other hand, poses many of the same questions as the dialogic approach—focusing our attention on the dynamic, relational, internally diverse nature of American evangelicalism—but goes much farther in offering us a robust set of empirically informed theoretical tools with which we may begin seeking answers to our questions. Of course, in the last analysis, the utility of any theoretical approach is determined by its ability to provide a more persuasive, penetrating, parsimonious, wide-ranging, and empirically supported account of its subject matter than its theoretical competitors.[253] In that regard, adjudicating between the field-theoretic and other approaches to the study of American evangelicalism(s) requires considering the entirety of this book's arguments in relation to its peers.

Proposition Two: The distinctive standpoints of agents in the evangelical field are constructed in relation to one another and to their position in the field.

The fundamental principle of field-theoretic analysis is to *"think relationally."*[254] The various standpoints of agents in the evangelical field are constructed in relation to one another through a "dialectic of distinction," in which agents define and differentiate themselves in a continuous series of oppositions, negations, modifications, and reversals of other standpoints in the field—both past and present—such that "there is no action by an agent that is not a reaction to all the others, or to one or another among them."[255] Thus, attempts to explain the theological and political standpoints of evangelicals as arising "straight from the Bible," on the one hand, or straight from economic or social position, on the other, are doomed to failure. Social positions and biblical texts do in indeed shape evangelical position-takings, but only through the mediating influence of the evangelical field as a whole, which is to say only through the objective structure of relations between distinctive positions and position-takings which obtain within the specific social universe of American evangelicalism.

Thinking relationally allows us to understand how the Christian Right can cast such a large shadow across the entire evangelical landscape, in spite of the fact that it does not represent all (or even most) evangelicals. As described above, the Christian Right/conservative evangelical point of view is characterized by an overwhelming emphasis on the politics of sexuality and the family. It forcefully champions single-issue voting against pro-choice politicians, to the point of questioning the religious integrity of Christians who consider voting for pro-choice candidates because of their stance on other issues. The conservative evangelical point of view regards America as a Christian nation founded on biblical principles, and a nation whose laws and culture should clearly reflect a "Judeo-Christian" point of view. It views America's political, economic, and military might as a sign of God's favor and blessing of America's Christian heritage. However, this blessing is now at risk due to the work of secular humanists and liberal elites—working through judicial activism, the entertainment industry, secular public education, and liberal media propaganda—who are eroding traditional Christian understandings of marriage, family, and sexuality. As a result, the United States is in the midst of a precipitous and unprecedented moral crisis and decline which threatens to destroy America and Western civilization. Conservative evangelicals are also staunch defenders of deregulated free-market capitalism, standing against "socialist" and "big government" perspectives on economic issues such as progressive taxation, the welfare state, and arguments against current levels of economic inequality in America as unjust—arguments which the Christian Right rejects as expressions of class resentment or class warfare.

We see the shadow of these viewpoints in the position-takings of each of the other four evangelical positions examined above, positions that often, like a mirror, reflect and reverse the original image. Jim Wallis and the evangelical left directly reverse the Christian Right point of view at almost every turn: flatly declaring "we are not single-issue voters," that "God is not a Republican," condemning the rhetoric of "righteous empire" as "dangerous religion," and aggressively advocating for economically progressive "pro-poor" tax policies and budget priorities.[256] While substantively oppositional to the Christian Right, the evangelical left point of view is in many ways structurally equivalent and significantly derived from the set of Christian Right position-takings, as summarized in table 3.2.

The table could be extended further, but it makes its point: the position-takings of the evangelical left are constructed in relation to the conservative evangelical point of view, typically taking the form of a direct reversal of the Christian Right perspective. Even on those issues where the evangelical left agrees with conservative evangelicalism—such as opposition to abortion in most cases, the importance of healthy marriages and families for healthy societies, and dismay over the increase in degrading and dehumanizing forms of entertainment in popular culture—the evangelical left still constructs its position-takings in terms of opposition to the Christian Right. For instance, while generally agreeing with conservative evangelicals on abortion, it nevertheless frames its position in oppositional terms, arguing

Table 3.2 Positions and Oppositions: Evangelical Left and Christian Right

Christian Right/conservative evangelicalism	Evangelical left
"Christian America"	Anti-Christian nationalism
Abortion priority	Anti-single-issue voting
Iraq = just war	Iraq = illegal and immoral war
"Islamic threat"	Islam not the enemy
Conservative economic policy	Left-liberal economic policy
Anti-gay marriage	Pro-gay civil rights
Anti-feminist	Gender egalitarian

against the Christian Right's promotion of single-issue voting and searching out ways to work with abortion advocates to reduce abortion rates.[257]
Furthermore, the texts examined above demonstrate how evangelical left
leaders forcefully emphasize their disagreements and disputes with the
Christian Right point of view in the foreground—devoting provocative section headings, prominent chapters, and hundreds of pages to oppositional
standpoints—while often leaving their agreements tacit, barely recognized,
or deeply buried in the text.[258]

Despite the fact that megachurch evangelicalism occupies a dominant position in the field, it too defines itself in relation and partial opposition to the
Christian Right. The megachurch texts analyzed above show leaders Rick
Warren and Bill Hybels distancing themselves from Christian Right standpoints such as the drive to "reclaim America for Christ" through politics, its
narrow focus on the politics of sexuality and the family, its general disregard
for pluralism, and its forceful advocacy of conservative Republican candidates
for public office. Instead, megachurch evangelicalism emphasizes the limits
of politics, the primacy of the church as the hope of the world, and, above all,
the need to prioritize the salvation of individuals through relevant communication of the gospel. In selecting and emphasizing theological individualism
from the evangelical religio-cultural toolkit in contraposition the Christian
Right point of view, megachurch evangelicalism simultaneously reproduces
a historically dominant position-taking in the field (theological individualism) and establishes its own distinctive position through opposition to the
Christian Right and to "traditional" churches that fail to prioritize culturally
relevant evangelism.[259] Of course, by citing the limits of government and the
miracle motif view of social change, megachurch evangelicalism often remains in tacit agreement with political conservatism, an agreement reflected
in the politically conservative attitudes of megachurch evangelicals and reinforced by a host of other social and religious factors.[260] Yet despite its many
agreements with the Christian Right point of view, megachurch evangelicals
nevertheless develop their distinctive position-taking through reference to
the Christian Right. Even dominant positions in the field cannot escape the
shadow of other dominant positions, but rather are compelled to distinguish
themselves from one another and from dominated positions through difference and opposition.

We see the same dynamics at work in the emerging church's dramatic
oppositions and reversals of megachurch evangelicalism (table 3.3). Megachurch evangelicalism revolutionized the experience of going to church
through the use of "seeker-sensitive" messages, music, and religious architecture designed to show that "Christianity is relevant and applicable to the

Table 3.3 Positions and Oppositions: Emerging and Megachurch
Evangelicalism

Megachurch evangelicalism	Emerging Church
Modern/contemporary	Postmodern/"vintage"
Suburban	Urban
"Seeker-sensitive"	"Post seeker-sensitive"
Church growth/"bring in a crowd"	Small "authentic" churches
Evangelism priority	Holistic mission
Professional staff and programming	"Participatory"/"raw"
Business culture	Arts culture
Anonymous individual	Spiritual community

world of middle class suburbanites."[261] By contrast, the emerging church identifies itself as a "post-seeker-sensitive" point of view, directly opposing megachurch evangelicalism in hundreds of pages of text.[262] Emerging churches oppose megachurch evangelicalism's "individualistic" rather than "communal" and "holistic" understanding of the gospel and Christian faith.[263] Where megachurches are said to offer a "consumptive," "programmatic," anonymous church experience, emerging churches emphasize a "participatory" and "relationally based" approach.[264] Where members of megachurches invite "spiritual seekers" to churches stripped of religious imagery made to look like office buildings or shopping malls, emerging churches make heavy use of religious imagery and emphasize bringing the gospel outside the walls of church buildings and into the everyday lives of "post-Christian" people. Where megachurch evangelicals promote the use of "laser-age" technology and professional programming in religious services, emerging churches promote "raw" and "simple" worship gatherings.[265] Whereas the megachurch point of view emphasizes church growth and "bringing in a crowd," emerging churches celebrate "authentic" relationships in small communities of faith.[266] Where megachurch leaders import organizational strategies and language from the world of marketing and business management, emerging churches use the language of creativity and the arts. And so on. Just as the evangelical left reflects the image of the (dominant) Christian Right point of view, so too the emerging church point of view is constructed in opposition to (dominant) megachurch evangelicalism.[267]

While the emerging church and evangelical left standpoints are largely constructed against a single dominant position in the evangelical field (megachurch and conservative evangelicalism, respectively), neo-monastic evangelicalism is constructed in opposition to them both. Against the Christian Right, Urban Monastery participants criticize single-issue voting, militarism, religious nationalism, and conservative standpoints on poverty and economic inequality. Against megachurch evangelicalism, Urban Monastery participants oppose the bureaucratic and professional organization of spirituality, theological individualism, the prioritization of evangelism over social justice, and religious consumerism. Likewise, the neo-monastic texts analyzed above strongly oppose "pop evangelicalism" and the "cultural and patriotic Christianity" it is accused of promoting and representing.[268] These texts oppose conservative evangelicalism's complicity with American militarism, nationalism, and imperialism, its opposition to public policies that benefit the poor and vulnerable, and its conflation of the "Christian story" with the "American story," while also opposing the theological individualism, religious consumerism, and separation from the poor it attributes to megachurch evangelicalism.[269] The language of monasticism itself symbolizes reaction, negation, and opposition to the dominant religious, social, and political positions of the day. It is impossible to explain the neo-monastic point of view without reference to the social-historical field of American evangelicalism and the dominant positions against which its own religious and political standpoints are constructed.

These largely oppositional position-takings reflect the different positions that evangelical agents occupy in the evangelical field. This is true for all actors but particularly so for new entrants to the field who occupy dominated positions:

> [New entrants] are the ones who are also the most deprived of specific capital, and who (in a universe where to exist is to be different, meaning to occupy a distinct and distinctive position) only exist in so far as . . . they manage to assert their identity (that is, there difference) and get it known and recognized ("make a name for oneself") by imposing new modes of thought and expression which break with current modes of thought. The "youngest" writers structurally . . . that is, the least advanced in the process of legitimation—reject what their most consecrated precursors are and do.[270]

Thus, we find the most vigorous and comprehensive negation of the (dominant) points of view of the Christian Right and megachurch evangelicalism among the newest entrants to the field (neo-monasticism), who distinguish themselves from these dominant positions and from other dominated positions by opposing both dominant positions directly. By contrast, the shadow of the Christian Right point of view is weakest in the position-takings of megachurch evangelicalism which, having already attained consecration and legitimation in the field (having already "made a name for itself"), is less compelled to define itself in terms of negation and opposition to the Christian Right.

The tendency for agents who occupy dominated positions in a field to "reject what their most consecrated precursors are and do" in order to "assert their identity (that is, their difference) and get it known and recognized ('make a name for oneself')" is clearly evident in the emerging church and neo-monastic points of view, which challenge and often reverse the most dominant and consecrated positions in the field (megachurch evangelicalism and the Christian Right).[271] Agents occupying dominated positions in the evangelical field tend toward *challenger strategies* defined by opposition to dominant positions, while agents in dominant positions tend toward *conservation strategies*. The decision by newcomers to adopt challenger strategies, however, is not automatic. Challenger strategies open up new possibilities for recognition and legitimation, but they also risk the evangelical version of excommunication, as we will see below. Newcomers can choose instead to appropriate the position-takings of dominants as their own, thereby positioning themselves for recognition and approval from dominant players who control significant amounts of capital (and who are more likely to "invest" their capital in those who share their view of the world).[272]

These "inheritor" or *preservationist strategies* more or less reproduce dominant position-takings and offer the possibility of speedy consecration and recognition by dominant agents. In the evangelical field, we can observe this process of "simple reproduction" at work in the mutual recognition between "Gen X" megachurch pastors and their forbearers.[273] For example, Gen X megachurch pastor Erwin McManus is effusively praised by Rick Warren in the foreword of McManus's first book:

> This book models what a postmodern, purpose-driven church can look like. . . . For twenty-five years I've taught pastors that "the church is a Body, not a business. It is an organism, not an organization! It is a family to be loved, not a machine to be engineered, and not a company to be managed." . . . I've read too many self-serving critics of the [mega] church who attack straw men, use their books to vent unresolved personal anger issues, and never really give any useful insights for helping churches change and be healthier. Erwin, like a true leader, wastes no time criticizing or attacking others.[274]

As the successful practitioner of the megachurch model for the post-Boomer population, McManus is recognized by Warren as a legitimate inheritor of his own position in the evangelical field and is consecrated as such. For his part, McManus lauds megachurches like Willow Creek and Saddleback for being "organically connected to the community" and for their success at motivating church members to bring their non-Christian friends to church.[275] This process of mutual recognition confers legitimacy on a new entrant to the field (McManus) while reinforcing the legitimacy and extending the relevance of a dominant agent's position (Warren) into the next generation.[276]

While McManus adopts a preservationist strategy that appropriates megachurch evangelicalism while adapting it to a new cultural context (urban young adults in Los Angeles versus suburban baby boomers in Orange County), Warren adopts a conservation strategy by attempting to define McManus's point of view as a version of his own: an example of "what a postmodern, purpose-driven church can look like." Warren is famous for successfully using business management and marketing strategies to organize and grow the church, yet claims McManus's organic and relational church metaphors as expressions of his own view. By claiming McManus's innovative, hip new perspective on the church as a version of his own, Warren safeguards the legitimacy of the megachurch position against its critics and extends its influence to the next generation. At the same time, he blasts emerging church leaders as "self-serving critics" who "attack straw men" and "use their books to vent unresolved personal anger issues" against megachurch evangelicalism.[277] The *challenger strategies* adopted by emerging church newcomers provoke reaction and response from dominant agents like Warren, who enact conservation strategies that attempt to preserve and extend the influence of their own position in the field.[278]

These conservation strategies may take countless forms, but the most direct and forceful way for agents occupying dominant positions in the evangelical field to preserve the existing state of the field—and thus preserve their dominant position within it—is to identify their own particular point of view with *orthodoxy* and define the position-takings of challengers as *heresy*.[279] Describing a challenger's point of view as heresy is the nuclear option of conservation strategies in the evangelical field, an attempt to deny a challenger his very existence as a legitimate participant in the evangelical field and banishing him to the outer darkness of the excommunicated heretic.

The emerging church has increasingly found itself confronted with exactly this sort of opposition. When Brian McLaren and others associated with Emergent Village began criticizing dominant conservative evangelical perspectives on the gospel, biblical interpretation, and the evangelical doctrine of substitutionary atonement,[280] conservative evangelicals perceived them as questioning the unquestionable assumptions that make one an evangelical. So long as the position-takings of avant-garde groups do not challenge the core theological commitments that define the boundaries of evangelical faith—the fundamental *doxa* of the field one must accept in order to be accepted as a participant in the field—innovation and criticism of dominant positions in the field is tolerated. However, while the emerging church's deconstruction of dominant evangelical approaches to evangelism and mission inspired praise, interest, and financial backing of the evangelical establishment; their theological criticisms resulted in widespread criticism and sanction. Thus, in a book titled *Becoming Conversant with the Emerging Church*, Dr. D. A. Carson—a widely respected conservative evangelical author and professor at Trinity Evangelical Divinity School—issues a dire warning against some emerging church perspectives on the Christian gospel: "I have to say, as kindly but as forcefully as I can, that to my mind, if words mean anything, [emerging church leaders] have largely abandoned the Gospel."[281] For evangelical Christians, there is no more severe charge than the judgment that one has abandoned the gospel. Similarly, Dr. R. Albert Mohler Jr. (President of Southern Baptist Theological Seminary) raises the specter of relativism in a review of Brian McLaren's book *A Generous Orthodoxy*: "Embracing the worldview of the postmodern age, [McLaren] embraces relativism at the cost of clarity in matters of truth and intends to redefine Christianity."[282] From the conservative point of view, the emerging church's attacks on dominant position-takings in evangelicalism are a heretical attack on Christianity itself.

Likewise, in politics, opposition to the Christian Right point of view is frequently viewed as opposition to Christianity and even to God. Just as Jerry Falwell publicly urged evangelicals to support George W. Bush as a matter of spiritual integrity, Christian Right leaders in 2008 repeatedly equated the decision facing evangelical voters in the 2008 presidential election with the biblical confrontation between the godly prophet Elijah and the pagan prophets of Baal, implying that God's choice for president was clear (the Republican candidate John McCain) and that evangelicals undecided on whom to vote for—which included many Urban Monastery participants such as Caleb and Lilith—were in danger of heresy.[283] When Caleb's childhood pastor heard that Caleb was questioning the wisdom of supporting the McCain/Palin ticket in 2008, the pastor sent him an urgent email "out of concern and curiosity" as to how Caleb, a devout Christian and religious leader, could possibly even consider voting for the Democratic Party's presidential candidate. Lilith, meanwhile, voted for George W. Bush in 2004 because, as she told me, "I felt coerced. I felt manipulated, spiritually manipulated: like I would be sinning if I voted for someone else."

At this point, two caveats are in order. First, the practical strategies adopted by agents in response to their position in a field are typically matters of subconscious intuition rather than conscious and explicit intention. I am not arguing that the theological and political position-takings of agents in the evangelical field are a matter of "cynical calculation" or "the conscious pursuit of maximum specific profit" (such as money, book sales, recognition, or a large following), as some Bourdieusian critics have argued.[284] Accusing Bourdieu of a form of "economism" which reduces all action to interest based on a "selfish rationality assumption," these critics denounce Bourdieu's theoretical language of fields, capital, and habitus as a sort of dystopian take on economistic rational action theory.[285] However, Bourdieu's theory of practice and oft-repeated denunciations of both Marxist and rational choice varieties of economic reductionism make these readings untenable.[286] For Bourdieu, the concept of "strategic action" does not reduce to the conscious, intentional action of a utility-maximizing agent.[287] Rather, these strategies typically take the form of "an unconscious relationship between a *habitus* and a field," that is, between the dispositions of agents and an agent's objective position in the structure of relations that constitute the field in question.[288] In other words, the degree to which the strategies of agents are implicit and subconscious versus conscious and intentional depends on the agent and field in question. It is a matter of empirical investigation rather than theoretical fiat.

The second caveat is that these strategies are not deterministic in nature. On the one hand, "in a state of equilibrium, *the space of positions tends to command the space of position-takings.*"[289] On the other hand, "*social agents are not 'particles'* that are mechanically pushed and pulled about by external forces."[290] That is, the position-takings and strategies of actors in the evangelical field cannot be deduced directly from their social position in the manner of a "reductionistic 'social physics'" which leaves no room for intention or agency.[291] The space of possible position-takings is characterized by a "certain structure of probabilities . . . but this structure always includes a share of indetermination"—that is, of freedom, unpredictability, surprise—given the complexity of human agents and social fields.[292] An agent's position in a field probabilistically governs her adoption of conservation or challenger strategies, without implying, for example, that "all small capital holders are necessarily revolutionaries and all big capital holders are automatically conservatives."[293]

Despite his own frequent denunciations of the practice, the charge of reductionism is common among Bourdieu's critics.[294] It is true that Bourdieu gives explanatory priority to the material and objective—as opposed to the symbolic and subjective—in much of his work, and claims that economic capital "is at the root of all other types of capital," thereby providing some fodder for such critics.[295] However, while Bourdieu accepts the "sound materialist principle" that an agent's position within the objective structure of a field generates a set of material and symbolic interests which causally influence an agent's standpoints and strategies of action,[296] he systematically rejects one-way materialist reductionisms which deny any autonomy to the cultural or subjective realms. For Bourdieu, (subjective) agents constitute fields as much as (objective) fields constitute agents.[297] Non-economic forms of capital have their own specific efficacy which cannot be reduced or translated without remainder to economic capital.[298] Fields of religious or cultural production have their own specific forms of capital and hierarchical classification systems which cannot be reduced to the economistic logic of the market.[299] And so on. Field theory is not reductionist, and Bourdieu is not a strict materialist in the final analysis.[300] If he sometimes appears so, it is partly because he deploys a "deliberate and provisional reductionism" to his analyses of sociological objects in the cultural sphere,[301] intentionally "twisting the stick in the other direction" in an attempt to dethrone the "myth of the uncreated creator" and demystify the social processes at work within the fields of cultural production.[302] Still, it is fair to say that Bourdieu's theoretical approach to culture, agency, and subjectivity is underdeveloped,[303] which is why, in the next chapter, I bring in other theories of culture to fortify my own field-theoretic analysis of how neo-monastic (and other) evangelicals construct their distinctive religious and political standpoints and strategies of action.

If field theory survives charges of reductionism, what of claims that Bourdieu is nothing more than a rigid "reproduction theorist," illuminating the processes whereby hierarchical class and social structures reproduce themselves through domination and misrecognition while leaving no room for resistance, creativity, or change?[304] That Bourdieu's human "agents" are not really agents at all, but rather oversocialized cultural zombies who lack the basic human capacity to resist unjust forms of domination, reflexively deliberate about personal life goals, organize one's actions in light of those goals, and creatively pursue ultimate concerns that may be at odds with one's location in the social structure?[305] That Bourdieu offers us an unrealistically fixed and gloomy "inverted sociodocy" in which "all is for the worst in the worst possible world?"[306] Here again, some of the criticism is fair. It is true that Bourdieu's sociology operates with a strong hermeneutic of suspicion, where nothing ever is what it seems and where inequality, domination, and misrecognized power relations seemingly lurk around every corner. Bourdieu devotes far more time to unveiling the mechanisms of social reproduction and domination than he does theorizing about the conditions and possibilities of social transformation, creativity, or resistance.[307] But again, as with his tendency to prioritize the material/objective over symbolic/subjective explanations, Bourdieu's focus on reproduction over transformation is more an attempt to "twist the stick" against naïve views of the egalitarian possibilities of an ascendant meritocratic ideology in the 1960s French educational system, for example, or against overly optimistic and naïve perspectives on the likelihood of radical social change, than it is an intrinsic feature of field theory itself.[308] Historical sociologists, for example, have found field theory to offer a rich source of conceptual tools for explaining historical social change, even while acknowledging Bourdieu's failure to develop a satisfactory account of democracy, democratic publics, transnationalism, or resistance.[309] I think they are right. For those who have eyes to see, field theory offers us powerful conceptual tools for understanding both reproduction and transformation, both continuity and change, in the field of American evangelicalism. A brief detour to consider the relationship between Pierre Bourdieu's and Max Weber's sociologies of religion may help us further clarify this complex, non-reductionist relationship between the religious standpoints of agents and the social positions from which they arise.

Excursus: Weber, Bourdieu, and the Social Roots of Religion

Among his many achievements in the sociology of religion, Max Weber's account of the influence of the specific social strata from which the world's major religions originated is one of the most enduring. Weber argued that each of the world's major religions bore the stamp of the material and cultural interests and worldviews of the particular social classes that were their original social carriers. For example, Buddhism's "world-rejecting" religious ethic reflected the social status of the "homeless, wandering" monks who first propagated it; Judaism's asceticism, legalistic rationalism, and intellectualism reflected the "petit-bourgeois intelligence" of its town-dwelling progenitors; while the Protestant ethic of "innerworldly asceticism" reflected Christianity's flourishing as an urban, civic religion of the middle-class—notwithstanding the more "magical," "anti-intellectual," and "world-rejecting" teaching of its charismatic Messiah and his "wandering brotherhood of artisans."[310] More generally, Weber argued that magical religions appealed to the peasant strata whose livelihood depended on the fickle gods of nature, "this-worldly" religious ethics developed in the "knightly warrior strata" for whom rationalistic and mystical religion was anathema, and the bourgeois strata gave birth to a broader and more inde-terminate range of religious ethics.[311]

There are two crucial things to note about Weber's understanding of the relationship between social positions and the religious position-takings asso-ciated with them. First, while there exists a certain "elective affinity" between the interests and worldview of a given social class and the type of religion that tends to flourish among members of that class, social position does not deter-mine religious position-taking.[312] It is worth quoting Weber at length on this point:

> Now it needs to be made very clear what is being advanced in the fol-lowing exposition. It is not being argued that a specific religiosity is a simple function of the social position of the stratum, which appears to be its characteristic carrier, as if it were the "ideology" or a "reflection" of the material and ideal interests of that stratum.[313] It would be diffi-cult to conceive of such a complete misunderstanding of what is being discussed here. The primary imprint of a religious ethic is received from religious sources—foremost being the content of its promises and message. It does not come from politically and economically de-termined social influences . . . however far-reaching these factors may be. . . . The influence of other [nonreligious] spheres of interest, while often quite emphatic and occasionally decisive, can only be of second-ary importance.[314]

Weber's historical sociology demonstrated that the interests and worldview of a religion's "socially decisive stratum" typically had "far-reaching signifi-cance" during a religion's formative stages.[315] However—and this is the second crucial point—once a religious tradition received its "typical imprint" from the class position of its early and decisive social carriers, religious ideas had the potential to transcend the social position from which they originated and exert influence over a wide range of social positions. As Ann Swidler aptly summarizes in her introduction to Weber's *The Sociology of Religion*, "once a religion is sufficiently 'rationalized'—that is, systematized and unified—its core religious ideas come to have a logic of their own."[316]

Bourdieu's debt to Weber—particularly with respect to the development of his core theoretical concepts of field, capital, and habitus—is significant and not frequently recognized.[317] What Weber observed concerning the ori-gins and development of the world's major religions, Bourdieu recognized as a recurring social process in the ongoing historical development of all social fields. New entrants who typically enter a field in a dominated position necessarily develop their particular points of view in reference to the points of view held by actors in dominant positions in the field, which—because of their accumulated capital—have a significant degree of power and influence on the field as a whole.[318] The points of view taken by new entrants to a field are at first narrowly limited to others sharing their dominated position, a situation akin to the elective affinity between social strata and religious standpoints during a religious tradition's formative stages. However, through the accumulation of capital, some occupants of dominated positions are able to increase their influence and recognition in the field over time and eventually come to occupy dominant positions themselves, at which point the points of view they developed while occupying a dominated position can be decoupled from their original social position and come to transcend and exert influence over a wide range of other social positions in the field. For both Weber and Bourdieu, social positions influence religious position-taking, but religious position-takings are not mechanistically determined by social positions, and they are capable of exerting influence on social positions other than the ones they originate from.[319]

Proposition Three: Innovations in American evangelicalism are typically initiated by the socially young, who relegate earlier innovations and social generations to the outmoded past.

The vast majority of neo-monastic and emerging church leaders and participants are in their twenties, thirties, or early forties.[320] However, it is not strictly biological age but rather social age in which the motivation for innovation is found.[321] Each successive *social generation*—a cohort of new entrants to a field who sometimes also represents a biological generation, but not always—faces an objectively structured space of possible position-takings hierarchically ordered according to the outcomes of prior (historical) struggles in the field.[322] As new entrants to the evangelical field encounter seeker-sensitive/purpose-driven megachurch evangelicalism as a dominant position in the field, some (i.e., Gen X megachurches) accept the received wisdom of the preceding generation's most consecrated positions and reproduce the existing order of positions and classification schemes in the field, while others (i.e., neo-monastics and emerging churches) oppose dominant positions and struggle to carve out new positions that are often more or less direct negations of dominant position-takings. As new entrants succeed in establishing their position as legitimate and begin accumulating capital in the field, they relegate previously dominant positions to the past, decreasing their influence over the entire field and especially among the newly arrived social generation.

Previously dominant positions become old, obsolete, the way of the past; while the new position is for the young, the relevant, the way of the present and the future.

For example, emerging church leader Dan Kimball builds his case against the "outdated" seeker-sensitive megachurch standpoint around an ironically told conversion story of a young "antichurch, anti-Christian" (i.e., not a "seeker" of the sort megachurch evangelicals speak of reaching) named Sky:

> Sky did not come to know Jesus and become part of a church because of a well-rehearsed drama sketch, polished four-point preaching, flaw-less programming, or new padded theater seats. It wasn't because we met in a well-lit, contemporary, bright and cheery church facility where we removed religious symbols, stained glass, and churchy at-mosphere to make "seekers" more comfortable.[323]

Kimball pokes fun at the megachurch point of view (and Rick Warren's position-takings in *Purpose-Driven Church* in particular)[324] while claiming that Sky became a Christian because "he experienced more of a 'post-seeker-sensitive' approach to ministry."[325] The message is simple: megachurch evangelicalism is old, outmoded, obsolete; emerging churches are new, cutting edge, the future. Not content to describe their innovations in merely genera-tional terms, however, Kimball and his fellow emerging church leaders breathlessly up the ante by arguing that the emerging church point of view is not just about a "generation gap"; rather, it is the only adequate response to the "major period of cultural transition" occurring across the entire land-scape of Western civilization, a transition akin to the Enlightenment in scope and thus requiring a radical deconstruction and reconstruction (by the emerging church) of the entire evangelical edifice.[326]

It is not that emerging church leaders are particularly hostile toward lead-ers of megachurch evangelicalism, or that they and certain neo-monastic leaders are unusually maladjusted discontents who overflow with self-righteous religious hubris. Indeed, emerging church and neo-monastic lead-ers like Brian McLaren, Dan Kimball, and Shane Claiborne have plenty of positive things to say about the dominant figures of megachurch evangelical-ism.[327] The process of social aging is rather a general property of social fields, from which the field of American evangelicalism is not immune.[328] Newcom-ers seeking to establish their identity and carve out a distinctive position in the evangelical field adopt challenger strategies which, when successful, in-evitably make those agents occupying dominant positions appear old and out-moded. Thus, "new entrants are bound to continually banish to the past—in

the very process by which they achieve existence . . . those consecrated producers against whom they measure themselves."[329] By announcing the need
for a "post seeker-sensitive" standpoint to reach "post-Christian" people living
in a "post-modern" culture with a "post-evangelical" gospel, megachurch
evangelicalism's "modern," "seeker-sensitive" standpoint is automatically
pushed into the past through the inexorable process of social aging: "Ageing
occurs among enterprises and authors when they remain attached (actively or
passively) to modes of production which—especially if they have left their
mark—inevitably become dated."[330]

Megachurch evangelicalism's seeker-sensitive mode of religious production has most certainly "left its mark" on the evangelical landscape, becoming
the dominant expression of evangelical religious organization and influencing an enormous swath of likely and unlikely religious communities.[331] In the
1980s and 1990s, however, the seeker-sensitive mode of religious production
was the new cutting-edge perspective in American evangelicalism, and megachurch evangelicalism was the innovative, experimental, controversial avant-
garde position in the field. *Rediscovering Church*'s insider account of the rise of
Willow Creek is full of the problems, polemics, and controversies of the newly
consecrated avant-garde. The book finds early progenitors of the megachurch
position being forced to defend their use of slick professional programming
and topical preaching style against "traditional" church critics who accused
Willow Creek of abandoning biblical preaching and "watering down the
gospel" in its attempts to be relevant to seekers. Bill Hybels notes, "In some
corners, Willow Creek has become known primarily for the avant-garde, laser-
age style of its pre-evangelistic events" and for helping evangelicals "build a
big church or create the latest laser-age programs."[332] The traditional defenders of orthodoxy attacked the young (biologically and socially) Willow Creek
experiment as "shallow" and "superficial," for "watering down the gospel"
and "compromising" biblical truth; while Hybels and other leaders of the
avant-garde seeker-sensitive standpoint defended their prioritization of evangelism as more faithful to the Bible than the "traditional," "formal," "insular,"
"boring," "out-of-touch" expressions of church it was seeking to replace.[333]

Fast forward a number of years and today megachurch evangelicalism occupies a dominant position in the evangelical field. It is the obvious, taken-for-
granted position of the evangelical establishment. Its leaders are frequently
viewed as representing American evangelicalism as a whole. In moving from an
avant-garde to dominant position in the field, the innovations introduced by
megachurch evangelicalism have become "common sense" to tens of millions of
evangelicals and tens of thousands of their churches, the only conceivable reference point from which to begin thinking about evangelicalism in America.[334]

However, the "spreading of the norms of perception and appreciation" accomplished through the widespread dissemination of the megachurch point of view is also "accompanied by a *banalization*" which produces an inevitable wearing-out effect that transforms the avant-garde into the commonplace.³³⁵ The historical trajectory of megachurch evangelicalism through the evangelical field is the embodiment of the social aging process. The megachurch point of view has moved from an avant-garde position-taking to a dominant position-taking against which the new evangelical avant-garde (such as the emerging church) positions itself. The emerging church is *emerging*—representing the *new*, the *now*, the *future*—while megachurch evangelicalism (which itself once represented the evangelical avant-garde) becomes *old*, "old news," and for the "old."

While the process of social aging is an inevitable and general property of all social fields, it is not an agent-less process. Rather, it is the product of the struggle among agents occupying distinctive positions in a field which defines the field itself:

> The ageing of authors, works, or schools is something quite different from a mechanical sliding into the past. It is engendered in the fight between those who have already left their mark and are trying to endure, and those who cannot make their marks in their turn without consigning to the past those who have an interest in stopping time, in eternalizing the present state; between the dominants whose strategy is tied to continuity . . . and the dominated, the new entrants, whose interest is in discontinuity, rupture, difference, and revolution.³³⁶

We saw a window into this struggle in Rick Warren's response to Gen X megachurch leaders, on the one hand, and to his emerging church critics, on the other. Warren recognizes those who recognize him and the ongoing legitimacy of his (dominant) megachurch position while harshly dismissing emerging church challengers who oppose the megachurch point of view. The oppositions inherent in the relationship between (dominant) established positions and (dominated) avant-garde positions "installs at the very core of the field a tension between those who try to overtake their rivals and those who wish to avoid being overtaken."³³⁷ It is these struggles that drive the process of social aging.

The Privilege of Youth

The first clause of proposition three states that "innovations in American evangelicalism are typically initiated by the socially young." The last half-century of American evangelicalism alone has witnessed movements such as megachurch evangelicalism, the evangelical left, neo-monastic evangelicalism, the emerging church, and the Jesus People movement, all of which were initiated by socially young evangelicals who developed innovative religious and political standpoints that transformed the evangelical field to greater or lesser degrees. However, we must distinguish between the fact that innovation is typically initiated by the young and the more general claim that transformations in the field of American evangelicalism are always the result of youthful innovation. The first is valid, the second is not. Although "it is true that the initiative for change can be traced back, almost by definition, to new (meaning younger) entrants," the fact that a change in the relationship between any two positions in a field transforms the whole field means that there is no single locus for change.[338] Transformations in a field can also arise out of struggles between (older) agents occupying dominant positions, or they be driven by demographic, cultural, or political changes occurring outside the field. Megachurch leaders Bill Hybels and Rick Warren's public attempts to break with the Christian Right in recent years are an example of transformation in the evangelical field being driven in part by struggles between actors occupying dominant positions.[339] So while new position-takings in American evangelicalism tend to originate among the socially young, we cannot therefore say that all transformations within the evangelical field are the result of these innovations, or even that the young are in general more central to global transformations in the field than the old.

The drive to remain relevant, current, a part of the present rather than the past, arises from a general property of social fields (the process of social aging) which—despite their initial lack of accumulated specific capital in the field—privileges youth.[340] However, this general privilege accorded to youth may take different forms depending on the specific characteristics of a field. Thus, in the nineteenth-century French artistic field, "the pre-eminence given to youth by the field of cultural production [came] down, once again, to the spurning of power and of the 'economy' that [was] at its root."[341] In the nineteenth-century French literary and artistic fields, the symbolic capital granted to youth was associated with the values of "change," "originality," and rejection of the bourgeois pursuit of economic and political power; oppositional values that constituted the origins and *doxa* of these fields of cultural production.[342]

"Youth" is also a form of symbolic capital in the evangelical field, but not for all the same reasons. As in the French literary field, the symbolic capital granted to youth in the evangelical field is connected to the specific genesis and *doxa* of the field itself, which we may partially capture with Christian

Smith's concept of *engaged orthodoxy*.[343] To be an evangelical is to be actively engaged with society. This engagement can take many forms, but the primary form it has taken in historic American evangelicalism is *evangelism*: sharing the gospel of Christ with non-Christians. The same passionate commitment with which American evangelicals have pursued the missionary task of preaching the gospel to "people of every tribe and tongue" around the world also drives them to reach the various demographic groups and subcultures of American society.[344] This *doxic* commitment to evangelistic engagement propels evangelicals forward in a constant search for new "unreached people groups" with whom to share the gospel. The more "unreached" a group is in terms of its exposure and acceptance of Christianity, and the greater the social and cultural distance between that group and mainstream evangelical Christianity, the more recognized and significant the evangelical members of that group become. In the United States, young people are less likely to identify with evangelical Christianity; therefore, young evangelicals become particularly significant and important as relatively rare and distinctive commodities. Urban, educated, progressive, and artistic young adults from the east or west coast are even less likely to identify as evangelicals, increasing the rarity and thus the symbolic capital granted to evangelicals sharing these demographic characteristics. Representing a sort of evangelical beachhead on an unreached cultural shore, these relatively rare evangelicals become the experts who teach the evangelical mainstream how to reach desirable "post-Christian" young people with the gospel, thereby fulfilling the Great Commission and aiding the survival and growth of the field and specific church congregations.

This privilege accorded to youth in the evangelical field is amplified by the structure of the American religious field. America's disestablishment of religion has promoted a culture of religious pluralism, voluntarism, and free-market competition in the religious field, where the competition between religious institutions for new adherents bears some resemblance to the competition between business institutions for new consumers.[345] American evangelicalism, in particular, is an exemplary case of the American religious model of religious pluralism, competition, and choice.[346] Because of its relative lack of strong denominational structures, centralized authority, and its historic identity as a popular religion focused on reaching the masses, "the evangelical field is structurally wide open for inventive leaders to emerge and launch new initiatives."[347] Particularly, it is open to new leaders and initiatives focused on reaching new generations, subcultures, and demographic groups with a relevant, appealing, and persuasive expression of the Christian faith. The necessity of remaining relevant to youth is an acutely felt reality for the pastors and leaders of evangelical churches, as expressed by their chronic alarmism concerning the "declining religiosity" of youth and ubiquitous phrases such as "the church is only one generation from extinction," phrases that press the urgency of reaching the next generation with the gospel.[348] Thus, the symbolic capital granted to youth in the evangelical field is both culturally and structurally determined, arising out of evangelicalism's *doxic* commitment to evangelistic engagement, on the one hand, and out of the pluralistic structure of the American religious field, on the other.

Proposition Four: Struggles between competing visions of evangelical Christianity create a state of permanent (partial) revolution in the evangelical field, simultaneously preserving and transforming the field as a whole.

As noted in proposition one, struggles between agents holding competing visions of the legitimate representation of biblical Christianity in the evangelical field do not threaten the existence of the field itself. Rather, they are partially responsible for preserving and reproducing it. The act of engaging with other positions in the evangelical field—even when such engagement is antagonistic and oppositional in nature—is itself an act of commitment to the field, its stakes, its value, and its particular view of the world. In proposition two we observed how preservationist and challenger strategies alike aid in the reproduction and growth of the evangelical field. The point is obvious in the case of conservation or preservationist strategies, which more or less reproduce dominant positions in the evangelical field and thereby guarantee its ongoing relevance, identity, and existence. More counterintuitively, agents who adopt challenger strategies also reproduce the field. Through the very act of struggling with dominant positions over the stakes of the field, they affirm their investment in its value and develop new position-takings which help keep evangelicalism relevant and significant to new biological and social generations.[349] The end result of these struggles between evangelical agents over the legitimate representation of biblical Christianity is a state of permanent partial revolution in the evangelical field, which simultaneously reproduces and transforms the field as a whole.

We can observe a distilled example of this process at work in the emerging church's struggle against the megachurch point of view. For all their passionate disagreements, the driving motivational force behind today's massive suburban megachurches and the emerging churches which oppose them is the same. Both have their origins and motivating impulse in the desire to engage non-Christians who are not interested in traditional churches or traditional Christianity.[350] Both seek to communicate and embody the Christian message in innovative ways to demonstrate the relevance and attractiveness of the Christian way of life to the particular demographic and cultural groups they identify with and live among. So while prototypical evangelical mega-churches such as Willow Creek and Saddleback "intentionally minimize the distance between the outside world and the church by showing how Christianity is relevant and applicable to the world of middle class suburbanites,"[351] emerging churches react against big-box suburban megachurches in search of more "intimate," "communal," "creative," and "authentic" expressions of evangelical Christianity that are more appealing to urban, educated young adults. As each group seeks to communicate the evangelical message to its particular demographic and cultural group, the message itself becomes transformed—toward individualism and "therapeutic personalism" in the suburban megachurch context and toward holistic communitarianism in the post-Boomer neo-monastic and emerging church context.[352] Emerging churches struggle against the megachurch representation of evangelical Christianity, yet their innovations are driven by the same *doxic* commitment to evangelistic engagement and evangelical orthodoxy that motivates megachurch evangelicalism, a striking example of how "the partial revolutions which constantly occur in fields do not call into question the very foundations of the game, its fundamental axioms, [or] the bedrock of ultimate beliefs on which the game is based."[353] Evangelicalism's *doxic* commitment to evangelistic engagement and its minimalist approach to orthodoxy enable it to be highly flexible in both content and form while maintaining its distinctive identity as a religious movement, a critical component of American evangelicalism's dynamic vitality.[354]

The emerging church's critique of evangelicalism and of the dominant megachurch position thus serves simultaneously to preserve and transform the evangelical field. It transforms the field by staking out within it a new legitimate position that challenges dominant positions and their representation of evangelical Christianity, sapping the influence of the dominants and increasing the influence of the emerging church position. So instead of participating in the conferences and church associations organized by megachurch evangelicals, some pastors and religious leaders begin attending emerging church conferences and join the "Emergent conversation."[355] The emerging church also preserves and renews evangelicalism by reinforcing *engaged orthodoxy* as the fundamental *doxa* of the field.[356] It does so while adopting new theological and cultural forms that appeal to demographic and cultural groups hostile to or disinterested in older versions of evangelicalism, thus preserving and expanding the field. Driven by evangelical agents' *doxic* commitment to evangelistic engagement, evangelicalism goes forward, but with transformed visage. And driven by evangelical agents' *doxic* commitment to biblical orthodoxy, evangelicalism maintains its distinctive religious identity and self-consciously preserves itself as a distinctive field within American religious and social space.

The oppositional position-takings of new entrants to the evangelical field often take the form of a call for "purity" and a "return to origins," which further strengthens the legitimacy and existence of the field (even among those actors who most vigorously oppose currently dominant positions within it). In this, American evangelicalism is similar to other fields of cultural production:

> In the fields of production of cultural goods—religion, literature, or art—heretical subversion [of dominant positions] claims to be returning to the sources, the origin, the spirit, the authentic essence of the game, in opposition to the banalization and degradation which it has suffered.[357]

In the evangelical field, the most common form of the "return to origins" trope is a call to return to the pure and ancient expression of biblical Christianity. As Dan Kimball argues, the emerging church's "post-seeker-sensitive" point of view "is really nothing new at all; in fact, it is simply going back to more of a raw and basic form of 'vintage Christianity.'"[358] *Vintage Christianity*, of course, is the title of Kimball's book, which captures the emerging church's argument that evangelicalism (and megachurch evangelicalism, in particular) needs to be purged of all the entrapments and influences of Western modernity corrupting the pure, "vintage" expression of authentic biblical Christianity in America and the West.[359]

Similarly, neo-monastic evangelicals appropriate monasticism—historic Christianity's earliest and most common expression of "return to origins" religious purity—to symbolize their opposition to the "over-accommodating" and "compromised religion" represented by American "pop evangelicalism."[360] Urban Monastery participants view their practices of hospitality, holistic mission, authentic community, prayer, justice, team leadership, and intimate spiritual family as "the truest representation of the dream church," practices just "like how the apostles used to have church" (Jasmine). They draw on biblical passages such as Acts 2:42–47 to describe how the Urban Monastery represents an authentic and pure form of biblical Christianity in contrast to the bureaucratic, judgmental, and separatist "traditional" churches which dominate the evangelical landscape.[361] Alex, who acts as point person for the Urban Monastery's core leadership team, describes the origins of the

Urban Monastery as inspired by the "simple" rhythms of the early church as recorded in the book of Acts:

ALEX: We were *really* inspired by the early church—the way that Jesus lived and the way the early church carried that on after he was resurrected. They ate meals house to house, read scripture, prayed, and went out to share with those who didn't know the Lord. That just really took hold of our hearts. So we started praying a lot, hanging out a lot, eating meals together. . . . Those were our beginnings. That was the seed that everything sprouted from.

While opposing the dominant standpoints of traditional evangelicalism, however, Urban Monastery participants also express solidarity and kinship with them, explicitly acknowledging a shared religious identity with all who profess faith in Christ and his Word. In the words of Caleb, one of Alex's closest friends and a founding leader of the Urban Monastery:

CALEB: Talking about the Urban Monastery specifically, I would hope that whatever form this takes in the years ahead, that there is never a sense of cornering the deal. Because there are amazing things in evangelical America that we need to learn from.

Evangelical *doxa* demands commitment to biblical authority and to a small but often explicit set of theological convictions as the price of entry to the field, which makes it more historically continuous—and its partial revolutions less tumultuous—than those in the artistic or intellectual fields, where the *original*, the *new*, and the *subversive* are more uniformly required and praised. Yet the dynamics of struggle, social aging, and permanent revolution, which are properties of all social fields, are properties of the evangelical field as well.

Excursus: Resolving the Traditionalists/Innovators Debate

At the beginning of this chapter, I introduced a prominent sociological debate concerning American evangelicalism: are evangelicals essentially dogmatic religious traditionalists at bottom, or are they innovative religious pragmatists? We are now in a position directly to address this debate in light of proposition four. Among their many disputes concerning evangelicalism and America's culture war, James Davison Hunter and Alan Wolfe offer opposing perspectives on evangelicalism's basic stance toward religious and social change.[362] Hunter emphasizes the traditionalist and conservative impulses of evangelicalism's perspective on religion and morality:

> One moral vision—the traditionalist or orthodox—is predicated upon the achievements and traditions of the past as the foundation and guide to the challenges of the present. . . . The order of life sustained by this vision is, at its best, one that seeks deliberate continuity with the ordering principles inherited from the past.[363]

Alan Wolfe, on the other hand, argues that the primary impulse of evangelicalism is innovation:

> The popular idea that Americans are attracted to conservative Christianity because they are traditionalists at heart who want to return to the morality prominent in America before the 1960s runs into the complication that evangelical Protestantism is anything but traditional in its outlook on the world. If I had to invent a term that meant the exact opposite of "traditional," I would use the phrase that evangelicals apply to themselves: "born again." . . . It is because evangelicals assign a relatively low value to tradition that their faith has grown in the decidedly non-traditional environment of American culture. Committed to spreading the good news of the Gospel, evangelicals rely on every innovative twist in the culture to reach those in need of salvation.[364]

What is going on here? How can two empirically based arguments about the evangelical view of the world yield such contradictory perspectives on American evangelicalism's stance toward tradition and innovation?

The first thing to note is that the dispute between "innovation" and "traditionalism" as described above is a false antithesis. Both "traditionalism" and "innovation" are fundamental features of the evangelical field, as propositions one through four make clear. Agents occupying dominant positions in the field tend to adopt conservative strategies of action that preserve the status quo, while agents in dominated positions are more predisposed to adopt challenger strategies that favor innovation. In addition to this general property of fields, the presence of both traditionalist and innovative impulses in evangelicalism also arises out of the evangelical *doxa* of *engaged orthodoxy*.[365] Evangelical agents' *doxic* commitment to *engagement*—particularly evangelistic engagement—drives innovation in the evangelical field, while their commitment to *orthodoxy* places limits on innovation and preserves the impulse toward evangelistic engagement by reinforcing evangelical self-identity as a "peculiar people" set apart by God and entrusted to be his witnesses in the world.[366] The commitment to both "innovative" evangelistic engagement and "traditional" orthodoxy is a fundamental feature of evangelical *doxa* and thus of the evangelical field itself, and both contribute to the preservation and renewal of the field through the process of permanent partial revolution. Thus, it is not surprising that scholars find evidence of both traditionalism and innovation in the evangelical field. However, by treating them as antithetical rather than complementary features of American evangelicalism, these disputes call to mind the old Indian proverb of the blind men and the elephant, in which the blind men cannot agree on whether an elephant is like a pillar, a brush, or a basket because they are examining different parts of the whole.

Proposition Five: Evangelical agents who occupy dominated positions tend to converge through opposition to dominant position-takings; while avant-garde groups fracture upon achieving consecration.

The tendency for new entrants in a field to adopt standpoints that oppose and reverse dominant standpoints has the effect of promoting agreements among agents in dominated positions: which explains one prominent source of collaboration across different movements within the evangelical field. Despite their widely disparate points of view, these agents find common ground in opposition to dominant forces. The emerging church, neo-monastic evangelicalism, and the evangelical left's common opposition to the Christian Right, on the one hand, and theological individualism, on the other, is reflected in a number of shared position-takings across these dominated groups. These similarities are acknowledged in the mutual recognition the evangelical left, neo-monasticism, and the emerging church grant one another. To take one example, evangelical left figurehead Jim Wallis wrote the foreword for Shane Claiborne's first book, in which Wallis recognizes and affirms Claiborne and the New Monasticism as something akin to the next generation of the evangelical left:

> I must admit that the young Shane reminds me a little of a young radical Christian about three decades ago when we were founding Sojourners magazine and community. We were also young evangelicals who found that neither our churches nor our society were measuring up to the way of Jesus—not even close. Our battle then was against a private piety that limited religion to only personal matters, then compromised faith in a tragic capitulation to the economic, political, and military powers that be. We desperately wanted to see our faith "go

public" and offer a prophetic vision with the power to change both our personal lives and political directions. . . . But then came the religious right with evangelical faith going public, but not in the ways we had hoped.[367]

Likewise, Shane Claiborne acknowledges his debt to evangelical left leaders and quotes them throughout his book, particularly in reference to their criticisms of the Christian Right.[368] In addition to Wallis's foreword, prominent evangelical left leaders Tony Campolo and Ron Sider also endorsed Claiborne's book, as did Brian McLaren, the emerging church's elder statesman and one of its most influential leaders.[369]

Mutual recognition is common among occupants of these three dominated positions in the evangelical field. Tony Campolo and Brian McLaren coauthored a 2003 book, titled *Adventures in Missing the Point*, which took on the evangelical establishment, and McLaren's other books are regularly recommended by prominent evangelical left leaders such as Wallis and Campolo.[370] Likewise, McLaren and other emerging church leaders frequently endorse the works of evangelical left leaders such as Tony Campolo, as does neo-monasticism's Shane Claiborne.[371] Indeed, Campolo, McLaren, Wallis, and Claiborne—along with a number of prominent Catholic, African American, and Latino Christian leaders—have increasingly begun to identify themselves as "Red Letter Christians" rather than "Evangelicals" in an effort to distinguish their positions from the dominant, politically conservative evangelical mainstream.[372] The Red Letter Christians blog has become a magnet for heterodox evangelical left, emerging church, neo-monastic, African American, and Latino female and male leaders united by common opposition to dominant expressions of politically conservative evangelicalism.[373]

Such *coalitions of the dominated* are typical among the avant-garde of all social fields.[374] Predisposed as they are toward oppositional subversion strategies that can appear to border on heresy from the point of view of dominant agents, these dominated groups tend to exhibit a greater degree of flexibility with respect to the boundaries of the evangelical field and thus create the conditions for a more inclusive and ecumenical flavor to their alliances. Thus, both the emerging church and neo-monasticism include a significant number of Catholic and mainline Protestant individuals and communities, while the evangelical left also includes significant African American, Latino, and other ethnic minority leaders and communities in its network of allies and participants.[375] Observed through the lens of field theory, the ecumenical flavor of these dominated evangelical positions is unsurprising on a number of counts. Dominated and avant-garde groups must fortify their position as much as possible in their attempts to gain recognition and legitimacy as challengers to dominant positions, and thus they have an interest in lowering boundaries and building alliances with those who share their opposition to dominant evangelical actors.[376]

Moreover, the tendency for agents in dominated positions to develop standpoints that oppose and reverse dominant standpoints can create similarities across the position-takings of dominated groups. For instance, both neo-monastic and emerging church leaders valorize their small, "simple," "authentic," "participatory," "relational," and "raw" religious communities against the large, "professional," "consumerist," and "anonymous" paradigm of megachurch evangelicalism. Celebrating the legitimacy, significance, or superiority of small religious communities over large ones is in the interest of these avant-garde groups (which are low in *specific (people) capital*) and also reflects their common opposition to the dominant model of megachurch evangelicalism, which alternatively valorizes church growth and size.[377]

The standpoints of these dominated evangelical positions also converge around the *holistic communitarianism* and the *contradictory cultural location* observed among Urban Monastery participants, who often find themselves stuck between the progressive Left and religious Right:[378]

MANUEL: My brother . . . likes to call me a social conservative and a monetary liberal. I love being completely Christian to my liberal friends and being completely liberal to my Christian friends. So I kind of take that strong stance in both ways.

LILITH: I'm not a Republican Christian. . . . I get really upset at a lot Republicans, and I get really upset at a lot of Democrats. It's always a mixed bag.

The content of Jim Wallis's *God's Politics* bears strong resemblance to the holistic communitarian politics of Urban Monastery participants, including homologies with the Urban Monastery's contradictory cultural location.[379] Equally opposed to both the "secular fundamentalism" of the Left and "religious fundamentalism" of the Right, *God's Politics* decries narrow ideological approaches to poverty, war, and family found on both sides of the political aisle.[380] More than 50 pages in *God's Politics* point to Wallis's contradictory cultural location with respect to the progressive Left and the religious Right, with other evangelical left texts containing over 75 examples each.[381] In his foreword to Shane Claiborne's *The Irresistible Revolution*, Wallis recognizes this same sense of occupying a contradictory cultural location as present in the neo-monastic point of view, writing that "the vision presented here can't easily be put into categories of liberal and conservative, left and right, but rather has the capacity to challenge the categories themselves."[382] And just as Urban Monastery participants expressed frustration and tension with both sides of America's culture war, Claiborne echoes the sentiment:

> I have a confession I'm sure many of you will find refreshing and fa-miliar: I don't really fit into the old liberal-conservative boxes, so it's a good thing we are moving onto something new. . . . Many of us find ourselves estranged from the narrow issues that define conservatives and from the shallow spirituality that marks liberals. We are thirsty for social justice and peace but have a hard time finding a faith commun-ity that is consistently pro-life or that recognizes that there are "moral issues" other than homosexuality and abortion, moral issues like war and poverty.[383]

Opposing the Christian Right but bound by a *doxic* commitment to biblical authority which leads them to relatively conservative positions on abortion, sexuality, and the family, the political standpoints of these dominated evan-gelical groups converge around the contradictory cultural location with re-spect to the progressive Left and religious Right.

Likewise, while *theological individualism* has been a dominant position-taking among evangelicals both past and present, these groups converge around an oppositional communitarian stance consistent with moral cosmol-ogy theory. Although less consistent and pronounced than it is among Urban Monastery participants and other neo-monastic communities,[384] the emerg-ing church and evangelical left also give voice to a strong communitarian message:

> America . . . becomes less and less communal every day. It is a harsh and cruel individualism that is now being forced upon us by our cor-porate, media, and political culture. And that is not good for family or community values. In fact, it destroys them.[385]

God's Politics contains 30+ references to society's "common good" and more than 100 references to America's need to strengthen and build "community" across America's families, neighborhoods, religious, and racial groups. The religious and political standpoints of the evangelical left, neo-monastic, and emerging church evangelicals converge in homologous points of view shaped by their homologous positions in the evangelical field.

The tendency for the standpoints of dominated groups to converge through shared opposition to dominant groups—and to form *coalitions of the dominated* more heterodox and ecumenical than is typical of other positions in the field[386]—is joined by a related but paradoxical tendency of avant-garde groups to fracture upon achieving consecration:

> Whereas the occupants of dominant positions . . . are very homogeneous, the avant-garde positions, which are defined mainly negatively, in opposition to dominant positions, bring together for a while (in the phase of the *initial accumulation of symbolic capital*) [agents] who are very different in their origins and their dispositions and whose interests, momentarily coming together, will later start to diverge . . . these dominated groups tend to enter into crisis, by an apparent paradox, when they achieve recognition.[387]

The historical trajectory of the emerging church over the last fifteen years is an exquisite example of this process of the formation and fracture of avant-garde groups. As noted above, the emerging church in America was born of a well-funded Leadership Network initiative that brought together a small cadre of dynamic young church leaders from around the country, leaders who were successfully engaging "Gen X" and "postmodern" culture with the gospel. This group included among others key emerging church leaders such as Brian McLaren, Tony Jones, Doug Pagitt, Dan Kimball, and Mark Driscoll.[388] The Leadership Network worked with the evangelical publishing giant Zondervan to facilitate an ongoing series of conversations and conferences featuring this disparate group of young "emerging" evangelical leaders, events that served as the platform for the initial accumulation of symbolic capital for the emerging church position in general and for this small group of emerging church leaders, in particular.

Initially held together through opposition to dominant "modern" expressions of evangelicalism and by the significant opportunity for capital accumulation and recognition afforded by Zondervan and the Leadership Network's backing, the group fractured upon achieving consecration, with one side accusing the other of heresy and the other defending itself against such attacks as expressions of a rigid, biblicist, intellectually naïve, and power-hungry representation of evangelical Christianity.[389] Mark Driscoll, a founding member of the emerging church movement, led the palace revolution against the liberal Emergent point of view. In *Confessions of Reformission Rev.: Hard Lessons from an Emerging Missional Church*, Driscoll throws down the gauntlet:

> The emergent church is part of the Emerging Church Movement but does not embrace the dominant ideology of the movement. Rather, the

emergent church is the latest version of liberalism. The only difference is that the old liberalism accommodated modernity and the new liberalism accommodates postmodernity.[390]

By equating the Emergent church point of view with theological liberalism, Driscoll evokes the early twentieth-century battles between fundamentalist and modernist Christians in which (from the evangelical point of view) being a theologically liberal Christian meant not being a legitimate Christian at all. In doing so, Driscoll instantiates a common strategy in struggles over the definitions and boundaries of fields: evoking the original, founding point of view of the field as a means of rejecting "heretical" or heterodox positions perceived to challenge the field's *doxa* and therefore seen as threats to the existence of the field itself.[391] Driscoll returns to the founding struggles of the twentieth-century conservative Protestant field in his attempt to deny the evangelical credentials of his Emergent church protagonists.

In his struggle against competing points of view in the emerging church movement, Driscoll takes on the role of the "self-appointed defenders of orthodoxy" who patrol the boundaries of evangelical field and "aim to ensure that 'none enter here'" unless they adhere to a particular point of view regarding the founding principles and *doxa* of the field.[392] Other evangelical leaders joined Driscoll in condemning the liberal Emergent perspective in popular books such as *Why We are not Emergent* and *Becoming Conversant with the Emergent Church*.[393] More recently, influential evangelical author and Reformed minister John Piper—one of the "New Calvinism's" founding figures—essentially accused Rob Bell of heresy for Bell's views on hell in his *New York Times* best-selling book *Love Wins*, infamously tweeting the abrupt and foreboding phrase, "Farewell, Rob Bell," upon publication of Bell's book.[394] Just as early twentieth-century fundamentalists viewed theological liberalism as an unacceptable violation of the boundaries defining the legitimate representation of biblical Christianity, many evangelicals have come to view the Emergent church as a threat to evangelicalism's essential vision of biblical orthodoxy. While contemporary evangelicalism tolerates diversity and innovation on many issues, the only acceptable standpoint with respect to the gospel is affirmation. For many evangelicals, the Emergent church's theological critiques represent a violation of the fundamental *doxa* of the field and therefore cannot be tolerated. This leads us directly into proposition six.

Proposition Six: Struggles between agents in the evangelical field involve ongoing contestations over the definitions, boundaries, and hierarchical classification schemes that structure the field.

Struggles among evangelical agents over the legitimate representation of biblical Christianity in America express themselves as recurring historical struggles over the *boundaries* of the field (in particular, the boundaries of evangelical orthodoxy), over the *definitions* which grant agents the right to participate in the field or to represent a particular position within it (such as the definition of "evangelical" or "emerging church"), and over competing views of how to organize and "rank" positions in evangelical social space: the *nomos* which determine the legitimate "principles of vision and division" that structure the field.[395] Agents who occupy different objective positions in the field—and who therefore have different points of view of the field—also have competing views of the legitimate principles of classification that should be used to structure the evangelical field, views that are often tied to their particular interests.[396] So while megachurch evangelicalism celebrates large churches and church growth as signs of legitimacy and significance, neo-monastic and emerging church evangelicals celebrate the "authenticity" of small spiritual communities as marks of legitimacy. Each hierarchical classification scheme (large > small or small > large) reflects the group's position in the field: dominant megachurch evangelicalism is rich in specific (people) capital and thus celebrates the large, while neo-monastic and emerging church evangelicals are low in specific (people) capital and thus celebrate the small. The fact that agents who occupy different positions in the evangelical field view the field through alternative and competing principles of vision and division means that there is no single, eternal classification scheme one can use to describe the field. The classification lenses through which different evangelical agents view the field are themselves stakes in the struggle between them.[397] Thus, the classification schemes that structure the evangelical field are historically variable, as are the definitions and boundaries of the field itself.

Definitions of groups and group boundaries are likewise stakes in the struggle between agents in the evangelical field. The fracturing of the emerging church movement is a case of the general principle that—across all social fields—"internal struggles inevitably take the form of conflicts over definition."[398] By the mid-2000s the emerging church had accumulated enough symbolic capital to be well-established as a recognized position in the evangelical field, whereupon previously tolerated differences between leaders in the movement became intolerable, resulting in the movement's fracturing. Mark Driscoll, an influential original participant in emerging church gatherings, began publicly to oppose other emerging church leaders for their views on a host of theological and social issues, to the point of questioning their standing and legitimacy as evangelicals. In a series of scathing rhetorical attacks, Driscoll claimed the mantle of the "Emerging Church Movement" for himself while defining his targets (Brian McLaren, Doug Pagitt, Tony Jones, and others associated with Emergent Village) as the "liberal emergent church" position flirting with heresy.[399] Rather than abandon the emerging church label—a designation that had come to hold a significant amount of symbolic capital in the evangelical field—Driscoll attempted to redefine the emerging church in a way that made his position the dominant position while marginalizing emerging church leaders with whom he disagreed. Driscoll's efforts to redefine the emerging church movement—and thereby to impose definitional boundaries most favorable to his convictions and interests[400]—have been largely successful. The distinction between the liberal "Emergent church" standpoint represented by Brian McLaren and Emergent Village and the "missional" emerging church standpoint claimed by Driscoll has become the normal, common-sense way of defining the emerging church movement among many evangelicals, with Driscoll's position being the favorite among agents occupying dominant positions in the evangelical field.[401]

As attacks on the emerging church have intensified over the last several years, emerging church leaders wishing to retain an evangelical identity have had to work increasingly hard to explain and defend the orthodoxy and legitimacy of their theological views. The more radical or heterodox the standpoint of an agent with respect to historically dominant position-takings in a field, the harder they have to work to present themselves as legitimate participants within it. This is true for neo-monastic and evangelical left leaders as well. Both Shane Claiborne and Jim Wallis have years of experience in mainline Protestant churches, and they are among the most aggressive critics of the Christian Right and conservative evangelicalism in the evangelical field. However, both were also evangelicals in their youth and attended mainstream evangelical colleges before breaking with politically conservative evangelicalism and beginning their struggle to redefine evangelicalism's place in the political field. This background reinforces their claims to an evangelical identity and enables them to fluently speak the language of the field, which provides the practical benefits of gaining access to the very large market that exists for evangelical books and gaining an audience among the largest religious group in the United States. Given evangelicalism's numerical growth and rising political prominence over the last forty years, it makes good practical sense for anyone seeking to write about religion and politics in America to engage with the evangelical position if they are in a position to do so. But in order to do so, one must prove that one is, indeed, an evangelical.

So in *The Irresistible Revolution*, Shane Claiborne assures his readers that he is indeed an evangelical, while also subtly redefining the meaning of the term in order to better represent his own position:

> Sometimes folks (usually of an older persuasion) ask me if I am an evangelical Christian. . . . I want to make sure we have a proper understanding before I answer. . . . If by evangelical we mean one who spreads the good news that there is another kingdom or superpower, an economy and a peace other than that of the nations, a savior other than Caesar, then yes, I am an evangelical.[402]

Claiborne places himself inside the boundaries of evangelicalism while simultaneously challenging its meaning, focusing on the gospel as a political critique of nationalism and a call to peace and economic justice in this world. He does not deny any core evangelical doctrines, but neither does his definition mention traditional evangelical theological positions like the humanity and divinity of Jesus, his death and bodily resurrection in history, the authority of the Bible, or the importance of personal faith in Christ for the forgiveness of sin. Claiborne believes all these things, but he also aims to promote a new definition of evangelicalism that better represents his own position.

The Irresistible Revolution could serve as a brilliant practical textbook on how the struggle over definitions can be used to defend and promote alternative position-takings in a field. In making his argument for neo-monasticism and against megachurch and conservative evangelicalism, Claiborne repeatedly redefines core theological symbols, concepts, and practices that lie at the heart of evangelical faith, including "conversion," "missionary," "the cross," "rebirth/born-again," and "tithing." For example, while the cross is typically viewed by evangelicals as a symbol of the effects of sin and possibility of salvation through faith in Christ, Claiborne appropriates it as his warrant for a peacemaking trip to Iraq during the second Iraq war:

> I am going to Iraq in the footsteps of an executed and risen God. . . . I have pledged allegiance to a King who loved evildoers so much he died for them (and of course, the people of Iraq are no more evil or holy than the people of the U.S.), teaching us that there is something worth dying for but nothing worth killing for. . . . I go to Iraq to stand in the way of war. Thousands of soldiers have gone to Iraq, willing to kill people they do not know because of a political allegiance. I go willing to die because of a spiritual allegiance.[403]

While calling Christians to move beyond charitable giving and into a fight against the structural causes of poverty, Claiborne pushes the symbolic meaning of the cross in another unfamiliar direction[404]:

> People do not get crucified for charity. People are crucified for living out a love that disrupts the social order; that calls forth a new world. People are not crucified for helping poor people. People are crucified for joining them.[405]

Likewise, for most evangelicals, the term "missionary" refers to a person sent overseas by a religious organization to preach the gospel and attempt to gain converts. For Claiborne, antiwar activism is a missionary endeavor: "I go to Iraq as a missionary. In an age of omnipresent war, it is my hope that Christian peacemaking becomes the new face of global missions."[406]

Regarding conversion, Claiborne laments, "It's a shame that a few conservative evangelicals have a monopoly on the word *conversion*" while promoting New Monastic Schools for Conversion, which teach people how to live "converted" lifestyles of economic redistribution, peacemaking, racial justice, radical hospitality, and environmentalism in the context of New Monastic communities.[407] Regarding tithing, Claiborne argues that "church offerings were part of God's economy of redistribution" and that tithing is "unmistakably intended to be used for redistributing resources to the poor and not go toward buildings and staff for the church" (as almost every evangelical church in America teaches): an argument he made against a building expansion project at Willow Creek Community Church while serving there as a college intern.[408] Finally, he expands the evangelical notion of being "born again" to include the practice of economic justice:

> As we consider what it means to be "born again," as the evangelical jargon goes, we must ask what it means to be born again into a family in which our sisters and brothers are starving to death. Then we begin to see why rebirth and redistribution are inextricably bound up in one another.[409]

In struggles between agents with competing visions of legitimate biblical Christianity, struggles over the definitions and boundaries of the evangelical field often take center stage.

Agents who occupy dominated positions in the evangelical field are often forced to expend much energy and effort persuading other evangelicals that they are in fact evangelicals in spite of their sometimes radical opposition to dominant standpoints in the field. For some of these actors, however, the struggle to be recognized as an evangelical by other evangelicals sometimes becomes more trouble than it is worth, and over time they choose to become what the evangelical establishment already accuses them of being: something other than an evangelical. After decades of fighting for his inclusion in the evangelical field despite his progressive political views, evangelical left leader Tony Campolo has moved from worrying about a split in the evangelical movement to actively cultivating an alternative religious identity as a "Red Letter Christian" over the last several years.[410] Campolo describes Red Letter Christians as theologically evangelical but politically progressive; or, perhaps more accurately using a concept developed in this book, as Christians who occupy a contradictory cultural location between the progressive Left and the Christian Right.[411] Emergent church leader Doug Pagitt speaks of moving "beyond evangelicalism" to a "post-Protestant" Christianity.[412] Urban Monastery participants struggle over the extent to which they are willing to self-identify as "evangelical." As evangelical agents consciously or subconsciously weigh the benefits and costs of adopting particular definitions and classifications in light of current structures of power in the American religious and political fields, they adopt different strategies of definition and classification to advance their particular positions and standpoints regarding the legitimate representation of biblical Christianity in America.

Proposition Seven: The field of American evangelicalism is relatively autonomous—neither completely independent nor reducible—with respect to the American social and political fields.

Attempts to deduce the religious and political standpoints of evangelicals directly from their economic or social position are doomed to failure and distortion. Proposition seven helps us understand why:

> The field is a critical mediation between the practices of those who partake of it and the surrounding social and economic conditions. The external determinations that bear on agents situated in a given field never apply to them directly, but affect them only through the specific mediation of the specific forms and forces of the field, after having undergone a *re-structuring* that is all the more important the more autonomous a field, that is, the more it is capable of imposing its specific logic, the cumulative product of its specific history.[413]

Against the various popular and scholarly versions of status resentment theory, it is impossible to account for the religious and political position-takings of American evangelicals without reference to the specific structure, history, and cultural meanings that constitute evangelicalism as a relatively autonomous field in the larger social space that is American society. American evangelicalism has a centuries-old history of struggle whereby it has established its particular distinctiveness, its boundaries and rules of entry, its institutional networks and structures, its specific stakes and forms of capital, and its distinctive view of the world, all of which set it apart from the larger fields of American social and political fields. As it has grown in vitality and volume through struggle over time, it has accumulated a specific history and relative autonomy with respect to the American social and political fields.[414]

Evangelicalism's relative autonomy with respect to external social and political determinations is both an already achieved fact and a source of ongoing struggle. Evangelicals have their own churches and church networks, colleges and universities, businesses, media, publishing houses, political organizations, and the like—not to mention a multi-billion dollar commercial subculture that has become a perpetual fount of profit and amusement for both insiders and outsiders alike.[415] American evangelicalism has an authoritative religious text and its own well-established traditions of interpreting that text, one of the evangelical field's most robust sources of autonomy with respect to other social fields. It has a distinctive historical relationship with Catholics and mainline Protestants, with business and the arts, with elites and popular culture, with whites and ethnic minorities, and with the Republican and Democratic Parties. American evangelicalism's debates and distinctions concerning evangelism and social justice, the spiritual and social gospel, and theological individualism and communitarianism only make sense in the context of the specific social history of evangelicalism in the United States, and they carry particular significance and meaning only for those personally invested in evangelical field and its stakes.

Politicization and Autonomy

At the same time, evangelicalism's autonomy with respect to the American social and political fields is also a source of ongoing struggle. A field's autonomy is compromised when the boundaries, standpoints, and classification principles from another field begin to dominate or replace the boundaries, standpoints, and classification principles endogenous to the field in question. The struggle for autonomy with respect to politics is particularly difficult and constant. This is generally true for all fields, and it is particularly true for the evangelical field in America over the last thirty years. A general increase in the politicization of American public and civic life has been matched by the rapidly increasing politicization of evangelical religion since the rise of the Christian Right in the early 1980s.[416]

There are countless examples of the politicization of American evangelicalism in the pages above. Religious consistency theory, for example, argues that differences between the religious, moral, and political perspectives of religious conservatives and religious liberals have superseded denominational differences in a major twentieth-century restructuring of the American religious landscape.[417] Among Urban Monastery participants, the identification of evangelicalism with "rigid Republicanism" (Caleb), the unquestioned assumption that being an evangelical means voting for the Republican Party, and the categorization of not voting for Republican Party candidates as "sin" are powerful examples of the politicization of the American evangelical field:

CALEB: I found myself really angry with "the church"—I guess with evangelical America—and the simplicity or the narrow-mindedness of it. . . . All I wanted was to hear something like: "This is more difficult than 'We vote Republican because we're Christians.'" And though I heard some other things . . . overall that's what I heard.

LILITH: I voted for Bush in 2004, and I felt coerced. I felt manipulated. Spiritually manipulated: like I would be sinning if I voted for someone else. And I actually cried when I left the voting booth, because I was *so* conflicted.

Urban Monastery participants struggled intensively with internalized messages from dominant conservative evangelicals who equated conservative voting with religious faithfulness.[418] As demonstrated by the experiences of these Urban Monastery participants, the conservative politicization of the evangelical field has made it difficult for many evangelicals to challenge Christian Right position-takings without having the authenticity of their own faith be called into question. This is a clear sign of politicization and erosion of autonomy in the evangelical field.

In *The Irresistible Revolution*, Shane Claiborne and Jim Wallis are clearly aware that their strong attacks on evangelical political conservatism have the potential to call their evangelical credentials into question. Since their goal is to challenge and displace the currently dominant representation of Christianity in political and social space, it is essential that they be accepted by evangelicals as "one of us." It is also essential that evangelicals become convinced that Wallis and Claiborne's opposition to the Christian Right is *biblically based* and *religiously inspired* rather than inspired by secular liberal politics, a necessity that points to evangelicalism's ongoing (relative) autonomy. If evangelicals decided that Wallis and Claiborne were actually liberal mainline Protestants, or that they were leftist political activists trying to recruit evangelicals to the Democratic Party, Wallis and Claiborne's position-takings could be written off as outsider perspectives to be ignored. Thus, Wallis reassures readers of *The Irresistible Revolution* that Claiborne's "disaffection from America's cultural and patriotic Christianity came not from going 'secular' or 'liberal' but by plunging deeper into what the earliest Christians called 'the Way'—the way of Jesus."[419] The conservative politicization of the field makes it difficult for evangelicals to justify left-liberal position-takings without putting their integrity and identity as evangelicals at risk.

When participants in the evangelical field use a core religious concept such as sin to describe a partisan political action, when questioning the Republican Party raises questions about the authenticity of one's Christian faith, and when being an evangelical means being a "rigid Republican" from the point of view of both participants and outsiders to the evangelical field, we have strong evidence that categories of classification and perception from the American political field have partially compromised evangelicalism's autonomy with respect to American partisan politics. At the same time, however, we must be careful not to overstate the degree to which evangelicalism can be explained in terms of political categories.

For example, both the autonomy and the compromise of autonomy through politicization are evident in recent attempts by a coalition of influential emerging church, neo-monastic, evangelical left, and ecumenical Christian leaders to build momentum around a new category of religious identity for theologically conservative but politically progressive Christians, an identity they call "Red Letter Christianity."[420] In his 2008 book outlining the religious and political position-takings of *Red Letter Christians*, long-time evangelical left leader Tony Campolo introduces the new position:

> Given the general contemporary meanings and connotations ascribed to the word "Evangelical," a group of us who are speakers and authors and who share an evangelical theology got together and confessed that we have a hard time applying the label to ourselves anymore.[421]

Because of his politically progressive standpoints, Campolo has spent decades defending his identity as an evangelical against his many conservative evangelical critics. In *Red Letter Christians*, however, he announces a break with "Evangelicals" for the first time, despite affirming that "Red Letter Christians hold to the same theological convictions that define Evangelicals" and "are Christians with a very high view of Scripture."[422] Campolo and his allies argue that the conservative politicization of the word "Evangelical" has advanced to such a degree that they have been forced to search for new terminology to describe their religious identity.[423]

In doing so, Campolo and his fellow "Red Letter Christians" announce that their political disagreements with conservative evangelicals have become so significant and acute that their theological agreements are no longer enough to hold them together. This is the essence of the politicization of a religious field: when political categories and classifications trump theological ones. Campolo goes on to explain that "what differentiates Red Letter Christians from other Christians is our passionate commitment to social justice— hence, our intense involvement in politics," and he affirms Gandhi's view that "those who say religion has nothing to do with politics do not know what religion is."[424] Red Letter Christians are not arguing against the politicization of evangelical religion per se but rather against the particular form that this politicization has taken since the rise of the Christian Right,[425] a point that is emphatically punctuated by former President Bill Clinton's prominently displayed endorsement on the book's front cover.[426]

At the same time, *Red Letter Christians* demonstrates both the existence of and the ongoing struggle for evangelicalism's autonomy from the American political field. Campolo and his coalition of the dominated believe they are fighting for the liberation of evangelical Christianity from political captivity:

> I want it to be known that there are millions of us who espouse an evangelical theology, but who reject being classified as part of the Religious Right. We don't want to make Jesus into a Republican. On the other hand, we want to say loud and clear that we don't want to make Jesus into a Democrat, either. . . . Jesus refuses to fit into any of our political ideologies. . . . We are to avoid partisan politics that lead to unnecessary, unproductive, and even dangerous divisions.[427]

Asserting autonomy and transcendence over partisan politics in the name of Jesus, Campolo admonishes his fellow Red Letter Christians: "At election time when you are asked, 'Are you a Democrat or a Republican?' your answer should be, 'Name the issue!'"[428] Here and throughout the book, *Red Letter Christians* echoes the standpoint of the Urban Monastery participants, other neo-monastics, and evangelical left leaders whose voices we have listened to throughout this book, a standpoint I refer to as their contradictory cultural location with respect to the American political field.[429] The contradictory cultural location of Red Letter Christians and their allies is one of the many indicators of the evangelical field's ongoing relative autonomy from the American political field.

Autonomy and Social Structure

Proposition seven also asserts the evangelical field's relative autonomy with respect to American society as a whole. In other words, it asserts that evangelical position-takings cannot be deduced directly from the economic (i.e., class) or social (i.e., status) position of evangelical actors in the larger social space which is American society.[430] This is part of the meaning of autonomy: that the religious and political standpoints of evangelical agents cannot be explained without reference to the specific history, relational structure, and culture of the evangelical field itself. At the same time, the external struggles and transformations that structure American society do exert influence on the evangelical field. One of the primary ways they do so is by influencing the outcomes of struggles in the evangelical field. Whereas status resentment and other reductionist theories view external social and economic conditions as the *cause* or *source* of evangelical position-takings, external forces are in reality more likely to influence the evangelical field by influencing the *outcomes* (versus the origins or content) of struggles between agents in the evangelical field.[431]

For example, the rise of megachurch evangelicalism to a dominant position in the evangelical field has been greatly aided by the rising affluence of evangelicals and the ongoing suburbanization of the white middle-class in late twentieth-century America.[432] At the same time, however, the origins of megachurch evangelicalism's distinctive "seeker-sensitive" approach to evangelism and church growth lie in a suburban Chicago youth group pastor's creative response to the spiritual needs of teenagers—as seen from the point of view of a participant in the evangelical field—rather than in the external demographic changes that were occurring simultaneously.[433] The megachurch point of view itself was not caused by suburbanization and the growing affluence of evangelicals, but its rise to a dominant position in the evangelical field would almost certainly not have happened without these external changes.[434]

Struggles and transformations in the political and social field, larger demographic and economic changes, and differences in the durable dispositions of individual agents arising in part from differences in demographic background all can and do exert influence on the standpoints of agents and the structure of the evangelical field. However, these "external" conditions do not determine changes in the evangelical field directly, but only through the mediating influence of the historically accumulated structure of the evangelical field itself.[435] Furthermore, this process of restructuration means that the influence of external forces on the evangelical field is not predetermined or static but instead "may take on completely unexpected routes."[436] For instance, one of evangelicalism's signature responses to the social upheaval of the 1960s counterculture was not rejection but an unpredictable form of cultural appropriation. While the "Jesus Freaks" appropriated the fashion, music, and communal lifestyles of 1960s hippie counterculture, they also practiced an intensely apolitical, apocalyptic, and charismatic brand of Christian fundamentalism.[437] The 1960s counterculture certainly had an effect on the American evangelical field, but its influence was filtered through the pre-existing structures and meanings of the field and gave rise to strange and unexpected position-takings and transformations (such as the rise of the contemporary Christian music industry) within it.

It has become commonplace for both internal and external observers to note the many similarities between evangelical culture and American culture.[438] The American version of evangelical Christianity clearly bears the marks of national character, a reminder that the autonomy of a religious field with respect to external social and political forces is always circumscribed. Paradoxically, a primary source of the evangelical field's heteronomy with respect to American society is simultaneously an expression of its autonomy: namely, its *doxic* commitment to spreading the Christian gospel. Historic American evangelicalism's prioritization of evangelism over other forms of social engagement has resulted in a tendency for evangelicals to reproduce rather than challenge existing social divisions in the United States.[439] In chapter 2 we saw how evangelists such as D. L. Moody and Billy Graham embodied this tendency in their intentional efforts to avoid social or political actions that might distract from their primary mission of preaching the gospel of salvation to individuals. This commitment to evangelistic engagement also makes the evangelical field uniquely sensitive to external social or political changes in American society, as every new demographic, cultural, or political trend results in a new group of people who need to experience a newly contextualized embodiment of the gospel.

Moreover, the pluralistic structure of the American religious field creates an open marketplace for competition among religious groups for adherents, a fact that makes evangelicalism's own structural openness to innovation particularly well-suited to the American religious environment.[440] Evangelicalism's historic prioritization of evangelism and church growth over other forms of social engagement is thus an ongoing source of heteronomy in the evangelical field, as evangelicals respond to external cultural and political shifts in order to reach people with the gospel; relying, as Alan Wolfe observes, "on every innovative twist in the culture to reach those in need of salvation."[441] At the same time, however, the heteronomy introduced into the evangelical field through evangelistic engagement with American society is constrained by this very same act of evangelistic engagement. Calling people to an evangelical faith in Christ is part of the specific and distinctive *doxa* of the evangelical field, an expression of autonomy that reinforces evangelicalism's distinctive "subcultural identity" set apart from the world.[442]

Finally, the degree of autonomy of the evangelical field with respect to the political or social field is not fixed and static; it varies over time and across different positions in the field. The autonomy of the evangelical field is itself a source of struggle; and its present degree of autonomy is a matter of debate. On the one hand, American evangelicals' firm commitment to the authority of the Bible, their defense of traditional views of Christian orthodoxy with respect to the person and work of Jesus Christ, and the growth and vitality of distinctive religious institutions over centuries are indicators of a high degree of autonomy for the evangelical field. On the other hand, the increasing politicization of American evangelicalism and its historic tendency to mimic the social conditions of its surroundings point to significant limits in evangelicalism's autonomy with respect to the social and political structures of the United States. Either way, proposition seven asserts the impossibility of deducing evangelical standpoints directly from external structures without mangling one's analysis of evangelicalism. *What's the Matter with Kansas?* and similar work may make for entertaining reading, but its narrow political and economic reductionisms do as much to distort as to illuminate the real relationship between politics and religion in America.[443]

PART II

The Urban Monastery

A particular case that is well constructed ceases to be particular.

—PIERRE BOURDIEU[1]

Having set the historical and theoretical stage for the emergence of evangelical neo-monasticism in Part I, Part II raises the curtain on the Urban Monastery. Against the theological individualism and political conservatism of dominant expressions of evangelical Christianity in America, neo-monastic evangelicals in the Urban Monastery have constructed a distinctive theological meaning system—*holistic communitarianism*—that has given rise to new religious and political standpoints and strategies of action among Urban Monastery participants. Part II explores the Urban Monastery's theological, political, and practical embodiment of holistic communitarianism in three chapters.

Theologically, Urban Monastery participants express holistic communitarianism in their refusal to prioritize evangelism over social justice activism, and in placing relationships and community—rather than the isolated individual— at the center of religious life. In chapter 4, I draw on sociological theories of culture to show how Urban Monastery participants have developed holistic communitarianism as a distinctive theological meaning system by reinterpreting relationships of priority among core symbolic elements within traditional evangelical theology, while still remaining safely within the boundaries of *doxic* evangelical understandings of the gospel and scripture.

Politically, Urban Monastery participants express holistic communitarianism in their refusal of "single-issue" Republican Party voting and their tendency toward left-liberal economic perspectives consistent with moral cosmology theory. Chapter 5 explores Urban Monastery participants' *contradictory cultural location* with respect to the Christian Right and the progressive Left and examines the subjective and objective elements of this tension-filled cultural location. Chapter 5 offers an in-depth look at the political standpoints

and voting behavior of Urban Monastery participants and considers their relation to other communitarian religious and political movements in the
United States.

Practically, the Urban Monastery's holistic communitarianism finds expression in new ways of *organizing community* and pursuing *holistic mission* in
the world. In chapter 6, I argue that Urban Monastery participants practice a
type of innerworldly asceticism similar to Max Weber's depiction of the ascetic Protestantism, but it differs in being a *celebratory asceticism* that is communitarian rather than individualistic in emphasis. Building on chapter 4's
discussion of cultural theory, I argue that the Urban Monastery's practice of
holistic communitarianism is an example of how the vigilant application of
relatively coherent and comprehensive cultural meaning systems can become
a unifying action principle of remarkable strength and scope under the right
social conditions. Urban Monastery participants explicitly draw on core symbolic elements of their distinctive holistic communitarian theology to construct lines of individual and collective action in the world, practicing holistic
communitarianism as a relatively comprehensive and coherent strategy of
action.

Chapter 4

Belief and Meaning in an Urban Monastery

AT FIRST GLANCE, the idea of an evangelical monasticism is startling. With its deep roots in the Protestant Reformation's celebration of everyday work in a "calling" (as opposed to cloistered monastic life), along with its individualist approach to religion and social engagement, American evangelicalism would seem to be inhospitable territory for monastic movements of any variety.[2] American evangelicals have traditionally taken the Reformation motto of *sola scriptura* as proof and justification of their Bible-centered approach to Christian faith and practice, believing that their own theological and ecclesiological standpoints and strategies of action are and ought to be taken "straight from the Bible," without recourse to religious tradition or church history. Given American evangelicalism's historic anti-Catholicism, most nineteenth- and twentieth-century American evangelicals would have been offended at the idea of drawing on models—particularly Catholic models—from church history to inform current evangelical religious practices.[3] While American evangelicals have proven to be quite flexible and innovative with respect to their efforts to spread the gospel and grow churches, the establishment and growth of a neo-monastic evangelicalism remains a surprising phenomenon that both exemplifies and is contributing to recent changes in American evangelicalism and its relation to Catholicism, mainline Protestantism, other religious traditions, and American politics and society more generally.[4]

The neo-monastic movement has proliferated since the early 2000s, with thousands of young American evangelicals becoming involved in short- and long-term religious work in association with hundreds of neo-monastic communities and multiple organizational networks. One of these networks has come to be recognized as the "New Friars" because of their shared commitment to lifestyles of voluntary poverty, community, service, prayer, justice, and evangelism in the urban slums and squatter communities of global metropolises such as Bangkok, Manila, Kolkata, and Johannesburg.[5] Inspired by the Moravian, Franciscan, and Benedictine missionary orders, New Friar communities typically consist of two to six long-term workers who live alongside residents of urban slum communities to build relationships and establish micro-scale indigenous house churches, businesses, education initiatives, community organizing efforts, and community development projects in collaboration with their disadvantaged neighbors. There are over two hundred full-time workers associated with the five primary organizations constituting the New Friars network. Most are young adults from the United States with college degrees and middle-class backgrounds who "make covenants to live lifestyles of non-destitute poverty and simplicity for the sake of identification with the poor."[6] While the majority of workers in these movements are white American evangelicals, New Friar communities have non-white, non-evangelical, and non-American workers as well.[7] Organizations in the New Friars network also sponsor internships ranging from two months to two years in length for thousands more young adults exploring a call to live and work among the urban poor.[8] New Friars practitioners have been featured in *Christianity Today* cover stories and authored over a dozen books outlining their religious and political beliefs and practices.[9] While there are several small communities associated with New Friar organizations in the urban United States, the New Friars network focuses primarily on working in urban slum communities outside North America.

Besides the New Friars, at least two other networks of neo-monastic communities have formed in the United States. The popularity and recognition of these networks has much to do with the fact that they are both headlined by visible, charismatic leaders who have become internationally recognized authors, speakers, and public figures in the evangelical world. One of these networks originally called itself the New Monasticism, while the other is part of an international organization called 24–7 Prayer.[10]

The New Monasticism

In June 2004 a small group of Christian community leaders and academics gathered in North Carolina to share experiences and vision for a new expression of radical Christianity in North America. They wrote and adopted a flexible common rule for community life called the "12 Marks of the New Monasticism" intended as "a prophetic witness within the North American church that is diverse in form but characterized by the following marks":

1. Relocation to the abandoned places of empire.
2. Sharing economic resources with fellow community members and the needy among us.
3. Hospitality to the stranger.

4. Lament for racial divisions within the church and our communities, combined with the active pursuit of a just reconciliation.
5. Humble submission to Christ's body, the church.
6. Intentional formation in the way of Christ and the rule of the community, along the lines of the old novitiate.
7. Nurturing common life among members of an intentional community.
8. Support for celibate singles alongside monogamous married couples and their children.
9. Geographical proximity to community members who share a common rule of life.
10. Care for the plot of God's earth given to us, along with support for our local economies.
11. Peacemaking in the midst of violence, and conflict resolution along the lines of Matthew 18:15–20.
12. Commitment to a disciplined and contemplative life.[11]

Representatives from over seventeen communities around the country were present at the 2004 gathering, including a few older Catholic Worker, Mennonite, and Anabaptist communities, and many new ones composed mostly of young evangelicals.[12]

Since this inaugural gathering, the New Monasticism has developed literature and a loose organizational structure to support emerging New Monastic communities including conferences, websites, dozens of books and a New Monastic Library book series, and New Monastic "Schools for Conversion." Schools for Conversion are a collaborative effort led by popular New Monastic author and Rutba House cofounder Jonathon Wilson-Hartgrove, who organized the inaugural New Monastic conference in 2004 while a student at Duke Divinity School. In 2008 Wilson-Hartgrove estimated that there are over one hundred evangelical New Monastic communities around the country, most of which are less than ten years old.[13] The number of communities listed in the primary online directory of new monastic communities has grown from sixty-four in 2010 to over two hundred in 2013, the vast majority of them in the United States.[14] Over half are located in the Midwest and Northeast, while the rest are distributed throughout the West, Southwest, and Southeast United States. A majority of neo-monastic communities are evangelical, along with some Mennonite, Catholic Worker, and ecumenical Christian communities. Approximately one-third of these communities have fifteen or fewer members, another third have between roughly fifteen and fifty members, and just over a dozen communities have more than fifty members.[15] Most of the communities consist of one or several community houses in close geographical proximity to one another, usually in a poor, ethnically diverse, urban neighborhood, and meet regularly for prayer (often daily, sometimes multiple times per day), worship, meals, and various other activities ranging from environmental and peace activism to soup kitchens, community gardening, after school programs, Bible studies, alternative seminaries, and neighborhood revitalization projects.

Shane Claiborne, a founding member of The Simple Way community in Philadelphia, has become the unofficial spokesperson for evangelical neo-monasticism as a result of publishing a Christian best-selling book titled *The Irresistible Revolution: Living as an Ordinary Radical* in 2006.[16] Claiborne has become an influential figure in American evangelicalism while championing the New Monasticism in his many books and speaking tours. *The Irresistible Revolution* was published by Zondervan, a leading evangelical book publisher whose many authors include megachurch pastors Rick Warren and Rob Bell. Claiborne's speaking engagements span mainline and evangelical churches, universities, and seminaries, including major evangelical conferences such as InterVarsity Christian Fellowship's Urbana Missions Conference—regularly attended by over 20,000 evangelical college students from around the country—and the National Pastor's Convention, where thousands of evangelical church leaders gather to hear talks from dominant evangelical leaders such as Bill Hybels, Chuck Colson, and Rick Warren.[17] Thus, despite the small size of its communities and its ecumenical flavor, the New Monasticism has become widely recognized in the field of American evangelicalism, particularly influential among younger evangelicals.[18]

24–7 Prayer/Boiler Rooms

24–7 Prayer is an international, interdenominational Christian organization spanning over 99 countries, with an international leadership team based in England and national resource centers in Canada, Germany, Ireland, Spain, New Zealand, Sweden, Switzerland, the United Kingdom, and the United States.[19] It has also given rise to an international network of neo-monastic evangelical communities sometimes referred to as "Boiler Rooms."[20] The organization 24–7 Prayer works in partnership with a wide range of leading evangelical churches and organizations to establish prayer, mission, and social justice initiatives around the world. With over five million page visits since its launch in 1999, the international 24–7 Prayer website serves as a catalyst for churches, neo-monastic communities, student ministries, and other organizations to participate in periods of non-stop prayer ranging from three days to many years in their local context.[21] Typically, over half of the groups who register prayer rooms through the website are located in the United States.[22]

Pete Greig, founding leader of the international 24–7 Prayer network, has been featured on the cover of *Relevant Magazine* multiple times as one the fifty most influential leaders among young evangelicals.[23] In addition to leading the 24–7 Prayer international leadership team, Greig is Director of Prayer for the influential Holy Trinity Brompton Church in London and its internationally acclaimed Alpha Course, a ten-week introduction to Christianity attended by over thirteen million people around the world.[24] He is also the author of numerous books including *Red Moon Rising: How 24–7 Prayer is Awakening a Generation* (the story of 24–7 Prayer's founding) and *Punk Monk: New Monasticism and the Ancient Art of Breathing*, which explains the origins and vision of 24–7 Prayer's neo-monastic communities. Andy Freeman—coauthor of *Punk Monk*—is a pastor, political activist, and web editor for the Christian Socialist Party in England who describes himself as "much too left wing for any of the mainstream parties in the UK."[25] Freeman led the team that established 24–7 Prayer's first neo-monastic community in Reading, England, in 2001.[26] He estimates that the international 24–7 Prayer network helps coordinate over fifty evangelical neo-monastic communities including the Urban Monastery, one of the first and largest of the new evangelical neo-monastic communities in the United States.[27]

Origins of an Urban Monastery

"It wasn't our intention to plant an Urban Monastery," Alex tells me with characteristic energy and intensity, his bright piercing eyes and fine features dramatically complemented by a sharp goatee and short, jet black hair. "We kind of got dragged into it by God." The young founders of the Urban Monastery first met at an unaccredited Bible school hosted by an influential, suburban, charismatic evangelical megachurch with a strong emphasis on prayer. Caleb and Mina were recently married childhood sweethearts from the West who spent months traveling internationally before relocating to the Midwest to attend the school. Alex came from the East Coast; Brad and Mindy from the Midwest. None had any intention of remaining in the city or pioneering a new religious community. "We just liked hanging out together," recalled Alex, "you couldn't keep us apart. Eating a meal together, we'd pray most mornings together, we were *really* inspired by the early church [as described in Acts 2 and 4]." Caleb concurs: "I think we unintentionally just looked at Acts 2 together and said, 'This sounds amazing. This is what we want.' So through our friendships we just explored what that meant. At first it wasn't super intentional. We were intentional in prayer together, but that was about it. Intentional in having fun! We just spent a lot of time together." "We really had no strong agenda or sense of what we were going to be doing with our lives. But it definitely didn't include 'church planting!'" added Mina. Eventually, these five founding members of the Urban Monastery found a foreclosed former drug house in the city and decided to move in together: "When we moved into the house together, that was the beginning of the idea that something could actually be built from our friendships and what God was doing. It just evolved naturally. We realized: we're living together, we're doing life together, we move into this house, and as we're *being* the church, suddenly all these people started gathering at our home. . . . One thing led to another, and that's kind of how we began the Urban Monastery." "When the house came up," adds Caleb, "we were like, 'This sounds like what they would have done in Acts.' . . . And out of that I would say—at the core of the Urban Monastery—is just these simple friendships. And hopefully that's being multiplied."

The charismatic evangelical megachurch where the Urban Monastery's eventual founders met had a reputation as an exciting and innovative place: according to Caleb, the church, "really felt and appeared like the cutting edge of Christianity." When Mina, Caleb, Brad, Mandy, and Alex arrived at the school, its host church was in the midst of launching a new "cutting edge" prayer ministry that involved a change in vision and leadership. "We found ourselves in the midst of these two extremes," said Caleb, "prayer versus mission, essentially, is how I would divide it." As various parties took sides and aligned themselves with one or the other of these "two extremes," Alex, Caleb, Mina, Brad, and Mindy met and became friends with 24–7 Prayer founder Pete Greig in 2003, first at a conference in England and then in the United States while he was on sabbatical. Alex and company resonated deeply with Pete's vision and experience as the "accidental leader of a worldwide prayer movement" involving "this beautiful fusion of friendship and mission and prayer." "He talked about friendship, he didn't take himself too seriously . . . and he talked about marrying prayer and justice and mission together," Alex recalled. As they became friends, Alex and company had the sense that "this is already us. . . . This is the lifestyle we want to live." In conversations with Pete and Andy Freeman about Celtic monasticism, Mina and the other Urban Monastery cofounders found a model that resonated with their desire to transcend religious antinomies between sacred and secular, spiritual and mundane, prayer and mission, work and rest, and spirituality and social engagement: "I think the basic framework that I agree with is this Celtic way . . . that's not super focused on grabbing people in an attractional style of doing church. But it's holistic. It's God in *everything*—not a sacred–secular split . . . in a community that's fluid and natural" (Mina).[28] Caleb concurred:

CALEB: The connection to the Celts was really attractive to us. We love what it looked like for St. Patrick to set up these communities that had a real monastic quality and yet also a strong sense of outreach and outwardness. Not wanting to hole up, but wanting to have some seclusion as well; have that sacred space. I think one of the things that also really drew us originally was the rhythmic lifestyle. I think that probably has been one of the biggest challenges as we've navigated through our idealism of what the Urban Monastery would look like. Like, "Ok, how does this urban monastic ideal work in modern Western society?"

Opposing the "attractional" megachurch style and the split between "two extremes" of prayer and mission in their local ministry field, sensing a challenge from God to "get out of the suburbs" and "stop using the city for your experiments" (Caleb) and seeking to live out a more "holistic" expression of Christian spirituality, community, and practice than they saw around them, the group of friends started having more intentional conversations, meals, and prayer gatherings focused on the possibility of pioneering a new urban monastic community in their city.

By this time the five friends had launched a year-long school of spiritual formation that welcomed young adults from around the world into the "holistic . . . way of life that we were already living" (Alex) in their intentional community house. Several of these students eventually became significant leaders in the Urban Monastery, including Kieren, a web developer from Scotland who teaches and does IT work for the Urban Monastery, and Devon, the Urban Monastery's hospitality guru who came to the school after modeling stints in New York and Europe. Other young leaders soon joined the emerging community. Lilith, a fine artist with an Ivy League M.F.A., whose parents were musical pioneers and commune members in the Jesus People movement, met Alex after giving a lecture on her work and her perspectives on the relationship between Christian spirituality and the arts:

LILITH: I did this lecture, and they were nice people. I didn't think I would see them again. But then through a series of circumstances I ended up hearing more about this Urban Monastery idea through Alex. And part of what made it stick in my mind was this community-centered thrust, hospitality, prayer, and then *such* a regard for creativity. And it seemed to me with my whole history and the way I grew up and the lifestyle I was leading at the time that—if there was anything that was a natural fit—it would be something like this. And certainly since it was almost kind of genetically embedded in my choices and character and expectations of life; that it would be fairly easy to help pioneer something like that. . . . So it started to be something I thought about. Then it started to be something I prayed about. And then as clearly as I'd ever heard anything I heard God say: "Go." And there are times when the only way you'll know if it was God's voice or your own imagination is to go! So I did it. And it's been great.

Lilith soon relocated to join the emerging Urban Monastery, buying a large, cheap house in the city whose rooms were quickly filled with young adults connected to the community. A thriving Urban Monastery Arts Collective would eventually grow up around Lilith's spiritual and artistic vision, unfolding "naturally . . . through relationships," in much the same way that Brad, Mandy, Mina, Caleb, and Alex describe the origins of the Urban Monastery. The Urban Monastery building itself was the result of Lilith's need for an art studio and Alex's need to find a space that could house the first cohort of students for their new school of spiritual formation. After a "desperate" search, Alex and Lilith finally found what has become the Urban Monastery's primary physical space just four days before the first students' arrival. Lilith's friend Anja, who met Alex and company while working as a ministry leader in a discipleship training school in another state, also sensed a strong call from God to relocate and join the emerging Urban Monastery. Anja soon became a member of the Urban Monastery's core leadership team and a national leader in the Urban Monastery's prayer and community network. Buoyed by these arrivals and encouraged by Pete Greig and other local spiritual elders, the Urban Monastery was officially launched in 2005.

We see many of neo-monastic evangelicalism's central themes—and some of the central themes of Part II of this book—reflected in embryonic form in the Urban Monastery's origin story. Stories of the "unplanned" and "unintentional" origins of the Urban Monastery—growing naturally out of "simple friendships" and "friends dreaming and praying together"—reflect neo-monastic evangelicals' emphasis on the "organic" emergence of authentic spiritual community as opposed to the "professionalized" emergence of strategically planned and demographically targeted megachurch franchises (Caleb, Mina, Alex).[29] The "seeds of the kingdom" out of which the Urban Monastery grew were communal and relational: the "natural overflow of loving relationships" (Alex, Mina) rather than the solitary dream of an ambitious individual or religious entrepreneur. The origin story of the Urban

Monastery thus reflects the origin story in the biblical book of Genesis as seen from the perspective of the Urban Monastery participants' Trinitarian theology, as we will see below.

Along with this communitarian theme, we see the Urban Monastery growing out of a desire for a "holistic" expression of Christian spirituality that seeks to overcome perceived oppositions between prayer and mission, sacred and secular, work and rest, spiritual and mundane, evangelism and social justice, which the Urban Monastery's founders saw at work in their local religious field and American evangelicalism more generally. We will explore each of these themes as we see them expressed in the Urban Monastery's religious and political standpoints and strategies of action in detail throughout the next three chapters.

Participants in an Urban Monastery

What sort of person becomes involved in an Urban Monastery? Most noticeably, they are young. A demographic survey administered at the Urban Monastery's Sunday worship gathering confirms what ordinary observation suggests: that the vast majority of Urban Monastery participants are under the age of 35. Roughly one-third (31 percent) are college-aged: between 18 and 23 years old. Over half (61 percent) are between the ages of 24 and 34. Only a handful of people are over the age of 50. Most are single (63 percent) and less than one-fifth (17 percent) have children. Over half (53 percent) of Urban Monastery participants have a bachelor's degree or more education, with 15 percent either in graduate school or already in possession of a graduate degree. Over 90 percent have spent at least some time in college and just over one-fifth (23 percent) are current college students. An unusually high percentage (29 percent) of Urban Monastery participants are artists, musicians, art students, or employed in an arts-related job, while 15 percent work in full-time Christian ministry. The large number of full and part-time Christian workers reflects the Urban Monastery's position of influence in a national network of neo-monastic communities.

In comparison to American evangelicals as whole, Urban Monastery participants are younger, more educated, more likely to be single, and have unusual job profiles, with an unusually large percentage of artists and religious workers. Over half of Urban Monastery participants have at least a bachelor's degree, compared to 21 percent of all evangelicals between the ages of 21–45.[30] While less than 15 percent of all American evangelicals in America are under the age of 30, 81 percent of Urban Monastery participants are under 30.[31] The Urban Monastery is located in the urban core of a

major metropolitan area, while less than a quarter of all conservative Protestants live in major cities.[32] However, just over half (52 percent) of Urban
Monastery participants grew up in rural areas, mirroring evangelicals as a
whole. The Urban Monastery also mirrors American evangelicalism in
terms of its racial (approximately 90 percent white) and gender (approximately 60 percent female) composition.[33] A significant majority (80 percent)
of Urban Monastery participants grew up in at least nominally Christian
homes, although almost one-fifth had no prior religious background before
becoming part of the Urban Monastery. Of those coming from Christian
families, two-thirds described their religious background as either evangelical (43 percent) or fundamentalist (24 percent) or both, while roughly one-
quarter (27 percent) grew up in either Catholic or mainline Protestant
homes. Half of those who grew up in Catholic or mainline Protestant families described their parents as nominal Christians who attended church
infrequently.

As discussed at length in chapter 3, innovation in social fields is often
driven by their youngest and most recent entrants, particularly when those
entrants possess specific forms of capital that can help them exert influence
in the field.[34] The demographic profile of the Urban Monastery is what one
might expect an *avant-garde* evangelical religious community to look like.
They are young, urban, well-educated, and possess relatively large amounts of
cultural capital in comparison to other evangelicals by virtue of their educational and artistic credentials. While not possessing formal seminary degrees, the Urban Monastery's cofounders were mentored by internationally
recognized evangelical leaders. The demographic profile of the Urban Monastery is thus similar to other neo-monastic and emerging church communities
in North America, which are typically composed of well-educated, middle-
class, mostly white young adults who tend to form relatively small but highly
committed religious communities in urban contexts.[35]

Although Urban Monastery participants fit the profile of an avant-garde
religious community for the most part, they appear to lack one key ingredient
common to successful pioneering agents in the religious or artistic fields: a
distance from necessity born of independent wealth or other sources of capital
that enable the pursuit of time-intensive creative action bereft of immediate
financial rewards.[36] As we will examine at length in chapter 6, Urban Monastery participants pour an enormous amount of time and energy into individual and collective expressions of their holistic communitarian vision of
Christian spirituality. Praying around the clock, hosting a steady stream of
travelers, pilgrims, and homeless neighbors, participating in multiple nested

micro-communities within the larger community of the Urban Monastery, and pursuing religious or artistic vocations (as nearly half of Urban Monastery participants do) all require large amounts of time and resources that are difficult to find within the typical lifestyle structure of a middle-class American adult. However, Urban Monastery participants do not typically come from elite families of financial ease, nor do they hold high-paying professional jobs that could generate the financial and temporal autonomy to do artistic or religious work for free (or for very little). How, then, are Urban Monastery participants able to get by while living their unorthodox, time-intensive religious and creative lifestyles?

Urban Monastery participants' ability to secure the avant-garde's necessary distance from necessity hinges on a combination of structural demographic characteristics and intentional cultural practices derived from their distinctive holistic communitarian spirituality. Demographically, Urban Monastery participants are much more likely to be young and single than other evangelicals or the general population, affording them more temporal and financial flexibility than older, mid-career, mid-family adults. And though they do not typically hail from upper-class families, they are also unlikely to come from disadvantaged families. Most Urban Monastery participants possess the skills, habits, and opportunities typical of the American middle-class, which, in global-historical context, is very much a privileged social class. Thus, despite their rejection of the American Dream and the individualistic pursuit of prestige, wealth, or power for its own sake, Urban Monastery participants tend to possess sufficient intellectual, social, economic, and educational resources to procure decent jobs and living situations. Many of the artists and religious workers in the Urban Monastery also hold part-time jobs as baristas, gallery managers, or artisanal trade workers (painting, carpentry, furniture construction, textiles, music, photography, etc.) that, in combination with religiously motivated intentional practices such as living communally in low-income neighborhoods, provide enough money for daily life while preserving free time for creative work and spiritual life in the Urban Monastery.

A large number of Urban Monastery participants live together in community houses within walking distance of the central Urban Monastery building, which is situated in a highly affordable transitional urban neighborhood that straddles the unofficial dividing line between white and black neighborhoods in the city. This close proximity to one another enables Urban Monastery participants to easily share time, space, and resources on a daily basis, creating a constant circulation of cars and bikes, meals and groceries, blankets and guest bedrooms, art supplies and job opportunities, and other personal resources throughout the community. Geographical proximity also facilitates community and collective action. Community meals and parties, informal art and music performances, prayer gatherings and book discussions, community service projects and holistic mission activities are ubiquitous—creating a low-cost, high-density, geographically strategic, place-based environment for the expression of creative avant-garde Christian community.[37]

Although living simply in intentional community houses of close geographical proximity in low-income neighborhoods makes it possible for Urban Monastery participants to live their avant-garde lives without the benefit of substantial economic resources;[38] their decisions about where and how to live are not merely pragmatic decisions driven by economic necessity. There are other ways to secure the avant-garde's necessary distance from necessity. Rather, Urban Monastery participants live their avant-garde lifestyles as a matter of faith and desire. Urban Monastery participants find great religious, moral, and aesthetic satisfaction in living simply, living in community, living in disadvantaged urban neighborhoods, and pursuing their religious and creative visions together to the fullest. They believe that people are, literally, made for living in loving community with one another; for creative expression; for the pursuit of justice, truth, and beauty together; for both worldly activity and spiritual ecstasy; and for the pursuit of God above all else. They sincerely believe in the superiority of spiritual, rather than material, rewards—in both the Bourdieusian and everyday evangelical meanings of those words. Their lives reflect these beliefs, which may be summed up (inelegantly, perhaps, but efficiently) under the rubric of *holistic communitarianism*.

Holistic Communitarianism in an Urban Monastery

The distinctive theological and political standpoints being developed by Urban Monastery participants and other neo-monastic evangelicals can be summarized using the concept of holistic communitarianism. As we consider how the theology, politics, social organization, and lifestyles of Urban Monastery participants embody holistic communitarianism in the next three chapters, it will be helpful to begin with some working definitions of what it means for a religious community to be *holistic*, and what it means to be *communitarian*. We may begin by listening to what neo-monastic evangelicals themselves say about the matter. Sitting outside her favorite café on a sunny spring day, Anja—with bright red hair, stud nose ring, and aqua green shirt and earrings matching her large sparkling green eyes—explains to me what exactly she finds attractive about how the Urban Monastery understands and practices Christian spirituality:

ANJA: One is the focus on a very Trinitarian understanding of God . . . the interplay of loving relationship between the Father, Son, and Spirit, and what that models for us in terms of what love and community and family really is: such as preference for one another, or delight and cherishing one another. I think that is a starting place for our theology and understanding of who God is, and then who we are, and then what we have to extend to the world. So I would say that's the first thing.

The second would be . . . the marriage of things that often aren't married together in the world—like the supposedly sacred and the supposedly secular, or the mundane with the spiritual—the marriage or indistinguishability [sic] of those things. Or holding in tension the values of prayer and spiritual journey with God, on the one hand, and mission and justice, on the other, for instance: the very "inward breath" of prayer with the "outward breath" of mission and justice in the world. And then add to that discipleship, and hospitality, and the arts and creativity: that God is inherently creative and that there are many ways to express who we are and who he is and how we interact with him. To me that's just a really whole and beautiful idea of how we can follow Jesus and of what [Jesus] models for us. Something whole: marrying things that aren't always held together in balance or in tension. . . . Living a rhythm of rest, work, prayer, mission—throughout the course of our normal days, weeks, months, year—individually and corporately. Both of those things are things I've loved about how the Urban Monastery works. So I'll live my life like this from now on. Wherever I go, whatever I do, I will attempt—because it's not always easy—to live according to these ideas and rhythms.

Anja's words closely resemble the vision presented in the book *Punk Monk*, where neo-monastic communities are described as being "holistic, not fragmented. We seek to live integrated lives that balance work, rest and prayer sustainably and that engage with society politically, economically and spiritually."[39] For neo-monastic evangelicals, being "holistic" is about overcoming a host of false antinomies and antagonisms, across multiple social domains (religious, political, cultural, and economic), that have come to define Christianity in the United States, and evangelicalism, in particular: such as the supposed oppositions between sacred and secular space, between the spiritual and social gospel, between evangelism and social justice activism, between

personal and social transformation, between prayer and activism, and between the politics of poverty/inequality and the politics of the family.

Neo-monastic communities also aim to be "corporate, not individualistic."[40] *Communitarian* religious communities such as the Urban Monastery
place relationships and communal practices, rather than the autonomous individual, at the center of religious life. Whereas dominant expressions of
twentieth-century American evangelicalism have emphasized evangelism
and personal piety as the hallmarks of faithful religion, communitarian religious communities believe that spiritual formation and human flourishing
are only possible in the context of community and authentic relationship.
Within the Urban Monastery, this communitarian ethos is undergirded by a
strongly Trinitarian understanding of God as a being whose intrinsic nature
involves the "interplay of loving relationships" among three distinct but inseparable Persons.[41] Participants in neo-monastic communities also tend to
be communitarians as defined by moral cosmology theory, believing that
social problems require state and community-based solutions that include all
members of a social group—as opposed to a libertarian perspective in which
individuals are left to fend for themselves and bear no responsibility for
others' social and economic well-being.[42]

Neo-monastic evangelicals have constructed their holistic communitarian meaning system in an attempt to transcend what they perceive to be false
antinomies and antagonisms—such as the antinomy between the spiritual
and social gospel—inherited from the religious past. However, in so doing,
they also create new antagonisms and oppositions, such as the opposition between "small, authentic, participatory" spiritual communities like the Urban
Monastery and "large, superficial, bureaucratic/professional" religious organizations like the prototypical evangelical megachurch. Some of these
newly created oppositions are no less "false" than the antinomies they seek to
overcome. For example, neo-monastic evangelicals often define themselves
in opposition to megachurch evangelicalism by describing evangelical megachurches as places that perpetuate a sacred/secular split in the lifestyles of
individual believers. They argue that by prioritizing an event-driven, profes-
sionally organized, once a week religious experience on Sundays, evangelical
megachurches foster a dualistic lifestyle that concentrates sacred "religious"
activity to a single day (or even hour) while leaving the rest of the week's activities in the realm of the "mundane" secular world. However, one could just
as easily argue that the whole *raison d'être* of megachurch evangelicalism is an
attempt to eliminate the sacred/secular divide in individual religious experience through strategies such as designing church buildings that resemble
the everyday world of secular business, crafting contemporary sermons and

worship music that connect with ordinary non-religious "seekers," and organizing lifestyle and interest-based small groups for attendees that range from "sacred" religious activities (such as Bible studies and prayer groups) to mundane "secular" ones (such as rock-climbing groups and financial management seminars).[43] In their attempts to transcend "false" dichotomies from the past through holistic communitarianism, neo-monastic evangelicals create new antinomies and oppositions that will themselves be challenged by other agents or movements in the evangelical field in the future.

The Urban Monastery and American Evangelicalism

The Urban Monastery's holistic communitarianism is a significant departure from dominant expressions of historic and contemporary American evangelicalism. Participants in the Urban Monastery are well aware that they are not like other American evangelicals, and they are happy about it. They referred variously to fundamentalist churches, evangelical churches, megachurches, and other Christian communities they had experienced as "traditional" churches that they were dissatisfied with for various reasons. Some of them had very strong reactions against traditional evangelical groups and told vivid stories about why they did not fit into those communities. Elle, who converted to Christianity while in high school, recalled being embarrassed by her pre-conversion sexual history and feeling alienated from the evangelical groups she tried to join as an undergraduate university student:

ELLE: There was a Campus Crusade for Christ group on campus, and I was like: "That's a terrible name!" The first time I went to Campus Crusade for Christ they played this game called "I Never." There were hundreds of freshman kids at this meeting. Someone would say, "Run around the circle if you've gotten a tattoo," and because I'd gotten a tattoo, I'd run around the circle. So out of all these hundreds of kids, this one girl yells, "I've never had sex!" So I take off running, and I'm the *only* one running, out of hundreds of kids! And I was like, "Oh my Gosh. I don't belong here. What am I doing here? I miss my stoner friends." So I just ran out of the circle and just kept running and was like, "I'm done." So church, to me, I did not fit in. And I was judgmental. I thought these people were hypocrites.

Jessica, an art school graduate and part-time gallery director who is new to the Urban Monastery, talks about distancing herself from megachurch evangelicalism among her non-Christian friends, "because it's better they think

I'm going to a cult than going to a megachurch . . . a cult might be more genuine!" In the secular urban art scene where Jessica works, being a Christian conjures up negative images of suburban megachurches marked by stifling conservatism and conformity.

Caleb, one of the Urban Monastery's founding leaders, has become so disenchanted with evangelical Christianity in America that he has at times refused to use those labels to describe his religious identity, telling people that "I'm not a Christian; I'm a follower of Jesus." Like Jessica, Elle, and other Urban Monastery participants, Caleb has cultivated a distinctive identity that is set apart from dominant expressions of American evangelicalism, and he is well aware of the non-traditional and avant-garde nature of the Urban Monastery with respect to the larger evangelical community:

CALEB: I just talked to my brother and he mentioned something that Rob Bell had said that was really controversial. And I just said, "Really? I didn't know he was getting into any controversy." And he laughed and was like, "You're in such a liberal Christianity Caleb, you have no idea! Rob Bell looks like the light stuff for you or something."

INTERVIEWER: How did that hit you, the comment about Rob Bell? How did you process that?

CALEB: I was just surprised that he was controversial! So many people told me about *Velvet Elvis*: that's the only Rob Bell book I've ever read. And I felt that it was—not in an arrogant way by *any* means—but I thought, "Yeah, it's good [shrugging shoulders in unimpressed, half-hearted interest]. I'm right with you." But my mom read it and it was just revolutionary for her! And so did my brother. It was really impacting. . . . I didn't think Rob Bell was that out there. Except maybe that he has a book called *Sex God* [laughing facetiously]. A lot of that stuff is just a front to offend religious people just for the sake of offending them. That's probably what Jesus would be like anyway.

Rob Bell is a *New York Times* best-selling evangelical author and megachurch pastor associated with the emerging church. From Caleb's perspective, Rob Bell's religious point of view is not seen as being particularly controversial—a perspective that his conservative evangelical brother viewed as representing "such a liberal Christianity" that a controversial figure like Rob Bell "looks like light stuff."[44]

As I argued at length in chapter 3, Urban Monastery participants' and other neo-monastic evangelicals' religious and political standpoints are constructed in (often oppositional) relation to other positions in the field of

American evangelicalism. However, while they have many strong critiques of dominant expressions of American evangelicalism, Urban Monastery participants are also careful not to sound overly harsh, negative, or dismissive of their evangelical kin. They are careful in their criticism, eager to avoid the rancorous, sectarian, and self-righteous tone that has characterized much of historic conservative Protestantism in America. In an extended conversation on the matter with Caleb over several pints of brown ale at a popular neighborhood pub, Caleb told me:

CALEB: One thing I fear would be the Urban Monastery, or the neo-monastic movement, or me or my wife or my closest friends, developing any sense of exclusiveness, like: "We've got the gospel cornered. We've got Jesus down, and other people don't." . . . I fear the gap [with other evangelicals] broadening, and that's why I'm so grateful for this pastor [a politically conservative pastor that Caleb debated with throughout the 2008 presidential elections]. We'll have exchanges, and I think in the end we agreed to disagree, but it was really honorable and meaningful for both of us.

Caleb and other Urban Monastery participants' critiques of other evangelical positions followed a common script—like Mina's below—in which their various criticisms of dominant expressions of American evangelism were joined by qualifying remarks that granted respect to other groups and acknowledged limitations in their own position. On the one hand, Urban Monastery leaders such as Mina and Caleb have strong convictions about not reproducing the dominant expressions of evangelical belief and practice of which they are critical. On the other hand, their words consistently expressed humility and reflexivity with respect to their own viewpoints and practices:

MINA: I feel like God's kept us on this hard line to not reproduce what we've always seen [in traditional and megachurch evangelicalism] . . . not just leaning into a consumptive form of church that's about receiving from professional ministers, and not becoming a removed subculture that has no relevance to society. But I see also, because some of us have such a history with traditional, formal ways of doing church, that you can quickly lean into doing what you've always known and building things the way they have always been built. I'm not saying that because I think we have some corner on how you *should* build or a better idea of how you should do church, but it's just something that God's convinced *us* of how we should build. It's not diminishing other expressions of church.

Of the hundreds of comments Urban Monastery participants made that were critical of dominant expressions of American evangelicalism, not one was made without some form of sincerely expressed qualification and mention of a positive attribute of the people, institutions, or movements being criticized. Urban Monastery participants are critical of many aspects of American evangelicalism; sometimes to the point of wanting to dissociate completely from any sort of evangelical identity. Yet they are also quick to acknowledge limitations in their own positions and work hard not to sound arrogant, closed-minded, or dismissive of those with whom they disagree.

Urban Monastery participants and other neo-monastic evangelicals actively struggle against dominant expressions of American evangelicalism in their attempts to construct alternative theological and political standpoints that they believe are more faithful and legitimate representations of biblical Christianity in America. However, despite their struggles against dominant positions in the field—struggles that sometimes lead them to question whether they are actually evangelical Christians at all—Urban Monastery participants remain firmly committed to the core elements of evangelical orthodoxy. In their understanding of the gospel, their commitment to biblical authority, and their belief in the importance of evangelism, Urban Monastery participants affirm the *doxa* of the American evangelical field while simultaneously challenging dominant positions within it; constructing holistic communitarianism as an alternative theological meaning system that challenges the theological individualism and political conservatism of dominant expressions of evangelical Christianity in America. In order to understand how they have done so, we must take a step back into the world of cultural theory, which will provide some more theoretical tools for understanding how religious and cultural meaning is constructed in the field of American evangelicalism, and how it can be transformed.

Studying Evangelical Religious Culture

Chapter 1 introduced two competing theories of how theological beliefs are related to the social, economic, and political attitudes of American evangelicals and religious believers more generally: namely, religious consistency and moral cosmology theory. While religious consistency and moral cosmology theory disagree about the exact nature of how theological and political standpoints are related, they are united in asserting that religious beliefs influence how people think about social and economic issues. In other words, they agree that religious culture—which includes moral perspectives concerning the good and how to know it—can and does influence the social, economic, and political standpoints of religious agents. Moral cosmology theory, in particular, argues that being a theological individualist or theological communitarian leads one to think differently about sexuality, gender, the nature of the family, economic inequality, racial inequality, and the government's role in addressing each of these matters.[45] While moral cosmology theory provides strong evidence that these alternative theological orientations influence the political attitudes of religious believers around the world, it is silent about the extent to which theological individualism and theological communitarianism has any effect on action.

Other studies of American evangelicals have examined how the cultural tools evangelicals use to make sense of the world influence their individual and collective strategies of action. For example—drawing on Ann Swidler's influential theory of culture as a "toolkit" that agents use to construct strategies of action[46]—Christian Smith and Michael O. Emerson argue in *Divided by Faith* that white American evangelicals' "accountable freewill individualism" limits their ability to pursue structural solutions to racial and economic inequality.[47] According to their argument, the "religiously based cultural tools" from which white evangelicals construct strategies of action to address racial problems are unremittingly individualistic, relational, and otherworldly. This leads white evangelicals to reject structural diagnoses and solutions to racial problems and limits their ability to effectively address problems of racial inequality.[48] In *American Evangelicalism: Embattled and Thriving*, Smith argues further that the subcultural tools white evangelicals use to address economic inequality are similarly limited by their "a priori relationalism," which leads them to consistently address social problems through a "personal influence strategy" that eschews structural solutions in favor of voluntary, individualist, and spiritual strategies of individual and collective action.[49]

While Swidler's approach to cultural analysis is helpful for understanding how cultural meanings are put into use by individuals in their daily lives, it leaves us with unanswered questions about how cultural meaning systems themselves are constructed, reproduced, and transformed. Treating culture as a pre-existing toolkit that people draw on to construct practical strategies of action can result in a static, black-box conception of culture that "ignores the internal structure of meaning systems, indeed the content of meaning systems" and "assumes that symbolic elements—and what they mean—do not change."[50] Against this view, culture theorist Anne E. Kane argues:

> Because meaning is embodied in the specific arrangements of symbols in cultural models, and cultural models are the first point of reference when people interpret experience, these structures should be the initial theoretical and analytic focus in studying meaning construction.[51]

Rather than treating cultural meaning systems and the symbolic elements that constitute them as a static stock of resources that agents draw on to construct ad hoc strategies of action, structuralist theories of culture such as Kane's argue that in order to understand culture and its influence, we must pay attention to the internal structure and interpretation of cultural (in our case, theological) meaning systems themselves.

Two Approaches to Cultural Analysis

Contemporary sociological approaches to cultural analysis thus fall into two broadly opposing camps with respect to their view on where cultural meaning is located and how it is constructed and used by social agents.[52] Structuralist theories of culture, on the one hand, emphasize the internal symbolic structure of cultural meaning systems and their interpretation by social agents as the primary locus of meaning construction and transformation, which in turn shapes individual and collective action in specific historical and material contexts.[53] Structuralist theories of culture emphasize the "semi-coherent" and "relatively autonomous" nature of cultural meaning systems,[54] whose influence on individual and collective action is neither reducible to nor completely independent of social structure, material interests, historical events, or the concrete "practices" of individuals or groups.[55] Since meaning is located in the relation between symbols in the symbolic structures of meaning systems—which are relatively autonomous with respect to both social structure and to how cultural meanings are "used" or enacted in concrete practices—structuralist theories of culture view the content of meaning systems and their interpretation as analytically indispensable elements for understanding how cultural meanings are constructed, transformed, and deployed in social action.[56]

Pragmatist theories of culture, on the other hand, "treat meaning as emerging from the contingencies of individual and collective action" and emphasize the multiple, fragmented, and often contradictory ways in which culture is put to use by social agents:[57]

A culture is not a unified system that pushes action in a consistent direction. Rather, it is more like a "tool kit" or repertoire from which actors select differing pieces for constructing lines of action . . . all real cultures contain diverse, often conflicting symbols, rituals, stories, and guides to action.[58]

Pragmatist theories of culture—such as Ann Swidler's influential work— focus on how individuals and groups draw on different elements from their available cultural repertoires to construct strategies of action in everyday life. These cultural repertoires typically consist of multiple, fragmented, and often contradictory cultural "vocabularies" drawn from various sources (such as "self-help" literature, political ideologies, religious beliefs, etc.).[59]

Although Swidler's toolkit conception of culture emphasizes the multiple, fragmentary, and often contradictory nature of the cultural repertoires people use to understand their world and construct strategies of action within it, she acknowledges that certain types of cultural "modalities" are more coherent, unified, and explicit than others.[60] Specifically, ideologies—which Swidler defines as "articulated, self-conscious belief and ritual systems aspiring to offer a unified answer to problems of social action"—are a "product of continuous, explicit construction" and have the ability to "influence action in powerful, direct ways."[61] This is particularly true in the context of "unsettled" lives or periods of social change:

> Culture takes a more explicit, coherent form when people are reorganizing their strategies of action or developing new ones. . . . In such periods, ideologies—explicit, articulated, highly organized systems of meaning (both political and religious)—establish new languages and styles for new strategies of action. When people are learning new ways of organizing individual and collective life, practicing unfamiliar habits until they become familiar, then doctrine, symbol, and ritual directly shape their action. . . . Such overt, ideological cultures might well be called "systems." While not perfectly consistent, they aspire to offer unified answers to questions of how human beings should live.[62]

Given that "trying to live out of a coherent worldview is especially characteristic of ideologically ordered communities such as Christian sects or radical political movements"[63]—in our case neo-monastic evangelicals—treating religious culture as a static stock of fixed theological meanings and religious practices while studying American evangelicals would be a mistake. Rather, because evangelicals take the meaning-content of theological systems seriously, and because the transformation of theological meanings is a primary way that evangelical groups develop their distinctive points of view on religious and political matters, studying evangelicals requires adopting a structural-hermeneutic perspective on culture that takes the content of cultural meaning systems seriously as a source of action.[64]

According to the structural-hermeneutic approach to cultural analysis, meaning arises from the interpretation of symbols and their relation to each other in a cultural system.[65] While the notion of a cultural "system" can elicit misleading notions of culture as a fully determined, logically consistent idea-tional structure, we may define cultural meaning systems simply as "cogni-tive schema intersubjectively shared by a social group";[66] a definition that makes no assumptions about the comprehensiveness, logical consistency, or inconsistency of any given cultural meaning system. The holistic communi-tarianism of new monastic evangelicals and the theological individualism of dominant expressions of historic American evangelicalism are examples of different types of theological meaning systems among evangelicals.

Symbols are the building blocks of cultural meaning systems.[67] Jesus, the Trinity, the gospel, the cross, evangelism, and sin are examples of religious symbols of particular importance to evangelical Christians.[68] Because the relationship between an object and its symbolic meaning is metaphoric in nature, symbols are polysemous, meaning that they can have multiple mean-ings that can change over time as social agents in concrete historical situa-tions (re)interpret symbolic meanings while using them to understand and act in the world.[69] The reinterpretation of symbolic elements in a cultural system is one mechanism whereby the meaning of cultural systems can be transformed. Another is by changing relationships of priority among one or more symbolic elements in a cultural system. Because "symbolic meaning is created by the relationship of one symbol to another" in any given cultural system, "alteration of one symbolic element [or altering the relation between symbolic elements] transforms the whole."[70]

Holistic Communitarianism, Theological Individualism, and the Transformation of Evangelical Religious Culture

Urban Monastery participants have developed holistic communitarianism as a distinctive theological meaning system that simultaneously challenges domi-nant expressions of historic American evangelicalism while at the same time adhering to core elements of evangelical *doxa*. They have done so by *rearranging relationships of priority* among key symbolic elements in the structure of evan-gelical theology. Whereas dominant expressions of twentieth-century Ameri-can evangelicalism have prioritized evangelism, personal salvation, individual moral transformation, and the individual's relationship with God as the hall-marks of faithful religion and the solution to social problems, Urban Monastery participants emphasize God's relational and communal nature as the pattern for human interaction and view the pursuit of social and economic justice in the world to be of equal spiritual significance to the practice of evangelism.

In chapter 2 we saw how dominant expressions of twentieth-century American evangelicalism have prioritized evangelism as the primary work of the church and the primary solution to social problems. The prioritization of evangelism over social reform is an expression of twentieth-century American evangelicalism's theological individualism, as exemplified by its spiritual and individualist analyses of social problems and strategies of social engagement.[71] As illustrated in figure 4.1a, evangelism is thus a controlling symbolic element in the theological individualism of dominant expressions of twentieth-century American evangelicalism. However, by rearranging the relationship between the symbolic elements of evangelism and social reform (figure 4.1a) and increasing the symbolic prioritization of the Trinity (figure 4.1b), Urban Monastery participants have transformed the meaning system of dominant expressions of American evangelicalism while at the same time retaining the core symbolic elements that define the boundaries, identity, and *doxa* of the American evangelical field.[72]

As evident in official mission statements and local practices, in informal conversations with both national leaders and local grassroots participants, and through explicit statements of theological conviction, neo-monastic evangelicals have rejected historic American evangelicalism's prioritization of evangelism and personal spiritual transformation over social justice activism, elevating the latter to a place of equal religious importance (figure 4.1a).[73] Whereas historic American evangelicalism has prioritized evangelism, personal salvation, individual moral transformation, and the individual's relationship with God as the hallmarks of faithful religion and the solution to social problems, the neo-monastic evangelicals in the Urban Monastery view working for social justice in this world as having equal religious value as practicing evangelism or pursuing individual spiritual transformation.

Urban Monastery participants have also elevated the symbolic priority of the Trinity as a model of religious practice and human flourishing, which is worked out in a comprehensively communitarian perspective on religion and social engagement as illustrated in figure 4.1b. For traditional evangelicals,

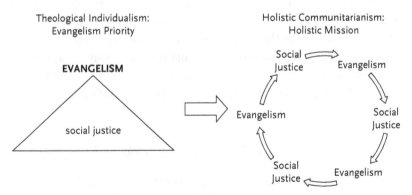

FIGURE 4.1A Evangelism priority to holistic mission

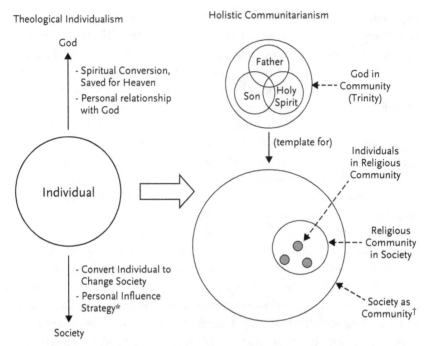

FIGURE 4.1B Individualism to communitarianism through symbolic prioritization of the Trinity

* (Smith 1998)

† This is a communitarian view of society as defined by moral cosmology theory, in which all members of society have a responsibility toward other members

the individual is the center of religious life and individual transformation is the key to changing society. In this view, converting individuals to Christ is both the primary responsibility of the church and the only hope for lasting social transformation.[74] However, by making the Trinity a controlling symbolic element in their distinctive holistic communitarian theological system, Urban Monastery participants have displaced the isolated individual from the center of religious life and established "community" as the symbolic element that sets the pattern for their understanding of how to practice faithful religion, how to engage with society, and the nature of society itself, as we see in figure 4.1b and as we will see played out again and again in Urban Monastery participants' religious and political standpoints and strategies of action over the next several chapters.

The Urban Monastery and the Bible

Urban Monastery participants and other neo-monastic evangelicals have constructed their holistic communitarian religious standpoints in opposition to dominant expressions of American evangelicalism, which tend toward theological individualism. However, despite their struggles against dominant positions in the evangelical field, Urban Monastery participants remain firmly committed to core elements of evangelical orthodoxy. In their understanding of the gospel, their commitment to biblical authority, and their belief in the importance of evangelism, Urban Monastery participants affirm the *doxa* of the American evangelical field while simultaneously challenging dominant positions within it.

Indeed, one cannot be an evangelical without having a high view of scripture as a trustworthy, authoritative, and divinely inspired source of truth about God, people, and the world. Over 95 percent of American evangelicals believe that the Bible is the inspired word of God and "true in all ways": roughly half of whom believe the Bible should always be interpreted literally word-for-word, and half who believe that the Bible is divinely inspired but not always to be interpreted literally.[75] While most evangelicals acknowledge that science, reason, nature, and other religions can also be sources of legitimate knowledge, biblical authority remains the final word on religious, political, and moral arguments in the evangelical field.[76] Of course, evangelicals disagree about how to correctly interpret the Bible and its relation to other sources of knowledge. But to be an evangelical is to be someone who believes that the Bible should be taken seriously as an authoritative guide to human meaning and practice. And in areas of potential contradiction or dispute about how the Bible relates to other sources of knowledge—such as in the case of the Genesis creation story versus evolutionary theory—evangelicals who accept evolutionary theory (as many do) must have a ready explanation for why it does not contradict the true meaning of the biblical message, which is still considered divinely inspired wisdom even where it is not interpreted literally. A strong belief in the inspiration and authority of the Bible remains one of the defining characteristics of evangelical *doxa*.

On the issue of the inspiration and centrality of the Bible for religious life, Urban Monastery participants are firmly evangelical. Biblical teaching permeates all aspects of life in the Urban Monastery, and all of the Urban Monastery participants I interviewed drew fluently on both specific passages and broad conceptual themes from Christian scriptures to explain their communal and personal religious perspectives. Examples abound. Neo-monastic and religious communities around the world use the "God Story" curriculum developed by Urban Monastery leaders: a year-long, cover-to-cover reading of scripture conceptualized as the narrative of God's interaction with humanity throughout history. Urban Monastery leaders have refined this narrative, chronological approach to teaching the Bible, spending an entire year teaching through the complete "God Story" at their Sunday Gatherings and re-presenting it in a condensed eight-week package on a regular basis. Teaching at the Urban Monastery's Sunday gatherings include months-long studies of single books of the Bible, as well as topical themes that draw extensively on biblical teaching. D-Group participants in the Urban Monastery read fifteen chapters of the Bible every week on their own.[77] The social organization of the Urban Monastery is explicitly inspired by the organization of the early church as recorded in the book of Acts and by Jesus's model of religious training as recorded in the first four books of the New Testament. Urban Monastery participants are people of the book.

All evangelicals view scripture as the ultimate source of meaning and authority in the world. However, because scripture is multivocal and because the interpretation of cultural meaning systems by agents in concrete social and historical circumstances is not predetermined,[78] this shared commitment to the Bible as the primary source of religious and moral authority does not automatically result in shared religious or political standpoints among different evangelical groups. Like other evangelicals, Urban Monastery participants believe in the importance of personal faith in Christ for salvation and in sharing the gospel message with others. However, while American evangelicals have traditionally prioritized evangelism and viewed social problems through the lens of theological individualism, neo-monastic evangelicals draw on other symbolic elements from scripture to construct holistic communitarianism as a distinctive and alternative theological orientation.

In particular, Urban Monastery participants prioritize the doctrine of the Trinity as a controlling symbolic element in their holistic communitarian interpretation of scripture. For Urban Monastery participants, the overarching message of the Bible—the "God Story" in Urban Monastery vernacular—is the story of relationships and restored community between God and people:

MINDY: The overarching message of the Bible is that there is a Triune God who values relationship so much that he created a people and decided to do whatever it takes to make them a part of Himself.

The God Story begins with a Trinitarian God who is "a community" in himself—Father, Son, and Holy Spirit—who "out of the overflow" (Mina) of love within the Trinity created humanity in the image of the Trinitarian God, whose very essence is relational and communal:

DEVON: There was a Trinity of love happening in the beginning: the original community of Jesus, God the Father, and the Holy Spirit. And there got to be too much love. What flowed out of that was the creation of humanity. . . . I think without going too deep into it, the simple thing is God loved us, showed us that love, and that love overflows into us, and the only thing we can do with it is to love other people, which causes us to love the world that God created.

Humanity's intended relationship with God, one another, and the earth is broken by sin, but eventually restored through the life, death, and resurrection of Jesus, the son of God:

MINA: The overarching message of scripture is the potency of what God had designed in the beginning, with the Trinity being in this place of community and engagement with each other, and God, out of the overflow of himself, wanting to reproduce and share this and let people know and see his love, his dream over humanity. . . . And the gospel is the reconciliation of our lives back to that origin. It's how God in Christ paved a way back to the beginning, to the original design: the reconciliation of humanity to God in our most alive, most joyful, most pure and true state of union with our Maker.

Urban Monastery participants consistently interpret each of the core doctrines of Christian theology—creation, the "fall" of humanity through sin, Jesus and the gospel, and the essential nature of God—in relational and communal, rather than individualistic, terms. All evangelicals believe in the Trinity, but Urban Monastery participants are distinctive in how central the doctrine of the Trinity is to their reading of scripture, and in their understanding of the communitarian implications of the doctrine of the Trinity as a template for how followers of Christ are called to interact with one another and the world.

For Urban Monastery participants, the God of the Bible is a God of love. This belief is expressed in the Urban Monastery's mission statement, to— "Love God, Love One Another, Love the World"—and announced with unanimity by all of the community members I spoke with. Whereas they responded to most questions with long, thoughtful pauses before answering, Urban Monastery participants responded rapidly, succinctly, and emphatically when I asked the question, "What is the overarching message of the Bible?"

JASMINE: The overarching message of the Bible is that God is love . . . God wants a people who love him and will interact with him, and he's going to do whatever it takes to make that happen.

CALEB: I would say the central message of the Bible is love. In a word: love. We just did this massive God Story review to try to condense it into eight teachings. . . . We were going, "OK, so we do this great presentation of the whole of Scripture, but will people really get the central message? What's something we could do at the close of each of these teachings where people could walk away going, 'That is the message of the Story.'?" What we came up with—the thing that we said at the end of each teaching— was: "And God asks: 'Will you love me with all your heart, soul, mind, and strength?'"[79] I would say from the beginning that's been the question.

Urban Monastery participants unanimously agree that the message of the Bible, the "God Story," is that God is a relational, communal being overflowing with love, and that God's intention for people is that their lives would likewise be characterized by loving relationship with God and others, thereby reflecting and participating in the divine "community of love" modeled in the Trinity.

The Urban Monastery and the Gospel

If the overarching message of the Bible is love, Urban Monastery participants are equally clear and unanimous that "the gospel is just the current picture of that overarching theme that God is love . . . in Jesus" (Jasmine), "The gospel is Jesus" (Elle), "to know Jesus" (Jason), "in a word: Jesus" (Caleb), "the gospel is Christ himself" (Manuel). On the core evangelical question of the meaning of the gospel, Urban Monastery participants stand firmly in the center of evangelical orthodoxy by affirming belief in the divinity, incarnation, death, and resurrection of Jesus as God's path to forgiveness, reconciliation, and eternal life for all who believe. They quoted classic evangelical passages from scripture regarding salvation such as Romans 10:9, "If you confess with your mouth Jesus is Lord, and believe in your heart that God raised him from the dead, you will be saved," and affirmed classic evangelical understandings of the doctrine of Christ's atonement for sin through his death and resurrection:

JASMINE: God had a son, and his son was Jesus. He came to this world, he lived a perfect, sinless life . . . and then he died. He died for you, and he died for me. And again, it's just a zoomed in picture of the fact that God is love, and he wants interaction with his people.

ANJA: The God who is love has made a way for all of our death and sin and alienation from God and from each other to die, through the death of Jesus, and we are now risen with Jesus in his life and in his power and in his authority. I would say that understanding or belief would be central to what it means to be a Christian.

Like other evangelicals, Urban Monastery participants consider faith in Christ and the gospel to be central to what it means to be a Christian.

In all these ways, Urban Monastery participants affirm historic evangelical *doxa* concerning the gospel. Yet their understanding of the gospel is also more this-worldly and communal than the more otherworldly and individualist view of the gospel that has dominated historic American evangelicalism; a view in which the gospel is primarily about the forgiveness of sins and going to heaven when you die. Urban Monastery participants' unanimous agreement that the gospel is "Jesus" or "knowing Jesus"—rather than a formula for how to be forgiven of sin or get to heaven—is an example of a subtle but significant shift toward a more relational and this-worldly understanding of the gospel:

INTERVIEWER: What is the gospel?

MINA: In Jesus, the reconciliation of humanity to God to our most alive, our most joyful, our most pure and true state in union with our Maker. That's the gospel to me I guess . . . that God is living and active present-tense reality in our lives today. It's not just for some eternal deadline where everything gets made better.

JASON: To know Jesus. For me, that is the gospel, the good news. That's everything: to know Jesus. Yeah. And it might mean you're gonna fly in heaven or something, but I don't know. I know that what it is *today* is knowing Jesus.

Jason, along with many other neo-monastic and emerging church evangelicals, has found himself re-evaluating the real meaning of heaven, hell, and what it actually means to be "saved":[80]

JASON: I'm just beginning to lately study a little bit of N. T. Wright's stuff about heaven and hell, and it's challenging typical views . . . of what heaven or hell is: eternal cloud-sitting or eternal burning.[81] Something about that doesn't seem like the nature of God. . . . I just think that our paradigm for what being "saved" means maybe is different than the typical: "You pray a prayer, invite Jesus into your heart, and now you're saved." That's kind of what Paul said . . . "Believe in the Lord and you'll be saved."[82] But I don't know if he's talking about being saved in the heaven sense, or if he means more, "You're life will be radically transformed. The darkness you are experiencing today will be no more." So really right now, I'm gray on what heaven and hell means. But I *do* know—and this where I'm resolute—God wants to know us and be known by us. So the mission doesn't change. If I'm going to somebody and sharing my life with them— whether they're going to get saved or not, I don't know—but I just know I want to tell them: "God loves you crazily and wants you to experience it." And I think that's pretty scriptural.

Jason does not deny the reality of heaven and hell or the need for salvation, but he does challenge typical evangelical definitions of those terms. He affirms the divinity, crucifixion, and resurrection of Jesus for the forgiveness of sins and eternal life, but holds a more relational and this-worldly view of salvation while questioning the exact literal meaning of the Bible's discussion of hell. However, his uncertainty about the exact nature of salvation, heaven, and hell does not cause him to question the importance of evangelism, because he firmly believes that "God wants to know and be known by us" in this life, regardless of what may happen in the next one. While Jason's views on these issues were more heterodox than most other Urban Monastery participants, they are similar in adopting a more this-worldly interpretation of core evangelical beliefs. On the meaning of the gospel, Urban Monastery participants affirm evangelical *doxa*, while at the same time focusing on more relational and this-worldly, rather than otherworldly, interpretations of the gospel message.

The Urban Monastery, Evangelism, and Social Justice: The Spiritual and Social Gospel United

As explored at length in chapter 2, dominant expressions of American evangelicalism have prioritized evangelism over progressive social reform throughout most of the twentieth century. While Catholics, mainline Protestants, and black Protestants helped mobilize mass protests and significant resources in support the civil rights movement, Vietnam antiwar movement, and Central American peace movement, most evangelicals did not join them.[83] When "plain-folk" evangelicals re-emerged as a political force in the late 1970s with the rise of the Christian Right, it was to fight for legislation that preserved traditional family values and prayer in public schools, not to combat inequality or injustice in American domestic or foreign policy.[84] In generating conservative Protestant suspicion and hostility toward theologically liberal Protestants and the social gospel movement, the early twentieth-century fundamentalist-modernist struggles led dominant expressions of twentieth-century evangelicalism to eschew social justice activism as an element of Christian social engagement.[85]

How do Urban Monastery participants think about the relationship between evangelism and social justice? The dominant point of view in twentieth-century American evangelicalism is unequivocal: evangelism is without question the most important responsibility of individual Christians and the church in the world. In the late 1980s, for example, four out of five students at America's leading evangelical colleges and seminaries believed that evangelism was more important than social justice activism, while nine out of ten believed that the primary focus of Christian missions should be spiritual conversion rather than "improving the material lot of the poor."[86] By contrast, only one Urban Monastery participant told me that she believed evangelism to be a higher priority for Christians than social justice activism. The rest refused to prioritize one over the other, emphatically repeating phrases such as "they're the *same*" (Lilith, Mina, Roland, Riley, Kieren, emphasis in original), "they go hand in hand" (Jasmine, Jessica, Manuel, Scarlet, Mindy, Mitchell), and "they're kind of inseparable" (Caleb, Helena, Jasper, Kay). Manuel, a Brazilian soccer player whose mother grew up in a socialist commune, voiced one of the Urban Monastery's stronger critiques of the prioritization of evangelism above social justice activism:

MANUEL: They go hand in hand. I think if you do evangelism without social justice you're basically doing colonization. You're just colonizing people. But at the end of the day if you're doing social justice work without evangelization then—I think that actually reflects more of the heart of God—but at the end of the day it's such a temporary thing. We're not for this world, we're for heaven. So you're presenting a false gospel. In the same way you'd be presenting a false gospel if you were to be like [using a mocking, sing-song voice]: "Oh here's Jesus. Oh, he made you in poverty so stay in poverty forever and ever. Ok, God loves you, good-bye!"

From the point of view of Manuel and other Urban Monastery participants, a Christian who practices evangelism without fighting for social justice presents a "false gospel," as does a Christian who fights for social justice but without ever practicing evangelism.

Urban Monastery participants believe that a Christian who practices evangelism without also working for social justice has not fully expressed the love, character, and will of God, or fulfilled her religious obligation in the world. They lament that American evangelicals have largely neglected the biblical call to social justice and transformation:

JASPER: Confrontation and prophetic ministry has been neglected by the church: confronting the powers, confronting the systems. . . . We have great champions of that in the history of the church—like Dr. Martin Luther King Jr.—but sadly he wasn't championed by the evangelical church at the time.

Nor do Urban Monastery participants view social justice activism as a means to an end; rather, it is an end in itself. Pursuing justice in the world is important because it expresses God's love for humanity regardless of a person or groups' religious beliefs, not as a means of trying to convert people to Christianity.[87] Urban Monastery participants' unwillingness to prioritize evangelism over social justice activism is a powerful indicator of the Urban Monastery's rejection of theological individualism and their holistic communitarianism.

Against dominant expressions of twentieth-century American evangelicalism, Urban Monastery participants are committed to political and structural solutions to social injustice alongside spiritual and social service-oriented approaches. For example, Anja and Mina's anti-human trafficking work involves practical help for victims of human trafficking, political and legal advocacy, and mass-based political organization for structural changes that would make human trafficking more visible, traceable, and rare. Likewise, Jason's plans to pursue a career as an economic advisor in developing nations arose out of a strong critique of neo-liberal trade organizations such as World Bank and International Monetary Fund:

JASON: I started reading a lot about economic injustice, especially as it related to debt and the IMF's and World Bank's role in creating debt—often in noble pursuit—but the outworking of it has become extremely corrupt and unjust. It has failed people. It hasn't alleviated poverty, it hasn't been effective. . . . If I'm doing what I'd ideally like to do in the future, I'm an economic advisor to the Zambian government on economic policy, so that there's less poverty, more people employed, higher income, less suffering, less disease—because I believe a lot of problems, especially in that area, stem from poor economic policy. Often people steal not because they're corrupt in nature but because their family is dying. Rape, or murder, items like that, could have come from years of economic desperation. You grew up in a family of economic desperation that creates an individual that's corrupt. I don't think that in the end there is somebody who just wants to murder—although there is some sickness, some sick minds out there.

Jason's structural diagnoses of social problems resulting from poverty and economic injustice are typical of the neo-monastic and evangelical left point of view, but stand in stark contrast to the "freewill individualism" through which American evangelicals typically view economic, racial, and social problems.[88]

Asking Protestants to prioritize between the importance of evangelism and social justice is one way of observing whether their religious ethic is oriented to more individualistic and otherworldly or communitarian and this-worldly concerns. While there is no inherent theological reason for Christians to draw sharp distinctions between these two orientations, opposition between them was a central feature of the struggle between conservative and liberal Protestants in the early twentieth century.[89] It is a distinction that has continued to delineate the opposing theological and political standpoints of conservative and liberal Protestants throughout the twentieth century. And it is a distinction that Urban Monastery participants, as an expression of their holistic communitarian theology, want nothing to do with. From their perspective, pursuing evangelism while neglecting social justice—or vice versa—is to practice a "false gospel" that severely truncates and distorts the true message of Christianity. And as we will see in the next chapter, Urban Monastery participants' holistic communitarianism is expressed in their political as well as their theological points of view. By reinterpreting relationships of priority among a few core symbolic elements of traditional evangelical theology, Urban Monastery participants have developed the framework for an alternative holistic communitarian vision of evangelical religion and politics in America.

Chapter 5

Politics and Religion in an Urban Monastery

IN CHAPTER 4 we saw that Urban Monastery participants are more theologically communitarian and more committed to social justice as a core element of evangelical religion than are dominant expressions of American evangelicalism. Given the American evangelical field's *doxic* commitment to evangelism, Urban Monastery participants' unwillingness to prioritize evangelism over social justice activism is a powerful indicator of their holistic communitarian theology and opposition to theological individualism and conservative evangelicalism. But what does this mean for their approach to politics? Just as it leads them to reject the prioritization of evangelism at the expense of social reform, Urban Monastery participants' holistic communitarianism leads them reject "single-issue voting" on the traditional Christian Right shibboleths of abortion and gay marriage: "I think Christians have gotten *way* too tied up with abortion . . . I don't think one isolated issue can be the only thing that matters" (Jason, emphasis in original). As holistic communitarians, they are highly critical of the Christian Right and conservative evangelicalism's focus on the politics of abortion and sexuality while neglecting issues of peace, poverty, and economic justice:

CALEB: You hear a *ton* about abortion from the church, but you *don't* hear a lot about injustice that's happening abroad in other ways, you *don't* have a lot of people who understand or have taken any effort to research, "What do these tax policies mean? What does it mean to help the poor?"

MINDY: A lot of things you find the Church impassioned about—they're important—but not more important than anything else. Abortion certainly isn't more important than the economic crisis.

In the same way that Urban Monastery participants refuse to prioritize evangelism over social justice, they vigorously denounce Christian Right arguments about a "hierarchy of morality" that unquestioningly place abortion and heterosexual marriage at the top of the list of political issues that evan-gelical Christians should care about (Caleb). As holistic communitarians, Urban Monastery participants believe that working for social justice in this world is as important as evangelism, and that poverty, economic injustice, and militarism are moral issues that Christians need to consider when decid-ing who to vote for—no less than other "moral values" issues such as abortion or gay marriage. The political standpoints of Urban Monastery participants are constructed in opposition to the Christian Right and conservative evan-gelicalism, and find many points of convergence with an earlier generation of evangelical left position-takings with respect to the legitimate representation of biblical Christianity in the American political arena.

The Urban Monastery and the 2008 Presidential Election

I was able to interview Urban Monastery participants shortly after the 2008 presidential election, which provided a methodologically advantageous con-text for asking Urban Monastery participants about their political attitudes and voting behavior. Because the election was fresh in their minds, interview respondents were able to recall specific conversations, thought processes, and emotions relating to their voting decisions. And because the election gener-ated much deliberation, conflict, and debate in the Urban Monastery, inter-view respondents had already spent considerable time thinking through their voting decisions, what political issues mattered to them, and how they trans-lated religious convictions into political standpoints. The 2008 election thus provided an excellent concrete window through which to examine the politi-cal attitudes and voting behavior of Urban Monastery participants.

The Urban Monastery participants that I interviewed were more likely to support the Democratic Obama-Biden ticket than they were the Republican McCain-Palin ticket—though there were also some "very vocal McCain sup-porters" in the Urban Monastery as well.[1] While the mere fact that a group of predominantly white evangelicals preferred Obama to McCain is significant in itself, the process that Urban Monastery participants went through in de-ciding who to vote for is even more interesting. Most Urban Monastery par-ticipants had an extremely difficult time deciding who to vote for:

MINA: I voted for McCain and Palin after a *grueling* process—*grueling*—of just thinking it through and not being entirely sure which way to go.
LILITH: I'm so colossally torn every time there's an election.
ALEX: I voted for John McCain, but it was a *heck* of a wrestle. I almost just didn't vote.

HELENA: It was *painful* to go and vote—really sad. I didn't like either option.

JASON: I've had a *lot* of these conversations this last year. I was excited for them to be over.

CALEB: It was a serious process for all of us.

By all accounts, the Urban Monastery was deeply engaged in political conversation and debate throughout the presidential primary and general election season, including a series of community gatherings where Urban Monastery leaders led discussions about how each of the candidates' positions on specific issues compared to a "biblical worldview":

ALEX: We had a huge open forum in which the people on our leadership team never declared who they were voting for. In fact we had people on our leadership team who voted for a third party, we had no voters, Democratic voters, Republican voters, all in our leadership circle. So it was an interesting election.

The intensity of these discussions and debates about the election was palpable as I interviewed community members, who groaned in real and mock despair when I started asking questions about politics.

What made deciding who to vote for such a grueling process for Urban Monastery participants? One common element was the theme of "life versus life" (Manuel, Alex, Caleb, Jason, Kay). Urban Monastery participants were unanimous in their opposition to abortion, believing that it results in the death of a person made in God's image, although their opposition to abortion was nuanced in ways we will discuss below. Because of their views on abortion, Urban Monastery participants felt that in voting for either major party ticket, they faced a brutal forced choice:

MANUEL: For me it was this: who do I kill? Do I kill babies? Or do I kill young people at war? It sucked. It sucked. . . . It's such a complicated, horrible decision that we have to make as humans. I was at a stalemate regarding *life*, and realizing that there was no life. And as far as capital punishment is concerned . . . I just don't think it's our job. I don't think it's our job to kill people.

CALEB: I found myself getting into numbers of deaths, going "OK, here's a guy with a Republican mentality who is going to persist in warfare." I love Obama's foreign policy, and I think there are a lot of lives that are going to be saved and a lot justice that is going to go forth with his type of foreign policy. And then I'm like, "OK, how many abortions versus how many war casualties?" And I'm just like, "I can't *do* this. This is too *hard* [shaking head grimly]."

Urban Monastery participants' unanimous anguish concerning abortion and near unanimous (all but two interview subjects) opposition to the Iraq war and the aggressive, militaristic foreign policy position they attributed to the Republican Party put them in a difficult position regarding how to best protect and preserve human life through their vote. Torn by this dilemma, a number of them refused to choose between what they viewed as two terrible options, either refusing to vote or voting for a third party candidate "so I could say: 'I want another voice. I'd love a third party here'" (Caleb).

Another reason most Urban Monastery participants had a difficult time deciding who to vote for involved the conflation of evangelical Christianity with political conservatism and Republican Party loyalty, an association that is as strong and widespread within many segments of the American evangelical field as it is in the popular imagination:

INTERVIEWER: Who is evangelical America for you?
CALEB: I could almost say it more from a political standpoint, and say hardcore Republicans, basically. . . . And that's definitely a harsh line to draw, but, yeah, evangelical America has become very associated in my mind with a pretty rigid Republicanism.

Like Caleb, many Urban Monastery participants experienced the conflation of evangelical Christianity with conservative Republican Party politics firsthand in their childhood families and churches. As Jasper—a former Bible college student who grew up attending a conservative megachurch in Texas— told me, "I've been involved in the Evangelical Right for as long as I can remember . . . and I have a lot of frustrations and disagreements with that sect." Scarlet, an Urban Monastery resident and studio artist, agreed:

SCARLET: I had an intensely political, fundamentalist Christian childhood. We spent a lot of time praying for George Bush—the first George Bush— to get elected. By the time I was eight I was handing out fliers for Republican Party candidates. A news anchor would mention something pro-choice and my parents would yell something belligerent at the television. It was very reactionary; not very thought out. Looking back on it, I wonder why we were so preoccupied with banning gay marriage and all these things that are really on the periphery of what it means to live a Christian life.

Because of significant and unavoidable past and present engagement with the Christian Right and conservative evangelicalism, Urban Monastery participants were forced to wrestle deeply with questions of religious and political identity.

The political deliberations of Urban Monastery participants vividly portray the subjective effects of politicization within the evangelical field as discussed in chapter 3, where external political categories come to impose themselves on the boundaries and classification schemes of the evangelical religious field. In many conservative evangelical circles in America, voting for Republican Party candidates is a given: the obvious choice for any truly faithful Christian. Voting for a Democratic Party candidate is unthinkable: enough cause to question the sincerity or integrity of someone's religious faith. Many Urban Monastery participants felt the tension of this association deeply:

LILITH: I voted for Bush in 2004, and I felt coerced. I felt manipulated, spiritually manipulated: like I would be sinning if I voted for someone else. And I actually cried when I left the voting booth, because I was *so* conflicted. I did not want George W. Bush! I did not want him. I wanted some of his *choices*, but not *him*, as a leader.

INTERVIEWER: But you felt compelled to vote for him at the time?

LILITH: Yeah.

INTERVIEWER: Because of what?

LILITH: Abortion. That was it. That was the only thing.

CALEB: My pastor back home caught wind that I wasn't 100 percent sold on the McCain-Palin ticket, and he emailed me "out of concern and curiosity." I found myself really angry with quote unquote "the church," I guess with evangelical America, and the simplicity or narrow-mindedness of it. . . . All I wanted was to hear something like: "This is more difficult than, 'We vote Republican because we're Christians.'" And though I heard some other things . . . overall that's what I heard.

Whether through anger or tears, Urban Monastery participants expressed deep frustration at the way in which many American evangelicals, including some of their closest friends and family members, had come to associate Republican voting preferences with religious faithfulness. This is the essence of politicization and the erosion of a field's autonomy with respect to the political field: when political beliefs and behaviors (e.g., voting for Republicans) come to define religious faithfulness and determine the legitimacy of one's claims to evangelical religious identity. However, while the equation of Republican Party voting with religious faithfulness among some evangelicals is a sign of evangelicalism's politicization and relative loss of autonomy with respect to the political field, Urban Monastery participants' *contradictory cultural location* with respect to the Christian Right and progressive Left is a sign of its ongoing (relative) autonomy.

The Contradictory Cultural Location of the Urban Monastery

Given the current structure of the American political culture and its two-party system, Urban Monastery participants find themselves torn between the left-liberal and conservative poles of the American political field. Although America's culture war may be at times exaggerated, it remains true that white American evangelicals overwhelmingly support Republican Party candidates and conservative positions on most political issues,[2] while the nonreligious overwhelmingly support Democratic Party candidates and left-liberal positions.[3] Evangelical views on health care, defense spending, and government aid all became increasingly conservative between 1980 and 2004—reflecting the increasing number of evangelicals identifying with conservatism and the Republican Party in general over this period.[4]

Against these trends, Urban Monastery participants were more likely to vote for Barack Obama than John McCain: opposing abortion while taking left-liberal positions on war and foreign policy issues, education, environmental protection, health care, and government involvement in reducing economic inequality. While it may be tempting to label Urban Monastery participants as part of the "muddled middle" in American politics given their political standpoints, this would be a mistake.[5] There is nothing "muddled" about the political views of Urban Monastery participants: they have clear and strongly held positions on most political issues. Rather, Urban Monastery participants have a difficult time deciding who to vote for because they have strongly held political beliefs that cut across the existing liberal-conservative divide in American culture and politics. In other words, Urban Monastery participants occupy a *contradictory cultural location* with respect to the American political field.

Erik Olin Wright developed the concept of "contradictory locations within class relations" to describe the increasingly complex class structure of advanced capitalist societies.[6] In Wright's influential formulation, the "middle class" in advanced capitalist nations is not merely a catch-all category for those who are neither wealthy capitalist elites, on the one hand, nor low-income wage earners, on the other. Rather, the middle class includes many individuals who have characteristics that place them in a contradictory relationship to both the capitalist and worker poles of class relations in advanced capitalist societies. Similarly, the political position-taking of Urban Monastery participants exhibits a contradictory pattern with respect to the objective structure of the American political field; a structure in which social, economic, and foreign policy conservatives oppose social, economic, and foreign policy left-liberals in an essentially two-party system. Urban Monastery participants' opposition to abortion, on the one hand, and to American militarism, imperialism, and global and domestic economic inequality, on the other, places them in a contradictory position with respect to the Christian Right and the progressive Left in the United States.[7]

There is both an objective and subjective element to the contradictory cultural location of Urban Monastery participants. Objectively, their political views are firmly conservative with respect to abortion, but left-liberal with respect to their positions on foreign policy, economic inequality, and many other political issues such as racial inequality and environmental protection. Over and over again, Urban Monastery participants expressed their difficulty in deciding how to vote and where to place themselves on the American political map. As Mina, one of the Urban Monastery's founding leaders told me, "There were things on the Democratic side that I *really* wanted to see influence our nation, and there were things on the conservative ticket that I wanted to see influence our nation." Other Urban Monastery participants similarly found themselves stuck between the two dominant poles of the American political system:

ELLE: I don't like to choose a party and say "I'm a Democrat" or "I'm Republican." . . . It was hard for me number one because I don't think abortion is right, so that makes me Republican. . . . But I feel completely Democrat on economic issues.

HELENA: My friend kept trying to get to come to this Republican political rally, and I told him: "That would be awkward since I'm a Democrat." But really, I'm not either. In either place—either group—I feel like a complete alien.

Almost one-third of the Urban Monastery participants that I interviewed either didn't vote or voted for a third party candidate because of their difficulty in choosing which of their deeply held political convictions to betray in order to vote for either candidate:

CALEB: Ultimately I voted independent because I thought Mr. Obama and Mr. McCain both had some pretty serious problems. I wanted to vote because I wanted my voice to count in our democracy, but I decided I'd rather have it count as a statistic that says, "I want other voices, not just these two."

Those Urban Monastery participants who did not vote or who supported independent candidates as a way to protest traditional Republican and Democratic Party politics did so because of their contradictory position-takings with respect to the liberal-conservative poles in American politics, not because they were confused, muddled, or apathetic in their political engagement.

Indeed, far from being apathetic, the contradictory cultural location of Urban Monastery participants was subjectively felt very deeply throughout the 2008 election process, as expressed in the significant levels of intellectual and emotional tension that they experienced while discussing their political views and voting decisions. They also demonstrated a high degree of self-awareness about their contradictory position in the American political field. As Jasper told me, "Some people have called me a socialist, an anarchist, a communist; but anybody in *those* circles would call me a religious fanatic!" (Jasper). The subjective tension of was particularly acute for Caleb, one of the Urban Monastery's founding leaders with some childhood ties to Sarah Palin:

CALEB: It was one of those times where I really felt the sacred–secular divide in my own life. Because at school anytime something would come up about McCain-Palin it became the center of laughter, the butt of a joke. And then I go to [the church where I grew up], and I mention, "You know, I'm not completely sold [on McCain-Palin]. I have some issues." And you'd think I'd have just shot my mother!

In the end, Caleb cast a protest vote for a third party candidate. While lacking Caleb's rare personal connection to the 2008 election, Elle found herself similarly torn between her pro-Obama medical school roommates and pro-McCain small group members:

ELLE: When I compare myself to other Christians I feel completely liberal. But when I compare myself to other atheists I feel really conservative. So I don't know.... When the elections were going on, there was a divide. There were people I talked to who were completely Republican, and there were people I talked to who were completely Democrat. I was going back and forth on it, and then made my personal decision.... It was difficult. When I went to the medical school I did not feel Democrat, but when I came here I did not feel Republican. I just felt completely stuck in middle ground. There was *so much* tension. I would go home and all my roommates—there are four girls, all going to be doctors in four years, extremely intellectual, and they love the Lord—but it was an Obama household. And then I come to my small group—all these intellectual people, love the Lord—but Republican. I was just so distraught throughout it.

The contradictory cultural location of the majority of Urban Monastery participants is a deeply felt subjective reality, as well as an objective description of their political standpoints with respect to the religious Right and the progressive Left.

Urban Monastery participants feel torn between the conservative and left-liberal poles of American politics because of their contradictory position-taking on issues such as abortion, poverty and economic justice, and war, and because of their social location. As evangelicals, they are immersed in a conservative political culture that often equates voting for Republicans with religious faithfulness. As urban young adults attending public universities and art schools and participating in the secular artistic field, they are also immersed in a left-liberal political culture where being a liberal Democrat "just sort of comes with the territory" (Riley), and where evangelicals and the Christian Right are seen as representing an intolerant, old-fashioned, possibly dangerous mixture of conservative religion and politics. Urban Monastery participants reject both of these extremes, and long for a viable alternative political position that better represents their holistic communitarian theology. However, as Alex told me, they are not particularly hopeful about the possibility of such a position emerging: "Given our system, there's not left much of a choice. I would love it if a Democrat could be pro-life, but I just don't see that happening. It's like a gridlock." In light of Urban Monastery participants' political attitudes, Alex's desire for a "pro-life Democrat" represents the type of alternative position that would appeal to many members of the Urban Monastery. From their vantage point, however, the possibility of such an alternative position emerging in establishment American politics seems remote given conservative evangelicalism's dominance in the evangelical field, on the one hand, and the progressive left's strong commitment to abortion rights, on the other. If the opposition between politically conservative orthodox religionists and politically liberal moral progressives in America really could be characterized as a culture war, Urban Monastery participants would be deeply conflicted noncombatants hoping for a cease-fire and the emergence of a "different voice" in the American political field (Caleb).[8] The Urban Monastery's contradictory cultural location is consistent with moral cosmology theory's expectations regarding the social and economic standpoints of theological communitarians, thus placing them at odds with both Republican economic conservatism and Democratic left-liberalism on "social issues" such as abortion.

Abortion, Pluralism, and the 2008 Presidential Election

Urban Monastery participants who voted for McCain-Palin cited abortion as the primary, and typically only, reason for their vote. As Kay told me, "For me the big issue is life. If a president doesn't value life and is promoting and supporting abortion, then we're in trouble" (Kay). Alex, one of the founding leaders of the Urban Monastery, agreed:

ALEX: For me it came down to—although I don't really champion being a one-issue voter—I felt like I had to prioritize the abortion issue. . . . There were many facets where I felt like I probably fell on the side of Obama, but for me it came down to that issue of life, that tragedy of innocent life. It just weighed on me real heavy, which I feel is probably a classic Christian answer. Yeah, I wrestled with it, but that's where I came down. I can say that I wasn't really that disappointed when Obama got elected.

Anja, another significant leader in the community, expanded Alex's emphasis on "classic Christian issue" of abortion to include opposition to gay marriage as well:

ANJA: I think the issues that were the most deciding for me in the election were the issues of abortion and marriage and family. I believe that the image of God is reflected in marriage first and foremost and that all of society is built on the individual and then on marriage and then on family and then on community. . . . So I think the design of God for marriage and family and for life is the bedrock on which all other things are built on. For me that was the core of why I voted the way I did. Although on the Democratic ticket and the kinds of things that Democrats have stood for, stand for, more quote "social justice" oriented things—education, health care, the poor, things that protect women and children—these kinds of things are *so* important to me too. But I had to vote the way that I did because of that.

Anja's comments are notable because of their singularity in how they reflect the family-centric view of society espoused by Christian Right advocates, who believe that abortion and gay marriage violate the "two great pillars" on which God has designed society: "marriage between a man and a woman" and the sanctity of human life beginning at conception.[9] Anja was the only interview subject who articulated this position, which she immediately qualified by pointing out how important "social justice oriented things" that "Democrats have stood for" were to her as well.[10]

The Urban Monastery participants I interviewed were unanimous in their opposition to abortion, and viewed abortion as an extremely significant political issue. Yet many voted for the pro-choice candidate Barack Obama nonetheless. They were able to do so for two reasons. First, their holistic communitarian theology leads them to reject single-issue voting or the existence a "hierarchy of morality" with abortion at the apex:

MINA: I think that I was really struggling with what you hear—especially in conservative and typically Christian circles—about there being a hierarchy of morality and trying to apply that to a political ideology. And it was just really difficult to me to say that abortion is more elevated and more of an important issue to address than how we go about our foreign policy and how we deal with other nations.

While Urban Monastery participants did, of course, have to prioritize among the importance of different political issues in deciding how to vote, only Anja and Kay automatically placed opposition to abortion at the top of the list.[11] Even those who ended up voting for the McCain-Palin ticket because of their position on abortion were against "single-issue voting" as a general principle, in direct and conscious opposition to hard-line Christian Right advocates who argue that "to vote for those who support the shedding of innocent blood [abortion] . . . or for those who would redefine marriage between a man and woman in defiance of Genesis 1:27, is actually an act of rebellion that brings one under the divine scrutiny and the warning of God."[12] Urban Monastery participants categorically reject such views.

The second reason that Urban Monastery participants were able to vote for Barack Obama despite their strong opposition to abortion in most cases was their respect for pluralism and democratic governance in the American political process. While they personally believe that limiting abortion is a human rights issue of grave importance, many Urban Monastery participants were ambivalent about efforts to pass anti-abortion legislation because of their commitment to pluralism and their view on the limits of the political process:

HELENA: How can I take a stand against a woman who wants to have an abortion because not doing so will ruin her life? Because it will—according to her perspective, her standard—it will. It'll destroy her. *I understand!* From a certain context and worldview, it makes complete sense to me. *Of course!* So how can I make a political stand for or against that?! I *can't* take a stand against these issues [abortion and gay marriage]. But from the reality of what Jesus says, he has more for you.

JESSICA: I don't believe in abortion. I wouldn't suggest it to somebody. I wouldn't advise them to do it. I do feel though that maybe it is peoples' right to choose. It's kind of a tricky thing . . . because I think people often don't have abortions because of Christian morals, yet I also feel like the meat and potatoes of Christian morals should be love. And love is compassion and understanding. So how can we possibly rule out situations [where abortion may be necessary]? I don't know. It's such a gray area. But saying: "No, this is the way. This is the only way. And you're a murderer"—that's not loving at all. So it's kind of confusing.

For some, a commitment to pluralism included recognition of gender as a political category that held significance for discerning what to legislate and who should be doing the legislating:

RILEY: I'm hesitant to speak about abortion because, well, I'm not a woman. It's not my body. So how do I have the right, as a man, to speak about that? At the same time, however, it *is* about preserving life. But in cases of rape or incest, how can we tell a woman what to do? It's tough.

While Urban Monastery participants opposed abortion in most cases based on Christian moral values regarding the sacredness of all human life; Christian moral values of love, compassion, respect, self-determination, and understanding also made them wary of judging women who have had abortions or who fight for abortion rights, and made them ambivalent about the legitimacy of enacting strong anti-abortion legislation.

With respect to pluralism, when asked the question, "Do you think Christians should try to pass laws that reflect Christian morality, or should laws in America reflect the diversity of religious and moral opinion in the population?" Urban Monastery participants voiced strong concerns about imposing Christian morality through legislation:

ANJA: I think laws in any country should reflect the majority of the population of that nation, and not [just Christians]. I think a biblical principle of government is that people choose what they want in terms of leaders and law. So if a nation is predominantly Christian and the nation chooses laws that reflect Christian beliefs then that can work for them, but if a nation doesn't *choose*, as a people, those kinds of laws, they shouldn't necessarily have those kinds of laws.

MANUEL: You're forcing people to become something they're not. But there are certain issues where I battle over that with myself: "Where do we take our stance as Christians, and where do we just let God's love overflow?" Abortion being the number one issue. . . . With abortion, the question is: "What's the value of life?" It's the ultimate value. . . . But then should we be Christian super-rulers [by legislating morality]? Then we become colonists again, colonizing people to live under our rules. So, I don't know. I don't think so.

Because they do not view America as a "Christian nation" and believe in the legitimacy of self-determination and the democratic model of government, Urban Monastery participants do not assume or expect that the laws governing the nation will or should always reflect their own particular moral vision.[13]

Like the vast majority of American evangelicals, Urban Monastery participants do not hold to a "dominionist" perspective on the relationship between Christian religion and politics.[14] Indeed, they are more likely to criticize "American imperialism" than they are to valorize the hegemonic spread of "Christian America" around the world or advocate a re-Christianization of the state:

JASPER: The early church lived under the rule and dominion of an oppressive [Roman] Empire, one that had some of the very same values systems that America does. Yet it didn't resort to power-grabbing as a means of social change. . . . They were much more subversive.

They do, however, believe that Christians should be involved in the political process, and that the positions Christians' take on political issues are and should be influenced by their religious beliefs and moral vision. Yet they also believe that Christians need to respect the choices, freedom, and alternative moral visions of other citizens:

CALEB: The election led me into the question, "How do the church and society interact?" My old pastor and I were talking about the separation of church and state. I was picturing a person who really loves Jesus coming into the chancellor position at my university and saying, "We're now going to pause every day at noon and pray, because I'm going to bring the kingdom of God to this place." And I was picturing how crazy that would be. I was having this thought in my anthropology class, and I'm picturing us pausing in the middle of the anthropology lecture and my professor saying, "Guys I'm sorry, we have this new chancellor, we've got to do this thing." And the Lord's Prayer or whatever comes on over the intercom and after we finish everybody's just bitter and angry and thinking, "This is so stupid and forced." And me now as a follower of Christ having all this junk to navigate through . . . and yet I'm praying *daily* that a chancellor who loves Jesus would come into power! So I'm like, "What do I expect from him then? To kind of tip-toe around and love some people and pray in secret?" That question just began to haunt me. To be honest it still does in a lot of ways, because I don't know that it is that clear.

Caleb, like other Urban Monastery participants, wants to see Christians have influence in mainstream political and social institutions, but is wary of imposing Christian perspectives on unwilling people.

On the issue of abortion, however, Urban Monastery participants are torn between their strong convictions about the need to protect vulnerable life and their commitment to democratic pluralism:

SCARLET: We have no right to govern morality. It can't be imposed. I *do* feel strongly about abortion, however, because it directly deals with life and defending the defenseless.

CALEB: Man, this is tough . . . it's what I spent the fall [before the election] wrestling through. One of the phrases that lingered on my heart was, "You can't mandate a heart position, or a heart condition." And if this is about the heart, then I have difficulty with the effectiveness of laws that dictate Christian values. And yet, does that mean I'm going to sit by and let innocent babies die? No way! . . . So ultimately I want to see Christian morals upheld . . . but I don't think that we can expect that to be the hope.

MINA: I think the abortion side of things is really hard for me . . . but then I go back to the question again: "How do you legislate morality? Can you tell people what is right and wrong?" . . . The thing I love about God is he did set in motion something that involves free will, so it makes sense to me that humanity would have a chance to engage their free will. . . . Oh, it's so hard. It seems like it's got to be both/and somehow.

Urban Monastery participants' back and forth deliberations on whether or not to push for anti-abortion legislation at the federal level are indicative of the dilemma that Christian Smith observes among American evangelicals more generally: a *voluntaristic absolutism* that simultaneously affirms the existence of universal moral truths while at the same time upholding individual moral freedom and a strong belief in personal choice.[15] Just as other American evangelicals' dual belief in the existence of universal moral standards and individual moral freedom leads them into strategic quandaries with respect to their political engagement, Urban Monastery participants struggle to reconcile how to translate religiously derived moral convictions into political behavior.[16]

Different community members resolved this dilemma in different ways. Some decided that although they were against abortion they did not believe in pursuing across the board anti-abortion legislation because of the existence of other moral perspectives on the issue. Others supported anti-abortion legislation because they believe strongly that "laws are supposed to protect the innocent, and for someone to be able to go down the corner and have [an abortion] has definitely normalized something that I do not believe should have been normalized" (Alex). Thus, although Urban Monastery participants unanimously opposed abortion in most circumstances, more Urban Monastery participants voted for pro-choice Barack Obama than John McCain, and community members disagreed on the extent to which anti-abortion legislation should be pursued, demonstrating a degree of nuance and complexity in their political reasoning that is generally absent from the blunt applications of biblical morality to American politics in the Christian Right.

The Christian Right perspective on the relationship between biblical morality and American politics was not, however, completely absent from the Urban Monastery. Two of my interview subjects, a married couple named Kay and Kieren, were very clear in their support of legislating Christian morality for all American citizens and the dire consequences of not doing so. Kay framed her argument in favor of legislating Christian morality as an opposition to moral relativism: "I would say we need to base laws on the word of God and upon the truth, on Christian morals, as opposed to what everyone thinks is good and right and feels nice and meets peoples' desires" (Kay). Kieren warned about what would happen to a nation that failed to base its laws on biblical morality:

KIEREN: Laws should reflect what is absolutely true. God says he absolutely detests when nations start saying that good is evil and evil is good.[17] That is like the last straw for God. So to legislate that good is evil and evil is good is on a course for—not the wrath of God—but for the hand of protection of God being lifted off a people, simply because we're not asking for it or desiring it. We're not allowing him to bless and protect us if we're legislating unrighteousness . . . and great failure and disaster will come within a few generations of unrighteousness being legislated as truth. And that's what we're beginning to see happen.

These two individuals were atypical of the Urban Monastery participants I spoke with, but they clearly articulate one side of the dilemma posed by American evangelicals' voluntaristic absolutism with respect to moral truth and freedom. Evangelical Christians believe that the Bible contains moral truth that is universally true, not just true for Christians or those who believe, and that it is therefore wise—a "no brainer" as Kieren told me—that it is in America's best interests to institute legislation based on "Christian" morality. Not surprisingly, both of these individuals voted for John McCain in the 2008 presidential election.

Political Attitudes in the Urban Monastery: Poverty, Patriotism, Peace, and Gay Marriage

While Urban Monastery participants are similar to other evangelicals in placing abortion near the top of their list of core political issues, the same is not true of their position on gay marriage. More of the Urban Monastery participants I interviewed favored the legalization of gay marriage than opposed it, and less than half even raised it is an important political issue for Christians. Like Manuel, those who support gay marriage believe that it violates God's design for marriage and family, but nevertheless believe that gay people should have the right to marry:

MANUEL: I don't agree with all the typical Christian things. Like the idea that we need to "protect marriage" by banning gay marriage. I think that we as a church are oppressing gay people. . . . If they want to be physically responsible for each other, financially responsible for each other, let them! It's oppression! If they're stepping into that commitment with each other, let them. If they want to visit someone on their deathbed, who are we to stop that? . . . I still think it's wrong, I still think it's a sin, and when I say that I mean it separates you from your relationship with God like anything else that is sin, but we've made too much of a hoopla about it. . . . You hear, "Oh, we have to stand up for family virtues." "Family virtues" is you going home at night and reading your Bible to your kids. It's you loving your kids. It's you making sure your kids know what to look for in a partner. It's you loving your wife to show your kids what that is. *That's* family virtue. It's not holding onto the meaning of a word. That pisses me off so much.

As with those Urban Monastery participants who are personally against abortion yet don't believe abortion should be banned, those community members who support gay marriage do so because they respect pluralism and believe in people's right to moral and religious self-determination:

JASON: I'm against gay marriage because I believe the behavior is wrong. But because I'm for less government, I don't think it should be the government to decide that over somebody, because that has so many implications. . . . So that's why I'm against [banning gay marriage].

ELLE: I think that the government should have nothing to do with a bunch of issues that Republicans try to get into. I think that the decision to be saved and follow God is a personal one. I don't think you can implement these laws over an entire country. So that's how I think about it. To say that all of gay marriage is illegal everywhere, I don't think you can do that, because it's a personal decision for people.

While Urban Monastery participants' strong belief that abortion leads to the death of a vulnerable person leads many of them to support anti-abortion legislation despite misgivings about the effectiveness of imposing legislation on the issue, they are less likely to take a similar position with respect to gay marriage. The overwhelming majority of Urban Monastery participants I interviewed either supported gay marriage or did not consider the issue to be a central issue for Christians, a view that is deeply at odds with the Christian Right and conservative evangelicalism.

If Urban Monastery participants are critical of the Christian Right position on the central importance of opposing gay marriage and civil rights for the LGBTQ community, what political issues are of central concern to them? Along with abortion, Urban Monastery participants cited war and poverty as the political issues that mattered most to them and that they believed should matter most to Christians. They unanimously supported President Obama's multilateral, diplomacy-oriented rhetoric on American foreign policy while opposing what they viewed as the militant and aggressive Bush/McCain approach:

ALEX: On foreign policy I was definitely more with Obama and building rapport with other nations as a means of solving problems. . . . As someone who travels internationally a lot, I spend a lot of time apologizing for American arrogance, and the idea of our president being a "maverick" doesn't appeal to me.

MINA: I was concerned about McCain because I felt like his brain was so hardwired pro-military that I was afraid he was going to emanate another, "America should police the world, we're going take out all the bad guys" view of the world. I appreciated what was coming from Obama: a willingness to engage in conversation and a different kind of diplomacy.

Urban Monastery participants' positions on US foreign policy stand in stark contrast to the Christian Right and conservative evangelicals, who are significantly more likely than other Americans to view having a "strong military," spreading democracy and "American values" around the globe, to distrust international institutions like the United Nations, and to support unilateral approaches to foreign policy.[18] None of the community members I interviewed mentioned fighting terrorism, "spreading democracy," or keeping a strong military as important issues, and everyone who spoke about the Iraq war opposed it.

One of the more dramatic illustrations of the opposition to militarism and religious nationalism among Urban Monastery participants came from Jasper. Jasper attended a large megachurch in Texas as a teenager and later spent time at a famous fundamentalist Bible college for a year before dropping out. Jasper used the word "frustrated" over fifty times to describe his experiences with the "evangelical right" during our interview—though like other Urban Monastery participants he leavened his criticism by pointing out positive attributes as well. Conservative evangelicals' uncritical patriotism and support for the Iraq war was at the top of the list of things that Jasper found "frustrating" with his church experience. It is worth recounting his response to this frustration in detail:

JASPER: When it comes to patriotic holidays, Southern Baptist churches are grotesquely loyal. Memorial Day services were particularly frustrating. In an effort to comfort families who had lost sons in the Iraq war, they would inadvertently villainize a whole other culture. In a service where there are more American flags than crosses, the church said, "It's OK that your son died, because he died for a good reason. In fact, he was exhibiting the qualities of Jesus Christ. In fact, he's a *perfect* embodiment of Jesus Christ." I just became really frustrated with that. Yes, comfort families who are in pain, but also remember that a whole other country now has a gaping wound and has far more casualties than we have. . . . A friend and I wanted to do something that would be a little controversial, obviously, but would speak into an area that is very neglected by the church. In prayer we got a vision of Christians being mediators of conflict—whether personal or international—standing between conflict and preaching the gospel of peace and reconciliation through Jesus Christ out of Ephesians, that Jesus "breaks down the wall of hostility" between peoples.[19] As a representation of that scripture we made these T-shirts. On the front it said, "War kills all," and on the back it said, "Jesus loves all." Over the top of that on the front there was an American flag, and on the back there was an Afghan flag. My friend's shirt was the same, except that on the front there was an Israeli flag and on the back a Palestinian flag. We just chose two religiously charged conflicts and wanted to stand in between that.Then we printed out the names of Iraqi victims, out of the half a million or whatever the exact number is that have died since the beginning of the war. We printed out five hundred names on strips of paper that said who they were, what they did for a living, where they were from, or if they were a son or father or mother. And we stood outside our church as the Memorial Sunday service let out, handing out these names and asking people to pray for the families of these people and to pray for the country of Iraq. We wound up getting kicked off church premises, and had a really weird run in with church security—*armed* church security at that—which was very revealing of the nature and structure of this church.

While not all community members had a story like Jasper's to tell, they shared his frustration with the religious nationalism and militarism common in conservative evangelical circles.

Urban Monastery participants were especially harsh in denouncing any notion of the United States being uniquely good or uniquely blessed by God as a nation. They used pejorative words like "arrogance," "colonialist," "imperialist," and "disgusting" to describe such views:

LILITH: Yeah, we're some kind of behemoth. But this nation, as much as it was sown in a desire for freedom, was also sown in violence. And that kind of sordid history is true of other nations as well. So I think it's reprehensible to have this high-minded view of ourselves.

JASPER: On the one hand, you have your conservative southern evangelicals talking about family values and Christian morality in politics. But I think even the most conservative of evangelicals would acknowledge that we're not God's chosen nation or something like that. America isn't the kingdom of God.

Urban Monastery participants flatly reject the "Christian America" ideology that marked early American Protestantism and has continued to hold sway as a dominant standpoint in the Christian Right and contemporary conservative Protestantism.

Along with abortion and anti-militarism, Urban Monastery participants place poverty and economic justice at the top of their list of important political issues. While most American evangelicals are in "no way troubled" by systematic economic inequality because of their deeply rooted individualism and belief in economic self-determination,[20] Urban Monastery participants are very troubled by poverty and economic inequality, both at home and abroad. Unlike most American evangelicals, their diagnoses of economic problems focus on structural and systemic injustices rather than the focusing exclusively on the individual:

MANUEL: Basically I don't mind giving money to the government. I guess that's the "communist" in me [smirking]. The majority of people who want to privatize things are people who have money. The poor don't. I think that in spite of all of the horrible things, the loopholes, the corruption, that can happen with giving money to governments, the poor still benefit from that. Because the rich don't give money to the poor until the poor take it. . . . And the rich are robbing them, sometimes by conscious decisions and sometimes just because of the things that they've implemented in the past. Like any of these cash-checking places near the Urban Monastery owned by rich people. They say, "Oh, we're helping out poor people be giving them loans." No they're not! . . . The poor are so vulnerable. I don't sympathize with the rich, that's my biggest thing.

While talking about the importance of pursuing systemic economic justice through progressive taxation, fair trade practices, and economic policy legislation, Urban Monastery participants spoke of both personal and political responsibility toward the poor and marginalized among Christians:

JASPER: As far as I know I'm supposed to provide for the widow and the orphan. Meaning, defend the defenseless. Which is one reason I don't know if I'm a pacifist or not. And as far as I know, if I *can* provide for a person in need, it's my responsibility to do so. I attempt to have the *gospel* shape my politics. So the God of the scripture's concern for the widow and the orphan and the foreigner plays a *huge* role—is paramount—to my political decisions and viewpoints.

From the perspective of the neo-monastic evangelicals in the Urban Monastery, working to end poverty and economic inequality is a major responsibility for all Christians and for any government or political system that claims to uphold justice.

Beyond their critique of unjust distributions of wealth and poverty in the United States and between Americans and citizens of other nations, Urban Monastery participants were quick to recognize the effects of economic policy in other areas of justice as well:

RILEY: In my opinion the most important political issue right now is the economic issue, because it's not just one issue. . . . For instance, it perpetuates urban decay. And that, to me, is *so* unjust. There are so many different ways that urban communities could work to rebuild, but they're not getting the funds and support they need. And that all circles back to the economic issue. . . . It also ties to the agricultural-industrial complex as well and the whole issue of "efficiency." . . . Economic imperialism has been perpetuated for centuries now and it's not going away anytime soon. . . . Wendell Berry wrote this essay about how the African American community after World War II—with the rise of urbanization and expansive metropolises and expansive suburbs—that a lot of working class people who were working out in these rural communities and keeping their local economies going were suddenly shifted to the cities because that's where the industry went in order to be more "efficient." That's such a big problem. . . . The environmental sustainability issue is also tied to economics. . . . We've really lost touch with agriculture and gardening, which is something that brings in touch with God and with our ancestors, with Israel: working in the fields, working for harvest, and then Sabbath. We've lost all these things that are really valuable from our culture. And I feel like that's all tied in with the economic issue.

Where Riley (above) pointed out the economic roots of racialized urban poverty, urban decay, and environmental justice issues, Jasper argued that "maybe one sustainable solution to the abortion issue is to pursue economic reform," given that abortion clinics "tend to be concentrated in lower income areas that are targets for this sort of action." Here again, we find Urban Monastery participants standing against dominant expressions of conservative evangelicalism, which sing the praises of deregulated free market capitalism while bashing progressive tax policies as "socialist," denying global warming and the need for environmental regulation, and attributing poverty to poor family dynamics and work habits.[21]

Urban Monastery participants are particularly sensitive to global economic injustices and the US role in helping to create and sustain economic inequality that harms people in less powerful nations while creating dependency on the United States:

MANUEL: We're the Babylon of our time. We're the Roman Empire, the American Empire. . . . As much I'd like think we don't conquer people, we conquer people. We enslave people to our finances. . . . I don't think our calling from God is to be colonizers. I don't think we're supposed to be imperial rulers.

When Urban Monastery participants talk about America's influence in the world, they are more likely to be critical of its use of military and economic power in pursuit of national self-interest than they are to praise America as a moral exemplar or champion of democracy. As in other arenas, however, they are balanced in their critiques, acknowledging the good as well as the bad and being critical of the radical Left's tendency to take absolutist "anti-American" positions at all times (Caleb, Lilith).

Urban Monastery participants also mentioned environmental preservation, universal health care, education reform, global feminism, systemic racism, and opposition to capital punishment among the political issues that mattered most to them, though these issues were named less frequently than abortion, poverty/economic justice, and anti-militarism. For a few white Urban Monastery participants, racial inequality and injustice was the defining issue of the 2008 election:

ELLE: I'm really involved in racial justice stuff . . . and people kept saying Barack Obama was going to get shot. . . . The cops are *racist*, the Christians are racist, *racist*. I had *so many* Christian friends telling me they're not voting for a black guy; because he's Muslim, because he's black. . . . It brought out racism, all this anti-gay stuff, all this stuff. This was my first election being truly saved and rooted in Christ, and I just was so shocked to see how our country reacted. So if anything I voted for Obama *because* he was black. I was like, "My kids are going to see the day when *truly*, the White House is not all white."

As with their views on war, poverty, inequality, education, and the environment, Urban Monastery participants tend toward left-liberal rather than conservative positions on racial issues.

The Limits of Politics and of Autonomy from Politics

Finally, while Urban Monastery participants engaged quite deeply in the 2008 presidential election and strongly affirmed a Christian responsibility to pursue justice through political engagement, they were wary of placing too much hope or emphasis on political systems as a means to accomplish good in the world. Although Urban Monastery participants largely supported Mr. Obama's presidential campaign, they were also critical of the "idolatry" and false hopes it engendered (Riley); or as Jasper put it, the "fashion show, the hype, the 'hail the messiah' feeling in the air. I don't want to hail the American messiah." Their political reflections were sprinkled with questions and comments such as, "Isn't there someone who has others' interests in mind?" "We have a broken political system" (Helena), and "I don't put a lot of hope in politics" (Roland):

MINDY: Politicians seek their own good, fame, and glory, and their party's fame and glory. Nobody's looking out for the people in a concerted way.

RILEY: My ideas about politics have radically shifted [since becoming a Christian]. I'm more apolitical now: my King is in heaven. Politics often just perpetuates everything that's wrong with the world. . . . So many Americans are disenchanted with government.

HELENA: Bureaucracy can't care for people. It's a machine. Creating these systems is not going to help people be fully cared for. . . . Government can't do heart to heart.

Like Jasper (below), they wrestled with scripture and history in their deliberations about politics, Christian responsibility toward politics, and the proper way for Christians to engage in the political process:

JASPER: Why didn't Paul openly rebuke government and social structures that were oppressive; like Paul's admonition for slaves to obey their masters? Because accepting slavery is *obviously* not part of the gospel that Jesus Christ preached. But then you read Philemon and the words he has for masters and slaves, and you realize he's doing something far more subversive. Think about slavery in the United States: we fought a civil war to end slavery, but really it was the nonviolent subversion of the civil rights movement that *really* changed people's minds. Top-down change—just changing the rules—doesn't change the heart. And of course the church didn't have power in Paul's day. But Galatians 3:28 is *incredibly* subversive.[22] And it worked! And it was revolutionary for that time. It cultivated love. Christians shouldn't be absent from politics, but by no means should we think that politics is *the* answer.

Urban Monastery participants did not neglect political structures or view Christian spirituality as a private matter which had no bearing on the state, but neither did they overburden their political engagement with expectations of quick or dramatic social transformation through electoral politics. They engaged in political action and debate, but were careful to maintain a certain degree of autonomy and critical distance from political process.

In articulating these concerns about the limits of electoral politics and bureaucratic systems for solving social problems, subverting unequal social relationships, and addressing poverty and inequality humanely, we hear echoes of the apolitical communalism that marked much of the Jesus People movement. It is instructive to note the similarities and differences between Urban Monastery participants' views on the limits of politics and those of the Jesus People. In their desire to replace bureaucratic systems with authentic human community, their emphasis on localism and face-to-face relationships over placelessness and social distance, their celebration of the small and informal over the large and formal, and their time-intensive communal lifestyles, communitarian movements such as the Jesus People and new monasticism have the potential to push participants away from mass-based political engagement.[23] In the case of the Jesus People movement, these tendencies were exacerbated by a strong premillennial dispensationalism that pointed to the futility of social reform (and concomitant emphasis on personal evangelism) in light of the coming apocalypse. A potent mixture of radical countercultural skepticism toward "the system," and conservative evangelical skepticism about the possibility of social reform in light of human depravity, produced a recipe for political disengagement for many Jesus People communities.[24]

Although we see some similarities between Urban Monastery participants and their Jesus People progenitors, neo-monastic evangelicals have largely resisted the latter's tendency toward political disengagement, not least due to their rejection of premillennial dispensationalism and more this-worldly interpretation of the gospel.[25] Still, systemic skepticism about large-scale political and economic institutions (particularly acute among neo-Anabaptists) and disillusionment with recent Christian Right forays into the political realm have left neo-monastic evangelicals vulnerable to the temptation of disengagement.[26] The temptation is exacerbated by frustration over their contradictory cultural location, which makes it difficult for many neo-monastic evangelicals to find politicians or political parties to get excited about. As noted above, almost one-third of the Urban Monastery participants that I interviewed either did not vote or voted for a third party candidate because of their difficulty in choosing which of their political convictions to betray in order to cast a vote. As Devon confessed to me:

DEVON: I didn't know who to vote for, which is why I didn't vote! . . . Part of my frustration is I was right in the middle. I don't agree with either one of their policies enough to vote for them. And I'm not going to just go, "Well, there are four things I agree with this candidate and five things I agree with this candidate, so I'm going to go with the five." I couldn't bring myself to do that.

Even among neo-monastic evangelicals who have been able to find a political home in the Democratic (or Republican) Party, their communitarian impulses and contradictory cultural location puts limits on the extent to which neo-monastic evangelicals are willing to commit resources toward partisan political activism. For example, while they devoted significant amounts of time and energy discussing political issues and their relation to faith and scripture, Urban Monastery participants did not join political campaigns or participate in get-out-the-vote drives. They did not volunteer or donate money to political parties or political action committees. Urban Monastery participants' political engagement was active but circumscribed, with many community members preferring more "subversive" approaches to social transformation centered on the proliferation of radical alternative communities and social institutions rooted in civil society (Jasper).[27]

The temptation to disengage from electoral political involvement in favor of a "new politics of spiritual community"—as historian David Swartz described the Jesus People's widespread abandonment of mass-based politics—remains a concern among some contemporary observers of neo-monastic communities and the "new evangelicalism" more generally.[28] While heartened by the social and political sensibilities being cultivated within "the new evangelical social engagement," sociologist R. Stephen Warner worries that growing evangelical disillusionment with Christian Right politics (and politics in general) could lead to a counterproductive abandonment of the pursuit of social transformation through political action altogether.[29] Indeed, this is precisely what James Davison Hunter calls for in his widely read book (in evangelical circles) *To Change the World: The Irony, Tragedy, and Possibility of Christianity in the Late Modern World.* Finding little more than nihilistic Nietzschean *ressentiment* and will-to-power in the political practices of the Christian Right, evangelical left, and neo-Anabaptist movements alike, Hunter suggests that American Christians might do well to exit the political arena for a spell in order to work "toward a new city commons" rooted in civil society.[30]

Neo-monastic and other evangelicals' struggles to strike the right balance between political engagement and disengagement, piety (whether individual or communal) and politics, otherworldly and this-worldly concerns, or working within or outside "the system," is another manifestation of the dynamic tension between politicization and autonomy in the American evangelical field. As I argued in chapter 3, evangelical religious and political standpoints cannot be deduced directly from social location or explained solely in terms of external political categories. While we cannot understand contemporary American evangelicalism without understanding how historical political struggles have shaped the boundaries, classification schemes, and structure of the evangelical field, evangelical religion is not exclusively, or even primarily, concerned with what goes on in the political arena. As much as it is about politics, evangelical religion is even more so about belief, worship, spiritual formation, personal transformation, and spiritual community. It is about pursuing a certain kind of relationship with God, with other people, and with the natural world. While the way that evangelicals engage in these activities are shaped by and have political implications, it is always a mistake to explain American evangelicalism exclusively in terms of political categories. To do otherwise is to ignore the (relative) autonomy of the evangelical field with respect to the American political field, which is a product of the specific and irreversible cumulative history of evangelical religion in the United States.[31]

The contradictory cultural location of Urban Monastery participants and other neo-monastic evangelicals also reflects American evangelicalism's relative autonomy with respect the political field, as well as the limits of that autonomy. The deeply held religious beliefs that drive Urban Monastery participants' frustration with both the Democratic and Republican Parties reflect this autonomy, while the difficulty of imagining a viable political platform which represents their holistic communitarian views demonstrates how evangelical political engagement is constrained by external political forces. For example, the "life versus life" theme in Urban Monastery participants' political deliberations echo earlier Catholic and evangelical left attempts to organize American Christians around a "consistent ethic of life" platform that combined conservative views on abortion with left-liberal views on racial, economic, and foreign policy matters in the 1970s and 1980s.[32] The failure of these efforts to gain traction—and the difficulty many evangelicals had in even conceiving of such a position as a legitimate expression of biblical Christianity in America—points to the limits of evangelicalism's autonomy with respect to the political field.[33] Conservative evangelicals dismissed "so called Christians like [Senator] Mark Hatfield" who opposed President Nixon on the Vietnam War in the 1960s and 1970s, just as some Urban Monastery participants felt "coerced . . . as if they would be sinning" by voting against George W. Bush in 2000 and 2004 (Lilith).[34] And just as progressive evangelicals received a cold shoulder from Democratic Party activists and the New Left due to their pro-life standpoints, Urban Monastery participants recognize that they often look like "religious fanatics" to their friends on the Left, even while being called "socialists," "communists," and "radicals" by their friends on the Right (Jasper, Caleb).[35]

Paying attention to politicization in the evangelical field also illuminates the processes through which distinctive movements within evangelicalism form coalitions with each other and with non-evangelicals, as well as the limits of these coalitions and how they dissolve. As discussed in chapter 3, it is common for agents occupying dominated positions in a field to form relatively heterodox and ecumenical *coalitions of the dominated* as a result of their shared opposition to dominant standpoints. Shared opposition to a common "enemy" is one of the primary drivers of coalition-making within the evangelical field, whether that be conservative evangelicals and Catholics uniting against pro-choice Democratic Party candidates, or young evangelical left activists uniting with mainline Protestants, progressive Catholics, and secular New Left activists against US interventionism in Nicaragua under Ronald Reagan.[36] Common enemies create common ground. This is particularly true among dominated and avant-garde positions within a field, where the pressure to accumulate sufficient economic, symbolic, and specific capital in order to survive creates strong incentives—sometimes even necessities—for agents in dominated positions to expand their search for partners beyond the traditional boundaries of the field. As illustrated by the struggles of evangelical left organizations such as Sojourners and Evangelicals for Social Action to remain solvent through the 1980s and 1990s, mundane demands for money, volunteers, and organizational resources can generate a strong impetus for ecumenical and heterodox coalition-building among dominated evangelical positions.[37]

The history of evangelical Christianity in America, then, suggests that opposition to common political enemies is a particularly potent driver of coalition-making in the evangelical field. However, while shared opposition to a common enemy is a powerful impetus for evangelical coalition-building, the absence or removal of that enemy is an impetus for fragmentation, as the early history of the evangelical left vividly portrays.[38] Organized under the banner of Evangelicals for McGovern and driven by strong anti-Nixon sentiment, the Thanksgiving Workshop of Evangelical Social Concern in 1973 brought feminist, African American, Anabaptist, Jesus People, Reformed, and "ethnic" evangelicals together in an attempt to mobilize quiescent midcentury evangelicalism toward progressive political engagement.[39] By 1975 however—with Nixon out of office and the American war in Vietnam concluded—the Thanksgiving Workshops had dissolved in the midst of internecine theological, denominational, racial, political, and gender disputes, foreshadowing the fragmentation and decline of the evangelical left through the late 1970s and 1980s.[40] The Christian Right, on the other hand, had little difficulty in holding together conservative evangelicals, Catholics, and other coreligionists against the specter of a diffuse, long-standing political enemy known as "secular humanism" (and left-liberal politics in general).[41]

If the loss of a common enemy is an impetus for fragmentation in evangelical coalition-building, so, too, is consecration. It was the 1973 Thanksgiving Workshop that put the evangelical left on the map and consolidated its status as a recognized, if dominated, position within the evangelical field. Just as the nascent emerging church movement brought together a diverse group of (socially) young evangelical religious leaders united in opposition to dominant conservative and megachurch expressions of American evangelicalism, the Thanksgiving Workshop brought together a diverse group of (socially) young evangelical religious leaders united in opposition to American evangelicalism's quietism and complicity in a host of social ills it associated with right-wing politics. And just as the emerging church movement fractured upon achieving consecration and distinction as a recognized position in the evangelical field, the nascent evangelical left coalition fragmented upon achieving consecration when, in both cases, internal differences and disagreements that were initially hidden by a shared opposition to dominant standpoints—and a shared interest in achieving recognition—were exposed as these avant-garde movements established themselves and began to accrue symbolic and specific capital in the field.[42] We may expect to see similar processes of fragmentation and internal differentiation unfold within evangelical neo-monasticism in the coming years, insofar as the new monasticism continues to accrue capital and grow in size and visibility within the evangelical field.

Conclusion: Communitarianism and the Urban Monastery

To summarize, then, Urban Monastery participants were more likely to vote for Barack Obama than John McCain in 2008 presidential election, but not overwhelmingly so. They are unanimously and strongly opposed to abortion in most cases, though they are split on whether they support anti-abortion legislation or not. Anti-militarism and economic justice—not gay marriage— are the other political issues of greatest importance to Urban Monastery participants. The Urban Monastery participants I spoke with more likely to oppose a ban on gay marriage than support it, in spite of the fact that they personally believe in traditional, heterosexual marriage for religious reasons. On other issues of importance to them, they overwhelmingly tended to support left-liberal political standpoints. Clearly, the Urban Monastery's view of politics does not fit comfortably within the political ideology of the Christian Right, conservative evangelicalism, or Republican Party conservatism; nor does it fit comfortably within the progressive Left. Like other emerging church, evangelical left, and neo-monastic evangelicals, Urban Monastery participants often find it difficult to negotiate their political and religious identities as theologically, but not politically, conservative Christians. They are deeply torn between the conservative and liberal poles of American politics, occupying a *contradictory cultural location* with respect to the Christian Right and the progressive Left.

In contrast to the theological and political position-takings of dominant expressions of twentieth-century American evangelicalism, the Urban Monastery's holistic communitarianism is consistent with moral cosmology theory: Urban Monastery participants tend to have conservative social attitudes but left-liberal economic attitudes. The Urban Monastery's holistic communitarianism puts them at odds with economic and political position-takings of the majority of American evangelicals and pushes them toward the more left-liberal economic attitudes anticipated by moral cosmology theory. This is true despite the fact that Urban Monastery participants are more highly educated than most evangelicals, which according to prior sociological research should push them toward greater economic conservatism.[43]

Communitarianism is also a philosophical and political position advocated by a host of prominent scholars such as the late Robert Bellah and Amitai Etzioni.[44] Urban Monastery participants did not express any awareness of communitarianism as a broader intellectual and political movement, but their political attitudes and reflections on personal voting decisions suggest some affinity with it. This affinity is partially captured by the concept of the Urban Monastery's contradictory cultural location with respect to the Christian Right and the progressive Left. In the words of Amitai Etzioni:

> Communitarianism is committed to fostering a greater sense of personal and social responsibility among individual citizens; to strengthening the cohesion of families and local communities; to encouraging reconciliation among different racial, ethnic, and religious groups; and to fostering a national policy debate more cognizant of humankind's moral horizon and the social responsibilities of the individual and the community. Its aim is to contribute to effective solutions, derived from democratic dialogue, through a careful elucidation of alternative policies and competing models of social conduct in light of their moral implications and their likely practical consequences for family and community life.[45]

Political communitarians favor "social formulations of the good" and argue that "today's problem in our societies is excessive individualism."[46] Etzioni describes "communitarianism as a 'third way' between capitalism and socialism or perhaps more realistically, a 'third way' between rampant liberalism and uncompassionate conservatism."[47] Political communitarians are committed to "emphasizing social responsibility and promoting policies meant to stem the erosion of communal life in an increasingly fragmented society"[48] and argue that modern Western political theory and practice overemphasizes individual "rights" at the expense of social "responsibilities."[49]

Much like political communitarians, Urban Monastery participants are critical of political conservatives for ignoring the state and society's responsibility toward the poor and reducing global and domestic economic inequality, while also being critical of political left-liberals who prioritize individual rights over social responsibility to "protect the innocent" as in the case of abortion (Alex). They are critical of excessive individualism in politics, the church, and society, and work to strengthen family and social bonds in their local context across racial, class, and political boundaries. Urban Monastery participants repeatedly expressed desire for a "different voice" in American politics that could better represent their own commitment to holistic communitarianism (Caleb), which, among other things, follows the pattern of social conservatism and economic left-liberalism anticipated by moral cosmology theory. Alex's wistful longing for a "pro-life Democrat" represents the sort of political position that Urban Monastery participants favor but express little hope for given the current structure of the American political field.[50] Urban Monastery participants are perhaps not so alone as they think, however, in their desire for a different voice in American politics, as suggested by the political communitarian movement, resonances between the "new evangelicalism" and long-standing Catholic social teaching,[51] and over thirty years of evangelical left activism that has increasingly made inroads among both megachurch and moderate American evangelicals.[52]

Indeed, the political standpoints of Urban Monastery participants bear some resemblance to the political profile of "populist evangelicals" who comprise approximately 35 percent of American evangelicals, more than any other evangelical opinion cluster.[53] Populist evangelicals are the largest and fastest growing segment within American evangelicalism.[54] Like moral cosmology theory's theological communitarians, populist evangelicals are socially conservative but economically left-liberal and favor government involvement in both economic and social issues.[55] Like most Urban Monastery participants, populist evangelicals are strongly opposed to abortion, have left-liberal standpoints on environmental protection and foreign policy issues, believe that Christians should be active in politics, and demonstrate a high degree of religious commitment.[56] Just as Urban Monastery participants' contradictory cultural location made political deliberations and voting decisions extremely difficult, the process of bringing faith to bear on political issues is an "agonizing experience" for populist evangelicals, given that their political views "are simultaneously at odds with the dominant forces in the Democratic and Republican coalitions."[57] Like R. Stephen Warner and other observers of the "new evangelicalism," political scientist John C. Green is both curious and cautious about the future political implications of the rise of the new evangelicalism and populist evangelicals in particular, wondering whether, "Faced with this agonizing choice, many populists may be especially tempted to become politically quiescent."[58] In Green's view, "it is the fate of the [evangelical] populists that is most likely to determine the place of evangelicals in American public affairs."[59] Urban Monastery participants may feel like a lonely minority with no political home, but their political standpoints and contradictory cultural location are in fact indicative of the political sensibilities of a large and growing population within contemporary American evangelicalism.

Chapter 6

Organizing Community for Holistic Mission: An Urban Monastery in Action

IN ADDITION TO expressing the theological and political standpoints of Urban Monastery participants, *holistic communitarianism* also functions as a relatively coherent and comprehensive strategy of individual and collective action within the Urban Monastery; a strategy that challenges dominant evangelical approaches to religious organization and social engagement.[1] Whereas the building projects and religious programs of megachurch evangelicalism are focused on the primary goals of evangelism, personal development, and church growth,[2] Urban Monastery participants pursue *holistic mission* in an attempt to address spiritual, social, economic, and political needs in the "abandoned places of empire."[3] The first part of this chapter focuses on the various expressions of *holistic mission* within the Urban Monastery. The Urban Monastery also practices a remarkably coherent and comprehensive style of *organizing community* that draws heavily on the Trinitarian elements of their holistic communitarian meaning system. The Urban Monastery is organized into a web of dense, nested micro-communities that reinforce the centrality of "community" as both the means and end of authentic Christian spirituality, as we will see in the latter part of this chapter.

In each of these ways, Urban Monastery participants explicitly draw on core symbolic elements of their distinctive holistic communitarian meaning system to construct lines of individual and collective action in the world, practicing holistic communitarianism as a relatively comprehensive and coherent strategy of action. In doing so, they demonstrate how cultural meaning systems can "influence action in powerful, direct ways" under the right social conditions, as religious and cultural sociologists such as Ann Swidler and Max Weber have long agreed.[4] Just as the vigilant application of a religious ethic enabled the early ascetic Protestant sects of Europe to organize many aspects of private and public life according to their distinctive religious *Weltanschauung*,[5] Urban Monastery participants practice a *celebratory asceticism* and a distinctive style of *anti-bureaucratic rational organization* derived from a careful and intentional application of holistic communitarianism to their individual and collective life, as we will see below.[6]

Practicing Holistic Communitarianism: Holistic Mission

Throughout most of the twentieth and early twenty-first century, dominant expressions of American evangelicalism have prioritized evangelism as their primary strategy of social engagement. The primacy of evangelism rests on two basic theological premises: that having a relationship with God through Jesus Christ is the only way to eternal life, and that society can only be as good as the individuals who comprise it. According to this second premise, good government and just social relationships are made possible primarily through the spiritual conversion of individuals rather than by attempting to change unjust political, economic, or social structures directly. If one wants to change society for the better, one should try to convert as many individuals as possible to Christianity because "the Gospel makes men good. [And] Good men make good societies."[7] Sociologist Christian Smith refers to this line of thinking as evangelicalism's "personal influence strategy" of social change:

> American evangelicals are resolutely committed to a social-change strategy that maintains that the only truly effective way to change the world is one-individual-at-a-time through the influence of interpersonal relationships.[8]

In this view, spiritual revival through effective evangelism is not just the only hope for the individual; it is the only hope for society as well.[9]

Neo-monastic evangelicals agree with the importance of sharing the gospel with individuals, but they disagree that it should be the only or primary strategy of social engagement for evangelical Christians. At both the individual and communal level, neo-monastic communities like the Urban Monastery emphasize "holistic" social engagement that places equal emphasis on evangelism and social justice action, "sacred" and "secular" activities, and individual and social transformation. The Arts and Homeless Youth Monastery runs two transitional houses for young adults coming out of the justice system, off the street, or out of serious addictions and who are looking for help with employment, life skills, and spiritual growth. The Recovery Monastery hosts middle-aged men battling addictions in a gritty working-class neighborhood. The Justice Monastery runs a recovery house for young women, volunteers with local landlords to offer services in the neighborhood's "slum hotels" where most poor residents live, and engages in public advocacy for clean affordable housing in the neighborhood at local government meetings. The Sanctuary Monastery fights city government over unjust immigration enforcement practices. Neo-monastic communities provide a wide range of services in their neighborhoods, varying from after-school programs to volunteer-staffed cafés, free meals, community organizing and other events, and simple friendship.

At the individual level, Urban Monastery participants practice holistic mission by pursuing careers in politics, law, social work, the arts, and public policy as legitimate expressions of Christian mission in the world that go beyond personal evangelism and traditional religious careers. Rather than valorizing foreign missionaries and full-time Christian workers as the highest expression of Christian vocation as is typical of many conservative Protestant churches, many Urban Monastery participants are drawn to careers that enable them to challenge poverty, inequality, and injustice.[10] This is one of many ways in which Urban Monastery participants reject the bifurcation of the world into "sacred" religious space and "profane" secular space, as we will explore further below.[11] Thus, for example, Jason views the pursuit of a career as economic policy advisor in developing nations as the best way for him to pursue Christ's mission to bring justice to the poor. Other Urban Monastery participants are social workers who serve as legal advocates for victims of domestic violence. Mina—one of the cofounders of the Urban Monastery involved in mobilizing grassroots advocacy and service efforts for victims of human trafficking—is pursuing a career in law devoted to fighting the human trafficking industry. As individuals, Urban Monastery participants believe that Christians must be involved in the transformation of social structures that lead to poverty and human oppression, and they view careers devoted to such endeavors as effective and religiously legitimate expressions of Christian mission.

As a community, the Urban Monastery engages in a wide variety of non-evangelistic activities as an expression of its mission to "love the world."[12] As part of their efforts to combat racial inequality in their highly segregated city, they participate in volunteer work days and mentoring programs at a nearby predominately African American public high school, where only 11 percent of students read on grade level and the dropout rate is above 50 percent (Alex). The Justice Collective, composed mostly of social workers, "pioneered . . . an Extreme Home Makeover thing at one lady's house. It was a blast" (Caleb). A team from the Urban Monastery traveled to New Orleans after Hurricane Katrina, providing water and spiritual support for victims of the hurricane.

A number of leaders serve as part of their city's Human Trafficking Rescue Project, a coalition led by the Department of Justice composed of social service agencies, local law enforcement, and the FBI to provide services to local victims of human trafficking. Whereas conservative evangelicals are often suspicious of Christians who work with religious outsiders to combat poverty, Urban Monastery participants practice holistic mission that attempts to engage social problems at the social and systemic—not just the individual and spiritual—levels.

Hospitality as Holistic Mission

The practice of hospitality—a core practice of most neo-monastic communities—is a particularly instructive example of holistic mission in the Urban Monastery.[13] The concept and practice of hospitality is loaded with complex variegated meaning that informs how the Urban Monastery interacts with its immediate surroundings. First, the practice of hospitality in Urban Monastery involves the personal, physical presence of a group of people who intentionally devote personal and communal resources and time to welcome the "stranger." Devon, 26, a former international model and the Urban Monastery's director of hospitality, developed a hospitality effort he called the Front Door:

DEVON: The vision was to have a floor in the Urban Monastery building where we could welcome the "stranger." And I defined the stranger as "a person without a place." A lot of people see strangers as maybe undefined or dangerous in light of that fact that they just don't know someone, they objectify someone, or they assume something about someone.

Devon referred to a book about the historical meaning and practice of Christian hospitality as a significant influence on his development of the Front Door and the practice of hospitality in the Urban Monastery. In it the author writes:

For much of church history, Christians addressed concerns about recognition and human dignity within their discussions and practices of hospitality. Especially in relation to strangers, hospitality was a basic category for dealing with the importance of transcending social differences and breaking social boundaries that excluded certain categories or kinds of persons. . . . Hospitality that welcomes "the least" and recognizes their equal value can be an act of resistance and defiance, a challenge to the values and expectations of the larger community.[14]

From the point of view of neo-monastic evangelicals, to practice hospitality of this sort in the radically class and race segregated United States means reloca-tion. Sharing meals, resources, work, and friendship across significant race and class divides is far more realistic when living in close geographical prox-imity. While transportation and housing costs make it practically impossible for marginalized groups to move into middle- and upper-class neighbor-hoods, the reverse is possible, albeit costly in terms of convenient access to the best schools, parks, jobs, and businesses. The Urban Monastery was in-tentionally established in a poor, racially diverse urban neighborhood with the hope of finding ways to become part of the neighborhood and practice reciprocal hospitality as opportunity allowed (Caleb).

This particular vision of hospitality leads neo-monastic communities like the Urban Monastery to think about church buildings differently than many evangelicals. Rather than building churches with large sanctuaries for Sunday services in the expanding middle-class suburbs, the Urban Monastery rents a large industrial building in the urban core of a large city where it is possible for some community participants to live on site. This allows the community to practice hospitality in ways that are impossible for churches that are re-moved from disadvantaged neighborhoods, are only used occasionally during the week for regularly scheduled religious events, and are only accessible by automobile. By occupying a building in a diverse, low-income neighborhood in which many community members actually live, the Urban Monastery is able to practice holistic mission in the form of hospitality in ways that others cannot:

DEVON: In the first year and a half I can say that at least once a weekend we had somebody staying with us. Could have been a person off the street, or there's a whole group of what I would call traveler youth who travel the United States hitch-hiking on freight trains: they would come and stay from one night to three months. At one point about two months after we opened the hospitality house we had forty people staying with us.

Because of its geographical location and live-in residents who intentionally make themselves available to neighbors and visitors, the Urban Monastery is able to practice a flexible form of hospitality that offers material, social, and spiritual resources in the context of informal personal relationships rather than formal social service programs:

DEVON: We're realizing a new definition of hospitality. It's not going to be the same for everybody. It can be a meal. It can be rest. It can be, "Hey, come in for a couple of hours, take a shower, clean up." It can be, "Hey, come in and stay for a month." Sometimes it's a glass of lemonade and a five minute conversation. Sometimes it's a person who needs a place to stay for three months. It's not my job to define it.

In the words of a leader of the Justice Monastery, "relocation to the abandoned places of empire" means that, unlike many religious and nonreligious people who work with disadvantaged populations: "We don't go home at the end of the day. We *are* home."[15]

Urban Monastery participants draw on biblical and monastic teachings in viewing hospitality as an opportunity to offer "home" to people by treating strangers and visitors as if they were family:

DEVON: Hospitality in the Greek is two words. The first word is *phileo*: that word in Greek means to serve a person of close kinship or family to you. The second part of the word hospitality in Greek is *xenia*, and that word means stranger. So the word hospitality that appears in the Bible comes from a Greek word that means to serve the stranger as if they were of close kinship or family to you. So we began trying to offer people that kind of hospitality.

Offering this type of hospitality to people on a regular basis requires community members to devote significant amounts of time and economic resources to welcoming strangers to the Urban Monastery. Practicing hospitality on the scale of the Urban Monastery cannot typically be done by traditional family households: it requires a collective effort to pay rent for extra living space, for food and other practical needs, and a willingness by some community members to live in the Urban Monastery not as traditional renters, but as an intentional community ready to share time and resources with one another and with strangers as "family":

DEVON: I invited five guys and said, "I need you to do three things. One, I want you to get rid of all your stuff. Second, if there is anything of financial, monetary, or sentimental value to you that you would be frustrated, sad, or mad if it got stolen: don't bring that here either. I'm not trying to say anything with that, but there's a good possibility that a laptop, an iPod, a gold coin, or whatever could get stolen. There are going to be a lot of people here, so you need to be OK with that. Third, I asked them to be willing to serve wherever they are able to serve, and to also fourthly get to a point where they don't think of their stuff as *theirs*, but *ours*. So we put some stuff in place. One, all of the food at the Front Door Hospitality

House is *ours*. It's not *yours*, it's not *mine*. If you buy food, we don't allow you to put your name on it, because when you are offering hospitality on a regular basis it's easier to say "any food you can find you can have." (Emphasis in original)

The practice of hospitality is one example of how the Urban Monastery and other neo-monastic evangelicals pursue social justice as part of a holistic communitarian strategy of action, establishing communities where "the practical needs of the local poor are met" and "sharing economic resources with fellow community members and the needy among us."[16]

In the Urban Monastery, practicing hospitality across racial and class-based social boundaries is an expression of the politics of recognition and the feminist axiom that "the personal is political," as well as a practical expression of the Christian understanding of human dignity.[17] Sharing a meal or one's home with the "stranger" or "other" is a way of challenging existing social hierarchies of domination. Rather than objectifying the stranger as an object of pity or a moral project, they are welcomed into community as friends and equals:

DEVON: In some ways hospitality can literally create or provide an opportunity for someone who is socially invisible to become visible. By inviting them into a family, you create visibility for an otherwise socially invisible person that someone would objectify. It's the difference between introducing someone as: "This is my homeless friend" versus "This is my friend from southern California." You get a completely different response. All of that person's definition of a homeless person comes in the baggage of shaking that person's hand, which is unfair to them.

Urban Monastery participants told me numerous stories of how their practice of hospitality challenged personal habits of objectifying marginalized "others" inherited from their middle-class religious backgrounds:

DEVON: In that first year we hosted a guy off the street that I became good friends with: African American guy, 48 at that point, and an alcoholic. He had come over for dinner Friday night and he was going to come over the next morning, and I went to bed realizing, "I don't know where my *friend*, Marcus, is sleeping tonight." And for the first time it hit me that I had been objectifying this guy for the last year, defining our relationship inaccurately, in that we constantly had people that would come and stay at the Urban Monastery for two days, three days, two weeks, three months, and I didn't know them. But for whatever reason I'm willing to fling the doors wide open, give them all of my food, and let them sleep wherever they want. But this guy that I've *known* for a year, that I know better than some people that I see every day, I didn't know where he was sleeping. So I went to bed just freaking out. I woke up the next day, he came over, and I was like, "Man, I don't know where you slept last night—it's really none of my business—but if you need a place to crash tonight you can sleep here." And he was like, "All right, that's sweet." So he came to live with us. We'd have other homeless guys that were sleeping in the lobby, that were drunk, and we'd invite them up, they'd crash on the couch and get up and have a meal with us or a cup of coffee. It really challenged me a lot, and it gave me an opportunity to challenge other people in that place of objectification.

While Urban Monastery participants look for ways to help people in need, they are wary of objectifying the "other" and turning disadvantaged individuals or groups into benevolence projects in the manner typical of many historic evangelical approaches to "helping the poor":[18]

DEVON: As Western Christians we often take on this responsibility to go find the most messed up person we've ever met and try to save them and to fix their problems. That's just not right. People convince themselves that somebody, first, wants their help, and second, needs their help, and then they go find the most jacked up person they've ever met and say, "Come live with me." Then they are surprised when that person rips them off or things go badly. . . . There is just so much objectification and so much responsibility that we think we have that we really don't.

Urban Monastery participants speak of how becoming neighbors and friends, rather than social service providers or evangelistic crusaders, has taught them to move beyond objectified relationships with the "other" into more mutually respectful and authentic interactions.

The Urban Monastery's pursuit of holistic mission through hospitality is both similar and dissimilar to standard evangelical practices of evangelism. As evangelicals, Urban Monastery participants believe that sharing the gospel is a religious imperative and primary way in which they pursue their mission to "love the world." However, they are careful not to attach any form of expectation or pressure around spiritual conversion to their practice of hospitality:

DEVON: Hospitality isn't overwatering someone with all of your information and knowledge. . . . Creating an environment of hospitality is really just allowing people to figure out *their* language and figure out *their* ideas. . . . It's not boxing someone in a corner and going, "This is what I believe: you have to believe because I'm giving you a place to stay" or whatever. I don't want to box somebody in. I don't want to meet somebody and say, "What do you believe? And does that match up with what I believe? Then we can be friends." No! I want to be like, "Hey, do you want to come hang out here?" . . . Before they know what they believe, before they know what they want to become a part of, they simply belong. And maybe they do become a part of this family. Maybe they do begin to believe similar things. But as Mother Teresa said: It's not my job to convert anybody. It's only my job to introduce people to God. Then it's up to them what they do with that.

Urban Monastery participants practice hospitality as a way to express God's love for the world by intentionally and often sacrificially offering material, social, and spiritual resources to those around them, while respecting the beliefs, autonomy, and dignity of the "stranger."

Holistic Mission and the Arts

With almost one-third of the community either attending art school or working in an arts-related job outside the evangelical subculture, many Urban Monastery participants are engaged in efforts to practice holistic mission among artists. Whereas American evangelicals have had a contentious relationship with the secular artistic field throughout most of the twentieth century—frequently protesting movies and television shows, boycotting the movie industry, and condemning public funding for the arts that evangelicals frequently find religiously and morally offensive—Urban Monastery members engage the arts community as participants in the field.[19] They spoke about the fear and difficulty of "coming out" as a Christian artist in a world where "Jesus or a cross or Christianity are so deeply offensive" (Helena). All of the Urban Monastery artists I interviewed talked about the history of mutual antagonism between conservative American evangelicals and secular arts community, and the hostility they experienced from other artists, art students, and professors toward Christianity:

JASMINE: We're required to take two Western thought classes at the Art Institute. . . . So we're in this philosophy class and someone says, "You can apply that idea to Buddhism!" And somebody adds, "You can apply it to Hinduism," and I was like, "You can apply it to Christianity, too." And someone responded in a mocking voice, "You've *got* to pull the Christian card." At this point no one in this classroom knew me, so I just said, "You don't even know me! I may or may not even be a Christian. Can we not just discuss the idea of Christianity, since we just spent twenty minutes talking about Buddhism?" But it's the one religion that you can't even *talk* about. You can't even bring it up without immediate negative reaction. It wasn't even like we were talking about it and they disagreed. Talking about it was not even allowed.

LILITH: Whole classes [at the Art Institute] are built around this venomous attitude towards our history of Christian culture, because there's this idea that to be an artist is to be a punk and a rebel. And the louder, the more violently you thrash against whatever barriers there are that happen to bother you, the more you get rewarded.

ALEX: I didn't realize how much these students didn't believe that Jesus could coexist with their world as an artist. I found out that there was a worldview of tolerance on campus that somehow didn't include or was not tolerant of those who follow Christ.

Artists in the Urban Monastery wrestle with the conflicting values of the artistic field and their own faith, such as the conflict between radical autonomy and self-chosen limits or between expressive individualism and holistic life in community:

LILITH: I don't think that questioning is bad. I think questions are extremely creative when they're spoken in the right spirit. *Extremely* creative, because they're probing for new information and they're creating something new. But oftentimes sadly the artist's attitude involves a predetermined dismantling. Some things deserve dismantling. Not everything does though!

There's this idea that part of the job description of an artist is to be a rebel. What's funny is that *that* idea is about being destructive: but to be rebellious in *this* culture is to be constructive. To be someone who values limits and who considers carefully building a life that is not susceptible to the whims of my fickle nature . . . *that's* kind of rebellious! To make decisions that aren't entirely wrapped around your career. To see your life as a whole. To recognize that all the ingredients of your life should contribute to something larger. I think that these are more difficult things to maintain than rebellion.

That's the way I've been trying to live my life. And I think people are drawn to a holistic existence, and I think it's fairly easy for artists to pull that off. Being an artist can be very, very healthy, instead of this fractured, roller coaster existence of a lot of artists where they're at the mercy of their own emotions and whims. Placing yourself in a community where you're seen and transparent puts a lot of tent pegs around you . . . I think that's healthy, to corner yourself a bit.

Rather than condemning or withdrawing from the mainstream arts community as a result of these tensions, however, Urban Monastery participants attempt to build relationships and overcome the distrust and anger directed toward evangelicals from many in the arts community.

The Urban Monastery attempts to bridge the chasm between evangelicals and secular artists in various ways. They host art openings for students from the nearby Art Institute in their first floor gallery. They invite their friends to meals with other artists in the Urban Monastery. The Urban Monastery's Arts Collective planned a prayer tent on the campus of the Art Institute to apologize and ask forgiveness for the ways that the church has rejected, harmed, and stifled artists. The community is also renovating the fourth floor of the Urban Monastery to open up studio space for working artists:

JASMINE: What we're trying to do on the fourth floor is provide this bridge between the church and the arts world in this city. . . . It's hard to explain where it all went wrong. But there's definitely this stigma among artists that "the church doesn't accept me." . . . I've been talking to a lot of people who are graduating from the Art Institute next semester who are looking for studio spaces and I'm like, "I've got some for you. I'll be in contact with you," and they're like, "Don't you have to be a Christian?" And I was like "NO! No you don't have to be a Christian to rent a studio! NO!"

Lilith welcomes a regular flow of visitors from the city's fine art scene to visit her studio in the Urban Monastery, along with visitors from churches and neo-monastic communities around the country:

LILITH: I think an incredible thing—as far as the church and the art world that have been so disenfranchised from one another is concerned—is to have my studio in the Urban Monastery building, which is a destination place and pilgrimage spot for a lot of people in the church from around the country, and they come in and they see an artist at work! How often do you see that? Never! You just never see an artist's studio: someone who is making a living at it essentially and who has been well-trained by the world. So many times people are like, "This is the first time I've seen anything like this, least of all in church." So it's really educational. I've had curators come in who've never been in church environments like this before, and they're like, "What is this thing? Who are all these people?!" I end up explaining myself a lot.

Urban Monastery leaders have been surprised by how successful some of these efforts to bridge the sacred/secular divide between "the church" and secular artists have been:

ALEX: At one point we had all but one or two resident assistants from the Art Institute dorms coming to the Urban Monastery. There's just been an incredible rapport and connection. . . . The administration at the Art Institute has taken notice and has given us an accredited six-month internship with them that they sponsor. Students can come spend a semester with us and get credit at the institute. And we've had administrators say, "Not only do we want you here, but we need you here, because a lot our students have left because there haven't been any faith organizations." We've started Priamus Studios now in our building which has eight or nine studios and is basically a home for artists, we have meals, we have professional artists working here, we have a gallery space on the first floor that art students use . . . we have a lot of dreams. Our heart is to re-present the kindness of Christ, the truth of Christ, the beauty of Christ among artists. And obviously not everyone will appreciate that, but we've found that many *have* appreciated that: including people with no faith background or who were very antagonistic towards what they had experienced in the church or had been hurt by the church.

By offering gallery and studio space in the Urban Monastery to non-Christian artists; establishing a presence at the nearby Art Institute; hosting regular meals, retreats, and gatherings for artists; and through Lilith's work and influence as a critically acclaimed fine artist working out of the Urban Monastery; community members work to educate Christians and overcome mutual misunderstanding and hostility between evangelicals and the arts community.

As with the practice of hospitality, the Urban Monastery's engagement with artists and the artistic field embodies the community's theology of holistic mission in multiple ways. For the Urban Monastery, the practice of "mission" includes but is not limited to sharing the gospel with individuals. Artists and art students in the Urban Monastery invite their friends from the art scene to meals and community gatherings to *"know* and *be known,* whether it involves becoming a believer at the end or not" (Lilith, emphasis in original).

They are more interested in building relationships, having dialogue, and participating in the secular artistic field than they are interested in condemning or separating from it. Through their participation in mainstream galleries and art schools and ready inclusion of non-Christian artists in their own studio space without censure, they take their practice of Christianity "outside the walls" of traditional church venues rather than creating an isolated subculture of evangelical artists trying to pull individuals into the evangelical subculture in an "attractional mode" (Caleb, Mina). In doing so, we see the Urban Monastery practicing holistic mission among artists while also vigilantly organizing community in such a way as to deconstruct traditional boundaries between the "sacred" religious world and the "secular" artistic one.

Excursus: Accounting for the Urban Monastery's Affinity with the Arts

How are we to make sense of the apparently strange affinity between a neo-monastic evangelical community and the decidedly non-conservative, nonreligious world of modern art? On the surface, the Urban Monastery's deep interconnectedness with individuals and institutions of the secular arts world is rather stunning, given American evangelicalism's historically antagonistic relationship with the artistic field.[20] However, social theorists have long recognized the homology between religious and artistic spheres of social life. For example, while acknowledging the tension between ascetic Protestantism's highly rationalized "religious ethics of brotherliness" and the "free-standing autonomous values" and "irresponsible enjoyment" of the artistic field, Max Weber also notes that:

> Magical [i.e., mystical or charismatic] religiosity stands in the most intimate relationship with the aesthetic sphere. From time immemorial religion has been inexhaustible source of artistic developments.[21]

The artistic sphere, as a "universe objectively oriented toward the *production of belief* in the work of art," with its "forms of artistic faith, whether blind belief or pharisaic piety," its "mystical representation of the artistic 'encounter,'" and its "primary cult of art and artist, with its holy places, its perfunctory rites, and its routinized devotions,"[22] carries many deep homologies with the religious sphere:

> Thus the analogy, which has often struck analysts, between the artistic field and the religious field. Nothing is more like a pilgrimage to a

holy shrine than one of those trips to Salzburg that tour operators will organize in the thousands for the Year of Mozart.[23]

For Pierre Bourdieu, the homology between the religious and artistic fields is such that "the sociology of culture is the sociology of religion of our time."[24] Indeed, Bourdieu first began developing field theory while reworking Weber's sociology of religion,[25] which he then immediately began applying to other fields of cultural production such as the intellectual, artistic, and literary fields.[26]

In addition to these more general homologies between the religious and artistic fields, Christian monasticism and the artistic sphere also share a *common opposition to the dominance of temporal power* as it is expressed in the world of business and the political economy of wealth. In the case of Christian monasticism, the struggle against the dominance of wealth and worldly power goes back to the very origins of the Christian faith, which Weber describes as "early Christianity's complete indifference to the world":

> Early Christianity . . . in the specific sense was world-rejecting.[27] [Becoming a disciple of Jesus] involved breaking all ties with the world, from family as well as property, as was the case with Buddha and other similar prophets. But obviously the attachment to "mammon" [wealth or money] remains one of the most difficult obstacles to being able to enter the kingdom of God, although with God anything is possible.[28] Wealth deflects from the attainment of religious salvation, on which everything depends. Although this is not explicit, it is assumed that wealth leads to a lack of brotherliness. . . . In short, absolute indifference to the world and its affairs is crucial for salvation.[29]

Moreover, according to Weber, the struggle against worldly temporal powers—and against the compromising influences of wealth on religious practice—is perhaps the defining characteristic of Christianity's monastic impulse (and of ascetic Protestantism more generally):

> In fact the whole history of monasticism is in a certain sense the history of a continual struggle with the problem of the secularizing influence of wealth. The same is true on a grand scale with the innerworldly asceticism of Puritanism. The great revival of Methodism, which preceded the expansion of English industry toward the end of the eighteenth century, may well be compared to such a monastic reform. We may hence quote here a passage from John Wesley himself . . . "I fear,

wherever riches have increased, the essence of religion has decreased in the same proportion. Therefore I do not see how it is possible, in the nature of things, for any revival of true religion to continue long. For religion *must necessarily* produce both industry and frugality, and these cannot but produce riches. But as riches increase, so will pride, anger, and love of the world in all its branches."[30]

For Wesley, as for Weber, there is an inescapable paradox at the heart of all monastic and ascetic movements that seek to restore Christian spirituality to its original glory: the practice of "true religion" produces discipline; discipline produces wealth; and wealth brings worldliness and compromise, polluting the practice of pure religion and creating conditions that call for new monastic and ascetic movements to arise.

Just as monastic, ascetic, and mystical Christianity stands in opposition to the dominance of wealth and worldly power, so the field of artistic production—in its purest and most autonomous form—constitutes itself against the pursuit of wealth and market logic in favor of the "pure" form of artistic production: "art for art's sake."[31] In its rejection of the tyranny of the market, the artistic field is "an economic world turned upside down," an "anti-economic" universe in which the purest, most consecrated, and most esteemed artistic products and producers are those which are the least economically viable and commercially successful.[32] As Bourdieu masterfully traces out in *The Rules of Art: Genesis and Structure of the Literary Field*, this inversion of the economic order lies at the very heart of the modern artistic field, whose origins are found in the "symbolic revolution through which artists free themselves from bourgeois demand by refusing to recognize any master except art."[33] Renouncing the pursuit of economic gain and commercial success, the artistic field—like the religious field—is a social space that "defines itself against ordinary vision and against the mercantile or mercenary ends . . . of the economic field."[34]

Thus, the religious and artistic fields each offer *symbolic* rewards that require the renunciation of the ordinary *temporal* rewards associated with wealth. For the Christian who seeks true spiritual riches, "in order to gain one's life, one must lose it," for "what good is it for someone to gain the whole world, yet forfeit their soul?"[35] Likewise, in the pure artistic field, "the artist cannot triumph on the symbolic terrain except by losing on the economic terrain."[36] With respect to the rejection of economic power, as it is for the Christian monastic, so it is in the field of artistic production.

The opposition between art and business, between symbolic capital and economic capital, and between spiritual and temporal power play themselves out in homologous fashion across a wide range of social spaces, from the intellectual and artistic fields to social provision and the field of power.[37] In the American evangelical field, this opposition is expressed in the struggle between neo-monastic and megachurch evangelicals over the legitimate representation of biblical Christianity in the United States. Urban Monastery participants—and neo-monastic evangelicals more generally—have constructed their distinctive holistic communitarian approach to Christian spirituality partially through opposition to more dominant expressions of evangelical religion in America, namely megachurch evangelicalism and the Christian Right/conservative evangelicalism. Both conservative and megachurch evangelicalism have strong relational and cultural affinities with corporate business and management practices.[38] Neo-monastic evangelicals, in keeping with the inexorable logic of the field as a structured "space of possibles" which encourages newcomers to define themselves against more established positions, reject the "bureaucratic," "market-driven," "business-management," "consumerist" style of religion they attribute to megachurch evangelicalism in favor of a more "creative" and "authentic" expression of Christian spirituality.[39] As a young, urban, creative community that defines itself partially in opposition to conservative and megachurch evangelicalism, the Urban Monastery's relational and cultural affinity to the artistic field makes perfect sense. Rejecting the consumption-oriented, business friendly, materialistic assumptions of their construction of megachurch evangelicalism and middle-class expectations concerning the American Dream, Urban Monastery participants find common cause with participants in the artistic field who have likewise renounced the tyranny of market-based materialism in favor of more symbolic and "spiritual" rewards.

Neo-monastic evangelicals' representation of megachurch evangelicalism as a bureaucratic, individualistic, superficial, market-driven expression of Christianity is not mere fantasy, but neither is it a fully reliable account of the megachurch point of view. The neo-monastic point of view concerning megachurch evangelicalism is rather, as Bourdieu reminds us, just that: a particularistic "view from a point" in social space that is influenced by the hierarchical structure of relations existing among different agents within the evangelical field.[40] Urban Monastery participants—like most dominated agents within a field—tend to selectively emphasize areas of *difference* and *distinction* which set them apart from other positions in an (often tacit) attempt to establish and enhance the legitimacy of their own position.[41] As argued at length in chapter 3, this *construction of difference* (i.e., the "creative/artistic" Urban Monastery versus the "corporate/market-driven" megachurch) *inside agreement* (i.e., on such fundamental matters as the divinity of Jesus, the authority of scripture, or the importance of evangelistic engagement) is a primary mechanism through which American evangelicalism is both reproduced and transformed. To take just one example, Urban Monastery participants are extremely vigilant in their efforts to deconstruct the "sacred/secular divide" in their practice of Christian spirituality, and they often contrast these efforts with conservative and megachurch evangelicals, whom Urban Monastery participants see as practicing a form of religion that unhelpfully reinforces this divide in the lives of many evangelicals. While some of these arguments are plausible, they also obscure the fact that megachurch evangelicals, for example, are no less committed to the cause of deconstructing the sacred/secular divide than are Urban Monastery participants themselves.

Holistic Mission: Deconstructing the Sacred/Secular Divide

Based on his study of primitive religious classification systems, classical social theorist Émile Durkheim famously argued that one of the fundamental features of religion is the classification of objects, events, and practices in the world into "sacred" and "profane" categories. According to Durkheim, religious beliefs and rituals together do the work of identifying and reinforcing the classification of objections into one or the other categories of this binary opposition, categories that Durkheim and his later followers argue are not limited to the religious sphere but also organize cultural meaning in the civic and political spheres as well.[42] For Durkheim, this opposition between the sacred and profane is forceful, absolute, and socially reinforced through ritual rules of conduct that govern interaction with sacred objects, thereby protecting them from pollution and publicly reinforcing the classifications of sacred and profane objects within a particular religion, community, or nation.

The division of the world into "sacred" religious space and "secular" profane space is particularly characteristic of fundamentalists and conservative evangelicals. Francis Schaeffer popularized the idea of "secular humanism" as the great modern enemy of biblical Christianity in his prolific writing and speaking career spanning the mid-twentieth century.[43] Christian Right rhetoric is filled with hostile and antagonistic references toward "secular public schools," "secular government," the "secular media," and the like.[44] For many conservative evangelicals, "secular" ideas and institutions are the enemy of Christianity and a constant, menacing threat to the Christian faith. For these conservative Protestants—using the language of Durkheim—the secular is profane.[45]

For much of the twentieth century, conservative evangelical churches reinforced the boundary between the profane and polluting secular world and the pure and sacred world of faith through social norms prohibiting swearing, alcohol and tobacco consumption, and abstinence from many forms of secular entertainment such as movies, music, and of course, extra-marital sexuality.[46] These "visible signs of salvation" clearly separated the saved from the unsaved and the sacred from secular.[47] In these conservative evangelical communities, unless one is a pastor, missionary, or full-time religious worker, work in the everyday world is seen as religiously inconsequential, ordinary, mundane: a necessary but essentially meaningless activity required for human sustenance. It is part of the profane secular world. While most contemporary evangelicals have abandoned the strict fundamentalism of their religious past, the conservative evangelical tendency toward suspicion of the secular remains strong, as exemplified, for instance, in the explosion of the commercial Christian subculture over the last thirty years, where one can go to Christian bookstores to buy Christian books, Christian music, and Christian clothing apparel; attend Christian rock concerts, coffee shops, and universities; and listen to Christian radio stations that are "positive" and "safe for the family" (with the not-so-subtle implication that "secular" bookstores, universities, and radio stations are often a polluting, dangerous influence on the family).[48]

Urban Monastery participants strongly reject Christian Right and conservative evangelical classifications of "secular" activities and institutions as profane. Through their teaching, their practice of hospitality, their efforts to participate in and build bridges to the arts community, and the organization of physical space and community life, among other things, Urban Monastery leaders engage in nearly constant efforts to "deconstruct the sacred/secular divide" in the minds of Urban Monastery participants (Caleb).[49] For them, practicing holistic mission includes "loving people," "representing Jesus," and practicing humility in social environments typically characterized by mutual antagonism and opposition between evangelical Christians and others (Alex). Rather than condemning lifestyle choices like drinking or smoking and considering abstinence from them as the "visible signs of salvation" that separate the saved from the unsaved in the manner of fundamentalist churches, Urban Monastery participants do not hesitate to have a beer at a house party or become cigar connoisseurs as they seek to sacralize secular space and engage people with the gospel:

DEVON: I got a job at a cigar shop this past December. . . . Coming from a crazy, living-the-dream nightlife, traveling around New York and Italy as a model—all that stuff—to the Midwest, was a bit of a shock to me. So as I was allowing the Lord to transform me, I needed an outlet. . . . I found this cigar shop in [a nearby restaurant-bar district] and I've been going there for three and a half years. . . . I have the opportunity to almost on a daily basis share the gospel with people, share church with people, share Jesus with people. And most people have a hard time working out in their minds how someone who is part of a Christian leadership community can work at a cigar shop. They can't wrap their heads around it. But it's attractive to them, because they don't see rules, they don't see regulations. . . . They're like, "Whoa, whoa, whoa. Why are we talking about church in a cigar shop? You don't talk about church in a cigar shop. What's the deal?"

CALEB: The second time we did a prayer tent on the university campus was in connection with this protest event called "tent state." Supposedly it's a national deal. Students set up all these tents and they protest everything from the war in Iraq to the cafeteria food. . . . They invited us to this big party at the end of the week at the "Jello-Shot King's House." That's what they called it [laughing]. . . . So we ended up at this party, and this became a pivotal moment in my theology and my life. I'm sitting on the couch with this kid, and I've got a beer, and he's got some hard liquor. And he's pretty well liquored up and he's going, "Now who are you man? Were you in the tent state?" I was like, "Did you see that prayer tent down the way?" He was like, "Oh yeah, yeah." And I was like, "You know this might be crazy, but we really love Jesus. He's completely changed our lives. We really want to share that reality with people. But it's really awkward trying to tell people sometimes." And he's like, *"Dude!"* He puts his hand on my knee and looks me right in the eye. "Let me tell you what you need to do. You've just got to hang out with us. Come to our parties like this man. We'll become friends, and you can tell us about Jesus. You tell us stories, and we'll tell you our stories. That's great man." I just raised my glass and said, "Cheers. Clink."

Caleb likes to retell this story when he teaches at the Urban Monastery as an example of open, participatory, non-judgmental Christian witness with people in natural social contexts, whether that is in an art gallery, a tobacco shop, a coffeehouse, or at a house party.

Indeed, the Urban Monastery and other neo-monastic communities seem to take special delight in living and working in places one might least expect to encounter evangelical Christians, including living and working among prostitutes in a red-light district in Mexico as friends and advocates, working with homeless drug addicts in numerous North American inner cities, or building relationships with dance club workers and partiers in Ibiza, a notorious European party destination for young adults. By intentionally participating in activities and social contexts that many evangelicals find offensive, morally suspect, and spiritually dangerous, Urban Monastery participants intentionally and loudly announce their rejection of the sacred/secular classification system of conservative evangelicalism in America.

The Urban Monastery's efforts to deconstruct the symbolic boundaries between sacred and secular space is not without conflict. When Urban Monastery leaders announced that a drawing class involving nude models would be held in the Urban Monastery's worship space as part of a wider offering of educational opportunities in the Urban Monastery, they received strong opposition from a vocal contingent of community members who believed the use of nude models to be unnecessary and inappropriate. On the other side of the spectrum, many others—particularly members of the Arts Collective— could hardly believe that the drawing class was controversial at all, because learning to draw using nude models is simply how it is done. After much debate and conversation among leaders and advocates of both perspectives, the leadership team decided in the end to hold the drawing class in an alternative location.

Other conflicts have arisen from the dual use of the Urban Monastery's first floor as both an art gallery and space for Sunday worship gathering, and over what it means to simultaneously affirm Christian and artistic values in the community:

HELENA: My friend Sara does these wonderful paintings of awkward people in weird circumstances. I love this one in particular: it's of this kind of raunchy looking guy, mustached, he has hair coming out of his V-neck shirt, he's smoking a cigarette, and at the top it says, "Do you love me?" And on his bare chest he has a tattoo that says, "Do you want me?" And it's this interesting thing, because the artist loves Jesus with all of her heart, and we put up her work here [in the worship/gallery space], but we had to take it down for a night because some leaders said, "We don't know about having her work up in the Urban Monastery during worship!" It became this huge conversation. We were like, "Are you serious? You want this to be a gallery for artists. But if you're stumbling over Sara's work then we're going to have to have a really long conversation, because what that girl has to say is good, and right, and beautiful." . . . It speaks into the identity crisis and need for love in this generation. And it is offensive. It is kind of raunchy. But man, is it *loud*, what she has to say.

In their attempts to deconstruct traditional boundary markers between sacred religious space and profane secular space in their community, Urban Monastery participants and leaders often meet resistance from more traditional members of their community—as well as from their own religious sensibilities—about holy and unholy, appropriate and inappropriate, and legitimate or illegitimate expressions of artistic creativity in the context of Christian life and worship. As Durkheim recognized, one cannot flaunt the taboos and boundary markers that protect the purity of the sacred from pollution by the profane with impunity or ease.

Moreover, the development of new cultural models for organizing individual or community life are always met with resistance, whether explicitly through competition with other cultural models or ideologies, or tacitly through the powerful forces of culture as it operates through habit and "common sense."[50] Urban Monastery leaders were quite cognizant of the difficulties of attempting to practice a "whole new way of doing 'church'" (Mina) that conformed to their holistic communitarian ideals, and of the power of habit and common sense to place limits on the transformative potential of their avant-garde expression of Christianity:

MINA: I see it [referring to the Urban Monastery's holistic communitarian way of practicing Christian spirituality] reproducing all around us. It's how people think. It's a grid that they function through. . . . But I see also, because some of us have such a history with traditional, formal ways of doing church, that you can quickly lean into doing what you've always known, and building things the way they have always been built. . . . There's always the temptation to lean into what's more comfortable. And I think that we've intentionally taken things out from under ourselves, hopefully in the leading of the Holy Spirit, so that we *won't* fall back into some of those old mindsets and ways of functioning. For example, we've chosen to gather as a whole community only twice a month as a way to resist letting people just lean into a consumptive form of church that's about receiving from professional ministers. . . . I'm seeing people begin to detox from a consumptive form of Christianity. But I also know that we're still so far from that being our only reality, because all of us—myself included—are still dealing with old mindsets and old patterns. (Emphasis in original)

Challenging well-established religious or cultural norms requires a level of consistent, vigilant, and intentional effort that is not casually or frequently achieved. The power of "settled" cultural patterns (such as American and evangelical individualism) to resist change, to shape thought and action tacitly through habit and common sense, is strong. We will discuss several examples of the obdurate nature of the cultural status quo in Urban Monastery life later in this chapter.[51] Nevertheless, the holistic communitarianism expressed in the theological, political, and organizational beliefs and practices of Urban Monastery participants displays an unusual degree of consistency and integration relative to the other individuals and communities in the postmodern West.[52] We will now turn to another classical social theorist to help us understand why.

Practicing Holistic Communitarianism "24–7": The Urban Monastery and Weber's Ascetic Protestantism

Culture's influence on action differs depending on its modality—whether it takes the form of religious or political ideology, tradition, or common sense—and on the social contexts in which it is situated and used.[53] It also depends on the coherence of cultural meanings and how completely and vigilantly social actors apply cultural meaning systems to everyday life.[54] Individuals and groups differ in how vigilantly they attempt to apply coherent cultural meanings to their lives. Classical social theorist Max Weber famously argued that the Calvinist-derived Puritan ethic helped revolutionize modern Western societies by developing a uniquely coherent and comprehensive theological system that adherents rigorously applied to all aspects of their daily lives.[55] Likewise, contemporary culture theorist Ann Swidler argues that the vigilance with which individuals attempt to apply cultural meanings to their everyday lives and experiences is a significant factor in how much cultural meanings influence action.[56] According to Weber and Swidler, the more coherent and comprehensive a cultural meaning system is, and the more vigilantly social actors attempt to apply cultural meanings to all aspects of their lives, the greater is culture's influence over action. Individuals who share the same relatively comprehensive and coherent cultural meaning systems—such as many evangelical Christians—can nevertheless differ in how much culture influences action depending on how vigilant they are in attempting to apply cultural meanings to everyday life.[57] Like Weber's Puritans, Urban Monastery participants are extremely vigilant in their attempts to apply a unified theological meaning system to all aspects of individual and communal life, magnifying the influence of their holistic communitarian theology on action in their community.

The Urban Monastery's holistic communitarianism is evident in community members' intentional efforts to organize their entire lives in devotion to their Trinitarian God; whether through their practice of radical hospitality and communal living, artistic expression, social justice oriented vocations, or prayer and worship. For Urban Monastery participants, dividing one's life or the world into sacred space (such as a religious service) where God is the focus and secular space (such as one's work or private life) that is left largely untouched by spirituality falls short of the radical, all-encompassing message of the gospel:

MINA: The basic framework that I agree with and that I see throughout our movement is this Celtic way and theology—or maybe ecclesiology—that's ... holistic. It's God in *everything*: not a sacred–secular split.

For Urban Monastery participants, following Jesus is a lifestyle to be lived twenty-four hours a day, seven days a week. The Urban Monastery's mission is "not a religious program, but just to live a life of following Christ":

ALEX: Jesus lived thirty-three years and only three of them were ministry. He's not offended by mundane life. . . . And we feel that the Urban Monastery is really that. It's just the way we live.

For some community members, the Urban Monastery's holistic approach to Christian spirituality is a continuation of early childhood experiences in the 1960s Jesus Movement:

LILITH: I grew up in a Christian commune. . . . My parents lived an unusual Jesus People lifestyle. The commune consisted of 75 people in the Cascade Mountain Range in Oregon. It was "common purse" style: financially everything was thrown in the same pot. It had lots of ministries—some of which were really cutting edge—one of which was one of the first Christian rock bands ever. They recorded seven albums and toured all over the world and had laser light shows and stuff. . . . So that was the environment I grew up in. It was what I saw: Christianity was more of a lifestyle than an event on Sunday. God was incorporated in the most basic life decisions.

Like Lilith's experience of living in a Jesus People commune, "24-7" is not just the name of a religious organization: it expresses Urban Monastery participants' efforts to organize all aspects of life into a consistent, continuous life ethic of whole-life discipleship in the way of Jesus as recorded in scripture.

According to Weber, the wholesale organization of life into a consistent and continuous personal religious ethic governing activity in the everyday world was a distinctive feature of ascetic Protestantism, which included the

English Puritan (Calvinist), Baptist, Pietist, and Methodist sects that are the principle ancestors of modern American evangelicalism.[58] Weber contrasted the *otherworldly asceticism* of Western Catholic monasticism—which encouraged monastic withdrawal from society in order to pursue a more disciplined and rigorous lifestyle devoted to God than was possible in the everyday world—with the *innerworldly asceticism* developed by Luther and Calvin in the Reformation and carried forward among the ascetic Protestant sects. Ascetic Protestants believed that "the only way of living acceptably to God was not to surpass worldly morality in monastic asceticism, but solely through the fulfillment of the obligations imposed upon the individual by his position in the world. That was his calling."[59]

Weber famously argued that the Puritan version of ascetic Protestantism played a particularly prominent role in the development of Western capitalism through its development of a religious ethic whereby living a systematically disciplined moral life and diligently working in a worldly occupation (one's "calling") was a sign of salvation:

> The God of Calvinism demanded of his believers not single good works, but a life of good works combined in a unified system. . . . The moral conduct of the average man was thus deprived of its planless and unsystematic character and subjected to a consistent method for conduct as a whole . . . a methodical, systematic rationalization of conduct for the purpose of attaining the certainty of one's salvation.[60]

According to Weber's argument, the Calvinist doctrine of predestination—that God chooses who is saved (the elect) and who is damned apart from any human initiative—placed enormous psychological pressure on its adherents to prove to themselves and to others that they were part of God's elect. For Weber, the Puritans' pursuit of the certainty of salvation through a life of "methodically rationalized ethical conduct" was carried out with "bitter seriousness," given that "Calvin viewed all pure feelings and emotions with suspicion."[61]

We may pause here for a moment to appreciate the irony—as Weber no doubt would—of a Protestant neo-monastic movement critiquing the descendants of ascetic Protestantism for being too removed from the world.[62] After all, the very foundation of the Protestant Reformation as inaugurated by Luther and Calvin involved a forceful rejection of the perceived Catholic rejection of the world as it was expressed in the practice of the Catholic monastic orders. From the Reformation point of view, Catholic monasticism had gone horribly awry in denying the spiritual significance of 'mundane' work in an occupation; instead favoring a world-rejecting withdrawal into monastic religious enclaves devoted to the practice of "pure religion" far removed from the distractions and degradations of ordinary society.[63] In neo-monastic evangelicalism, the Reformation's rejection of world-rejection has had the deeply ironic result of producing a twenty-first-century Protestant movement that champions *inner-worldly monasticism* as a correction to the worldly individualism and the sacred–secular dualism of twenty-first-century evangelical Protestants. One can imagine Luther shaking his head in wonderment at such a notion.

The point here is not simply to tell an interesting little story about the shifting meanings of monasticism since the time of the Reformation. Rather, it is an example of how struggles within the field of American evangelicalism— in this case, the neo-monastic struggle against the perceived sacred/secular divide within the conservative and megachurch expressions of American evangelicalism—can have the simultaneous effect of reinforcing the fundamental beliefs and values of the evangelical field as a whole. Since the time of the Reformation, one of the defining characteristics of Protestantism has been its affirmation of the religious significance of everyday life and its commitment to *engagement*—rather than withdrawal—from the world.[64] Urban Monastery participants (fairly or unfairly) perceive conservative and megachurch evangelicals to be promulgating an expression of Christianity that creates false and harmful boundaries between the sacred and secular world. However, in struggling against these dominant expressions of American evangelicalism, Urban Monastery participants simultaneously strengthen and reproduce the evangelical worldview by affirming its *doxic* assumptions about the importance of engagement with the world.[65]

A Communitarian and Celebratory Asceticism

One may doubt whether the obsessive drive to prove one's individual salvation through asceticism was as characteristic of Puritan social psychology as Weber claims. It is certainly absent from the Urban Monastery. However, Urban Monastery participants do practice a type of innerworldly asceticism as defined by the "methodical penetration of conduct with religion" in everyday life.[66] They hold each other accountable to challenging moral standards with respect to sexuality, money, truth-telling, substance abuse, and the practice of positive Christian disciplines like prayer and evangelism in their weekly D-Groups. They see their careers and occupations in the world as opportunities to express the love and justice of God in society. They practice Christianity as an all-encompassing lifestyle rather than as a set of beliefs or as the ritualistic attendance of a weekly religious event. For Urban Monastery participants, the call for a "new monasticism" is not a call to withdraw from the world into sheltered religious enclaves, but rather a call to whole-life religious devotion in the context of radical Christian community alongside the poor and oppressed.[67] The *inner-worldly monasticism* of the Urban Monastery is perfectly illustrated by the cover art of the book *Punk Monk*, which depicts a peaceful monastic scene of old stone walls, natural beauty, and a dove with the word "Monk" overlaying what look like an angel's wing on one half of the cover, while the other half depicts an urban scene of skyscrapers and graffiti splatter (or is it blood?) in crimson red overlaid with the word "**Punk**" in bold gothic script.[68]

Like Weber's Puritans, then, the Urban Monastery practices a form of innerworldly asceticism by attempting to rationalize the conduct of everyday life toward religious ends. At the same time, however, the Urban Monastery's drive to "rationalize worldly activity" in accordance with their religious beliefs is markedly different than the individualistic attempt to prove one's own salvation through rigorous discipline in worldly activities as characterized by Weber's portrayal of the Puritan ethic.[69] One of these differences lies in the communitarian, rather than individualistic, orientation of the Urban Monastery's practice of innerworldly asceticism. Where Weber emphasized the "inner isolation" of the Puritan seeking to prove her salvation through personal moral discipline in worldly activity,[70] the social organization of the Urban Monastery is aimed at helping participants pursue whole-life discipleship in the context of Christian community. The Urban Monastery is organized into a series of nested micro-communities of varying sizes. First, there are Discipleship Groups (D-Groups) of two to three people, then the Collectives with ten to forty people, which all take part in the large Gathering where the entire community of one hundred fifty Urban Monastery participants comes together. At the leadership level, there is a five-person core team and a sixty-person Leadership Community composed of the core team, Collectives leaders, and other key leaders in the Urban Monastery.

Urban Monastery participants take part in several micro-communities simultaneously. For instance, when Lilith led the Arts Collective, she was involved in three D-Groups with "people I wanted to make into leaders," the Leadership Community, the Arts Collective, and Sunday gatherings. Alex is part of the five-person core leadership team, leads the Leadership Community, is involved in one or two D-Groups at a time, and teaches at the Sunday Gathering. Manuel is in a D-Group and attends the University Collective and Sunday Gatherings. Jason sits on the Urban Monastery's legal board, co-leads the Young Professionals Collective with his spouse, and takes part in the

Leadership Community and Sunday Gathering. Since D-Groups and Collectives meet once a week and the Leadership Community and Sunday Gatherings meet every other week, the typical Urban Monastery member participates in at least three Urban Monastery related gatherings each week. Many participate in more than three, especially those who are involved in leadership. Lilith describes her involvement in the Urban Monastery as being a part of "four of five communities on top of each other." This does not include participation in conferences, retreats, meals and prayer meetings in community houses, outreaches, and other activities such as the Urban Monastery's dedicated prayer weeks, during which time Urban Monastery participants sign up to pray for multiple hour-long shifts in the prayer room in order to fill an entire week with non-stop night and day prayer. These weeks of 24–7 prayer happen every six weeks in the Urban Monastery.

Clearly, Urban Monastery participants demonstrate a high level of commitment to one another and the community as measured by the amount of time they devote as leaders and participants in the Urban Monastery's multiple levels of community life. For community members, this is part of the attraction of the Urban Monastery:

ELLE: I think the Urban Monastery exists for people who honestly just want to live life completely *awake*. I've lived life asleep for so long, and I'm so tired of just being awake on Sundays and being asleep the rest of the week. And I think there are a lot of people who feel that way. It doesn't just end with Sunday service, it's continued through the week. And that's a core goal of the Urban Monastery. We have these things called Discipleship Groups and Collectives, and throughout the week people will independently lead their own worship groups. I like to go to Discipleship Group. Huge growth is instilled in me by these people, as opposed to just a Sunday meeting where there's not a real big challenge. . . . To have this week-long thing that wasn't just a Sunday event, to live life completely in love with each other, to have brothers and sisters in Christ: that's what I saw when I came here. (Emphasis in original)

Like Elle, each of the new participants I interviewed cited the high level of commitment among both leaders and participants in the community and the many opportunities to participate in Christian community throughout the week as reasons they joined and remain part of the Urban Monastery.

In addition to its communitarian rather than individualist focus, the Urban Monastery's practice of innerworldly asceticism also differs from Weber's Puritan ethic in terms of the individual's motivation for practicing

Christian asceticism. Where Weber's Puritans practiced asceticism to prove their individual salvation in the afterlife, Urban Monastery participants demonstrate no anxiety about their eternal fate when they talk about their motivations for comprehensively organizing everyday life in the world according to their religious beliefs. Rather, they talk about faithfully and consistently demonstrating the "three loves" as their logical and heartfelt response to the love that God as demonstrated in the life, death, and resurrection of Christ.[71] That is, their asceticism is aimed at experiencing and demonstrating the love of God in this world, rather than proving their worthiness as individuals for salvation in the next one.

Third, Weber's Puritans practiced an asceticism characterized by a "grim seriousness" and deep suspicion of emotion and mystical experience as a legitimate guide or goal of religious practice.[72] By contrast, the type of inner-worldly asceticism practiced by Urban Monastery participants is a *celebratory asceticism* that embraces emotion and mystical experience as both a means and an end of the disciplined Christian life. All of the Urban Monastery participants I interviewed spoke about how powerful, emotional, and personal encounters with the Holy Spirit played a significant role in their conversion and ongoing pursuit of greater levels of faithfulness and commitment to living lifestyles of complete devotion to God. Rather than being suspicious of emotion or mystical experience, Urban Monastery participants believe that such experiences are to be celebrated as the natural result of having a genuine relationship with God and devoting one's life to him:

ELLE: I believe that what we read is really important, and what we listen to is really important, and what we watch on TV is really important. I used to feel like such a prude person when I first went to this lifestyle. Obviously I've relaxed a little from the intensity of it, but it's honestly the best, truly alive life you can have. . . . God says, "Seek for me and I'll be found," but it's when you search for me with *all* your heart![73] There's this verse in Timothy that says: "Don't put your hope in money, but go to God for your complete enjoyment."[74] Go to God for your enjoyment?! Instead of going to get a drink, pursue God for enjoyment! Instead of going for these temporary highs, go to God! . . . I work 20 hour shifts as a medical resident, and I get exhausted, but we still need to focus on God. Even this party that I'm going to after this interview, I want it to be focused on *God*! Someone's birthday party: to be focused on *God*! . . . I went through a lot when I first became a Christian, but God said, "My good will always completely trump the bad." That means my fun, my love, my laughter, instead of negativity and pessimism. Approach life with childlike faith! Be happy that you're loved and beloved! Be happy that you're going to heaven, and that Christ has won! I want to see the church be a happier place. I've been through so much death and hard times, and I'm attracted to happy people.

For Elle and the Urban Monastery participants, joy, gratitude, and experiencing the love of God are both the motivation and result of practicing a life of celebratory asceticism that is completely devoted to God. In this regard, the Urban Monastery is more like the Pietist and Methodist types of ascetic Protestantism than it is Puritanism. Both German and Continental Pietism—the former represented by Count Zinzendorf's Moravian brotherhood and the latter by the Wesley's Methodist movement in England and the United States—practiced "an emotional but still ascetic type of religion" that "through intensified asceticism wished to enjoy the blissfulness of community with God in this life."[75] Indeed, Urban Monastery leaders explicitly cite the Moravians as inspiration for their own contemporary expression of *celebratory asceticism* (Alex, Caleb, Manuel, Anja, Mina).

Anti-Bureaucratic Collective Organization

According to Weber, the rationalization of conduct in everyday life through the practice of innerworldly asceticism is not the only way that ascetic Protestantism contributed to the "rationalization" of religion and society in the West. They also contributed to rationalization of the world through "the elimination of magic as a means to salvation," by which Weber meant the elimination of reliance on church sacraments such as baptism and priestly confession as a means to salvation within the ascetic Protestant sects.[76] In a related argument, Weber also established the significance of *bureaucratization* as a defining feature of Western modernity. According to Weber, modern bureaucracy is characterized by clear, official hierarchies of subordinate and supervisory positions with clear "channels of appeal" for decision-making and conflict resolution; "full-time career jobs" requiring specialized training; and organized, written, and general rules that regulate interaction between persons operating in the modern bureaucratic organization.[77] Modern bureaucratic organizations seek to optimize efficiency through calculation and a focus on objective results "without regard for persons."[78] The life of the modern bureaucratic official is strictly separated into the private sphere of personal life and the professional sphere of official organizational responsibility. Weber observed this process of the rationalization of social institutions through modern bureaucratic administration taking place across the whole spectrum of political, economic, and religious organizations in modern Western societies.[79] For Weber, bureaucratization is what rationalization looked like in the social institutions of Western modernity.

The social organization of American evangelicalism's churches and religious organizations has not been immune to the modern tendency toward bureaucratization. While Catholic and mainline Protestant denominations have more fully developed denominational bureaucracies, evangelical churches and denominations follow a similar pattern of official hierarchy, clear channels of appeal, full-time career jobs (the senior pastor and, depending on the size of the church, a small team of specialized full-time pastors and office workers), specialized graduate level training of ministers at one of many evangelical seminaries, legal charters and elder boards delineating clear authority over budgeting procedures, personnel and operations decisions, and clear distinctions between the professional religious worker and the members of his congregation. Evangelical churches have access to a vast army of professional paid consultants to help them plan church growth strategies, raise money for building projects, perform demographic studies of potential sites for new church plants, and search for qualified candidates to fill positions on pastoral staff teams.

Urban Monastery participants, on the other hand, strongly oppose the encroachment of bureaucratic processes into the organization of religious life. They are critical of conventional, congregational approaches to the organization of religious life in evangelical churches and organizations:

JESSICA: There are organizations like Hilltop [a large evangelical church in the city] that always throws the word "community" around—but look at my experience with the pastor alone! . . . We had been going to Hilltop for a year and we were re-introducing ourselves again to the main pastor, and he asked, "What are your names again?" And I was like, "We should get together and have dinner or something! We've been going here for a year." And he said, "Well, I can't eat dinner with everybody," or something like that. I didn't like that. Maybe that's true, but I don't want to go to a church where I don't know the pastor at all. . . . That's just not the type of community that I have in mind when I'm thinking about church. That's like the mayor! The secular mayor can't have lunch with everybody, that's obvious. But at a *church*; we're a family! We're a family under God in the end! . . .

In opposition to the pastor-as-CEO business model of church perfected by evangelical megachurches, Urban Monastery participants use family metaphors to describe what they believe Christian community should look like:

JASMINE: I feel like the Urban Monastery is the truest representation of the dream church. I hate to use that term because I don't want to put any group of people on a pedestal. That's not what I'm trying to do. But if I had to describe to you the ideal church, I feel like this is as close to that picture as anything I've witnessed to this point.... It's just such a beautiful family here. If you had to ask me why I go to the Urban Monastery, it's because of the way people love each other. It's the real deal.... I had the opportunity to do some "church shopping" when I moved to this city. A lot of churches say they have this commitment to relationship and relational values, but they don't act it out.

Urban Monastery participants believe that Christian communities and churches should be places where people experience intimate, personal relationships with one another and with leaders similar to what one would experience in an idealized family, rather than being inflexible rules-based organizations led by religious professionals who are set apart from the rest of the community.

Urban Monastery leaders and participants constantly use words such as "fluid," "relational," "organic," "natural," "simple," and "family" to describe their community and what they believe Christian community in general ought to look like, as opposed to what they view as the impersonal, hierarchical, efficiency-based structure of evangelical churches influenced by modern bureaucratization processes:

JASMINE: The church I grew up was like: "Things aren't really going very well so we have to work hard to get more people to come to church to make it function. There's a structure that's set in place and we have to find people to fill that structure." But Alex talked out of this place of, "We have these people, and it's our job to formulate some sort of structure that fits them." And I was like, 'That's so beautiful!' That's the way it should be!"

MINA: We're a community that's fluid, natural, people built together who are spiritual family in a locale who are going after Jesus, who are praying together, who are engaging the heart of God through mission and going after the people that he misses.

Urban Monastery leaders emphasize the "unplanned" and "unintentional" origins of the Urban Monastery and its initiatives, preferring to view organizational growth as a creative, flexible, unpredictable process that emerges naturally from a foundation of "simple friendships" and "real relationships," as opposed to following the calculated, predictable, and impersonal logic of bureaucratic organizational growth (Alex, Lilith, Caleb, Mina). They are also opposed to the bureaucratic impulse to draw distinctions between personal and private or sacred and secular space, and between "religious profession-als" possessing specialized training and skill and nonprofessionals who func-tion as religious "consumers" rather than full and equal participants in the spiritual work of the community (Anja, Mina).

The distinctions Urban Monastery participants use to contrast their reli-gious standpoints with other evangelicals—such as the opposition between "fluid" and "rigid" or "organic" and "bureaucratic" organizational structures, between church as "family" or church as "business," between "uninten-tional" spontaneity and calculating control, between "authentic relationship" and "impersonal" or "superficial" interactions between church members, be-tween spiritual "community" and programmatic religious "events," and be-tween "decentralized" versus "hierarchical" leadership structures—is typical of how different movements within American evangelicalism are constructed in relation to one another. While the tendency to construct positions through opposition is often tacit and subconscious rather than explicit and conscious, some Urban Monastery participants clearly grasp the oppositional nature of some of their religious practices and position-takings with respect to other evangelicals:

SCARLET: I enjoy the emerging church a lot, and all of these grassroots move-ments back towards community, back towards the earth, back towards just a simpler way of living. . . . And I know that a lot of these things that I'm excited about—I know that what we're doing is a reaction. The pendu-lum always swings. A lot of the people that I talk [to] in the Urban Monas-tery grew up in megachurches! Either that or their parents were sort of leftovers from the Jesus Movement. . . . But I do really enjoy that I have the option to go to about four different community meals a week. That I live in a community where there are always people around. That if I want to strike up a God-centered conversation it's generally welcomed by my friends; and that we don't segregate our spirituality to a certain part of our lives.

Like the other movements within the field of American evangelicalism, Urban Monastery participants construct their distinctive religious stand-points and strategies of action through a dialect of agreement and opposition with the other positions in the contemporary and historic American evangel-ical field.

The fact that the Urban Monastery stands against the bureaucratization of evangelical religious communities does not mean that it is unorganized or anarchic. On the contrary, Urban Monastery leaders are highly intentional and reflexive about how leadership and community life is organized in the Urban Monastery, as evident in its innovative, extensive, and clearly purposed multi-layer organizational structure of nested micro-communities described above and in the section. Participants are highly committed and highly integrated into the multiple levels of community organization present in the Urban Monastery, and they demonstrate a strong sense of identification with the Urban Monastery's mission and values. In these ways (and borrowing from Weber's conceptual language), the Urban Monastery expresses a type of *anti-bureaucratic rational organization.* Just as individual community members practice innerworldly asceticism by rationalizing worldly activity in pursuit of their mission to love God, love each other, and love the world, the social organization of the Urban Monastery is rationalized toward the end of helping community members experience authentic Christian community and aid them in engaging the world in holistic mission. The organization of the Urban Monastery is highly intentional, but it is a more informal, relational, and flexible than professional, impersonal, and rules-based style of organization.[80]

Practicing Holistic Communitarianism: Organizing Community

The Urban Monastery embodies holistic communitarianism as a strategy of collective action in its practice of holistic mission, its communitarian leadership structure, and its strong emphasis on "community" as both the means and end of authentic biblical Christianity. The Urban Monastery's commitment to community as an essential element of religious practice is visible in the oft-repeated official slogan of the Urban Monastery as a community that practices "Love in Three Directions and Community in Three Expressions." "Love in Three Directions" refers to the Urban Monastery's holistic mission to "Love God, Love People, and Love the World," often referred to as the "Three Loves" by community participants. "Community in Three Expressions" refers to how the Urban Monastery organizes community life in its attempt to live out its holistic mission. These "three expressions" include: (1) the Urban Monastery's Sunday evening gatherings for worship and teaching, (2) smaller groups of ten to forty individuals with various emphases called "Collectives" that meet every week, and (3) "Discipleship Groups" (commonly referred to as "D-Groups") composed of two or three individuals that also meet weekly. While Urban Monastery participants are constantly gathering for other meals, parties, prayer times, special events, and projects in addition to these three expressions, the Sunday Gathering, Collectives, and D-Groups form the backbone of community life in the Urban Monastery.

The fact that there are "three loves" and "three expressions" of community in the Urban Monastery is not an accident: this formulation of the Urban Monastery's overarching mission and structure intentionally and explicitly evokes the "Three in One" nature of the Christian Trinity, the "template" from which the Urban Monastery patterns its communitarian leadership structure and social organization (Mina, Anja, Alex). Applied with the creativity, flexibility, and symbolic efficiency of the "fuzzy" logic of practice,[81] the Urban Monastery's Trinitarian theology is expressed in everything from the community's founding myths to its mission statement and from leadership structures to the organization of spiritual community at multiple levels:

ROLAND: I think what makes the Urban Monastery and other neo-monastic communities distinctive is how far they take and how far they implement the theological sentences that are spoken in evangelical culture. I mean, I've never been part of a church that hasn't believed that God exists as a Trinity, but I think the Urban Monastery and similar communities are one of the few contexts in which that becomes not just a statement about how God is structured as a being, but how the rest of the universe is structured as well. I think the way that the Urban Monastery applies historic doctrines to specific social and economic systems is unique.

More than many other religious communities, the Urban Monastery translates core symbolic elements from the community's holistic communitarian theological meaning system into a wide range of religious, philosophical, and political standpoints and practical strategies of action with focused intentionality.

The Trinitarian Template: "Community in Three Expressions"

As opposed to "going to church" on Sunday morning every week, the Urban Monastery's Sunday evening gathering occurs every other week in a conscious attempt by community leaders to promote a different way of thinking about what it means to practice holistic Christian spirituality. Urban Monastery leaders constantly aim to "send people" and "get them out of the walls of our building" (Caleb), rather than being "focused on grabbing people in an attractional style of doing church" and "leaning into a consumptive form of church that's about receiving from professional ministers" (Mina). Instead, they work to convince community members that:

MINA: I'm actually commissioned into society by God. I'm not leaning into [professional religious leaders] to do it for me or to articulate my faith to me. I'm called to embody it. And my unique expression may be in the business world, or in the art institute, or at the university, or at a coffee shop, or whatever.

Rather than trying to attract people to a "formal, traditional church" experience in a religious building led by "professional ministers" who do most of the religious work (e.g., studying and teaching the Bible, leading worship, spreading the gospel, caring for the poor, etc.) (Mina), the Urban Monastery expects participants to be more than just passive consumers of religious experience attending religious events. By only gathering to meet as a whole community every other week for worship and teaching, the Urban Monastery intentionally interrupts religious expectations of participants shaped by the almost universal adoption of the weekly congregational model by religious communities in the United States.[82]

Urban Monastery leaders de-emphasize the primacy of Sunday worship gatherings in order to encourage participants to meet in smaller groups throughout the week that facilitate deeper levels of relationship, accountability, and support than is possible in a larger gathering. Meeting in smaller groups enables more Urban Monastery participants to take on leadership roles and develop more diverse ways of pursuing the Urban Monastery's mission to love God, love people, and love the world. Many Urban Monastery participants refer to Discipleship Groups (D-Groups), not the Sunday gathering, as the most important way in which they participate in religious community:

LILITH: D-Groups are one of the most important aspects of the Urban Monastery.... They're really powerful. *So* powerful. You meet once a week in groups of two or three. It's voluntary. There's a pact of total honesty. You read fifteen [Bible] chapters a week together. If one of you doesn't finish the fifteen chapters, you all start over from the same spot until you've all read the fifteen chapters. So it keeps you immersed in the Word. Then there are three groups of questions: one about loving God, one about loving people, one about loving the world. So these questions are pretty penetrating. Questions about finances: how are your decisions about them contributing to the kingdom of God and conforming to it? There are questions about sexuality, questions about your thought life, questions about loving your neighbor, and questions about your prayer life. Just knowing that you're going to be answering all these questions puts a knife edge of consciousness on your life. What's also really exciting about D-Groups is that you pray for three people in your acquaintance that they might come to Christ. . . . D-Groups foster a lifestyle of transparency and praying for people. We're not talking about a program; we're talking about building disciples.

Figure 6.1 is a reproduction of the Urban Monastery's guide for participating in a D-Group. The questions are organized around the "Three Loves" (Love God, Love One Another, Love the World) and each question is heavily fortified with scripture references to provide context, inspiration, and justification for the importance of the spiritual practices associated with each question. Even a cursory reading of the document reveals its deeply evangelical nature: from the heavy use of scripture references to its emphasis on evangelism, scripture reading, and personal piety.

D-Groups are seen as serving a variety of functions in the Urban Monastery. They provide a place for participants to enter into authentic relationships with other members of the community rather than pursuing spiritual growth as isolated individuals. They challenge community members to organize their entire public and private lives around the three loves: loving God, loving people, and loving the world. They reinforce the centrality of studying the Bible and sharing the gospel in one's personal life on a regular basis. D-Groups are also intended to multiply as new people become Christians through the prayer and personal witness of Urban Monastery participants, who then start new D-Groups with new converts. Urban Monastery leaders also start D-Groups with people they recognize as potential leaders as a way of developing new leaders through friendship and personal interaction. Urban Monastery leaders estimate that about 70 percent of the community is involved in a D-Group.

D-Groups embody the Urban Monastery's theological convictions that the Christian faith is essentially holistic and communitarian rather than individualistic. They also embody the Urban Monastery's attempts deconstruct the sacred/secular divide between professional ministers who do religious work and passive religious consumers. By participating in a D-Group, all members of the community are encouraged to practice all the essential elements of Christian discipleship in their own lives: studying the Bible, sharing the gospel, praying, practicing personal moral discipline, and engaging in acts of mercy and justice. D-Groups are a strategy of collective

D-Group Questions

D-Groups provide a simple way to live and reproduce the life and ministry of Jesus through intentional, accountable relationships of two or three people. The conversation questions below are meant to focus us on the central teachings and commands of Jesus, which can best be lived out through the grace, instruction, and empowerment of the Holy Spirit. We aim to be and make disciples so that Christ is formed in us and the kingdom is extended through us.

D-Group Conversation Questions:

Core Values Questions: Jesus Central Commands
Great Commandment (Mark 12:30-31)
Great Commission (Matt. 28:18-20)

Love God
1. Am I receiving God's love for me and growing stronger in my relationship and obedience to Him? Am I daily seeking and listening to Jesus, intentionally spending time with Him, and involving Him in every aspect of my life?

Love One Another
2. What have I done to love, serve and prefer others above myself
(specifically those closest to me)? How can I grow in this? Have I withheld forgiveness, remained frustrated or damaged another person with my words?

Love The World
3. Am I taking opportunities to share Jesus and reproducing my life in others through making disciples? Am I praying for and remembering the sick, hurting and needy? Am I informed about global issues and seeking to advance God's Kingdom in the nations of the earth?

Integrity Questions

4. Strongholds and Patterns: Am I pursuing freedom from destructive patterns, strongholds and hopeless areas in my life? Explain.
5. Sexuality: Am I honoring God with my sexuality? Have I lusted after anyone and not valued God's image in them? Have I exposed myself to sexually alluring material or allowed my mind to dwell on inappropriate thoughts?
6. Money: Am I being a faithful and generous steward of my (God's) money and possessions? Am I worrying about or being controlled by a love for money or materialism, instead of trusting God?

God's Story Reading and Prayer Questions:

7. Did I do my Bible Reading this week? (15 Chapters)
8. Did I do Daily Prayer this week? (Morning, Noon & Evening)
9. Did I faithfully Pray by Name for 1-3 people who are not yet in a relationship with Jesus? (Individually and with my D-group)

D-Group Scripture References
Jesus said, "'Love the Lord your God with all your heart and with all your soul and with all your mind and with all your strength.' The second is this: 'Love your neighbor as yourself.' There is no commandment greater than these."
(Mark 12:30-31)

Jesus said, "All authority in heaven and on earth has been given to me. Therefore go and make disciples of all nations, baptizing them in the name of the Father and of the Son and of the Holy Spirit, and teaching them to obey everything I have commanded you. And surely I am with you always, to the very end of the age." (Matt. 28:18-20)
"...Train yourself to be godly" (1 Timothy 4:7)

1. Love God: This is love: not that we loved God, but that he loved us and sent his Son as an atoning sacrifice for our sins. And so we know and rely on the love God has for us. God is love. Whoever lives in love lives in God, and God in him. We love because he first loved us. (1 Jn. 4:10;16;19) Come to me; hear me, that your soul may live. Your face, Lord, I will seek. (Is 55:3; Ps 27:8)

2. Love One Another: My command is this: Love each other as I have loved you. Greater love has no one than this, that he lay down his life for his friends. (John 15:12-13) For if you forgive men when they sin against you, your heavenly Father will also forgive you. (Matt. 6:14) Do not let any unwholesome talk come out of your mouths, but only what is helpful for building other up according to their needs. (Eph 4:29)

3. Love The World: As you go, share this message: 'The kingdom of heaven is near." Heal the sick, raise the dead, cleanse those who have leprosy, drive out demons. Freely you have received, freely give. (Matt. 10:7-8) Pray for us, too, that God may open a door for our message, so that we may proclaim the mystery of Christ...pray that I may proclaim it clearly, as I should. Be wise in the way you act toward outsiders; make the most of every opportunity. (Col. 4:3-5) If you spend yourself on behalf of the hungry and satisfy the needs of the oppressed, then your light will rise in the darkness (Is 58:10). (Also Eph. 6:19-20)

4. Strongholds and Patterns: Do not give the devil a foothold. (Eph. 4:27) The thief comes to steal, kill and destroy; I have come that they may have life and have it to the full. (Jn.10:10) He sent me to heal the broken hearted, to proclaim freedom for the captives and release from darkness for the prisoners. (Is 61:1) (Also 2 Tim. 2:25-26)

5. Sexuality: So God created man in his own image; he created them male and female. (Gen.1:27) I made a covenant with my eyes not to look lustfully at (another). (Job 31:1) Flee from sexual immorality. Do you not know that your body is a temple of the Holy Spirit. Therefore honor God with your body. (1 Cor. 6:18-20) (Also Phil. 4:8; Matt. 5:28)

6. Money: Each person should give what he has decided in his heart to give, not reluctantly or under compulsion, for God loves a cheerful giver. (2 Cor. 9:7) Keep your lives free from the love of money and be content with what you have, because God has said, "never will I leave you; never will I forsake you." (Heb. 13:5) You cannot serve both God and Money. (Matt. 6:24) (Also Acts 2:45)

7. Bible Reading: Let the word of Christ dwell in you richly as you teach and exhort one another. (Col. 3:16) (Also Acts 2:42; 2 Tim. 3:16-17)

8. Daily Prayer: Devote yourselves to prayer being watchful and thankful. (Col. 4:2) And pray in the Spirit on all occasions with all kinds of prayer and requests. (Eph. 6:18) (Also Lk. 18:1-8)

9. Pray by Name: I urge, then, first of all, that requests, prayers, intercession and thanksgiving be made for everyone...this is good and pleases God our Savior, who wants all people to be saved and come to the knowledge of the truth. (1 Tim. 2:1-4) (Also Acts 17:27)

FIGURE 6.1 D-Group questions

action that enables Urban Monastery participants to be unusually vigilant in their attempts to apply holistic communitarian Christian faith to all aspects of their lives.

The second way in which the Urban Monastery organizes community "outside the walls" of dedicated religious buildings and apart from a traditional Sunday church service is through weekly gatherings called Collectives (Caleb). Collectives are groups of ten to fifty Urban Monastery participants who share particular interests, vocational areas, or are in similar life stages. Urban Monastery Collectives have included an Arts Collective, Young Professionals Collective, University Collective, Prayer Collective, Justice Collective, Social Work Collective, and other geography- and interest-based groups. While varying somewhat in form, the goal of the Collectives is to provide another context for Christian community and engagement with different areas of society through different means (such as social work, the arts, or evangelism):

> Our collectives are small Jesus centered communities that pray together, eat together, grow in love together and share Jesus with the world around them. They provide a context for a simple and beautiful form of church where everyone can be known, heard and valued. We believe that church can be collective as every person participates through contributing who they are and the gifts they've been given. Collectives are distinct from one another based on unique missional focuses, leadership and the particular passions of individuals in the group. They are unified in their commitment to loving God, loving each other and loving the world.[83]

Sharing life and pursuing God's mission together in "real relationship" and "simple friendships" in the context of everyday life is contrasted with the "formal," "traditional," "attractional," and individualistic approach of dominant expressions of American evangelicalism (Mina).

The largest Collective in the Urban Monastery is the Arts Collective, which typically involves between twenty-five to fifty participants from a variety of arts backgrounds: "It's mostly art students at this point, but people are graduating and we have some curators and some other artists: we have an aerial acrobat, designers, animators, sculptors, painters, interdisciplinary artists, fibers. If anyone is a musician, it's in addition to their visual art" (Lilith). Others manage galleries or are involved in the local arts community in other ways. Lilith describes the beginning of the Arts Collective with the same anti-bureaucratic language that the founders of the Urban Monastery use to describe how it was established: unintentional beginnings, eating dinner together, and developing friendships with like-minded people:

LILITH: The Arts Collective; I didn't go out trying to start anything. God did that, and people came. Some people came knowing it was "church," some people didn't. . . . People just started showing up to the larger Sunday meetings and they were all from the Art Institute . . . and ended up realizing this is a place that was really good for artists. And so within the span of three weeks twenty to twenty-five people from the Art Institute began attending the meetings on Sunday. So we started meeting together—essentially just having church—on Thursdays once a week. . . . Then people started meeting outside of our official meetings together, people started praying on campus, and people started coming back to Christ or coming to Christ.

Participants in the Arts Collective and other Collectives refer to them as "church," intentionally elevating the status of these informal gatherings in homes to the same level as traditional Sunday worship services at designated religious buildings:

LILITH: [The Arts Collective] is essentially a church. It's the basic ingredients of church. You open the Bible, you pray, you worship, you share stories. The order would always be changed up. Sometimes we'd just have communion and come down to the prayer room and pray the whole time, sometimes we'd just worship, sometimes we'd share stories. When we first started out we would hear "testimonies" of people's lives: whether it involved becoming a "believer" at the end of the story or not. It was just an invitation to *know* and *be known*, and to invite God into the process of comprehending who you're supposed to be and what you're going through.

These Arts Collective practices exemplify how the Urban Monastery attempts to organize the practice of evangelical spirituality into more "holistic," "relational," and "fluid" structures that blur the lines between sacred religious activities and the mundane activities of everyday life (Mina).

Although Urban Monastery leaders often de-emphasize their Sunday worship services in a conscious effort to deconstruct the divide between sacred and secular space, the community still meets every other week for worship, scripture teaching, and communion. Apart from the hip urban location, the youth of those in attendance and those delivering the sermon each week, the prominence of women leading from the front, and the occasional use of liturgical prayers and readings, the Urban Monastery's Sunday gathering looks a lot like a typical evangelical church service—albeit a more lively and fashionable one. A worship band opens the service with some loud, hard-driving music for about thirty minutes. Those in attendance worship in a variety of ways. Many sing along fervently with eyes closed and arms lifted in the air. Others sit in chairs with eyes closed in quiet meditation. A few jump and dance to the beat. Young children chase each through the aisles of gray plastic chairs, creating a slightly chaotic atmosphere that bothers no one. Some hold conversations in the back or in the aisles throughout the worship set. After worship there are some announcements, and then a message. The majority of the teaching is done by one of the members of the Urban Monastery's five-person core leadership team, two of whom are women. Other trusted leaders in the community, women and men, are also invited to teach at the Sunday Gatherings on topics in which they have special interest or expertise.

They are all unusually charismatic personalities and effective communicators, especially for people in their late twenties. Alex, who leads the core leadership team, is a particularly dynamic teacher and speaker who teaches more frequently than others, but still speaks at less than half of the Sunday Gatherings. None have formal seminary degrees, but all have had extensive leadership training and Bible instruction with various evangelical churches or parachurch organizations. All have extensive knowledge of the Bible. The messages draw heavily on biblical themes while also addressing a wide range of personal and social issues depending on the week, including messages on the arts and creativity and various justice issues. Some examples include a sixteen-part teaching series titled "Life of a Disciple" that introduces the different elements of D-Groups, a two-year overview of the entire Bible approached as a narrative called the "God Story," and an eight-week condensed version of the God Story. While challenging dominant expressions of American evangelicalism in many of their religious and political standpoints and strategies of action, the Urban Monastery exemplifies evangelicalism's *doxic* commitment to scripture across all levels of its distinctive practice of "community in three expressions."

Communitarian Leadership: Trinitarian Theology in Practice

The Urban Monastery's approach to leadership also embodies holistic communitarianism in its team orientation, its gender egalitarianism, and in the large proportion of community members who hold significant leadership responsibilities. The community has sixty highly committed leaders out of a group of one hundred fifty people, which means that a very large proportion of Urban Monastery participants are involved in leadership in some capacity.

The Urban Monastery's Leadership Community meets every other week to report on various aspects of community life, to pray together, and to discuss major community decisions. Urban Monastery leaders make much of the way that Jesus pursued his ministry as recorded in the first four books of the New Testament. Alex is often heard saying phrases such as, "When Jesus decided to change the world he invested 70 percent of his time in twelve people." The statement expresses the Urban Monastery's strategy of investing heavily in leadership development and multiplication through close personal relationships, as opposed to the more common evangelical practice of focusing one's time and energy as a religious leader on attracting people to Sunday events and providing religious services for crowds. Urban Monastery leaders devote significant time and energy to the sixty people who are part of the Leadership Community, with the goal that each of those sixty people in turn develops a small group of leaders, who then develop their own leaders, and so on. Against a bureaucratic and "consumptive form of church" that relies on a small group of professional religious leaders, Urban Monastery leaders work hard to empower participants to become leaders themselves who are able to reproduce more leaders (Mina). This focus on empowering participants to become leaders is evident to new participants in the Urban Monastery. Each of the new community members I interviewed cited the unusually high number of leaders and the decentralized, empowering leadership structure of the Urban Monastery as a significant reason they became part of the community.

The Urban Monastery's model of communitarian leadership is derived from theological beliefs about the Trinitarian nature of God and is enacted within the structure of its core leadership team:

MINA: The overarching message of scripture is the potency of what God designed in the beginning: with the Trinity in this place of community and engagement with each other, and then God, out of the overflow of himself, wanting to reproduce, share, and let people know and see this love and this community. That is his dream for humanity. Then God commissioned people to reproduce and multiply that template of the Trinity's existence in the beginning.

A Trinitarian reading of the creation story provides the model for how Urban Monastery leaders understand the history of their community and serves as the template for how they organize leadership and community in the Urban Monastery. All of its founding leaders emphasize how the Urban Monastery was established "unintentionally" as a result of relationships and community, rather than through a single individual's entrepreneurial vision and energy. Just as the Trinity enjoyed love and community with one another before creating the world and humanity "out of the overflow" of that initial love, the founding leaders of the Urban Monastery frequently recount how they built deep friendships with one another before inviting others to join them in community, which then began the "organic" process that led to the establishment of the Urban Monastery. They celebrate interdependency and spiritual family rather than the heroic acts of individual religious leaders or believers. And instead of having a single senior pastor or leader possessing a high degree of authority as in typical evangelical churches, the Urban Monastery is led by the five-person core team who share leadership responsibilities.

The Urban Monastery's views on gender egalitarian leadership are also rooted in their Trinitarian reading of the creation story in which God created women and men equally as bearers of the divine image:

ANJA: The image of God is male and female both, in equality. . . . I think we have distorted the true image of female and the true image of male.

MINA: I want to see women raised up—not in an antagonistic, reactionary way against men—but I have *such* a desire in my heart, that I feel is from the Lord, that his image would be fully represented and that the disparity of a woman's voice in comparison to men would not be so marked anymore. That she would begin to speak out, she would step into who she was made to be, whether it's a mom at home or a CEO or starting a small business in Africa.

For Urban Monastery leaders, gender egalitarian communitarian leadership is modeled after the Trinitarian "template" established in Genesis 1–2, in which God creates male and female together to represent His image on the earth; an image that is communal (i.e., Trinitarian) in its very essence and can be fully represented only when women and men are empowered to fully express both femininity and masculinity in mutual interdependence and authentic relationship.

In addition to being on the Urban Monastery's core leadership team, a number of women are also national leaders who travel and speak frequently around the country, often working with other evangelical churches and organizations that are not used to seeing women in national leadership positions. Unsurprisingly, these women have experienced a great deal of tension and conflict as a result of their high profile leadership roles:

INTERVIEWER: So, you mentioned co-ed leadership as something you like about the Urban Monastery, and you've been in that position. Over the years, what has that been like for you as a female leader?

ANJA: You're opening up a large can of worms right there! I could talk for hours about this. It's been one of the most difficult and absolutely incredible, rewarding aspects of being part of the Urban Monastery. . . . I found that being a woman who is stepping into national influence as a leader was something I was unprepared for. . . . Leadership in the church in America is mostly male. And it's mostly older than my generation as well. And in some respects that's fine. But I found myself being regarded as a secretary or administrator, as Brad's assistant—a guy who is my peer, my age, who I was working with full time—when really we were leading together. Those kinds of things I wasn't prepared for. I began to encounter a lot of difficult interaction with male leaders from all over the country. Guys who wouldn't make eye contact with me when we were having meetings, or who wouldn't ask me a question but would ask Brad all the questions. I felt like they didn't think that I could be a leader or that I had answers to offer. . . . Nothing seems to say, "You're not valuable" more than somebody not even paying you the time of day when you're in a meeting with them. So those things were difficult for sure.

MINA: As far as how that's affected me on the national leadership and Urban Monastery front, it's been a very tumultuous but rewarding process. It just hasn't been smooth. . . . These [gender equality issues] go the very centerpiece of God's image—male and female—and bring some sort of unspoken undercurrent of division. It can be a subtle thought process that you have, a subtle animosity or distrust or compartmentalization of what women are supposed to do and what they are not. I know most people kind of think, "Oh that's so old. We're not dealing with that anymore." But it's still there in so many subtle, different ways.

While asserting themselves as leaders in both national contexts and in the Urban Monastery has been difficult, both Mina and Anja have been encouraged by the success of their efforts to overcome gender inequality in leadership:

MINA: We've had such breakthrough in the ideas that we have of how men and women can lead together, and there is such a freedom to feel honored both ways and to lead in freedom together. That's happened with all the men and with us. . . . We told God, "We don't want to reproduce this [gender inequality] in our generation. Would you do a different thing? Would you put your image on display in its fullness? Would you teach us how to work together?"

As a core symbolic element in the Urban Monastery's holistic communitarian meaning system, Trinitarian themes of love, community, relationship, and mutual interdependence are used to explain and organize a wide range of religious practices in the Urban Monastery according to the "fuzzy logic of practice," in which individual and collective agents use a small set of cultural symbols and representations in order to construct practical strategies of action across a wide range of activities.[84]

Along with the satisfaction of being part of an egalitarian leadership team for the Urban Monastery, these women have particularly enjoyed seeing how their position as female leaders has inspired and empowered the women and men that they speak to and work with around the country:

ANJA: Many people—as we team-lead in co-ed situations—*many* men and women have remarked to us about how unique it is to see us working together in the way we do, or to see Brad defer to us. . . . I see women's eyes light up when I talk in front of a group or when Mina speaks in front of a group. I see the women engage in a different way. We've had so many young girls especially come to us and be like, "This is amazing! I've never seen this model before!" Or, "I don't have models of women who are leaders like you. I want some of what God's doing in your life in *my* life." So it's been an incredible journey. Difficult, but good.

MINA: We've shared about struggling with feeling undervalued and overlooked because of our femininity and because we just aren't expected to be in these places or do these things. We share with women: "This doesn't have to be the story line." . . . Just the fact that we are *there*, that *we* were the ones speaking: you'd watch the eyes of the women light up. Suddenly they had fresh courage and fresh desire to *do* something and to be something because they're watching someone else do it as well. Because most of us have grown up watching a bunch of men lead. Those have been our role models. We haven't seen women or interacted with women who even *want* to do what we want to do.

In an evangelical world dominated by male authority, Urban Monastery leaders draw on a communitarian, Trinitarian interpretation of the nature of God and the creation story as the biblical grounds for gender egalitarianism in leadership.

Ironically, the creation account that Urban Monastery participants use as the warrant and template for their communitarian, gender egalitarian leadership practices is used by conservative evangelicals to justify restricting certain leadership positions in the church to men. Drawing on biblical passages such as Ephesians 5:21–33 and 1 Timothy 2:11–15, conservative evangelicals argue that the Trinitarian creation story in Genesis 1 and 2 teaches male headship and authority over women in marriage and the church.[85] In its metaphoric Trinitarian interpretation of the egalitarian implications of the Genesis 1 and 2 creation story, the Urban Monastery's application of the Trinitarian template to problems of gender equality follows the inexact and metaphoric logic of practical theology, rather than logician's logic of systematic theology.

The Urban Monastery's approach to gender equality is typical of how neo-monastic evangelicals adhere to the rules of the evangelical field while simultaneously challenging dominant perspectives within it. The Urban Monastery's argument for gender egalitarianism is a theological argument based on the authority of scripture, not primarily a political argument based on abstract philosophical principles. The Urban Monastery challenges dominant perspectives on male authority among conservative evangelicals in its theology and practice of gender egalitarian leadership, but does so without violating any of the core theological commitments concerning biblical authority that define the boundaries of the evangelical field.

Conclusion: Holistic Communitarianism, Limits and Contradictions

The development of holistic communitarianism as a relatively coherent and comprehensive strategy of action in the Urban Monastery is an example of how the "ideological" culture of a reform-oriented social movement can influence action in direct and powerful ways in the right social context, particularly when group members are vigilant about applying a relatively coherent cultural meaning system to all aspects of everyday life.[86] Neo-monastic evangelicals in the Urban Monastery explicitly draw on their distinctive holistic communitarian theology to develop new strategies of collective action that challenge traditional evangelical religious practices, recover communitarian elements of biblical theology and evangelical religious practice, deconstruct distinctions between sacred and secular space in individual and communal life, and expand the meaning of "mission" to include holistic personal and social transformation as a strategy of social engagement. The Urban Monastery's holistic communitarianism is a type of Weberian innerworldly asceticism, but is distinctive in its pattern of *anti-bureaucratic rational organization* and in being a *celebratory asceticism* that is communitarian rather than individualistic in emphasis. In organizing community for holistic mission, the Urban Monastery enacts holistic communitarianism through concrete individual and collective religious practices.

Urban Monastery participants' self-conscious efforts to apply holistic communitarianism to all aspects of individual and collective life is an example of how "culture takes a more explicit, coherent form" in unsettled contexts, when social actors are actively challenging and reorganizing existing strategies of action while constructing "new languages and styles for new strategies of action."[87] Of course, culture does not always have such an explicit and direct influence on action. In more "settled" contexts when people are operating within well-established strategies of action, culture influences action in more complex and contradictory ways, making culture's influence over action less direct and more difficult to observe.[88] For example, congregations in the same Christian denominations who share common theological doctrines often adopt diverse "group styles" that often bear little direct relation to explicit theological doctrines or beliefs.[89] Similarly, while black Protestant churches are perhaps the prototypical example theologically communitarian religious communities as defined by moral cosmology theory, their communitarian theology does not result in a comprehensive communitarian strategy of social organization as it does in the case of neo-monastic evangelicals. Instead, black Protestant churches adopt congregational styles of social organization typical of most religious communities in the United States.[90]

The difference between black Protestant and neo-monastic strategies of religious organization lies in the fact that neo-monastic evangelicals are engaged in an explicit, self-conscious, comprehensive struggle to develop new theological meanings and strategies of action that challenge the common-sense practice of organizing religious community according to the dominant congregational pattern. In the absence of direct ideological challenges to established meaning systems and strategies of action, common sense prevails.[91] However, because holistic communitarianism functions as the ideological framework of a new religious movement that is directly and explicitly challenging dominant expressions of American evangelicalism, neo-monastic evangelicals' holistic communitarian theology has a more unified and direct influence over action than is typical of religious culture in other contexts.

To argue—as I have done over the last three chapters—that religious culture can have a direct and powerful influence over action through the vigilant application of a relatively comprehensive and coherent theological meaning system is not, however, to deny the existence of contradictions or limits in the Urban Monastic point of view. Indeed, Urban Monastery leaders themselves speak of the "idealism" and uncertain future of their young avant-garde community and its holistic communitarian spirituality:

CALEB: I think that probably one of our biggest wrestles has been navigating through our idealism of what the Urban Monastery would look like. Like,

"Ok, how does this urban monastic ideal work in Western society?" . . . I could probably start every one of my answers with the comment: "We've wrestled with the idealism" of some of this. Take our location for example. We thought that a ton of stuff was going to happen immediately . . . that it was just going to bust loose. We thought there wasn't a Christian presence here. I think we had high hopes about homeless people coming in, just being a home for them; knowing that there are a lot of people who are out on the streets in this part of the city. I think some of that idealism was challenged by the fact that, while the Urban Monastery itself—the building—is here, we [Caleb and Mina] don't live here. I think that was a big wake up call. And still is. That's something that I've really wrestled through on a personal level.

So I think some of my idealism was broken in that way. And just security factors with homeless guys. Early on I think we had a much more open door policy before realizing "this is a little sketchy." Then we had girls in the mix [living in the Urban Monastery building] and were like, "O man, this is really difficult." Then we tried doing a thing for a while where we'd do a meal every month and we called it the "F-Bomb" (laughing). It was on the fourth Friday of the month on the first floor; and we would fast that day and then feast and invite everybody in the community and off the street to come. It was a great theory! We did it a couple times and it just didn't work. The most exciting part was the F-Bomb! The moment where we realized we were going to call something the F-bomb we were like "*Yes!*" (laughing with emphasis at the "F-Bomb's" alliterative and expletive-evoking connotations). But that was as good as it got.

According to Caleb, the "F-Bomb didn't work" because the Urban Monastery hadn't built sufficient relational credibility with their homeless neighbors, and because they lacked sufficient material resources and expertise to sustain the activity over the long haul. They also realized they had been "blind" to other churches and groups in the city who "fed 500 people a day" and "could do it a lot better than we can."

Urban Monastery leaders worried about the "longevity" of their highly "incarnational" and communal style of living; about "quality of life" and sustainability issues as more Urban Monastery participants grew older, got married, and had children; about how growing larger as a community had the potential to compromise the "fluid" and "relational" character of the Urban Monastery; about the constant temptation to slide back into "old habits and patterns" derived from "traditional" church expressions; and about whether their vision of holistic communitarian spirituality "was even possible in this context. Is it applicable to us in our Western context . . . with our Western set-up and our fragmented lifestyles? I don't know!" (Caleb, Alex, Roland, Mina).

From the point of view of cultural theory, these concerns are warranted. The limits of holistic communitarianism as a cultural meaning system capable of transforming Urban Monastery participants' strategies of action in a sustainable way go beyond the explicit concerns of community leaders. In general, the influence of new cultural ideologies over action is also limited by the quiet power of the cultural status quo—those elements of tradition and common sense that are so deeply embedded into the cultural and material organization of everyday life so as to go unnoticed and unchallenged.[92] Take, for example, the Urban Monastery's participation in "D-Groups": groups of two or three individuals who meet weekly to read scripture, pray, and answer a series of questions designed to encourage the vigilant application of biblical teachings to everyday life. As we have seen, D-Groups are a foundational part of the tripartite communitarian structure of life in the Urban Monastery; an attempt to integrate individuals into multiple nodes of spiritual community as an antidote to the individualistic orientation of American evangelicalism and American society more generally.[93] However, the Urban Monastery's practice of D-Groups also contains a notable, though largely unrecognized, element of individualistic voluntarism common to Americans and American evangelicals alike.[94] D-Groups are not "required" of Urban Monastery participants—they are purely voluntary. They are not tracked or counted by community leaders. Indeed, Urban Monastery leaders intentionally refrain from encouraging participants to join D-Groups while teaching or speaking from the front at community worship gatherings, fearful that doing so might cause community members to feel pressured into participating or come to view D-Groups as just another example of pre-planned, "programmatic" religiosity (Alex, Mina). Although it is a neo-monastic community that opposes individualism and prioritizes intentionality, commitment, and community as central markers faithful Christian spirituality, the right of the individual to choose for herself how to participate in community life remains sacrosanct.

This is but one example of the voluntaristic individualism that lies beneath the surface of the Urban Monastery's explicit and active communitarian religious orientation. As moral cosmology theory notes, theological communitarians tend to establish religious communities that are authoritarian and traditional in nature, emphasizing respect and submission to authority over individual autonomy in the interpretation and practice of religious faith.[95] A recent American example would be the 1960s and 1970s Jesus People movement, whose communitarian religious orientation led to a strong emphasis on submission to authority in many Jesus People communes.[96] The Urban Monastery, however, is decidedly anti-authoritarian. In talking with Urban Monastery leaders, one gets the impression that even the slightest exertion of pressure or directive leadership would be highly destructive to the sense of trust, equality, and mutuality that exists within the community. Because of the multi-level, team-oriented approach to leadership in the Urban Monastery, authority is spread widely and there is a decidedly democratic and participatory feel to community decision-making. The arts community, in particular, is fiercely independent and self-directed, unafraid to challenge or resist core community leaders when they deem it necessary. Speaking of her primary leadership role within the arts community, Lilith laughed: "Sometimes it feels like herding cats!" Lilith is not bothered by this. Creative freedom and nonconformity rule the day. There is a high degree of tolerance for independence, individual expression, and autonomy in the Urban Monastery that contrasts with the emphasis on order, submission to authority, and regularity typical of other monastic and communitarian expressions of Christianity. The Urban Monastery is deeply committed to community, but community entered into (and exited) willingly, with the presumption of a high degree of individual freedom and autonomy to engage as one pleases without invasive, heavy-handed leadership from above.

These latent strains of experiential and expressive individualism underlying the Urban Monastery's dominant holistic communitarian orientation demonstrate the obdurate nature of pre-existing cultural structures and strategies of action, which are no less powerful in their effects on action for their lack of explicit articulation.[97] It should come as little surprise, therefore, to discover latent elements of expressive individualism among Urban Monastery participants (despite their very earnest, explicit, and vigilant opposition to individualism in general). Urban Monastery participants are, after all, evangelicals. And American evangelicalism, while calling individuals to lives of vigilant moral discipline, has always also been a religion of the heart.[98] Urban Monastery participants are also Americans; and as the late Robert Bellah reminds us:

> Individualism lies at the very core of American culture. . . . There is a biblical individualism and civic individualism as well as a utilitarian and an expressive individualism. Whatever the differences among the traditions and the consequent differences in their understandings of individualism, there are some things they all share, things that are basic to American identity. We believe in the dignity, indeed the sacredness, of the individual. Anything that would violate our right to think for ourselves, judge for ourselves, make our own decisions, live our lives as we see fit, is not only morally wrong, it is sacrilegious.[99]

Urban Monastery participants have constructed a powerful, well-organized, and vigilantly applied holistic communitarian meaning system concretely expressed in individual and collective strategies of action; yet they also remain committed to the dignity, sacredness, and self-determination of the individual. Cultural meaning systems are never perfectly coherent or consistently applied. Even powerful, direct, and well-organized challenges to the cultural status quo cannot completely scrub away the residual influence of history, tradition, and common sense over individual and collective action.[100] While the Urban Monastery's relation to dominant expressions of American evangelicalism involves a great deal of explicit challenge and opposition, it involves much tacit agreement as well, as both field theory and cultural theory would lead us to expect.

Chapter 7

Conclusion
The Transformation of American Evangelicalism

WHEN CITIZENS OF the United States hear conservative Christians talk religion and politics, they are accustomed to hearing something about America's moral decline, the erosion of the family, God's judgment, and the betrayal of America's heritage as a Christian nation founded on biblical principles. When citizens of the United States hear evangelical Christians talk about religion and politics in the future, they may hear something about the importance of families or having a "consistent of ethic of life," but they may just as likely hear about global and domestic economic injustices, demands for greater environmental responsibility, and the dangers of militarism and religious nationalism:

> We are interested in the poor, in racial reconciliation, in global poverty and AIDS, in the plight of women in the developing world. . . . People who might be called progressive evangelicals or centrist evangelicals are one stirring away from a real awakening.
> —Bill Hybels, Senior Pastor and Founder of Willow Creek Community Church[1]

That was a turning point in my life two-and-a-half years ago where God basically said to me – and I've never heard God speak audibly; it's in my mind – "The purpose of influence is to speak up for those who have no influence. The purpose of influence is to speak up for those who have no influence." And in religious terms I had to say, "God, I repent, because I can't think of the last time I thought of 'widows and orphans.'" I live in a very affluent Southern California neighborhood. There aren't any homeless people lying on the streets where I live. And I said, "I can't think of the last time I cared about the homeless." And so I went back and I began to read scripture, and it was like blinders

came off. Now, I've got three advanced degrees. I've had four years in Greek and Hebrew and I've got doctorates. And how did I miss 2,000 verses in the Bible where it talks about the poor? How did I miss that? I mean, I went to two different seminaries and a Bible school; how did I miss the 2,000 verses on the poor?
     —Rick Warren, Senior Pastor and Founder of Saddleback Church[2]

If Rick Warren had been listening to Jim Wallis or other leaders of the evangelical left over the past thirty years, he would have heard all about the "2,000 verses in the Bible where it talks about the poor."[3] However, like most other middle- and upper-middle-class white evangelicals in the twentieth century, Warren's local social context, deep-seated theological individualism, and conservative politics kept him—in his interpretation of the Bible—from "seeing" or acknowledging the ubiquitous demands for economic justice found throughout Christian scriptures.[4] For decades, the evangelical left's accusations that evangelicals had created an "American Bible" that was "full of holes" due to its neglect of biblical teaching on economic justice largely fell on deaf ears.[5] That is no longer the case.

This book has been about "the transformation of American evangelicalism" in two senses. First, it has explored recent religious and political transformations associated with the "new evangelicalism" that have been taking place in the American evangelical field in recent years, with a specific focus on evangelical neo-monasticism.[6] Second, in using field theory to analyze neo-monasticism as a particular case of transformation in the American evangelical field, it offers a sociological analysis of the dynamic social processes through which American evangelicalism is reproduced and transformed. This final chapter will summarize each of these arguments with the help of some additional reflections that will make it somewhat more theoretically substantial than a typical concluding chapter.

A Practical Social Hermeneutic of American Evangelicalism

In chapter 1, I argued that we need a theoretical approach to the study of American evangelicalism that takes the meaning-content of religious culture seriously, rather than deducing the religious and political standpoints of evangelicals directly from social structure.[7] At the same time, I argued that we need an approach that better specifies how external social forces influence evangelical position-takings. The approach must help us make sense of the distinctive religious and political standpoints of different movements within

American evangelicalism and their relation to one another, rather than analyzing evangelicalism in terms of monolithic generational, religious, or political categories. And it must account for how the specific social history of
American evangelicalism continues to exert influence on the diverse evangelical standpoints in the present.

To that end, this book has drawn on field and cultural theory to develop
an original *practical social hermeneutic* approach to understanding the religious and political standpoints and strategies of action of American evangelicals.[8] To say that we need a practical social *hermeneutics* of evangelicalism
is to say that the meaning-content of religious culture and its interpretation
is a causally relevant factor in evangelical agency. In other words, this book
supports the "strong program in culture" that views culture (religious and
otherwise) as a relatively autonomous causal factor in human agency.[9]
Building on the work of Max Weber, Christian Smith, Anne Swidler, Jeffrey
Alexander, and others, I have argued that a structural-hermeneutic approach to cultural analysis is an essential element of any adequate model of
evangelical agency.[10] Chapter 4 employs the structural-hermeneutic model
to analyze how Urban Monastery participants have developed their distinctive holistic communitarian meaning system by changing the relational prioritization of a few, historically significant, core symbolic elements within
evangelical theology: namely evangelism, social justice, and the doctrine of
the Trinity.

Evangelicals would heartily affirm the claim that one must deploy hermeneutics in order to make sense of their religious and political standpoints, as a
stroll through the vast biblical hermeneutics section of any self-respecting
evangelical seminary library could attest. However, to say that we need a practical *social* hermeneutics of American evangelicalism is to argue that the process of biblical interpretation and theological meaning construction is also
bound up with social and historical processes, and that the religious and political standpoints of evangelicals are causally influenced by social forces.[11] I have
argued that Bourdieusian field analysis provides the best theoretical framework for understanding how social and historical forces influence evangelical
position-takings, and conducted a field-theoretic analysis of neo-monasticism's
relation to other theoretically and substantively relevant movements within
American evangelicalism in chapter 3.

Finally, to say that we need a *practical* social hermeneutic of evangelical
agency is to affirm that culture influences action not through the "logician's
logic" of the scholar or academic theologian, but through the "fuzzy" logic of
practice, in which a minimalist set of symbolic elements can be used to generate meaningful interpretations of an almost infinite range of actions and

social objects.[12] Here we find Bourdieu in agreement with both Kane and Swidler concerning the polysemous nature of symbols and the fuzzy logic of their application in practice.[13] Thus, it is that a relatively small number of adjustments to the theological meaning system of traditional evangelicalism (such as amplifying the symbolic priority of the Trinity and the symbolic priority of social justice relative to evangelism by Urban Monastery participants) are able to generate relatively comprehensive and radical transformations in the religious and political standpoints and strategies of action of neo-monastic evangelicals, as described in Part II.

This feature of the symbolic elements of cultural meaning systems helps explain how there can be so much diversity—and even contradiction—in the religious and political standpoints of different movements within American evangelicalism despite their *doxic* commitment to the authority of the Bible and its historically orthodox interpretation. The meaning-content of evangelical theologies contains a vast array of symbolic elements drawn from scripture, elements whose rearrangement and reinterpretation have the potential to generate a near infinite set of distinctive evangelical theologies without thereby contradicting any of the *doxic* theological commitments that set the boundaries of the evangelical field. For example, the doctrine of the Trinity is only one of hundreds of constitutive symbolic elements in the evangelical theological repertoire, yet changing its priority relative to other elements allows Urban Monastery participants to generate a whole alternative system of religious and political standpoints and strategies of action which challenge dominant expressions of American evangelicalism, while remaining safely within the boundaries of evangelical *doxa*.[14] Other evangelical agents can (and do) do the same with any of the hundreds of other elements contained in historic evangelical interpretations of the Bible to generate other distinctive standpoints and strategies of action. A practical hermeneutic approach to American evangelicalism helps explain the cultural sources of evangelical diversity, unity, and transformation.

Adding the *social* element to the practical hermeneutic approach explains them further, as demonstrated in chapter 3. The fact that the evangelical field (like all fields) is structured by a series of "synchronic oppositions between antagonistic positions"—and the related fact that the position-takings of evangelical agents are constructed in relation to other positions in the field— further expands the possibilities and complexity of transformations in the meaning-content of distinctive positions within the evangelical field.[15] The standpoints of evangelical agents are oppositions, not necessarily of an entire alternative position, but of some element or elements within it. In their search for distinction and *doxic* efforts to communicate the gospel to new subcultures, evangelical agents are able to construct a near infinite variety of new position-takings by selecting different positions and position-takings from within the field to stand against. Almost any theological, ecclesiological, or social feature of an alternative position—suburban location, boring buildings, style of music, organizational structure, specific doctrines, evangelistic (in)effectiveness, political standpoints, and so on—can be chosen as the target of opposition from which evangelical agents are able to construct a new and distinctive position in the field. At the same time, the *doxic* commitments, boundaries, and structure of the evangelical field make some positions and oppositions more possible, or more risky, than others. For example, challenging traditional evangelical understandings of the gospel or biblical authority is more risky than challenging traditional modes of Sunday worship, as emerging church leaders have discovered. A practical social hermeneutic of American evangelicalism reveals the dizzying array of cultural elements from which evangelicals construct their distinctive theological meaning systems and strategies of action, while at the same time revealing how the specific *doxa* and structure of the evangelical field narrows down these options to a more limited "space of possible" position-takings depending on an agent's particular position in the field.[16]

Although the cultural resources evangelicals use to construct distinctive standpoints and strategies of action are vast, there are rules for how evangelicals put them to use. The biblical text is far and away the primary cultural resource evangelicals use to construct their theological and political standpoints. However, they also draw on external cultural resources to challenge alternative standpoints and to develop their own. In chapter 3, we saw the emerging church use popularized versions of postmodern philosophy and literary theory to challenge modern megachurch evangelicalism, witnessed neo-monastic evangelicals use historical models of religious community to develop a "new monasticism" that confronts dominant religious and political powers of the present, and saw how megachurch evangelicals incorporate linguistic idioms, strategies, and organizational structures from American business culture. While it is acceptable for evangelicals to use external cultural resources to develop their particular points of view, they must not be seen to contradict *doxic* evangelical interpretations of the Bible, or they will face expulsion. The Bible is not the only cultural toolkit from which evangelicals extract the symbolic tools they use to construct religious standpoints and strategies of action, but any cultural tool borrowed from a different toolbox (be it science, politics, business, the arts, other religions, etc.) must be able to fit into the toolbox of evangelical *doxa* concerning the Bible, else it will be banished from the field.[17]

Figure 7.1a provides a stylized visual model of evangelical position-takings from the perspective of the practical social hermeneutic approach developed in this book. The far left of the diagram displays two common but inadequate reductionist approaches to explaining evangelical religious and political standpoints: the upwards conflation that explains evangelical position-takings solely in terms of biblically derived cultural meanings, and the downwards conflation that ignores the meaning-content of evangelical interpretations of scripture and explains evangelical position-takings solely in terms of external social, economic, or political structures.[18] As the diagram makes explicit, both approaches err by ignoring the fact that external forces and the biblical text influence evangelical position-takings *only after having been restructured* through the critical mediating influence of the specific history and present structure of the American evangelical field. The specific history, *doxa*, and structure of the evangelical field constitute the social context—which can be understood as a field of social forces—in which evangelical agents appropriate cultural resources from the Bible and external sources to construct their distinctive religious and political position-takings.

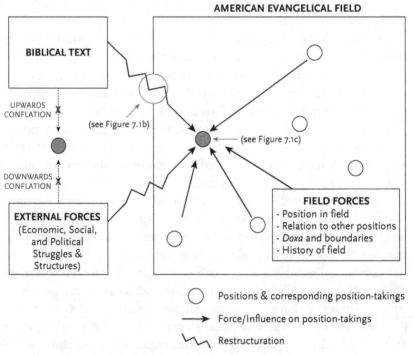

FIGURE 7.1A Unified model of evangelical position-takings

If the vector angle of each black arrow in the diagram indicates a specific force or influence on a position, one can see how the very same configuration of forces will be experienced differently depending on an agent's objective location in the field (i.e., dominant/dominated, volume and type of capital possessed, etc.), thus making certain types of strategies and position-takings more likely than others. As evangelical agents who occupy distinctive positions in the field engage different subcultures with the gospel, they interact with different sets of external structures, subjecting each agent to unique external influences on their position-takings—forces that remain subject to restructuration by the field. For example, the emerging church's engagement with educated urban young adults, or megachurch evangelicalism's engagement with suburban baby-boomers, subjects them to different sets of external cultural and social structures, which influence their respective position-takings indirectly through the mediating influence of the evangelical field, as explored at length in chapter 3.

Figure 7.1b takes a closer look at the process of theological meaning construction from the perspective of the practical social hermeneutic model. The biblical text is the primary (but not only) source of the cultural signs and

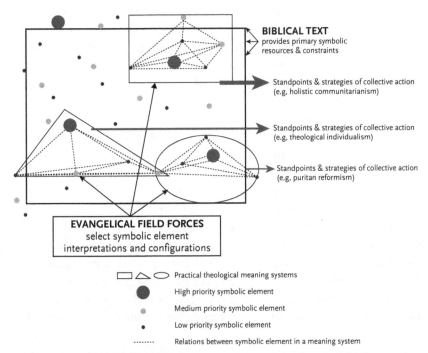

FIGURE 7.1B Practical social hermeneutic model of evangelical meaning construction

symbols that evangelicals use to construct their distinctive theological meaning systems. Different symbolic elements from the Bible are given different
degrees of emphasis or priority (represented by the varying size of the circles
in figure 7.1b) in different practical meaning systems. The specific relational
configuration of these symbols in different theological meaning systems
gives rise to a range of distinctive practical theologies among evangelicals
(represented by the three different shapes in figure 7.1b). Furthermore, the
Bible contains hundreds of powerful religious symbols, not all of which are
actively used in the construction of the various theological meaning systems
of evangelical agents: these "unused" symbolic elements are represented by
the circles which stand outside the three shapes in figure 7.1b. This allows for
a great deal of flexibility and potential for innovation among evangelical theologies, while still keeping them safely inside the boundaries of evangelical
orthodoxy concerning the authority of the Bible, the historicity of Christ's
death and resurrection, the need for forgiveness and the possibility of salvation, and the like. Changing the intensity, interpretation, or relational priority
of any one or a number of symbolic elements used to construct theological
meaning can change the shape or structure of an entire meaning system and
give rise to radically altered standpoints and strategies of collective action, as
illustrated in figure 7.1b and described in detail for the neo-monastic evangelicals in the Urban Monastery in Part II. Figure 7.1b also illustrates how
different practical theological meaning systems can overlap by sharing
common symbolic elements, while remaining distinctive due to the unique
configuration and prioritization of the elements used to construct theological
meaning within each system.

The interpretation and selection of the biblically derived symbolic elements used to construct distinctive practical theologies is influenced by the
specific forces of the evangelical field, which vary depending on an agent's
location in the field as displayed in figure 7.1a. Once again, external forces and
cultural resources influence the interpretation and selection of symbolic elements, but they do so only through the mediating influence of the evangelical
field. For example, Americans' "new quest for community" in the face of post-
industrial dislocation, social mobility, and social fragmentation is no doubt a
contributing factor to the development of holistic communitarianism as a
practical evangelical meaning system, but this more general search for the
experience of "community" is given specific force and shape by Urban Monastery participants' appropriation and application of the Christian symbol of
the Trinity in practical action.[19]

As discussed in chapter 4, the application of the word "system" to cultural
analysis is controversial among social theorists, but the concept is appropriate

for analyzing theological meaning construction among evangelicals, when used with the right qualifications.[20] Describing holistic communitarianism and other practical evangelical theologies as "theological meaning systems" does not mean that they are perfectly logically consistent, or that they are the only cultural elements evangelicals use to construct strategies of action in the world. Rather, it is to argue that the internal structure and meaning-content of evangelical practical theologies are relatively coherent, comprehensive, and organized systems of meaning that "aspire to offer unified answers to questions of how human beings should live" and that, under the right social conditions, can and do causally influence the standpoints and strategies of action of evangelicals through the fuzzy logic of practice.[21] Because of their *doxic* commitment to the reliability and authority of the Bible as God's uniquely inspired revelation concerning the nature of God, humanity, and the world, evangelicals tend to construct relatively rationalized, coherent, and comprehensive meaning systems that they attempt to apply to all aspects of life. As I argue in chapter 6, the more coherent a meaning system is and the more vigilantly and comprehensively social actors attempt to apply it, the more direct and powerful are its effects on action. The varying intensities of the gray arrows in figure 7.1b represent this variability in culture's influence on action—or, in the specific case of evangelicals—the varying degrees to which different theological meaning systems influence action depending on their degree of rationalization and the social conditions in which they are enacted.[22] As described in chapter 6, the Urban Monastery's *celebratory asceticism* and various ways of organizing community for holistic mission is an example of what this can look like in practice.

Figure 7.1c zeroes in on the relationship between religious and political standpoints among American evangelicals. Chapters 1 and 2 discussed the two dominant sociological perspectives on how to think about this relationship: religious consistency theory, on the one hand, and moral cosmology theory, on the other. The former equates theological conservatism with across the board social, economic, and political conservatism, while the latter argues that theological conservatives tend toward left-liberal economic perspectives. Although both theories correctly note that political standpoints are influenced by religious standpoints, religious consistency theory offers an oversimplified and outdated picture of the relationship between religious and political standpoints, while moral cosmology theory suffers from a lack of social and historical realism.[23]

Moral cosmology theory logically deduces the political standpoints of religious believers from their formal theological/moral standpoints. While deductive reasoning has its place in the development of social theories of

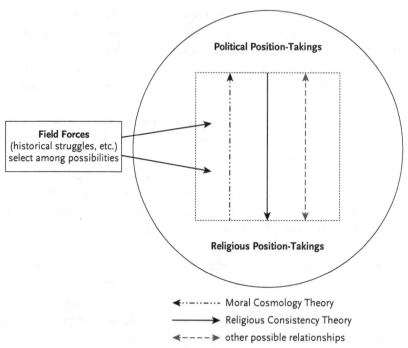

Political Position-Takings

Field Forces
(historical struggles, etc.)
select among possibilities

Religious Position-Takings

◄··—··—·· Moral Cosmology Theory
─────────► Religious Consistency Theory
◄── ── ─► other possible relationships

FIGURE 7.1C Space of possible relationships between religious and political position-takings

culture, it must be joined by concrete empirical analyses of the social and historical contexts in which cultural meanings are constructed and the practical logic with which they are enacted.[24] As I argue in chapter 2, American evangelical exceptionalism with respect to moral cosmology theory is rooted in the early twentieth-century struggles between fundamentalists and modernists over the legitimate representation of Christianity in America, struggles that helped set the pattern for a thoroughgoing theological individualism and political conservatism among theologically conservative Protestants throughout the twentieth century.

Whereas moral cosmology theory can lead analysts to overestimate the autonomy of theological position-takings with respect to historical religio-political struggles (represented by upward pointing arrow in figure 7.1c), religious consistency theory falls into the opposite trap (represented by the downward pointing arrow) of overestimating the degree of politicization and polarization of American religion into two neatly opposed monolithic camps consisting of theological and political conservatives, on the one hand, and theological and political liberals, on the other. By analyzing the "rationality" or "consistency" of evangelical position-takings *from the point of view of histor-ically contingent political categories and position-takings* as if they were obvious logical necessities, religious consistency theory fails adequately to account for the relative autonomy of the evangelical field with respect to American politics.[25]

Though inadequate in themselves as theories of evangelical position-takings, religious consistency and moral cosmology theory each point to em-pirically and logically probable potential relationships between theological and political position-takings among evangelicals (represented by the dashed box in figure 7.1c). However, the actual relationship between them will always be mediated by the specific social history of the American evangelical field and by ongoing struggles between agents in the field over the legitimate rep-resentation of biblical Christianity in America: struggles that involve the spe-cific *doxa*, forms of capital, and relatively autonomous categories of perception and meaning that constitute the field. The gray dashed line in figure 7.1c represents other potential relationships between the theological and political position-takings of evangelicals, with the historically variable degree of au-tonomy or heteronomy of theological position-takings with respect to the po-litical position-takings represented by the double-sided arrow.

The Transformation and Future of American Evangelicalism

If lessons from the past hundred years of American history are to be believed, one of the worst things that can happen to a sectarian religious movement in the United States is political success. Just as fundamentalist Protestantism's fall from grace followed its powerful political mobilization against evolution-ism and its social dangers in the early twentieth century, the Christian Right and conservative evangelicalism's successful consolidation of political power over the last thirty years has created a tidal wave of backlash and opposition from evangelical insiders and opponents alike. Close observers of the religion and politics scene in America argue that the Christian Right's influence peaked in 2004 in terms of both its impact on national politics and its posi-tion in the evangelical field itself.[26] While the evangelical left positioned itself as gadfly to a near-hegemonic conservative evangelicalism for over thirty years, recent years have witnessed dominant mainstream evangelical leaders and institutions publicly and explicitly breaking with the Christian Right/ conservative evangelical position for the first time.[27] Young evangelicals are even more likely to oppose the Christian Right and knee-jerk political conservatism.[28] It is not too much to say that American evangelicalism is experiencing a significant political transformation that is undermining conservative evangelicalism's long-standing hegemony over the field.[29]

If the monologue of the Christian Right is indeed coming to an end, what might be the future of evangelical engagement in politics?[30] While predicting social and political futures is a fool's game, Parts I and II of this book offer some clues. Chapter 3 explores the growing interconnections and agreements among *coalitions of the dominated* such as the one forming under the banner of "Red Letter Christianity"—a coalition that includes politically left-leaning evangelicals along with significant African American, Hispanic, and Catholic Church leaders.[31] The contradictory cultural location of Urban Monastery participants in chapter 4 is echoed in the political standpoints of the evangelical left, emerging church, and neo-monastic evangelicals more generally. These groups tend to advocate left-liberal political standpoints in the areas of foreign policy and militarism, religious nationalism and pluralism, poverty and economic inequality, race and immigration, and environmental issues, while maintaining moderately conservative standpoints on abortion and support for marriage and families. They tend to be ambivalent on the politics of homosexuality: firmly supporting gay civil rights, protections, and unions but taking mixed positions on gay marriage.

Beyond these streams, there is also significant momentum toward the consolidation of an "evangelical center" represented by dominant megachurch leaders and institutions such as Rick Warren and Joel Hunter, the National Association of Evangelicals, *Christianity Today*, InterVarsity Christian Fellowship, and the Council for Christian Colleges and Universities, an ensemble of leading evangelical higher education institutions including Wheaton, Calvin, and Gordon.[32] Since 2004, leaders from these institutions have published significant political statements such as the "Evangelical Climate Initiative" and "For the Health of the Nation" that have directly challenged the Christian Right and taken moderately progressive stances on issues relating to environmental protection, immigration, poverty, religious pluralism and freedom, and American militarism.[33] While this "evangelical center" remains firmly opposed to abortion and gay marriage, displays fondness for traditional patriotic religious language, and tends toward conservative economic policies, it also condemns automatic Republican Party partisanship, single-issue voting, and uncritical Christian nationalism.[34]

All this suggests significant changes in the style and substance of evangelical public and political engagement in the years to come. It is no longer possible to assume that being an evangelical means being a Republican or an across-the-board conservative, and current trends suggest a slow but steady decline in Republican Party identification among evangelicals as the scope of their political concerns continues to broaden beyond the politics of sexuality and the family.[35] This would mark a significant political transformation and restructuring of the role of religion in American electoral politics. At the same time, the Christian Right and conservative evangelicalism are not going away. Conservative evangelicalism continues to occupy a dominant position in the evangelical field despite its recent decline, and it will continue to be a dominant—though perhaps no longer hegemonic—force in the evangelical field for the foreseeable future.[36] Nor is evangelical opposition to abortion in most cases going away. The vast majority of evangelicals—whether left, center, or right—continue to believe that protecting the life of the unborn is a grave moral imperative and a significant human rights issue.[37] The political center of gravity of twenty-first-century evangelicalism is moving leftward— particularly among young evangelicals—yet evangelical political standpoints remain anchored in the specific history and struggles of the twentieth-century American evangelical field, which will continue to limit the speed and magnitude of the shift to the left in evangelical politics in America.

It remains to be seen how far this transformation in American evangelicalism will go and the extent to which it will engender new styles of political and social engagement among evangelicals in the United States. American evangelicals are increasingly concerned about the injustices of global and domestic poverty, for example, but there are many questions about how they will respond to these injustices.[38] Will more evangelicals begin actively supporting government-based responses to economic inequality, or will the majority continue to believe in small government and church-based responses to poverty and economic change? Will the majority of American evangelicals shift toward more communitarian economic and political position-takings as moral cosmology theory suggests, or will theological individualism and evangelical exceptionalism continue to hold as the dominant position-taking among evangelicals? Will evangelicals find new ways to address race and gender inequality, or will they continue to struggle with inadequate analyses and responses to inequality?[39] For example, despite their more progressive theological and political orientations, emerging church and neo-monastic evangelicals continue to struggle with problems of racial inequality and exclusivity in their communities and institutions, problems they themselves acknowledge.[40] And despite some success in addressing gendered power inequalities in progressive evangelical churches and organizations, white men continue to be the predominant faces and leading authorities within these institutions.[41] Will the theological and political transformations in American evangelicalism, as described in this book, lead to more widespread, sophisticated, and successful responses to these issues among evangelicals? And will evangelicals find new ways to articulate their distinctive moral and political visions without unnecessarily alienating or marginalizing non-evangelical Americans?

An even more basic question concerns whether American evangelicalism is heading toward a split. While there is a very real sense in which evangelicalism is in a constant state of permanent revolution and change, some transformations are larger than others. Sometimes struggles over the legitimate representation of biblical Christianity in America result in the genesis of new religious subfields that split off from old ones. Will history repeat itself in modified form? Are we witnessing the beginning of a break between politically conservative evangelicals and theologically conservative but politically progressive "Red Letter Christians" and the like, as many evangelical leaders have increasingly come to expect (and reluctantly advocate)?[42] Or will evangelicals hang together despite increasingly divergent social and political perspectives? These are some of the important questions raised by the transformation of American evangelicalism for the future religion and politics in America, questions whose answers will unfold through the same dynamic social processes that have driven reproduction and transformation in the American evangelical field since its inception.

In-Depth Interview Guide

Introduction

How long have you been a Christian?

How did you become a Christian?

What type of church did you attend growing up?

The Urban Monastery

Why did you become involved in the Urban Monastery?

How would you describe the Urban Monastery? Why does it exist? What is its mission or purpose?

Is there anything specific that you like about the beliefs or theology of the Urban Monastery?

Is there anything specific that you like about how the Urban Monastery is organized?

How does the Urban Monastery reach out to people in the community? To non-Christians? How do you do it (activities, events)? What are your goals in reaching out? What do you hope to accomplish?

How many Urban Monastery activities are you involved in during a typical week? What kinds of Urban Monastery activities are you involved in or have you been involved in?

Does your faith influence the type of work that you do or how you do your work? If so, how? Can you give me some examples?

Have you been involved in other churches or Christian groups in the past? How similar or dissimilar is the Urban Monastery to those groups? Can you give me some examples?

What books, ideas, or ways of practicing Christianity, from either the past or present, have you or the Urban Monastery been most influenced by?

Theology/Bible

What is the overarching message of the Bible?

What is the gospel?

What would you say a person has to believe to be a Christian?

What's more important: evangelism or social justice?

Politics, Culture, and Morality

Did you vote in the 2008 presidential election? Who did you vote/would you have voted for? Why? Was it easy for you to decide who to vote for, or difficult? Why? What issue or issues were most important to you?

Do you consider yourself to be more liberal or more conservative in general? What specific political issues matter most to you?

What political issues do you think should be most important for Christians in general? What other political issues should be important for Christians?

Should Christians try to pass laws that reflect Christian morality, or should laws in America reflect the diversity of religious and moral perspectives in the population?

America and the World

What do you think are the most important problems facing the world today? Facing America? How do you think people can best work to fix these problems, if at all? What role should Christians play in addressing these problems, if any?

What do you think about how America relates to the rest of the world? How should it relate? Do you believe that America has a unique calling from God in the world? If so, what is it?

The Church in America

What do you think are the biggest problems facing the church in America?

What developments in Christianity in America are you excited about? What developments concern you?

If you could change just one or two things about the way that American Christians typically live or think about their faith, what would you change?

Demographic Survey

Age:

Sex (M/F):

Race/Ethnicity:

Are you married?

Do you have children? If so, how old are they?

What is your current job/occupation?

If not your current job, what do you consider to be your primary work or vocation? (e.g. "I work at a coffee shop but I'm primarily an artist," etc.)

Are you currently a student? If so, what school or college do you attend? What is your major or course of study?

If you are currently a student, what year of school are you in? (high school junior, college sophomore, etc.)

If you are not a student, what is the highest year of education you have completed?

If you went to college/graduate/technical school, what school(s) did you attend? What was your major or course of study?

Do you have a college or graduate school degree? If so, what is your degree? (Bachelor's in Marketing, Associate Degree in ?, MBA, etc.)

Where did you spend most of your childhood? (city, state, region, etc.)

How would you describe where you grew up? (city, inner city, suburb, small town, rural)

Did you grow up in a religious home? If so, what kind of religion?

If Christian, what type of church did you attend? (Baptist, Non-denominational, Pentecostal, Catholic, etc.)

If you grew up in a Christian home, would you consider the type of church you attended "evangelical"? (yes, no, probably, don't know)

If you grew up in a Christian home, would you consider the type of church you attended "fundamentalist"? (yes, no, probably, don't know)

What type of church did you attend prior to becoming involved in the Boiler Room? If none, say none. If another religion, say what religion.

Books Used for Textual Analysis
Christian Right/Conservative Evangelicalism

*For Faith and Family: Changing America by Strengthening the Family

*How Would Jesus Vote?: A Christian Perspective on the Issues

*The Ten Offenses: Reclaim the Blessings of the Ten Commandments

Imagine! A God-Blessed America: How It Could Happen and What It Would Look Like

What If America Were a Christian Nation Again?

How Now Shall We Live?

Against the Night: Living in the New Dark Ages

The Gates of Hell Shall Not Prevail: The Attack on Christianity and What You Need to Know to Combat It

Courting Disaster: How the Supreme Court is Usurping the Power of Congress and the People

Listen America!

Megachurch Evangelicalism

Rediscovering Church: The Story and Vision of Willow Creek Community Church

The Purpose-Driven Church: Growth without Compromising your Message and Mission

Building a Contagious Church: Revolutionizing the Way We View and Do Evangelism

Becoming a Contagious Christian

The Purpose Driven Life: What on Earth Am I Here For?

Making Life Work: Putting God's Wisdom into Action

Who You Are When No One's Looking

The Life You've Always Wanted: Spiritual Disciplines for Ordinary People

If You Want to Walk on Water, You've Got to Get Out of the Boat

An Unstoppable Force: Daring to Become the Church God Had in Mind

The Case for Christ: A Journalist's Personal Investigation of the Evidence for Jesus

Inside the Mind of Unchurched Harry and Mary: How to Reach Friends and Family Who Avoid God and the Church

Evangelical Left

God's Politics: Why the Right Gets It Wrong and the Left Doesn't Get It

I Am Not a Social Activist: Making Jesus the Agenda

Speaking My Mind

Red Letter Christians: A Citizen's Guide to Faith and Politics

The Scandal of Evangelical Politics

Rich Christians in an Age of Hunger: Moving from Affluence to Generosity

Letters to a Young Evangelical

Everybody Wants to Change the World: Practical Ideas for Social Justice

The God of Intimacy and Action: Reconnecting Ancient Spiritual Practices, Evangelism, and Justice

With Justice for All: A Strategy for Community Development

Let Justice Roll Down

The Great Awakening: Seven Ways to Change the World

Emerging Church

*The Emerging Church: Vintage Christianity for New Generations

*Church Re-Imagined: The Spiritual Formation of People in Communities of Faith

*A New Kind of Christian: A Tale of Two Friends on a Spiritual Journey

Confessions of a Reformission Rev.: Hard Lessons from an Emerging Missional Church

The Radical Reformission: Reaching Out Without Selling Out

Listening to the Beliefs of Emerging Churches: Five Perspectives

Emerging Worship: Creating Worship Gatherings for New Generations

They Like Jesus but Not the Church: Insights from Emerging Generations

Adventures in Missing the Point: How the Culture-Controlled Church Neutered the Gospel

A Generous Orthodoxy

A New Kind of Christianity: Ten Questions that are Transforming the Faith

Everything Must Change: Jesus, Global Crises, and a Revolution of Hope

The New Christians: Dispatches from the Emergent Frontier

The Great Emergence: How Christianity is Changing and Why

Jesus Wants to Save Christians: A Manifesto for the Church in Exile

Neo-Monasticism

*Punk Monk: New Monasticism and the Ancient Art of Breathing

*School(s) for Conversion: 12 Marks of a New Monasticism

*The Irresistible Revolution: Living as an Ordinary Radical

Jesus for President: Politics for Ordinary Radicals

Becoming the Answer to Our Prayers: Prayer for Ordinary Radicals

Follow Me to Freedom: Leading and Following as an Ordinary Radical

New Monasticism: What It Has to Say to Today's Church

Inhabiting the Church: Biblical Wisdom for a New Monasticism

God's Economy: Redefining the Health and Wealth Gospel

The New Friars: The Emerging Movement Serving the World's Poor

Living Mission: The Vision and Voices of New Friars

The Vision and the Vow

*Starred books are coded and analyzed in Chapter Three (three books per position)

Notes

CHAPTER I

1. Freeman and Greig (2007): 20.
2. E.g., Freeman and Greig (2007): 20 and Rutba House (2005).
3. Falwell (1980): 63. On the complex, multiple discourses associated with Jerry Falwell over the course of his ministry and public life, see Harding (2000).
4. Falwell (2001, September 13), http://archives.cnn.com/2001/US/09/14/Falwell.apology/.
5. Quoted in Wilcox et al. (2006): 56.
6. Ibid.
7. See, e.g., Hunter (1991) and James Buchanan's speech at the 1992 national Republican Party Convention (Buchanan 1992).
8. Marsden (2006): 175.
9. Marsden (2006): 141,148; see also Harding (2000), Hankins (2010), Dochuk (2011).
10. Marsden (2006): 159.
11. On the many parallels between conservative evangelical political mobilizations in the 1920s and 1980s, see, e.g., Hankins (2010).
12. Hunter (1987): 151.
13. I refer to the scholarly version of this argument as *religious consistency theory*. See Wuthnow (1988) and Hunter (1991) for the most influential statements of this position.
14. See, e.g., Niebuhr (1929) and Wald et al. (1989).
15. E.g., Hunter (1991), Noll (2001), Dochuk (2011).
16. Quoted in Marsden (2006): 184–185.
17. Wald et al. (1989); see also Lorentzen (1980), Wood and Hughes (1984).
18. Quoted in Fowler (2008).

19. On *ressentiment* as a source of Christian morality and Christian political engagement in the United States, see Nietzsche (1989) and Hunter (2010).

20. On the culture war debate, see Dimaggio et al. (1996), Davis and Robinson (1996a, 1996b), Wolfe (1998), Smith (2000), and Hunter and Wolfe (2006).

21. E.g., Steensland and Goff (2014a), Green (2014): 129, Pally (2011), Farrell (2011).

22. Wallis (2005): 386, 395. See also Dionne (2008) and Gushee (2008).

23. E.g., Goodstein (2006), Luo and Goodstein (2007), Kirkpatrick (2007), and Kristof (2008).

24. Kristof (2008).

25. Kirkpatrick (2007).

26. "Myths of the Modern Megachurch" [Event Transcript]. *The Pew Forum on Religion and Public Life*, May 23, 2005. http://pewforum.org/Christian/Evangelical-Protestant-Churches/Myths-of-the-Modern-Megachurch.aspx.

27. Quoted in Kirkpatrick (2007).

28. E.g., Greeley and Hout (2006).

29. Warren (2008).

30. Cutrer (2000).

31. Lindsay (2007); see also Conger and Racheter (2006) and Green, Rozell, and Wilcox (2006).

32. E.g., Karnes et al. (2007), Sargeant (2000), Luhr (2009), Wilcox (2012).

33. See Smith (1998), Park and Reimer (2002), Steensland and Goff (2014a): 14–15.

34. See Part I below.

35. Claiborne (2006): 363.

36. Ibid. and chapter 3.

37. Samson (2014) and http://communityofcommunities.info.

38. E.g., Bielo (2011): 25–26, Packard (2012): 9, Steensland and Goff (2014a): 3, 13–14, Marti and Ganiel (2014): 8–11.

39. Anderson (2013); see also Moll (2005, 2007), Armstrong (2008), Worthen (2008), Claiborne (2009), Wolpert (2010), Galli (2009), Beaven (2010), Bielo (2011), Annan (2013), Samson (2014).

40. This study marks the first sociological monograph that takes up evangelical neo-monasticism as its primary subject matter. The new monasticism makes an appearance in section or chapter-length discussions in Hunter (2010), Bielo (2011), Samson (2014), and Marti and Ganiel (2014).

41. Hunter (1987): 141.

42. For example, in the most recent and exhaustive treatment of evangelical engagement with American public and political life—a massive two-volume series titled *Evangelicals and Democracy in America* (Brint and Schroedel 2009a, b)—all but four of the twenty-two chapters in the series focus specifically on the Christian Right and conservative politics. None focus on the

evangelical left or related positions, whose existence is barely acknowledged in over 700 dense pages of otherwise exemplary scholarship.

43. Smith (1998, 2000).
44. Davis and Robinson (1996a, 1999a, 1999b, 2006) and Greeley and Hout (2006).
45. Smith (2000): 8; see also Smith (1998).
46. Smith (2000): 13.
47. E.g., Wuthnow (2007) and Smith (2009). Flory and Miller's *Finding Faith: The Spiritual Quest of the Post-Boomer Generation* (2008) uses a fourfold typology to describe how young American Christians are practicing their faith, but focus exclusively on religious practices while ignoring the political standpoints of the different evangelical groups that they study. This approach is problematic for several reasons, not least because many of the new positions being developed by young evangelicals are explicitly political in nature. Neglecting the political perspectives of emerging evangelical communities means neglecting a core element of their self-identity, and missing a key variable that helps explain the development of their distinctive approaches to religious practice (see chapter 3 and Steensland and Goff 2014a, b).
48. Swartz (2012); see also Gasaway (2014).
49. E.g., Flory and Miller (2008), Bielo (2011), Packard (2012), Marti and Ganiel (2014).
50. E.g., Engelke and Tomlinson (2007), Bielo (2008, 2009, 2011), Elisha (2011). For an anthropological study that also recognizes the multiplicity and dynamism inside conservative evangelicalism and the Christian Right, see Harding (2000).
51. Elisha (2011): 23 (21–24), Bielo (2011): 99–103. On the bourgeoning "lived religion" literature, see, e.g., Hall (1997), Orsi (1997), Bender (2003), Ammerman (2006), McGuire (2008).
52. Bielo (2011): 197–203 and Elisha (2011): 24–28.
53. Steensland and Goff (2014a): 2 and Warner (2014): 282–284.
54. Ibid., 14–19. Indeed, it has become somewhat common among observers of American religion to note that "evangelicalism is the new mainline" in American Protestantism.
55. Ibid., 15–16.
56. This is not a criticism of Steensland and Goff's excellent introduction to *The New Evangelical Social Engagement*, just an acknowledgment that one can only do so much theoretical heavy lifting in the introduction of an edited volume.
57. On the capacity of the "well-constructed" case study to contribute to general social theory, see, e.g., Bourdieu and Wacquant (1992): 75–76; also Burawoy (1998) and Steinmetz (2004).
58. On the dynamic boundaries and internal differentiation of *social fields* as opposed to closed *social systems*, see Bourdieu and Wacquant (1992): 100–104.

On the dynamic boundaries and decentralized institutional structure of American evangelicalism, see, e.g., Hatch (1989), Smith (1998): 86–87, Swartz (2012): 263–264, Worthen (2013), Steensland and Goff (2014a): 20–22.

59. Social theorists disagree on the extent to which Bourdieusian field theory is just another form of economistic or materialist reductionism—albeit a more sophisticated version of the genre (see, e.g., Bourdieu and Wacquant (1992): 24–26, 115). I believe Bourdieu is somewhat ambiguous on this point and argue for the non-reductionist pole (see chapter 3, proposition two). On the "downwards" and "upwards conflations" relating to structure, culture, and agency, see Archer (1988).

60. Calhoun (1991).

61. E.g., Hunter and Wolfe (2006). See chapter 3, proposition four.

62. Namely, subcultural identity and religious economies theory (e.g., Smith 1998, Finke and Stark 1988, Warner 1993); see chapter 3, proposition one.

63. See chapter 7, figure 7.1. The practical social hermeneutic model developed in this book is interested in the more collective and macro-level, rather than individual and micro-level, aspects of evangelical culture and agency.

64. E.g., Alexander and Smith (1993), Alexander (2003, 2004), Emirbayer (2004), Sewell (1985, 1999).

65. See chapter 3.

66. E.g., Bourdieu (1977): 110, 221, Bourdieu ([1980] 1990): 86–87, and chapters 4 and 7 below. On the flexibility of evangelical uses of scripture in preaching and in everyday life, see, e.g., Harding (2000), Malley (2004), and Bielo (2009).

67. Davis and Robinson (2006): 167; see also Hart (1992), Hitlin and Vaisey (2013), Beyerlein and Vaisey (2013).

68. E.g., Gorski (2009), Swartz (2012): 265–266, Warner (2014): 284, Gasaway (2014).

69. On the specific brand of theological individualism that is dominant among American evangelicals, see Smith and Emerson (2000).

70. The Urban Monastery is a pseudonym.

71. E.g., Kane (1997); see also Ricoeur (1974, 1976) and Alexander (2004).

72. E.g., Swidler (1986, 2001) and Kane (1997).

73. E.g., Weber (1958): 138.

74. With the exception of already well-known national leaders and organizations, all organizational and personal names in this book are fictitious.

75. Miles and Huberman (1994): 28.

76. See the Appendix for a copy of the survey.

77. Glaser and Strauss (1967): 58, 69.

78. See Appendix for a copy of the interview guide.

79. Glaser and Strauss (1967): 58, 69.

80. Strauss (1987): 18–19.

81. See chapter 3. While I began this study following standard techniques of grounded theory, my analytic focus quickly shifted toward something more akin to the "relational ethnography" approach discussed in Desmond (2014). Relational ethnography and field theory are, of course, in many ways made for each other, rooted as they are in the relational modes of social-scientific theory and practice (e.g., Cassirer 1923 [1910], Bourdieu and Wacquant 1992, Emirbayer 1997).

82. Campbell and Gregor (2004); see also Martin (2011).

83. E.g., Smith (1987), Bourdieu and Wacquant (1992).

84. E.g., Shea (2004) quoted in Greeley and Hout (2006): 3.

85. Weber (1958): 183.

86. Smith (1998): 119.

87. Ibid., emphasis original.

88. On this fundamental contribution of feminist scholarship to social science research, see, e.g., Smith (1987). Of course, when it comes to the production of sociological monographs such as this one, this is a matter of degree. By retaining the power to select, frame, explicate, and contextualize my research subjects' quotations, conversations, and contributions to this study, there is a very real sense in which I am still, unavoidably, "speaking for" them.

89. For a defense of "person-centered ethnography," see Bielo (2011): 26–27. On the centrality of "first-person" explanations in the social sciences and their relation to field theory, see Martin (2011). For some sociological reasons not take people's accounts of their actions as the gospel truth—reasons that apply to sociologists as much as anyone else—see, e.g., Vaisey (2009) and Jerolmack and Khan (2014).

90. Bielo (2011): 27.

91. On realism, see, e.g. Lawson (1997) and Gorski (2004, 2013a); on instrumentalism, see, e.g., Friedman (1953).

92. E.g., Hedstrom and Bearman (2009): 3–14.

93. Indeed, one might sum up the whole history of the natural and social sciences—not least the "critical" social sciences—with the aphorism "things are not always as they appear." In sociological language, concepts such as *symbolic domination, ideology, hegemony,* and *misrecognition* speak of the sometimes systematic and intentional, sometimes accidental and unintentional, misunderstandings of the social world that we mistakenly take for granted as "common sense" or "the way things naturally are." If one prefers biblical language, one might speak similarly of the Paul's discussion of the "principalities and powers" in Ephesians 6 and elsewhere (e.g., Ephesians 6:12 and 2 Corinthians 10:4–5).

94. On the distinct advantages and disadvantages of analyzing elements of one's own social world, see Bourdieu ([1984] 1988): 1–6.

CHAPTER 2

1. Bourdieu and Wacquant (1992): 90.
2. Bourdieu ([1992)] 1996): 156–157, 242–243.
3. Hunter (1987): 46.
4. Harper (2008).
5. E.g., Steensland and Goff (2014b), Greeley and Hout (2006), Clydesdale (1999), Davis and Robinson (1996b).
6. Davis and Robinson (2006): 167.
7. Ibid.
8. Davis and Robinson (1999a, b, 2001, 2006).
9. Davis and Robinson (1999a, b, 2001, 2006); on the salience of individualism and communitarianism as attitude and action shaping moral worldviews, see also Hart (1992), Hitlin and Vaisey (2013), Beyerlein and Vaisey (2013).
10. E.g., Noll (2001) and Hankins (2010).
11. Marsden (2006): 11.
12. Ibid., 21.
13. E.g., Marsden (2006), Lichtman (2008), Hankins (2010): 23–25.
14. Marsden (2006) and Lichtman (2008).
15. Standing against dominant theological interpretations of the day, dispensational premillennialism—a nineteenth-century British-American theological innovation concerning the "end times"—predicted a steady demise of morality and human civilization prior the return of Christ (e.g., Sandeen 1970, Noll 1988, Carpenter 1997, Marsden 2006, Dochuk 2011).
16. Sandeen (1970) and Dochuk (2011).
17. Findlay (1969).
18. Ibid., 220–221.
19. For Moody, conversion involved three straightforward steps: being convicted of one's sin, making a commitment to repent or turn from sin, and making a decision to accept Christ as one's personal savior (Findlay 1969: 240, 242).
20. E.g., Findlay (1969) and Sandeen (1970).
21. Marsden (2006): 38.
22. E.g., Noll (2001) and Smith and Emerson (2000).
23. Marsden (2006): 38. On the popularity of this perspective in contemporary conservative Protestantism, see, for example, the best-selling *Left Behind* book series.
24. Smith and Emerson (2000).
25. E.g., Greeley and Hout (2006), Smith and Emerson (2000), and Davis and Robinson (1996a, b). This is not to say that white evangelicals are racial progressives, however. For example, according to McVeigh and Sobolewski (2007), blacks (and women) who live in areas with high concentrations of white evangelicals tend to be worse off than those who don't.

26. Wallis (2005).
27. Wood (1991).
28. Smith and Emerson (2000): 22–23.
29. Ibid., 22–27, Marsh (1997).
30. White evangelicals have been apologizing for their role in promoting and sustaining racial inequality for decades, from the Chicago Declaration in the 1970s to the Southern Baptist Convention's statement of apology in 1995.
31. Smith and Emerson (2000): 27–30.
32. Essig quoted in Smith and Emerson (2000): 29.
33. Smith and Emerson (2000): 32.
34. Lesick quoted in Smith and Emerson (2000).
35. Smith and Emerson (2000): 33.
36. Charles Finney is often cited approvingly by evangelical left figures such as Tony Campolo, Ron Sider, and Jim Wallis as an example of a more holistic and faithful representation of evangelical Christianity than that offered by the Christian Right, who sometimes distinguish themselves from dominant expressions of contemporary conservative evangelicalism by describing themselves as "19th century evangelicals" (e.g., Campolo 2004 and Wallis 2005).
37. Smith and Emerson (2000): 36–37; see also see Myrdal (1944).
38. Archer (1988) and figure 7.1a below.
39. E.g., Sandeen (1970), Marsden (2006), Hankins (2010): 63–82, Dochuk (2011): 15.
40. Hankins (2010): 69; see also Carpenter (1997) and Marsden (2006).
41. Hankins (2010): 63–69 and Marsden (2006): 14–15.
42. Marsden (2006): 16.
43. Sandeen (1970): 130–131.
44. Marsden (2006): 103 and Dochuk (2011).
45. Ibid., 117; see also Sandeen (1970): xiv–xv and Hankins (2010).
46. Bourdieu and Wacquant (1992): 98.
47. Marsden (2006): 119; see also Dochuk (2011): 43–50 and Hankins (2010): 65.
48. Sandeen (1970): 203.
49. Ibid., 204–206.
50. I.e., the idea that good democratic government depends primarily on individual spiritual conversion. Smith and Emerson (2000): 117.
51. Bourdieu and Wacquant (1992): 98.
52. See chapter 3, proposition seven.
53. Marsden (2006), Lichtman (2008), Dochuk (2011).
54. E.g., Kazin (2006), Marsden (2006), Hankins (2010): 84, Dochuk (2011).
55. Marsden (2006): 142.
56. Ibid., 151.
57. Ibid., 142.
58. E.g., Sandeen (1970), Marsden (2006), Lichtman (2008).

59. Lichtman (2008).
60. Dochuk (2011): 53.
61. Marsden (2006) and Lichtman (2008).
62. E.g., Sandeen (1970), Marsden (2006), Hankins (2010): 83–104.
63. Harding (2000), Marsden (2006), Hankins (2010).
64. Marsden (2006): 161, Dochuk (2011): 43–50, Harding (2000): xv–xvi, 63, 102, 268–271.
65. Hankins (2010): 84.
66. Numbers (1998), Harding (2000): 210–222, Marsden (2006), Hankins (2010): 87, Dochuk (2011).
67. Dochuk (2011): 53; see also Harding (2000): 216 and Marsden (2006).
68. Numbers (1998).
69. Numbers (1998), Harding (2000), Marsden (2006), Dochuk (2011).
70. Sandeen (1970) and Hankins (2010).
71. Dochuk (2011).
72. Including new evangelical leaders such as revivalist Charles Fuller (an immensely popular radio revivalist and founder of Fuller Theological Seminary), Harold Ockenga (cofounder of Fuller and first president of the National Association of Evangelicals), and Billy Graham.
73. Marsden (1987): 86; see also Carpenter (1997): 30–31, Harding (2000), Dochuk (2011): 121–122.
74. Marsden (1987): 17.
75. Carpenter (1997): 78, Harding (2000), Lichtman (2008), Hankins (2010), Dochuk (2011).
76. Marsden (1987): 93, 153–156; see also Lichtman (2008) and Dochuk (2011).
77. Carpenter (1997): 63 and Dochuk (2011).
78. Dochuk (2011): 52.
79. Wells quoted in Dochuk (2011): 167.
80. E.g., Dochuk (2011): xviii–xxiv, 112–114, 160–161.
81. Dochuk (2011): 148–152, 237–240; see also Hunter (1987) and Diamond (1995): 95–97.
82. Lichtman (2008): 346 and Dochuk (2011).
83. Lichtman (2008): 78–81 and Dochuk (2011): 112–114, 128–129.
84. Ibid., 75 and Dochuk (2011): 63–65, 75–76.
85. Lichtman (2008): 2, 204; see also Dochuk (2011).
86. Lichtman (2008): 30–31; see also Harding (2000): 16, Hankins (2010), Dochuk (2011).
87. Lichtman (2008).
88. E.g., Smith and Emerson (2000): 76, Smith (1998): 191, Smith and Emerson (2000): 117, 126–127.
89. Lichtman (2008): 28; see also Harding (2000), Marsden (2006), Dochuk (2011).

90. E.g., Hunter (1987), Carpenter (1997), Marsden (2006), Dochuk (2011): 43–50, 110, 237–240, 270–272.
91. E.g., Marsden (1987), Smith (1998), Dochuk (2011): 118–120.
92. Henry (1947).
93. Ibid., 17, 78; see also Marsden (2006) and Swartz (2012).
94. Marsden (1987): 29; see also Harding (2000), Lichtman (2008), Dochuk (2011).
95. Marsh (1997), Smith and Emerson (2000), Dochuk (2011).
96. E.g., Hofstadter (1963, 1965), Smith 1998: 2–3, Marsden (2006), and Hunter (1987).
97. E.g., Marsden (1987), Carpenter (1997), Dochuk (2011).
98. Marsden (1987) and Dochuk (2011).
99. Lindsay (2007), Luhr (2009), Dochuk (2011).
100. Swartz (2012).
101. E.g., chapter 3.
102. E.g., Diamond (1995), Carpenter (1997), Harding (2000), Marsden (1987, 2006), Dochuk (2011).
103. Falwell quoted in Harding (2000): 22.
104. Harding (2000): 242; see also 61–62, 75–79, 228–231 and Swartz (2012): 18.
105. E.g., Diamond (1995), Carpenter (1997), Marsden (1987, 2006), Hankins (2010), Dochuk (2011), Swartz (2012): 2–3, 23.
106. Wuthnow (1983); see also Harding (2000), Hankins (2010), Swartz (2012).
107. Wuthnow (1983).
108. Dochuk (2011): 337, 332–347.
109. Himmelstein (1983): 16; see also Harding (2000) and Dochuk (2011): 331–332.
110. Liebman and Wuthnow (1983), Harding (2000): 18–21, 79–80, 128–129, 156–181, Dochuk (2011): 383–387.
111. Harding (2000): 14–15, 105–109, 257–258, and Dochuk (2011): 51–76.
112. E.g., Conger and Green (2002), Conger and Racheter (2006), Green, Conger, and Guth (2006).
113. Wald and Scher (1997).
114. Green et al. (2000, 2003).
115. Harding (2000): 22, 120, 153–165.
116. Harding (2000): 18–21, 79–80, Lichtman (2008), Hankins (2010), Dochuk (2011).
117. Guth (1983) and Dochuk (2011).
118. E.g., Guth (1983) and Lichtman (2008): 344–346.
119. Green et al. (2003).
120. E.g., Green et al. (2000,), Green, Rozell, and Wilcox (2006), Lichtman (2008), Harding (2000), Hankins (2010), Dochuk (2011).
121. E.g., Brown (2002), Teles (2008): 16–17, Smith (2009).

122. Teles (2008): 1–3, 22–57, 88–89.
123. Dr. James Dobson, quoted in Brown (2002): 27 (see also 28–45).
124. "History" (n.d.), http://www.alliancedefensefund.org.
125. A regular advocate before the Supreme Court, Sekulow is a frequent guest and show host on Pat Robertson's Christian Broadcasting Network and Paul Crouch's Trinity Broadcasting Network, who "helped Sekulow become a mini media mogul in his own right by subsidizing Sekulow's Sonlight Broadcasting System, a network of television stations in Alabama, Mississippi, and Tennessee" Brown (2002): 127. For more on Pat Robertson's public rhetoric regarding the "liberal takeover" of America's judicial system, see chapter 3.
126. E.g., Brown (2002): 138–145 and Smith (2009): 329–331, 348–351. According to most legal scholars, the courts have had more impact on shaping the Christian Right than vice versa. Notwithstanding the alarmist cries of their most ardent political foes, America is in no danger of a theocratic takeover by the religious Right.
127. E.g., Greeley and Hout (2006): 46, 71, Smidt and Kellstedt (1992), Wuthnow (1983), Kellstedt et al. (1994), Dochuk (2011), Swartz (2012): 216–218.
128. Guth et al. (2003).
129. E.g., Gold and Russell (2007); see also Green, Rozell, and Wilcox (2006) and Smidt and Kellstedt (1992).
130. E.g., Gold and Russell (2007) and Greeley and Hout (2006): 45.
131. E.g., Sherkat (2007), Green et al. (2006), Campbell (2007), Guth et al. (2003), Keeter (2007).
132. Harding (2000), Marsden (2006), Lichtman (2008), Hankins (2010), Dochuk (2011).
133. Chaves (2006) and Ellingson (2008).
134. Ellingson (2008).
135. Dochuk (2011); see also Luhr (2009).
136. Dochuk (2011) and Wilford (2012).
137. Karnes et al. (2007), Luhr (2009), Dochuk (2011).
138. Karnes et al. (2007), Ellingson (2008), Luhr (2009), Elisha (2011).
139. Ellingson (2008): 3.
140. Ibid.; see also Luhr (2009), Elisha (2011), Wilford (2012).
141. Kellstedt and Green (2003).
142. Ibid.
143. Elisha (2011) and Wilford (2012).
144. Kellstedt and Green (2003): 557, Ellingson (2008), Luhr (2009), Elisha (2011), Wilford (2012).
145. Kellstedt and Green (2003).
146. E.g., Kellstedt and Green (2003), Luhr (2009), Elisha (2011), Wilford (2012).
147. Ellingson 2008: 6–7; see also Sargeant (2000): 58–73, Thumma and Travis (2007): 39–40.

148. E.g., Smith and Emerson (2000), Ellingson (2008), Luhr (2009): 5–6, 17, 72–73, 78, 158, 199, 288–289, Elisha (2011): 26–35, 45–56, Wilford (2012): 128, 153–157.

149. Swartz (2012): 47–67.

150. Sojourners Annual Report (2009).

151. Barber (2008).

152. Swartz (2012).

153. Sider (2005); see also Regnerus and Smith (1998) and Swartz (2012).

154. Excerpt from the Chicago Declaration of Evangelical Social Concern (1973).

155. Young (2002).

156. Although, as Swartz (2012) notes, earlier drafts of the Chicago Declaration were more strident and specific in laying blame for evangelicalism's and America's woes at conservative political and religious leaders' feet, with much animus directed at Richard Nixon and associates in particular.

157. IFES is acronym for the International Fellowship of Evangelical Students, to which InterVarsity Christian Fellowship (USA) belongs. FTL is acronym for the Fraternidad Teológica Latinoamerica, or Latin American Theological Fraternity in English, an indigenous fellowship of Latin American theologians which combined elements of evangelical and liberation theology (e.g., Swartz 2012).

158. Swartz (2012): 1–9.

159. Ibid., 117–124.

160. Richard Mouw quoted in Swartz (2012): 135.

161. Ron Sider quoted in Swartz (2012): 156.

162. Bill Pannell quoted in Swartz (2012): 33.

163. Swartz (2012): 65 and 47–67.

164. Ibid., 187–254; see also chapter 5.

165. Ellwood (1973), Richardson and Davis (1983), Luhr (2009): 73–82, Dochuk (2011): 309–316, 326–329, Swartz (2012): 86–110, Eskridge (2013).

166. E.g., McDannell (1995).

167. Ellwood (1973).

168. Goldman (1995) and Stewart and Richardson (1999).

169. Goldman (1995) and Ellwood (1973).

170. Richardson (1982), Goldman (1995), Stewart and Richardson (1999), Swartz (2012).

171. Swartz (2012): 89–107, 195–202.

172. Richardson and Davis (1983), Goldman (1995), Luhr (2009): 72–73.

173. Streiker (1971) and Dochuk (2011).

174. Goldman (1995) and Dochuk (2011): 388–391.

175. Richardson and Davis (1983).

176. Gordon (1984), Goldman (1995), McDannell (1995), Luhr (2009), Dochuk (2011), Swartz (2012).

177. 1971 *Time* magazine article titled "The Alternative Jesus: Psychedelic Christ," http://content.time.com/time/magazine/article/0,9171,905202,00.html.

178. Graham (1971): 16–21.

179. E.g., Noll (1988).

180. E.g., Luhr (2009) and Swartz (2012).

181. "The Alternative Jesus: Psychedelic Christ."

182. E.g., Swartz (2012): 92, 97–100.

183. Goldman (1995).

184. Gordon (1984).

185. Luhr (2009): 23–24, 72–82, 191–195; see also Goldman (1995), McDannell (1995), Lindsay (2007), Dochuk (2011).

186. Davis and Robinson (2006).

187. Ibid., 168.

188. Ibid.

189. Ibid., 167.

190. Ibid.

191. E.g., Davis and Robinson (1996a, b, 2001, 2006), Smith (2000), McConkey (2001), Guth et al. (2003), Greeley and Hout (2006), Gold and Russell (2007), Wuthnow (2007).

192. E.g., Greeley and Hout (2006): 130, 146; see also Gold and Russell (2007), McConkey (2001), Guth et al. (2003).

193. Davis and Robinson (2006).

194. Liebman and Wuthnow (1983), Hunter (Wuthnow 1987, 1991), Hunter and Wolfe (2006) Barker and Carman (2000), Greely and Hout (2006), Felson and Kindell (2007), Gold and Russell (2007).

195. E.g., Sandeen (1970), Carpenter (1997), Harding (2000), Marsden (1987, 2006), Lichtman (2008), Dochuk (2011), Swartz (2012).

196. E.g., Hunter (1991, 2006), Kellstedt and Green (2003), Brown (2002), Guth et al. (2003).

197. Gold and Russell (2007), Felson and Kindell (2007), Greeley and Hout (2006), Barker and Carman (2000), Smith and Emerson (2000), Smith (1998), Davis and Robinson (1999a): 341.

198. E.g., Smith (1998): 197 n. 5 and Swartz (2012).

199. E.g., Davis and Robinson (1996a).

200. E.g., Hollinger (1983), Marsden (1987, 2006), Smith (1998), Smith and Emerson (2000), Carman and Barker (2000), Luhr (2009).

201. E.g., Bellah et al. (1996) and Swidler (2001).

202. E.g., Smith (1998): 191 and Marsden (2006): 38.

203. E.g., Smith and Emerson (2000): 117, 126–127, Luhr (2009): 72–73, 188–189, Hunter (2010), Swartz (2012): 135.

204. Smith and Emerson (2000): 46–47.

205. E.g., Smith (1998), Smith and Emerson (2000): 47, Swartz (2012): 18, Marsden (1987, 2006).

206. E.g., Smith and Emerson (2000): 46–47, Marsden (1987), Dochuk (2011): 162–165, 274–289.
207. E.g., Marsh (1997), Smith and Emerson (2000), Swartz (2012).
208. Marsh (1997): 5–6, 89.
209. Ibid., 6.
210. Ibid., 90.
211. Ibid., 6.
212. Dochuk (2011): 285, 288; see also Swartz (2012): 21–23, 26–27, 38–40.
213. See also chapter 3, proposition four.
214. Smith and Emerson (2000).
215. Ibid., 95–101.
216. Ibid., 120–125, 63, 179, Bartkowski (2004).
217. Smith and Emerson (2000): 109.
218. Ibid., 110; see also Barker and Carman (2000).
219. Hart (1992): 124.
220. Davis and Robinson (2006): 186.
221. Swidler: (2001): 169, 171.
222. Ibid., 211.
223. See Bourdieu ([1992] 1996): 223.
224. E.g., Noll (2001), Young (2002), Marsden (2006); see also Gorski (2009).
225. Himmelstein (1983) and Dochuk (2011): 383–391.
226. E.g., Greeley and Hout (2006): 84–85, Felson and Kindell (2007): 684–685, Guth et al. (2003).
227. E.g., Rutba House (2005), Bessenecker (2006), Freeman and Greig (2007).
228. Claiborne (2006): 363.
229. See Rutba House (2005) and below.
230. E.g., Addams (1961), Carson (1990), Davis (1984, 2000).
231. Schneiderhan (2009): 100–101.
232. Ibid., 100.
233. E.g., Schneiderhan (2009): 107 and Addams (1961, [1899] 2002).
234. E.g., Addams (1961) and Freeman and Greig (2007).
235. See chapter 3, proposition five.
236. Wuthnow (1989).

CHAPTER 3

1. The author is using violence as a metaphor for something like a radical and uncompromising break with the past, not literal violence, as the context of the quote makes clear.
2. Freeman and Greig (2007): 35.
3. Monasticism is radical in its call for uncompromising challenge to the existing order; it is traditional in that it has been a well-established historical model of religious activity and protest in the Christian tradition for over 1,500 years.

4. E.g., Hunter (1987), Hunter and Wolfe (2006), Green (2009).
5. E.g., Wolfe (1998, 2003), Hunter and Wolfe (2006).
6. Ibid.
7. E.g., Diamond (1995), McDannell (1995), Carpenter (1997), Hunter and Wolfe (2006),.
8. E.g., Findlay (1969) and Sandeen (1970).
9. E.g., Sargeant (2000).
10. E.g., Ellingson (2008): 3.
11. This formulation is ubiquitous among evangelical pastors and preachers; see, for example, Warren (1995) and Driscoll (2006).
12. E.g., Findlay (1969), Marsden (1987, 2006), Hunter (1987).
13. See Bourdieu and Wacquant (1992): 97.
14. Bourdieu ([1997] 2000): 96.
15. Bourdieu and Wacquant (1992): 102.
16. Ibid., 99–101, 108.
17. See, for example, Bourdieu ([1984] 1993): 72–73.
18. Bourdieu ([1997] 2000): 187.
19. Bourdieu ([1992] 1996): 87.
20. Bourdieu and Wacquant (1992): 105.
21. Bourdieu ([1984] 1993) and Bourdieu ([1984] 1988): xvii.
22. Ibid.
23. Bourdieu and Wacquant (1992): 96, emphasis in original. On relational sociology, see also Emirbayer (1997) and Mische (2011).
24. Bourdieu ([1984] 1988): xvii.
25. See, for instance, Lindsay (2007) and Bielo (2011).
26. On the populism, market-orientation, and nondenominationalism of American evangelicalism, see, for example, Hatch (1989), Smith (1998), Campolo (2004), Marsden (2006), and Lindsay (2007).
27. E.g., Campolo (2004) and Marsden (2006).
28. E.g., Bielo (2009, 2011).
29. Bielo (2011): 8–16, 23, 33, 38–39, 42–43, 47–48, 52–53, 62, 68, 114–116, 125, 150. On "deconversion" and the emerging church, see also Packard (2012) and Marti and Ganiel (2014).
30. Bielo (2011): 9, 23.
31. Hunter and Wolfe (2006) and Hunter (2010); on the crucial role of elites in American evangelicalism, see also Lindsay (2007, 2008).
32. Smith (2000): 7–9.
33. Ibid. See also Bielo (2011): 102.
34. E.g., Bielo (2011): 101–103, Harding (2000), Elisha (2011).
35. E.g., Marti and Ganiel (2014), Bielo (2011), Elisha (2011), Harding (2000), Ammerman (1987).

36. E.g., Smith (2000): 7–9 and Bielo (2011): 99–101.

37. Bielo (2011): 99 and Marti and Ganiel (2014).

38. See below and Bielo (2011): 115; on *social generations*, see proposition three.

39. E.g., Claiborne (2010) and Rutba House (2005).

40. See Bielo (2011): 98–117, Marti and Ganiel (2014), and figure 3.1.

41. E.g., Elisha (2011).

42. Bielo (2011): 199. Indeed, his own ethnographic data suggests the significant influence that movement elites and the texts that they write have on ordinary emerging evangelicals' practice of everyday lived religion, e.g., Bielo (2011): 8–16, 23, 33, 38–39, 42–43, 47–48, 52–53, 62, 68, 114–116, 125, 150.

43. Ibid., 98, 103, 105, 114–115; see also Marti and Ganiel (2014).

44. Empirically, the fact that a small ethnographic sample happened to turn up individual neo-monastics who had previous ties to the emerging church is hardly representative, as, of course, Bielo himself would acknowledge. As we will see below, there are clear differences (as well as overlaps) between the founding points of view of evangelical neo-monasticism and the emerging church. More importantly, even if it were the case that all neo-monastics were or used to be associated with the emerging church movement (which it isn't), it would not necessarily mean that neo-monasticism was a type of emerging evangelicalism, just as the fact that many emerging church individuals and institutions were associated with conservative evangelical megachurches does not mean that the emerging church is a type of megachurch evangelicalism. Theoretically, the fact that the emerging church and neo-monasticism have distinctive origins, movement leaders, institutional networks, position-takings, and trajectories through the field is significant for understanding their respective religious and political position-takings, as should be clear from the analysis which follows in the rest of this chapter. At the very least, it is useful to distinguish among the neo-monastic and emerging church points of view when it comes to studying knowledge production in the evangelical field over time, as in the field-theoretic approach taken here.

45. Thus, the wisdom of drawing on both "on-the-ground" ethnographic data and "birds-eye-view" textual analysis of elite knowledge production in studying the processes through which neo-monastic evangelicals have constructed their distinctive religious and political points of view in relation to other positions in the field.

46. To be selected for coding, a book had to: (1) be written by an influential and nationally recognized representative of a given position (as demonstrated by media recognition and recognition by other evangelical leaders); (2) provide a relatively comprehensive statement of a recognized position and be recognized as such; and (3) include books that are widely recognized as signature statements of a given position (i.e., Brian McLaren's *A New Kind of Christian*

for the emerging church, Jim Wallis's *God's Politics* for the evangelical left, and Shane Claiborne's *The Irresistible Revolution* for the new monasticism).

47. As is done, for example, in Susan Harding's (2000) analysis of the complex and evolving political standpoints of Jerry Falwell and the emergence of the Christian Right; in Omri Elisha's (2011) examination of social activism within megachurch evangelicalism, or in Marti and Ganiel's (2014) discussions of the plurality of "religious orientations" within the emerging church movement.

48. See, for example, Gushee (2008) on the "evangelical center" and http://www. thegospelcoalition.org.

49. See proposition five.

50. See, for example, Marti (2005), Thumma and Travis (2007), and Elisha (2011).

51. Lynn and Bill Hybels are examples of the former, Jon Piper of the latter.

52. Focusing on the founding point of view a field or of new positions within a field is not an arbitrary decision. It is a theoretical move justified by the particular significance of founding points of view in the reproduction and transformation of social fields (Bourdieu [1992] 1996: 223).

53. E.g., Ellingson (2008) and Elisha (2011). Still, Elisha's discussion on evangelism and the near-ubiquitous attempts to make him a convert—along with the difficulty his small group of social activists had in mobilizing their churches for more "social justice" oriented causes—provides confirming evidence of the theological individualism and prioritization of evangelism described below.

54. For an example of a growing alliance among post-emerging church, neo-monastics, and others, see the Parrish Collective (http://www.parishcollective. org/). On political diversity in the emerging church, see also Burge and Djupe (2014).

55. See also Bielo (2011): 197–203, who makes a similar point. Let us hope that the recent turn to a more relational or "dialogic" approach to the study of American evangelicalism which recognizes this diversity bears much fruit in future scholarship that engages the whole iceberg.

56. E.g., Smith and Emerson (2000), Steensland et al. (2000), McRoberts (2003). Social scientists typically treat "evangelicals" and "black Protestants" as distinct religious groups in light of their radically divergent social histories, political attitudes, and the historic and contemporary segregation of black and white religious institutions in the United States.

57. For example, Dr. John Perkins—an African American civil rights leader and founding father of the Christian Community Development Association—has become a widely recognized and influential figure among the evangelical left, neo-monasticism, and other white evangelicals, just as Dr. Tony Evans has become a widely recognized and influential figure among conservative and megachurch evangelicals, particularly in the South (e.g., Marsh 2005 and Perkins [1982] 2007).

58. The intersection of race and religion among evangelicals has become the subject of increasingly intensive investigation among social scientists (e.g., Diamond 1998, Smith and Emerson 2000, DeYoung et al. 2003, Christerson et al. 2005, Emerson and Woo 2006, Lichterman et al. 2009). Social movement scholars have long recognized the prominent role of the black Protestant church (and white evangelical absence) in the 1950s–1960s civil rights movement (e.g., Morris 1984 and McAdam [1982] 1999).

59. Gorski (2013a): 356.

60. On American evangelicalism's history as a populist religion of the masses and anti-intellectualism, see Hatch (1989), Noll (1995, 2001), Marsden (2006).

61. On *recognition*, see, for instance, Bourdieu ([1992] 1996): 157, 287.

62. E.g., Hatch (1989), Smith (1998), Noll (2001), Marsden (2006).

63. The boundary of the American evangelical field itself, of course, constitutes a dynamic and overlapping space with respect to other fields or positions in American religious space, and thus should also be marked by porous boundary lines in figure 3.1, were it not for the confusing aesthetic effect that would result. Also note that each of these five positions—and the three dominated positions in particular—are not completely circumscribed by the field of American evangelicalism, but rather include some individuals and institutions from outside the field. Our primary focus here, however, is on the structure, reproduction, and transformation of the field of American evangelicalism, rather than on its relation to other positions in American or international religious space.

64. E.g., Bielo (2011), Marti and Ganiel (2014), Burge and Djupe (2014), and below.

65. See chapters 1 and 7; also Elisha (2011) and Harding (2000).

66. Thumma and Travis (2007).

67. Kellstedt and Green (2003), Karnes et al. (2007), and Ellingson (2007, 2008), Luhr (2009), Dochuk (2011), Elisha (2011), Wilford (2012).

68. Hunter and Wolfe (2006).

69. E.g., Conger and Racheter (2006), Green, Rozell, and Wilcox (2000, 2003, 2006), Green, Conger, and Guth (2006), Conger, and Green (2009).

70. E.g., Harding (2000) and Dochuk (2011).

71. Diamond (1998): 24.

72. Gilgoff (2007).

73. See Gilgoff (2007) and Arnold (2009).

74. See Smith (2000): 21 and Banerjee (2007).

75. These include his writing the now infamous "Land Letter" in 2002, which encouraged President George W. Bush to pursue a "just war" in Iraq to remove Saddam Hussein (Land 2002).

76. See Gushee (2008): 23–56 and Hunter (2010): 111–131 for an expanded list of Christian Right organizations and leaders.

77. Kirkpatrick (2007).

78. "Sojourners Annual Report" (2008); see also Swartz (2012) and Gasaway (2014).

79. "Sojourners Annual Report" (2007).

80. E.g., Wallis (2005), "Sojourners Annual Report" (2008), Hunter (2010): 143–145.

81. Swartz (2012): 7–9; see also Gasaway (2014), "How the Faithful Voted" (2008), http://www.pewforum.org/2008/11/05/how-the-faithful-voted/#1, Green and Clement (2010).

82. E.g., "For the Health of the Nation: An Evangelical Call to Civic Responsibility" (2004), "Climate Change: An Evangelical Call to Action" (2006), "An Evangelical Declaration against Torture: Protecting Human Rights in an Age of Terror" (2007), and "Christians for Comprehensive Immigration Reform: Statement of Principles" (2010). On the Chicago Declaration, see Swartz (2012): 1–9 and Sider (2005).

83. The battle over The Evangelical Climate Initiative's statement on global warming, for example, reveals both the growth and limits of the evangelical left's influence in the field (Gushee 2008).

84. Gibbs and Bolger (2005): 32, Bielo (2011): 8–9, "Leadership Network News" (2005), Marti and Ganiel (2014).

85. Some notable names from this group include Brian McLaren, Tony Jones, Dan Kimball, Mark Driscoll, Karen Ward, and Doug Pagitt; all of whom have become widely cited and recognized authors and leaders in the emerging church movement.

86. See Gibbs and Bolger (2005), Flory and Miller (2008), Bielo (2011), Packard (2012), Marti and Ganiel (2014).

87. Bielo (2011): 25–26 and Marti and Ganiel (2014): 8–11.

88. For a sample of national media coverage on the emerging church in such outlets as the *New York Times, Wall Street Journal, U.S. News and World Report, Christianity Today,* see Bielo (2011): 9, 70–73.

89. E.g., Bielo (2011): 100–101 and Samson (2014): 96–97.

90. E.g., Moll (2005), Worthen (2008), Claiborne (2009), Galli (2009), Beaven (2010), Anderson (2013).

91. This is Willow Creek Community Church's mission statement; see Mittelberg (2001): 25.

92. E.g., Smith and Emerson (2000), Sargeant (2000), Ellingson (2007, 2008), Luhr (2009), Elisha (2011), Wilcox (2012); see also chapter 2.

93. E.g., Hybels and Mittelberg (1994), Hybels and Hybels (1997), Warren (1995), Mittelberg (2001).

94. Hybels and Mittelberg (1994): 119–132, 223.

95. Mittelberg (2001): 367, Hybels and Hybels (1997): 213.

96. Warren (1995).

97. Ibid., 20, emphasis in original.
98. See chapter 2.
99. Ibid., back cover, contents, 165, 103.
100. E.g., Mittelberg (2001): 12; Warren (1995): back cover; Warren (2002): 9; Hybels and Mittelberg (1994): 39. See also Sargent (2000) and Ellingson (2008) for the therapeutic and strategic management cultures in evangelical megachurches.
101. E.g., Bielo (2011), Packard (2012), and below.
102. Rutba House (2005): x.
103. Ibid., 21.
104. Ibid., 45.
105. Ibid., xii.
106. Freeman and Greig (2007): 232–234.
107. Claiborne (2006): 354.
108. Ibid., 269.
109. Ibid., 39.
110. Ibid., 22, 38, 95, 102–107, 193, 326–328.
111. Claiborne (2006): 23–24.
112. Ibid., 356.
113. E.g., Gibbs and Bolger (2005), Flory and Miller (2008), Bielo (2011), Packard (2012), Marti and Ganiel (2014).
114. Ellingson (2008): 6–7.
115. Kimball (2003): 13.
116. Ibid., 7.
117. This despite the fact that it has become commonplace for critics to condemn the emerging church lacking sufficient evangelistic focus and effectiveness (e.g., Stetzer 2006, Driscoll 2006, DeYoung and Kluck 2008).
118. Kimball (2003): 5–6.
119. Ibid., 15.
120. Ibid., 26, 60–61, 95, 105, 248, 202.
121. Literally: Part One's title is "Deconstructing"; Part Two's title is "Reconstructing."
122. Ibid., 31–32, 62, 103–104.
123. Kimball (2003): 57 and chapter 5.
124. Ibid., 42, 44, 39–66.
125. Ibid., 37, emphasis in original.
126. Ibid., 44, 50, 59–61, 95, 105, 122–123, 187, 201–202, 215, 229, 249. See chapter 7, proposition four.
127. McLaren (2001).
128. Ibid., 66–86.
129. Ibid., 148–155, 188, 147–157.

130. Ibid., 106–119, 177–190.

131. Ibid., 117–135, 177–192.

132. Ibid., 86–96.

133. Ibid., 157, 185.

134. Ibid., 165.

135. Pagitt (2005): 70 and chapters 3 through 9.

136. Ibid., 22, 21, 29, 25–27.

137. Ibid., 23.

138. Ibid., 146.

139. Ibid., 42.

140. Robertson (2004): xii.

141. See chapter 5.

142. Ibid., 23, 28, 34, 36, 83, 94, 199–204.

143. Ibid., 204.

144. Land and Perry (2002): 61–62.

145. E.g., 11–12, 142, 191–193.

146. Kennedy and Newcombe (2008): 7, 187.

147. Ibid., 17, 206–207.

148. Ibid., 31; see also 28–31, 222–231.

149. Ibid., 82–83, 112–113, 157.

150. Jim Wallis quoted in Claiborne (2006): 12.

151. Claiborne (2006): 18, 26, 32, 197–198, 207, 330, 344.

152. Rutba House (2005): ix.

153. Ibid., 151, emphasis original.

154. Wallis (2005): vii–ix.

155. Ibid., 308.

156. Ibid., viii–ix. These are the subheadings to Parts Three through Five of *God's Politics*, respectively.

157. Campolo (2004): vii–viii.

158. Ibid., 138–139 and chapter 9.

159. Ibid., 174–176 and chapter 11.

160. Ibid., 144, 153, and chapter 10.

161. Land and Perry (2002): ix.

162. Ibid., 59; see also pp. 45–49 on feminism, pp. 10–11, 23, 28, and chapter 2 on secular humanism.

163. Ibid., 94, 5–6, 1.

164. Ibid., 77.

165. Ibid., 12.

166. Ibid., 77.

167. Ibid., 2.

168. Ibid., 1.

169. Ibid., 14, 45, 80.
170. Ibid., 43–76.
171. Ibid., 100.
172. Ibid., 103.
173. Ibid., 97.
174. Ibid., 103.
175. Ibid., 77; see also 77–90, 111–129.
176. Ibid., 131–163.
177. Kennedy and Newcombe (2008): 48, 58, 101–102.
178. Ibid., 47.
179. Ibid., 166; see also Land and Perry (2002): 62, 91, and 194 for more references to Dobson.
180. Hybels and Hybels (1997): 14.
181. Ibid., 16, 203, emphasis in original.
182. Smith and Emerson (2000): 117, 126–127; also see chapter 2 above.
183. Hybels and Hybels (1997): 212.
184. See chapter 5.
185. Claiborne (2006): 18, 44. Megachurch and emerging church texts are similarly silent on these issues for the most part, as reported in figure 6.2.
186. Wallis (2005): xix.
187. Ibid., xxvi–xxviii.
188. On progressive Catholic and evangelical arguments in support of a political platform based on a "consistent ethic of life," see, for example, Swartz (2012), Gasaway (2014), Elisha (2014), Williams (2014), and chapter 5 below.
189. Ibid., xvii, 4, 11, 74, 299–300.
190. Ibid., 331.
191. Ibid., 332–335.
192. See chapter 5.
193. Campolo (2004): 55,70, 73.
194. Ibid., 190.
195. Ibid., 192–194.
196. Ibid., 196–200 and chapter 12.
197. Sider (2008): 103.
198. Ibid., 123, 203.
199. Ibid., 193.
200. Ibid., 136, emphasis in original.
201. Kennedy and Newcombe (2008): 113.
202. Ibid., 107.
203. Ibid., 114; see also pages 100–117.
204. E.g., Robertson (2004): 42–43, 61, 127, 167–168.
205. Ibid., 169–170.

206. Ibid., 171.
207. E.g., Land and Perry (2002): 44–45, 62, 72–73.
208. Rutba House (2005): 30.
209. Ibid., 21, 22, 24, 32, 137, 146, 165, 170–171.
210. Claiborne (2006): 152.
211. Ibid., 163.
212. Ibid., chapters 4 and 12.
213. Ibid., 157.
214. Ibid., 28, 159, and chapter 6.
215. Ibid., 139.
216. Sider ([1977] 2005).
217. Sider (2008): 115–116.
218. Wallis (2005): 264.
219. There are over 380 nontrivial references to "community" in these three neo-monastic books, along with many direct criticisms of theological individualism. On *holistic communitarianism*, see Part II.
220. Smith (2000): 13.
221. References to scripture are ubiquitous across all five positions analyzed here: neo-monastic texts contained 500+ references to the Bible; megachurch texts 500+ references; evangelical left texts 400+ references; Christian Right texts 200+ references, and emerging church texts 200+ references.
222. Bourdieu and Wacquant (1992): 40.
223. See McGrath (1997) for an evangelical theologian's perspective on the role of social struggle in doctrine formation.
224. Bourdieu ([1992] 1996); see also Gorski (2013a).
225. See chapter 7. The practical social hermeneutic model developed in this book is an examination of the more collective and macro-level, rather than individual and micro-level, aspects of evangelical culture and agency.
226. E.g., Bourdieu ([1992] 1996): 231–234 and Bourdieu and Wacquant (1992): 97–101.
227. Bourdieu ([1992] 1996): 232.
228. See also Bielo (2011): 198 and Worthen (2013). This assumes, of course, that these struggles take place within the boundaries of the explicit and implicit *doxic* commitments which make someone an evangelical in the first place; such as belief in the historical death and resurrection of Jesus, for example.
229. On *illusio*, see, for example, Bourdieu and Wacquant (1992): 98, 115–117.
230. On Bourdieu's interminable quest to overcome theoretical antinomies in the social sciences, see, for example, Bourdieu ([1992] 1996): 179–180, 183 and Bourdieu and Wacquant (1992) 15–19.
231. Smith (1998): 151–153.
232. Ibid., 121.

233. Ibid., 121–126.
234. See, in particular, propositions four and five. Along with its sensitivity to the role of internal struggles in reproducing and transforming American evangelicalism, another advantage of the field-theoretic approach is its ability to incorporate both material and cultural factors into a unified, non-reductionist account of evangelical agency and transformation.
235. Bielo (2011): 197–203; see also Garriot and O'Neill (2008).
236. Ibid., 197. Note the similarities between Bielo's ethnographic analysis of several grassroots emerging church communities and individuals, and the position-takings of emerging church leaders in the books analyzed in this chapter; which among other things, offers more confirming evidence of the utility of textual analysis for studying the position-takings of the evangelical "elites" who in large part structure the field (e.g., Hunter and Wolfe 2006, 2010; Lindsay 2007, 2008). On the centrality of opposition and resistance to the identity of the emerging church—and more confirming evidence for the field-theoretic arguments I develop in this chapter—see also Packard (2012), Marti and Ganiel (2014), and Burge and Djupe (2014).
237. Bielo (2011): 197–198; see also Marti and Ganiel (2014).
238. Ibid., 198.
239. "Cultural critique," Bielo argues, ought to be universally accepted by religious scholars as a "foundational condition in the study of Christian culture, history, and identity" (2011: 198). I agree; and it is my argument in this book that a field-theoretic approach to American evangelicalism gives us the best analytical tools for the job.
240. E.g., Bielo (2011): 200–201.
241. Ibid., 198.
242. Ibid., 202.
243. While scholars recognize distinctions among the "fundamentalist," "evangelical," and "charismatic" varieties of conservative Protestantism (and appropriately so), it is common scholarly practice to subsume both groups under the category of "conservative Protestantism" or "evangelicalism" for analytic purposes; recognizing that, relative to other varieties of American Christianity (i.e., mainline Protestantism, black Protestantism, Catholicism, etc.), conservative Protestants are more similar than they are dissimilar with respect to their social, institutional, theological, and political trajectories through history (notwithstanding the sometimes fierce disagreements among them) (e.g., Hunter 1987, 1991, Steensland et al. 2000, Ammerman 2005, Marsden 2006, Greeley and Hout 2006). Of course, the decision on whether to separate out the "fundamentalist" and "evangelical" varieties of conservative Protestantism also depends on one's particular research questions.
244. Bielo (2011): 27, 202.

245. Ibid.

246. Bourdieu and Wacquant (1992): 97.

247. E.g., Bourdieu and Wacquant (1992): 104 and Bielo (2011): 199–202.

248. Bielo (2011): 199–202.

249. See Bielo (2011): 198–202 for a list of some of these characteristics drawn from decades of evangelical scholarship in the "discrete definitional" mode, such as "Biblicism," "conversionism," "activism," evangelistic fervor, having a "born-again conversion" experience, denominational affiliation, and the like.

250. Ibid., 201–202.

251. Ibid., 202.

252. Ibid., 198–199.

253. E.g., Lakatos (1980) and Gorski (2004).

254. Bourdieu and Wacquant (1992): 96, emphasis in original.

255. Bourdieu ([1992] 1996): 126.

256. See Wallis (2005): xxvi–xxviii.

257. Ibid., 297–300.

258. For example, despite Jim Wallis's own pro-life position (see page 11), *God's Politics* devotes a grand total of four pages (out of 374 pages total) to the pro-life argument, much of it trying to convince Democratic politicians that it is in their pragmatic interests to soften their position on abortion just a little so that evangelicals will feel better about voting for them (297–301). This miniscule pro-life argument is near the very end of the book, shares a chapter with opposition to capital punishment, and is located in a section titled "When Did Jesus Become a Selective Moralist?" (a section that slams the Christian Right position on abortion even while agreeing with it). Similarly, the book's "pro-family" section is buried in a penultimate chapter whose careful, irenic discussion of gay marriage stands in stark opposition to its guns-blazing polemics against Christian Right stances on poverty, peace, and Republican Party partisanship (despite Wallis's own very thinly veiled Democratic Party partisanship).

259. E.g., Warren (1995): 41, 80, 194 and Hybels and Hybels (1997): 31–32, 64, 168.

260. On megachurch political conservatism and the *miracle motif* view of social change, see chapter 2 and Kellstedt and Green (2003), Karnes et al. (2007), and Ellingson (2007, 2008), Luhr (2009), Dochuk (2011), Elisha (2011), Wilcox (2012).

261. Ellingson (2008): 6–7; see also Luhr (2009), Dochuk (2011), Wilcox (2012).

262. E.g., chapter 6 in Kimball (2003).

263. E.g., Pagitt (2005): 22, 21, 29, 25–27.

264. Ibid.

265. E.g., Hybels and Hybels (1997): 17 and Kimball (2003): 26, 246.

266. Warren (1995): Part Four and Pagitt (2005): 55.

267. This is despite the fact that the origins of the emerging church movement and its original preoccupation with reaching postmodern individuals with the

gospel are deeply rooted in megachurch evangelicalism (see, for example, Gibbs and Bolger 2005).

268. Claiborne (2006).

269. E.g., Rutba House (2005): 17.

270. Bourdieu ([1992] 1996): 239–240.

271. Bourdieu ([1992] 1996): 240.

272. See Flory and Miller (2008): 52–83 for more examples of preservationist strategies among new entrants to the evangelical field.

273. Bourdieu ([1992] 1996): 253. On "Gen X" megachurches, see, for instance, Gibbs and Bolger (2005).

274. McManus (2001): 6–7.

275. Ibid., 16.

276. On mutual recognition, see, for example, Bourdieu ([1992] 1996): 253.

277. This is precisely the language that other emerging church critics use to dismiss the movement as a sort of adolescent tantrum thrown by the "angry white children of evangelical megachurches" (Stetzer 2006). On dominant agents' disdain for challengers, see also Bourdieu ([1992] 1996): 240.

278. While proposition two emphasized how agents occupying dominated positions are forced to construct their distinctive points of view in relation to dominant positions, dominant position-takings are also continually (re)constructed in relation to the dominated positions that challenge them.

279. E.g., Bourdieu (1993): 73.

280. Briefly, the doctrine of substitutionary atonement has to do with the question of how Jesus's death on the cross on behalf of humanity can result in the forgiveness of sin for all who believe. On the debate over emerging church views of this doctrine, see, for example, McLaren (2001), Driscoll (2006), and Webber (2007).

281. Carson (2005): 86.

282. Mohler (2005); see also McLaren (2004).

283. E.g., Wallis (2005): xvi, "A Man of Destiny: Article about Lou Engle" n.d., Kennedy and Newcombe (2008). On Elijah's confrontation with the prophets of Baal, see 1 Kings 18.

284. E.g., Bourdieu ([1984] 1993): 76 and Fiske (1991).

285. Bourdieu and Wacquant (1992): 115–117 and Schusterman (1999).

286. Bourdieu ([1980] 1990, [1997] 2000) and Bourdieu and Wacquant (1992).

287. E.g., Wacquant (1993): 31 and Bourdieu (1986).

288. Bourdieu ([1984] 1993): 76.

289. Bourdieu and Wacquant (1992): 101, 105, emphasis in original.

290. Ibid., 108, emphasis in original.

291. Ibid., 101 n. 52.

292. Bourdieu ([1992] 1996): 239.

293. Bourdieu and Wacquant (1992): 109.

294. E.g., Archer (2012), Smith (2003), Schusterman (1999), Postone et al. (1993).
295. Bourdieu (1986): 252.
296. Bourdieu and Wacquant (1992): 115.
297. E.g., Gorski (2013a).
298. E.g., Bourdieu (1986).
299. E.g., Bourdieu and Wacquant (1992): 101–106 and Bourdieu ([1992] 1996).
300. Gorski (2013): 355–356.
301. Bourdieu and Wacquant (1992): 116.
302. Bourdieu ([1992] 1996): 28, 188–189; see also Gorski (2013).
303. E.g., Archer (2000, 2012) and Gorski (2013).
304. E.g., Gorski (2013), Emirbayer and Schneiderhan (2013), Burawoy (2008), Bohman (1999), Schusterman (1999), Postone et al. (1993), Elster (1990).
305. E.g., Archer (2012): 66–82, Burawoy (2008), and Bourdieu and Wacquant (1992): 10.
306. Elster (1990): 113.
307. E.g., Gorski (2013a) and Emirbayer and Schneiderhan (2013).
308. E.g., Bourdieu and Wacquant (1992): 79–82.
309. E.g., Gorski (2013b) and Emirbayer and Schneiderhan (2013).
310. Weber (2004): 57–58, 97–98.
311. Ibid., 72–73.
312. Ibid., 73.
313. Here we see Weber, like Bourdieu, arguing forcefully against Marxist versions of economic reductionism while developing more nuanced "sound materialist principle[s]" of agency and religious culture (e.g., Bourdieu and Wacquant 1992: 115).
314. Ibid., 58.
315. Ibid., 58–59.
316. Weber ([1922] 1993): xiii.
317. This is so despite the fact that Bourdieu himself points out (on pages 182–183 in *The Rules of Art*) that it was through engagement with Weber's *The Sociology of Religion* that he first came to develop his concept of the *field* (see Bourdieu 1987). For more on Bourdieu's appropriation of Weber, see also Bourdieu and Wacquant (1992): 115 and Wacquant (1998): 218.
318. E.g., Bourdieu and Wacquant (1992): 99–102.
319. On social determinism, see Bourdieu ([1992] 1996): 238–239 and Bourdieu and Wacquant (1992): 101 n. 52, 108–109. Against a social reductionist reading of Bourdieu, this book advocates the "strong program in culture," which asserts religious culture's causal efficacy and relative autonomy with respect to social structure (e.g., Alexander 1990, Alexander and Smith 2003).
320. E.g., Gibbs and Bolger (2005), Flory and Miller (2008), Bielo (2011), Packard (2012), Samson (2014), Marti and Ganiel (2014).

321. While many recent investigations of American religion *describe* the religious practices of *biological generations*, none *analyze* the processes of social aging between *social generations* which drive transformation in the evangelical field. The former are examples of the "substantialist" mode of thinking which takes common-sense objects (such as biological generations) *prima facie* as the subject of social research, whereas the latter remembers that "the real is relational" (e.g., Hegel in Bourdieu and Wacquant (1992): 97). By studying biological generations as substantive social entities more or less in isolation from their relation to previous generations—and more or less ignoring the objective structure of relations within them—a strictly substantialist mode of thinking makes it impossible to recognize the relational social forces which drive transformation in the evangelical field (e.g., Bourdieu ([1992] 1996): 181 and Bourdieu and Wacquant (1992): 96–97).

322. Ibid., 150–154.

323. Kimball (2003): 24–25.

324. *The Purpose-Driven Church* devotes multiple chapters to the importance of cheerful lighting, comfortable seats, clean bathrooms, orderly parking lots, upbeat music, and the presence of plants in the church sanctuary for creating the ultimate seeker-sensitive church service (Warren 1995: 251–292).

325. Kimball (2003): 26.

326. Kimball (2003): 42, 44, 57; and chapters 3 through 5.

327. E.g., Kimball (2003): 23–27, 103–104, Crouch (2004), Claiborne (2006): 99–104.

328. On the difficult sociological task of pursuing the "science of the sacred," see Bourdieu ([1992] 1996): 185.

329. Ibid., 157.

330. Ibid., 156.

331. These unlikely religious communities include everything from small country churches with part-time pastors to large mainline Lutheran congregations in the San Francisco Bay area (see, for example, Ellingson 2007 and Kellstedt and Green 2003).

332. Hybels and Hybels (1997): 17.

333. E.g., Warren (1995): 41, 80, 191, 194, 231, 293 and Hybels and Hybels (1997): 31, 32, 64, 92.

334. E.g., Bourdieu ([1992] 1996): 253.

335. Ibid., 254.

336. Ibid., 157.

337. Ibid., 126.

338. Ibid., 239.

339. Megachurch evangelicalism's break with the Christian Right has been influenced by the evangelical left, as Bill Hybels makes explicit (e.g., Kirkpatrick 2007).

340. Bourdieu ([1992] 1996): 154–156.
341. Ibid., 154.
342. Ibid.
343. Smith (1998): 10.
344. Revelation 5:9 in the *New American Standard Bible* (1995).
345. E.g., Finke and Stark (1988), Smith (1998), Warner (2005).
346. Here, as elsewhere, the field of American evangelicalism displays homologies with the larger social field of American society, mirroring its competitive free-market economic model, its celebration of "youth" and youth culture, and its recognition of hierarchical status distinctions between urban/nonurban and coastal/noncoastal geographical and cultural locations. On homologies between fields, see Bourdieu ([1992] 1996): 161, 182. For more on the existence and limits of autonomy of the evangelical field with respect to America's larger social and political fields, see proposition seven below.
347. Smith (1998): 86–87; see also Harding (2000): 273–274, Luhr (2009): 20, Swartz (2012): 263–264.
348. E.g., Goodstein (2006, October 6) and Kimball (2003).
349. Bourdieu ([1992] 1996): 167.
350. E.g., Sargeant (2000), Gibbs and Bolger (2005), Marti (2005), Dionne (2008): 6–7, Elisha (2011), Bielo (2011), Wilcox (2012), Marti and Ganiel (2014).
351. Ellingson (2008): 6–7.
352. Ibid.
353. Bourdieu ([1984] 1993): 74.
354. See Smith (1998): 118 on the subcultural identity theory of evangelical vitality.
355. Crouch (2004) and Marti and Ganiel (2014).
356. Smith (1998).
357. Bourdieu ([1984] 1993): 74.
358. Kimball (2003): 26.
359. E.g., Kimball (2003) and McLaren (2001).
360. E.g., Freeman and Grieg (2007): 37–38 and Claiborne (2006): 269.
361. See chapter 4.
362. E.g., Hunter (1991), Wolfe (1998, 2003), Hunter and Wolfe (2006).
363. Hunter and Wolfe (2006): 14.
364. Hunter and Wolfe (2006): 61–62.
365. Smith (1998).
366. Ibid.
367. Wallis quoted in Claiborne (2006): 12–13.
368. Claiborne (2006): 33, 46, 102, 117, 269, 353.
369. Ibid., 1–2.
370. E.g., McLaren (2004, 2006, 2007) and McLaren and Campolo (2003); McLaren also explicitly recognizes and thanks Campolo in *Finding our Way Again* (2008).

371. E.g., Campolo (2004, 2008).

372. Campolo (2008): 21–29.

373. http://www.redletterchristians.org.

374. Bourdieu ([1992] 1996): 267.

375. See, for example, McLaren (2004), Campolo (2008), Sider et al. (2008), and Tickle (2008); and contributing authors to redletterchristians.org and *Sojourners* magazine.

376. The particular importance of political struggles in creating the conditions for collaboration (and the disintegration of collaboration) among evangelicals will be revisited in chapter 5.

377. E.g., Gibbs and Bolger (2005), Flory and Miller (2008), Bielo (2011), Packard (2012), Marti and Ganiel (2014), and below.

378. See chapter 5 for an extended discussion of Urban Monastery participants' *contradictory cultural location.*

379. Wallis (2005).

380. Wallis (2005): 7, 346; also 3–19.

381. Campolo (2004) and Sider (2008).

382. Wallis quoted in Claiborne (2006): 15.

383. Claiborne (2006): 18, 20 and chapter 5.

384. The emerging church, in particular, has a strong bent toward religious individualism even as it also prioritizes the importance of "authentic" community and relationality (e.g., Marti and Ganiel 2014).

385. Wallis (2005): 340.

386. On the emerging church tendency to form "pluralist congregations" that encompass multiple expressions of religious belief and identity, see Marti and Ganiel (2014): 34–56.

387. Bourdieu ([1992] 1996): 267.

388. Gibbs and Bolger (2005) and Marti and Ganiel (2014).

389. See, for example, Driscoll (2006) and Pagitt (2007): 41–44.

390. Driscoll (2006): 21.

391. Bourdieu ([1992] 1996): 223.

392. Ibid.

393. E.g., Carson (2005), DeYoung and Kluck (2008).

394. See Eckholm (2011) and Galli (2011) for coverage in *The New York Times* and *Christianity Today* on the controversy over Rob Bell's *Love Wins.* Although he does not claim the label himself, Bell acknowledges the significant influence of the emerging church's Brian McLaren on his personal theological position-takings (e.g., Crouch 2004).

395. Bourdieu ([1992] 1996): 132.

396. As discussed in proposition three above, the fact that the classification schemes of different groups in the field often reflect their interests does not imply that they are *determined* by interests without remainder or that agents

consciously develop classification schemes which fit their interests. More often, the agreement between agents' position-takings and their interests given their position in the field arise out of a practical "feel for the game" and their place within it; that is through the learned, corporeal, and intuitive practical understanding of the habitus (e.g., Bourdieu [1984] 1993: 76, Bourdieu and Wacquant 1992: 129–135).

397. Bourdieu ([1992] 1996): 132, 223–224.
398. Ibid., 223.
399. E.g., Driscoll (2006): 21–23; and 14–25.
400. Bourdieu ([1992] 1996): 223.
401. E.g., McKnight (2007), Stetzer (2006), Driscoll (2011).
402. Claiborne (2006): 23.
403. Ibid., 365–366.
404. That is, in a direction that is unfamiliar to evangelicals.
405. Ibid., 129.
406. Ibid., 367.
407. Ibid., 149–150.
408. Ibid., 326–331.
409. Ibid., 163.
410. E.g., Campolo (2004, 2008).
411. Campolo (2008): 21–29.
412. Pagitt (2005): 43.
413. Bourdieu and Wacquant (1992): 105, emphasis in original.
414. Bourdieu ([1992] 1996): 242–243.
415. See, for instance, Balmer (2000), McDannell (1995), Lindsay (2007), Luhr (2009).
416. E.g., Hunter (2010).
417. E.g., Wuthnow (1988) and Hunter (1991).
418. See chapter 5.
419. Claiborne (2006): 12.
420. See Campolo (2008) and redletterchristians.org.
421. Ibid., 21. *Red Letter Christians* is another example of the standard evangelical practice of making major theological and political announcements, statements, and position-takings by taking their arguments straight to the people in the form of popular books, an empirical feature of evangelicalism that recommends its own methodology (i.e., textual analysis of popular books).
422. Ibid., 22–23.
423. Ibid., 15–24.
424. Ibid., 23.
425. See also Jim Wallis's foreword in Claiborne (2006).
426. The endorsement from Clinton is, of course, a provocative shot across the bow of the conservative evangelical ship, as conservative evangelicals were furiously opposed to the former Democratic president during his time in office.

427. Campolo (2008): 17.
428. Ibid.
429. Ibid., 15–29 and chapter 5.
430. Pace status resentment theory and other versions of economic or materialist reductionism.
431. Bourdieu ([1992] 1996): 127.
432. E.g., Smith (1998), Karnes et al. (2007), Luhr (2009), Dochuk (2011).
433. See Hybels and Hybels (1997).
434. Bourdieu ([1992] 1996): 239.
435. Ibid., 232.
436. Ibid.
437. E.g., Richardson and Davis (1983), Goldman (1995), McDannell (1995), Luhr (2009), Dochuk (2011).
438. To give just one example, evangelical sociologist Dr. Tony Campolo attributes evangelicalism's displacement of mainline denominations to its entrepreneurialism and superior marketing techniques, its focus on meeting the needs of individuals, its engagement in politics, and its avoidance of progressive position-takings on social issues that could alienate its majority constituency. Of course, entrepreneurialism, marketing, individualism, populism, opinion polling, and politicization are also widely noted features of American society (Campolo 2004; also Hatch 1989, Smith and Emerson 2000, Dochuk 29–31).
439. E.g., Smith and Emerson (2000).
440. E.g., Smith (1998).
441. Hunter and Wolfe (2006): 61–62.
442. Smith (1998).
443. E.g., Frank (2004). This is a classic example of Archer's (1988) "downwards conflation."

CHAPTER 4

1. Bourdieu and Wacquant (1992): 77.
2. Weber (1958): 117.
3. Hunter (1987, 1991).
4. E.g., Diamond (1995), Hunter and Wolfe (2006): 62, Steensland and Goff (2014b).
5. Bessenecker (2006) and Annan (2013).
6. Annan (2013) and Bessenecker (2006): 23.
7. ·Ibid., 24.
8. These organizations and internships include Word Made Flesh (wordmade-flesh.org), InnerCHANGE (innerchange.org), Servant Partners (servantpartners.org), Urban Neighbors of Hope (unoh.org), Servants to Asia's Urban Poor

(servantsasia.org), and InterVarsity's Global Urban Trek (http://globalurbantrek. intervarsity.org/).

9. E.g., Annan (2013).

10. Claiborne (2006).

11. Claiborne (2006): 363–364.

12. E.g., Moll (2005).

13. Worthen (2008).

14. "Community of Communities" (n.d.), http://communityofcommunities.info/ indexphp and Samson (2014).

15. Ibid.

16. Claiborne (2006).

17. E.g., "Shane Claiborne's Itinerary," (n.d.), http://www.thesimpleway.org/shane/ schedule/; "The Urbana Heritage," (n.d.), http://www.urbana.org/archives/ history; "National Pastors Convention" (2008).

18. E.g., Steensland and Goff (2014a).

19. Harding (2009).

20. Freeman and Greig (2007).

21. "24–7 Prayer: Operations" (n.d.). [PowerPoint slides]. http://wiki.247prayer. com/images/OpsPresentation2008.pdf.

22. "24–7 Prayer" (n.d.), http://www.24-7prayer.com.

23. Freeman and Greig (2007).

24. "The Alpha Course: Facts and Figures" (2010). http://uk.alpha.org/media-room/facts-and-figures.

25. Freeman (2008).

26. Freeman and Greig (2007).

27. Andy Freeman, personal communication (May 23, 2009) and "24–7 Prayer: Communities" (n.d.), http://www.24-7prayer.com/communities.

28. See also Freeman and Greig (2007).

29. Caleb, Mina, Alex; see also Dochuk (2011), Wilcox (2012), and chapters 3 and 6.

30. Wuthnow (2007): 83.

31. Ibid., 73.

32. Greeley and Hout (2006): 93.

33. Greeley and Hout (2006): 93 and Smith (1998): 80.

34. See Bourdieu (1996) and chapter 2.

35. E.g., Bielo (2011), Flory and Miller (2008), Bessenecker (2006), Gibbs and Bolger (2005).

36. Bourdieu (1996): 84.

37. On *holistic mission*, see chapter 6.

38. The idea of "living simply"—or consuming and spending less on oneself as a personalized religio-political expression, in order to practice "environmental

stewardship" and devote more time, money, and other resources to mission and justice in the world, has a long history within American evangelicalism (i.e., Swartz 2012: 153–170, in particular).

39. Freeman and Greig (2007): 232.

40. Ibid.

41. See figure 5.1b.

42. E.g., Davis and Robinson (2006).

43. E.g., Sargeant (2000) and Ellingson (2008).

44. This interview took place before the publication of Rob Bell's extremely controversial (among evangelicals) book *Love Wins*.

45. E.g., Davis and Robinson (1996a, b, 1999a, b). On the general point regarding the social and political consequences of religious-moral worldview differences such as the individualism/communitarianism binary, see for example Hunter (1991), Hart (1992), Vaisey (2007), Vaisey and Lizardo (2010), Beyerlein and Vaisey (2013), Hitlin and Vaisey (2013),

46. E.g., Swidler (1986) and Swidler (2001): 82.

47. Smith and Emerson (2000): 105–106; for an example of the deployment of religious strategies of action in black Protestantism, see Patillo-McCoy (1998).

48. Ibid., 96.

49. Smith (1998): 192.

50. Kane (1997): 254.

51. Ibid., 251.

52. With Alexander (2004), this study takes pragmatist and structuralist theories of culture to be analytically complementary, rather than competing or mutually exclusive, approaches to how culture relates to action. Also note that Alexander's use of the term "pragmatism" in cultural analysis does not refer to the pragmatist school of American sociology related to John Dewey, George Herbert Mead, Jane Addams, and other social theorists in the Chicago tradition.

53. Kane (1997): 250, 259.

54. Ibid., 254.

55. E.g., Sewell (1985), Alexander (1990), Alexander and Smith (1993, 2003), Kane (1997): 250, 252, Alexander (2004): 527.

56. Kane (1997): 251.

57. Alexander (2004): 527.

58. Swidler (1986): 277.

59. Swidler (2001): 112, 24–26.

60. Ibid., 22, 96.

61. Ibid., 96, 98, 99.

62. Swidler (2001): 99.

63. Ibid., 66.

64. E.g., Kane (1997): 254, Smith (1998): 119, and Hunter (1987).
65. Kane (1997): 250–251; see also Alexander and Smith (2003).
66. Ibid., 255.
67. Ibid. Following Saussure, Ricoeur, and Geertz, I accept Kane's definition of symbols as "shared understanding[s] of empirical objects, conditions, and events" including both their literal and metaphoric elements.
68. To refer to Jesus, the Trinity, the gospel, etc. as "symbols" says nothing about the ultimate ontological status of these subjects. To refer to Jesus as a symbol in this sense is simply to say that, in addition to signifying a first-century Jewish religious leader, for evangelicals, the name Jesus also evokes many other meanings, such as "Savior," "Lord," "Son of God," "Lamb of God," "Messiah," sacrifice, mercy, the love of God, the forgiveness of God, and the like.
69. Ibid., 256–259.
70. Ibid., 256.
71. See figure 4.1b.
72. See chapter 3 and figure 7.2.
73. See chapter 3 and below.
74. See chapters 2 and 3.
75. Smith (1998): 98, 264 and Greeley and Hout (2006): 15.
76. Wuthnow (2007): 105.
77. On "D-Groups" or "Discipleship Groups," see chapter 5.
78. E.g., Davis and Robinson (1996b), Smith (1998): 196 n. 5, Kane (1997), Malley (2004), Bielo (2009).
79. Deuteronomy 6:5.
80. E.g., Bielo (2011), Bell (2011), and chapter 3.
81. Wright (2008).
82. Romans 10:9.
83. Regnerus and Smith (1998).
84. Dochuk (2011).
85. See chapter 2 and Hunter (1987): 42, Marsh (1997), Smith and Emerson (2000), Swartz (2012).
86. Hunter (1987): 44.
87. This issue is explored further in chapter 6's examination of the Urban Monastery's practice of hospitality.
88. Smith and Emerson (2000): 76.
89. Smith (1998): 196–198 n. and Steensland and Goff (2014a).

CHAPTER 5

1. Caleb and other Urban Monastery leaders concurred that this preference for the Democratic ticket was true for the majority of the community.
2. E.g., Davis and Robinson (1996b), Hunter (1991), and Green (2009).

3. National Election Study data from 1980 to 2004 shows a steady convergence of evangelicalism and Republican Party identification (Gold and Russell 2007; see also Green, Rozell, and Wilcox. 2006; Smidt and Kellstedt 1992).

4. E.g., Gold and Russell (2007), Layman & Hussey (2007), Greeley and Hout (2006): 45.

5. Hunter (1994): 106.

6. Wright (2000): 255.

7. The concept of *contradictory cultural location* might be easily extended to other situations in which an individual or group adheres to cultural understandings that refuse to accept pre-existing, binary, oppositional cultural structures in favor of "contradictory" cultural formulations that attempt to fuse particular elements from two supposedly incompatible cultural poles. It is particularly useful for cultural theorists in the semiotic-hermeneutic tradition who accept the existence of objective cultural structures (e.g., Alexander 1990, 2004). In this context, the analogy between Wright's concept of a contradictory class location with respect to an objective economic structure, and a contradictory cultural location with respect to a particular objective cultural structure becomes even more robust.

8. Caleb and Hunter (1991).

9. Engle (2009).

10. In addition to Anja, two other interview subjects used Christian Right language to describe their conservative views on abortion and gay marriage; however, they did not make the "bedrock of society" argument that is ubiquitous among Christian Right leaders (e.g., Land and Perry 2002).

11. Interestingly, both of the people who automatically placed opposition to abortion at the apex of their political concerns were women.

12. Engle (2009).

13. Smith (2000).

14. Diamond (1995) and Smith (2000): 48, 60.

15. Smith (1998).

16. Ibid., 210–217.

17. A reference to Isaiah 5:20.

18. Wuthnow (2007): 180 and Liebman and Wuthnow (1983).

19. Ephesians 2:14–18.

20. Smith and Emerson (2000): 109–110 and Liebman and Wuthnow (1983).

21. See chapter 3.

22. In the New International Version of *The Holy Bible*, Galatians 3:28 reads: "There is neither Jew nor Gentile, neither slave nor free, nor is there male and female, for you are all one in Christ Jesus."

23. On the "communitarian," "small is beautiful," "antitechnocratic," anti-bureaucratic, anti-system ethos of the Jesus People, see, for example, Swartz (2012): 4, 89, 104–109.

24. E.g., Richardson and Davis (1983), Goldman (1995), Dochuk (2011).

25. Here again neo-monastic evangelicals find common cause with the emerging church's emphasis on the "gospel of the kingdom" and evangelical left critiques of premillennial dispensationalists (e.g., Gibbs and Bolger 2005, Bielo 2011, Swartz 2012, Gasaway (2014).

26. E.g., Hunter (2010).

27. See also Hunter (2010), Wright (2010), Davis and Robinson (2012). An example of such an alternative social institution would be the "relational tithe" network described in Claiborne (2006): 332–334, in which relationally connected individuals from around the world give money to a common fund to address specific personal and communal needs—everything from personal health expenses and birthday parties to energy bill assistance and tsunami victim relief.

28. Swartz (2012): 89 and Warner (2014).

29. Warner (2014): 289–290.

30. Hunter (2010).

31. Bourdieu and Wacquant (1992): 105.

32. E.g., Swartz (2012): 243–250 and Gasaway (2014)

33. Swartz (2012)

34. E.g., Swartz (2012): 77–78.

35. E.g., Swartz (2012): 233–254.

36. E.g., Wuthnow (1988) and Swartz (2012): 228–232, 234–243.

37. Swartz (2012): 238–243, 247–256.

38. E.g., Swartz (2012): 188.

39. Ibid..

40. Ibid., 187–212.

41. See chapter 3.

42. E.g., Bourdieu ([1992] 1996) and Swartz (2012): 1–9.

43. E.g., Clydesdale (1999), Greeley and Hout (2006), Felson and Kindsell (2007).

44. Bell (2009).

45. See "The Institute for Communitarian Policy Studies: About Us," n.d.

46. Beichman (2003).

47. Ibid.

48. Bell (2009).

49. Glendon (1991).

50. On "pro-life progressives" and the new evangelicalism, see Williams (2014).

51. Swartz (2012) and Elisha (2014).

52. Elisha (2011), Swartz (2012), Steensland and Goff (2014b).

53. Green (2014): 140.

54. Ibid., 149.

55. Ibid., 131.

56. Ibid., 140–142, 145.
57. Ibid., 129, 149.
58. Ibid., 149 and Warner (2014).
59. Ibid., 149. See also Steensland and Goff (2014a): 19–21.

CHAPTER 6

1. "Strategies of action" is a technical term used by Ann Swidler to describe how culture shapes action by shaping the "patterns into which action is routinely organized," rather than by providing ready-made ends for actors to pursue (Swidler 2001: 82).
2. E.g., Ammerman (2005): 25, Marsden (2006), and Ellingson (2008): 3–7.
3. Claiborne (2006): 363.
4. E.g., Weber (2004) and Swidler (2001): 99.
5. The most common English translation of the German concept *Weltanschauung* is "worldview."
6. This is one way that Urban Monastery participants—and evangelical neomonastic communities more generally—differ from many emerging church communities. Whereas Marti and Ganiel (2014) find that emerging church communities tend to form loosely connected "pluralist congregations" which prioritize the autonomy of individual religious experience and belief, Urban Monastery leaders and participants work extremely hard to organize their individual and communal lives around a common, coherent, and integrated expression of Christian spirituality.
7. Lewis Smedes quoted in Smith (1998): 191.
8. Smith (2000): 187.
9. See also Hunter (2010).
10. Ammerman (1987).
11. Durkheim (1995).
12. Combining the "Great Commandment" and the "Great Commission" as recorded in Matthew 22:35–40 and Matthew 28:18–20, the Urban Monastery's mission statement is to "Love God, Love People, and Love the World." Community members often refer to these as the "Three Loves"—which, not accidentally, mirror the tripartite, Trinitarian template at the center of the Urban Monastery's holistic communitarian theological system.
13. Freeman and Greig (2007): 236. The six practices are prayer, mission, hospitality/pilgrimage, creativity, learning, and justice/mercy.
14. Pohl (1999): 19, 62.
15. Andrew and Claiborne (2006).
16. E.g., Freeman and Greig (2007): 154 and Claiborne (2006): 363.
17. Pohl (1999).

18. Marsden (2006): 21.

19. E.g., Hunter (1991) and Lindsay (2007).

20. E.g., Hunter (1991) and Lindsay (2007).

21. Weber (2004): 230–231.

22. Bourdieu and Wacquant (1992): 86, emphasis in original.

23. Ibid.

24. Ibid., 86 n. 32.

25. Bourdieu ([1992] 1996): 182–183.

26. Ibid.; see also Bourdieu and Wacquant (1992): 85–88.

27. Weber (2004): 97.

28. Weber is here quoting Jesus as recorded in Luke 18:24–26: "When Jesus saw this, he said, 'How hard it is for the rich to enter the Kingdom of God! In fact, it is easier for a camel to go through the eye of a needle than for a rich person to enter the Kingdom of God!'"

29. Weber (2004): 99–100.

30. Ibid., 29, emphasis in original.

31. Bourdieu ([1992] 1996): 85.

32. Ibid., 81, 82.

33. Ibid.

34. Ibid., 223.

35. Matthew 16:25–26, paraphrased.

36. Bourdieu ([1992] 1996): 83.

37. E.g., Bourdieu ([1984] 1988, [1992] 1996, [1989] 1998), Embirayer and Williams (2005), Schneiderhan (2009).

38. As we saw in chapter 2, the historic affinity between American evangelicalism and conservative business in America is nothing new.

39. Bourdieu ([1992] 1996): 234–240.

40. Ibid., 87.

41. E.g., Bourdieu ([1979] 1984) and chapter 3.

42. E.g., Durkheim (1995) and Alexander (1988).

43. Schaeffer (1982).

44. E.g., Himmelstein (1983) and Falwell (2001).

45. Durkheim (1995).

46. Ammerman (1987).

47. Ibid., 82.

48. E.g., McDannell (1995) and Balmer (2000).

49. See also Bielo (2011): 101–102 and Marti and Ganiel (2014): 12–14, 109–133.

50. Swidler (2001): 100–104.

51. Swidler (1986, 2001).

52. On the difficulty of achieving cultural integration or "fusion" in the late modern context, see Alexander (2004).

53. Swidler (2001): 93–107.
54. E.g., Swidler (2001): 45 and Weber (1958).
55. E.g., Swidler (2001): 69, Gorski (2003), Weber (1958).
56. Swidler (2001).
57. Ibid., 60–66.
58. E.g., Weber (1958): 95 and Noll (2001).
59. Weber (1958): 80.
60. Ibid., 117.
61. Ibid., 114, 118, 125.
62. So, too, does James Bielo (2011): 107.
63. Ibid.
64. E.g., Weber (1958) and Smith (1998).
65. E.g., Bourdieu (1996), Smith (1998), and chapter 3 above.
66. Ibid., 138; see also Bielo (2011): 101.
67. E.g., Rutba House (2005), Bessenecker (2006), Freeman and Greig (2007).
68. Freeman and Greig (2007).
69. Ibid., 138.
70. Ibid., 108.
71. Based on the "Great Commandment" (Matthew 22:36–40) and the "Great Commission" (Matthew 28:18–20) in Christian scriptures, Urban Monastery participants describe the "Three Loves" as loving God, loving one another, and loving the world.
72. Weber (1958): 118.
73. Jeremiah 29:13.
74. 1 Timothy 6:17.
75. Weber (1958): 138, 130.
76. Ibid., 117.
77. Weber (2004): 209, 245–249.
78. Ibid., 248.
79. Ibid.
80. For a related discussion of religious organization in the emerging church, see Bielo (2011), Packard (2012), and Marti and Ganiel (2014).
81. Bourdieu ([1980] 1990).
82. Ammerman 2005: 3.
83. Urban Monastery website, n.d.
84. See chapter 7, Bourdieu (1977): 110, 221, and Bourdieu ([1980] 1990): 86–87.
85. E.g., Piper and Grudem (1991) and Land and Perry (2002).
86. Swidler (2001).
87. Ibid., 99.
88. Ibid., 103.
89. E.g., Becker (1999) and Lichterman and Eliasoph (2003).

90. Ammerman (2005).
91. Swidler (2001): 102.
92. Swidler (2001): 99–104.
93. E.g., Bellah et al. (1996) and Smith and Emerson (2000).
94. Ibid.
95. Davis and Robinson (2001, 2006).
96. E.g., Richardson and Davis (1983) and personal conversations with Lilith, Steve, Peter, and other Urban Monastery participants involved in the movement.
97. On expressive individualism, see Bellah et al. (1996): 27, 32–35. On the ability of cultural "common-sense" to influence action and resist challenges from new cultural ideologies, see Swidler (2001).
98. E.g., Hatch (1989) and Noll (2001).
99. Bellah et al. (1996): 142.
100. Swidler (2001).

CHAPTER 7

1. Bill Hybels quoted in Kirkpatrick (2007).
2. "Myths of the Modern Megachurch" [Event Transcript]. *The Pew Forum on Religion and Public Life*, May 23, 2005. http://pewforum.org/Christian/Evangelical-Protestant-Churches/Myths-of-the-Modern-Megachurch.aspx.
3. See, for example, Wallis (2005): 212–214.
4. On "local social context" and its effects on the 1960s Jesus Movement, see Gordon (1984).
5. Wallis (2005): 214; see also Sider (2008): 115–117.
6. Steensland and Goff (2014a).
7. For evangelicals, taking the meaning-content of religious culture seriously includes taking evangelical understandings of the Bible and its interpretation seriously as a source of evangelical position-takings.
8. The practical social hermeneutic model developed in this book is an examination of the more collective and macro-level, rather than individual and micro-level, aspects of evangelical culture and agency.
9. E.g., Alexander and Smith (1993, 2003), Alexander (2003, 2004), Emirbayer (2004), Sewell (1985, 1999).
10. See chapter 4 and Ricoeur (1974, 1976), Malley (2004), Bielo (2009).
11. In other words, the autonomy of evangelical interpretations of the Bible is a relative, not an absolute, autonomy with respect to external social forces (e.g., Harding 2000, Malley 2004, Bielo 2009). Also note that this claim says nothing about the ultimate truth or falsehood of evangelical claims about God, the Bible, or the world; just that these claims are socially and historically conditioned.
12. E.g., Bourdieu (1977): 110, 221 and Bourdieu ([1980] 1990): 86–87.

13. See, for example, Bourdieu (1977, [1980] 1990), Kane (1997), and Swidler (1986, 2001). The polysemous nature of symbols refers to the fact that the symbolic elements of cultural meaning systems can be given multiple meanings by concrete socio-historical agents, while the fuzzy logic of practice refers to the inexact and metaphoric use of cultural elements by agents to construct lines of individual or collective action in practice.

14. See figures 3.1 and 7.1b.

15. Bourdieu ([1992] 1996): 239.

16. Ibid., 232–239.

17. Swidler (1986).

18. Archer (1988).

19. See Wuthnow (1994).

20. See, for example, Skocpol (1985) and Swidler (1986).

21. Swidler (2001): 99; see also Bourdieu and Wacquant (1992): 42–43.

22. See chapter 6 for the full development of this essentially Weberian argument. It is also important to note that, with respect to the "rationalization" of culture and its application, neo-monastic evangelicals (as a newly minted "radical" movement in an already vibrant ideological subculture) are on the "high end of the high end" of the rationalization spectrum, as compared to other cultural and religious groups. See Smith (1998), Swidler (2001), and Weber (1958, 2004).

23. On religious consistency theory, see, for example, Wuthnow (1988) and Hunter (1991). On moral cosmology theory, see Davis and Robinson (1996a, 1999b, 2006).

24. On the historicity of reason and historical rationalism, see Bourdieu and Wacquant (1992): 188–189 and Bourdieu ([1997] 2000): 120–122.

25. E.g., Hunter (1987): 40–51, 117 and Hunter and Wolfe (2006).

26. See, for example, Gushee (2008) and Hunter (2010): 128.

27. See Gushee (2008): 93–98, 175 for a fascinating insider account of internal struggles between Christian Right power players and moderate evangelicals over the 2006 Evangelical Climate Initiative.

28. Hunter (2010): 128, Green and Clement (2010), Farrell (2011), and Steensland and Goff (2014a).

29. Indeed, evangelical theologian Scot McKnight called it "the biggest change in the evangelical movement at the end of the twentieth century" (quoted in Pally 2011: 107).

30. Wallis (2005).

31. See Campolo (2008): 1–28. Political scientist John C. Green estimates that slightly less than 1 in 10 adult Americans could be classified as "red-letter Christians" by virtue of the (conservative) theological and (left-liberal) political standpoints (Green 2008, Green and Jackson 2007).

32. Gushee (2008): 87–117.

33. See "For the Health of the Nation: An Evangelical Call to Civic Responsibility" (2004), "Climate Change: An Evangelical Call to Action" (2006), Gushee (2008).
34. See, for example, Gushee (2008): 88–92.
35. E.g., "How the Faithful Voted" (2008) and Hunter (2010).
36. E.g., "Election 2012 Post Mortem: White Evangelicals and Support for Romney" (2012) and "How the Faithful Voted: 2014 Preliminary Analysis" (2014).
37. E.g., Steensland and Goff (2014b) and, for young evangelicals, Farrell (2011).
38. Ibid.
39. Wallis (2005): 307–308. See also Smith and Emerson (2000), Christerson et al. (2005), Emerson and Woo (2006), Lichterman (2005), Lichterman et al. (2009).
40. E.g., McLaren (2001): 16, Rice (2005), Rah (2009), McLaren et al. (2010).
41. E.g., Rah (2009) and McLaren et al. (2010). The fact that only three of the fifteen of the books analyzed in chapter 6 were coauthored by women (and none were written solely by women) is a reflection of racial and gendered power inequalities in the evangelical field itself.
42. Campolo (2008); see also Campolo (2004) and Kirkpatrick (2007).

References

Addams, J. (1961). *Twenty Years at Hull House*. New York: Signet Classic.

———. (2002). *Democracy and Social Ethics*. Urbana: University of Illinois Press. (Original work published 1899)

Alexander, J. C. (1988). "Cultural and Political Crisis: 'Watergate' and Durkheimian Sociology." In J. C. Alexander (Ed.), *Durkheimian Sociology* (pp. 193–209). Cambridge: Cambridge University Press.

———. (1990). "Introduction: Understanding the 'Relative Autonomy' of Culture," In J. Alexander and S. Seidman, (Eds.), *Culture and Society: Contemporary Debates* pp. 1–27. Cambridge: Cambridge University Press.

———. (2003). *The Meanings of Social Life: A Cultural Sociology*. Oxford and New York: Oxford University Press.

———. (2004). "Cultural Pragmatics: Social Performance between Ritual and Strategy." *Sociological Theory 22* (4): 527–573.

Alexander, J. C., & Smith, P. (1993). "The Discourse of American Civil Society: A New Proposal for Cultural Studies." *Theory and Society 22* (2): 151–207.

———. (2003). "The Strong Program in Cultural Theory: Elements of a Structural Hermeneutics." In J. C. Alexander (pp. 11–26) *The Meanings of Social Life: A Cultural Sociology*. Oxford and New York: Oxford University Press.

Ammerman, N. T. (1987). *Bible Believers: Fundamentalists in the Modern World*. New Brunswick, NJ: Rutgers University Press.

———. (2005). *Pillars of Faith: American Congregations and their Partners*. Berkeley and Los Angeles: University of California Press.

———. (Ed.). (2006). *Everyday Religion: Observing Modern Religious Lives*. Oxford and New York: Oxford University Press.

"An Evangelical Declaration against Torture: Protecting Human Rights in an Age of Terror." (2007). National Association of Evangelicals. Retrieved from http://www.nae.net/government-relations/endorsed-documents/409-an-evangelical-declaration-against-torture-protecting-human-rights-in-an-age-of-terror

Anderson, M. L. (2013, March 15). "Here Come the Radicals!" *Christianity Today* [March cover story]. http://www.christianitytoday.com/ct/2013/march/here-come-radicals.html.

Annan, K. (2013, August 29). "Chaos and Grace in the Slums of the Earth." *Christianity Today* [September cover story]. Retrieved from http://www.christianitytoday.com/ct/2013/september/chaos-and-grace-in-slums-of earth.html

Archer, M. (1988). *Culture and Agency: The Place of Culture in Social Theory*. Cambridge and New York: Cambridge University Press.

———. (2000). *Being Human: The Problem of Agency*. Cambridge and New York: Cambridge University Press.

———. (2012). *The Reflexive Imperative in Late Modernity*. Cambridge and New York: Cambridge University Press.

Armstrong, C. (2008, February 8). "Monastic Evangelicals." *Christianity Today*. Retrieved from http://www.christianitytoday.com/ct/2008/february/23.28.html

Arnold, L. (2009). "Fostering Families: Beverly LaHaye." *Christian Examiner*. Retrieved from http://www.cwfa.org/images/content/LaHayeReprint.pdf

Balmer, R. H. (2000). *Mine Eyes Have Seen the Glory: A Journey into the Evangelical Subculture in America*. Oxford and New York: Oxford University Press.

Banerjee, N. (2007). "Rev. D. James Kennedy, Broadcaster, Dies at 76." *New York Times*. Retrieved from http://www.nytimes.com/2007/09/06/us/06kennedy.html

Barber, L. (2008). "Pursuing Beloved Community: Mission Year Annual Report 2007–2008." Retrieved from http://www.missionyear.org/pdf/Mission_Year_AR_0708.pdf

Barker, D.C and Carman, C.J. (2000). "The Spirit of Capitalism? Religious Doctrine, Values and Economic Attitude Constructs." *Political Behavior* (22) 1:–27

Bartkowski, J. (2004). *The Promise Keepers: Servants, Soldiers, and Godly Men*. Piscataway, NJ: Rutgers University Press.

Beaven, S. (2010, September 25). "Young Christians Seek Intentional Community among the Poor." *The Huffington Post*. Retrieved from http://www.huffingtonpost.com/2010/09/24/christians-new-monasticism_n_738729.html

Becker, P. E. (1999). *Congregations in Conflict: Cultural Models of Local Religious Life*. New York: Cambridge University Press.

Beichman, A. (2003, April 21). "The Communitarian: Amitai Etzioni on his Life and Times." Review of the book *My Brother's Keeper*. *The Weekly Standard*. Retrieved from http://www.amitaietzioni.org/MBKreview.html

Bell, D. (2009, January 22). "Communitarianism." *Stanford Encyclopedia of Philosophy*. Retrieved from http://plato.stanford.edu/entries/communitarianism/

Bell, R. (2011). *Love Wins: A Book About Heaven, Hell, and the Fate of Every Person Who Ever Lived*. New York: HarperOne.

Bellah, R. N., Madsen, R., Sullivan, W. M., Swidler, A., & Tipton, S. M. (1996). *Habits of the Heart: Individualism and Commitment in American Life* (2nd ed.). Berkeley and Los Angeles: University of California Press.

Bender, C. (2003). *Heaven's Kitchen: Lived Religion at God's Love We Deliver.* Chicago: University of Chicago Press.

Bessenecker, S. (2006). *The New Friars: The Emerging Movement Serving the World's Poor.* Downers Grove, IL: InterVarsity Press.

Beyerlein, K. and Vaisey, S. (2013). "Individualism revisited: Moral worldviews and civic engagement." *Poetics 41* (4): 384–406.

Bielo, J. S. (2008). "On the Failure of 'Meaning': Bible Reading in the Anthropology of Christianity." *Culture and Religion 9* (1): 1–21.

———. (2009). *Words Upon the Word: An Ethnography of Evangelical Group Bible Study.* New York: New York University Press.

———. (2011). *Emerging Evangelicals: Faith, Modernity, and the Desire for Authenticity.* New York: New York University Press.

Bohman, J. (1999). "Practical Reason and Cultural Constraint: Agency in Bourdieu's Theory of Practice." In R. Schusterman (Ed.), *Bourdieu: A Critical Reader* (pp. 129–152). Oxford: Blackwell.

Bourdieu, P. (1977). *Outline of a Theory of Practice.* (R. Nice, Trans.). Cambridge and New York: Cambridge University Press. (Original work published 1972)

———. (1987). "Legitimation and Structural Interests in Weber's Sociology of Religion." (C. Turner, Trans.). In S. Whimster & S. Lash (Eds.), *Max Weber: Rationality and Modernity* (pp. 119-136). London: Allen & Unwin. (Original work published 1971)

———. (1984). *Distinction: A Social Critique of the Judgment of Taste.* (R. Nice, Trans.). Boston, MA: Harvard University Press. (Original work published 1979)

———. (1986). "The Forms of Capital." In J. G. Richardson (Ed.), *Handbook of Theory and Research for the Sociology of Education* (pp. 241–258). New York, Westport, CT, and London: Greenwood Press.

———. (1988). *Homo Academicus.* Stanford, CA: Stanford University Press. (P. Collins, Trans.). (Original work published 1984)

———. (1990). *The Logic of Practice.* (R. Nice, Trans.). Stanford, CA: Stanford University Press. (Original work published 1980)

———. (1993) *Sociology in Question.* (R. Nice, Trans.). London: SAGE Publications. (Original work published 1984)

———. (1996). *The Rules of Art: Genesis and Structure of the Literary Field.* (S. Emanuel, Trans.). Stanford, CA: Stanford University Press. (Original work published 1992)

———. (1998). *The State Nobility.* (Polity Press, Trans.). Stanford, CA: Stanford University Press. (Original work published 1989)

———. (2000) *Pascalian Meditations.* (R. Nice, Trans.). Stanford, CA: Stanford University Press. (Original work published 1997)

Bourdieu, P., & Wacquant, L. J. D. (1992). *An Invitation to Reflexive Sociology.* Chicago: University of Chicago Press.

Brint, S. G., & Schroedel, J. R. (Eds.). (2009a). *Evangelicals and Democracy in America,* Volume 1: *Religion and Society.* New York: Russell Sage Foundation.

Brint, S. G., & Schroedel, J. R. (2009b). *Evangelicals and Democracy in America, Volume 2: Religion and Politics*. New York: Russell Sage Foundation.

Brown, S.P. (2002). *Trumping Religion: The New Christian Right, the Free Speech Clause, and the Courts*. Tuscaloosa, AL: University of Alabama Press.

Buchanan P. (1992). "1992 Republican National Convention Speech." Houston, Texas, August 17, 1992. Retrieved from http://buchanan.org/blog/1992-republican-national-convention-speech-148

Burawoy, M. (1998). "The Extended Case Method." *Sociological Theory* 16 (1): 4–33.

———. (2008). "Conversations with Pierre Bourdieu." Lecture Series and Working Papers delivered in April 2008 at the Havens Center for Social Justice, University of Wisconsin-Madison.

Burge, R. P. and Djupe, P. A. (2014). "Truly Inclusive or Uniformly Liberal? An Analysis of the Politics of the Emerging Church." *Journal for the Scientific Study of Religion* 53 (3): 636–651.

Calhoun, C. J. (Ed.). (1991). *Comparative Social Research, A Research Annual: Religious Institutions*. Greenwich, CN: JAI Press.

Campbell, D. E. (Ed.). (2007). *A Matter of Faith? Religion in the 2004 Presidential Election*. Washington, DC: The Brookings Institution.

Campbell, M., & Gregor, F. (2004). *Mapping Social Relations: A Primer in Doing Institutional Ethnography*. Walnut Creek, CA: Alta Mira Press.

Campolo, A. (2004). *Speaking My Mind*. Nashville, TN: Thomas Nelson.

———. (2008). *Red Letter Christians: A Citizen's Guide to Faith and Politics*. Ventura, CA: Regal.

Carpenter, J. A. (1997). *Revive Us Again: The Reawakening of American Fundamentalism*. New York and Oxford: Oxford University Press.

Carson, D. A. (2005). *Becoming Conversant with the Emerging Church: Understanding a Movement and Its Implications*. Grand Rapids, MI: Zondervan.

Carson, M. (1990). *Settlement Folk: Social Thought and the American Settlement Movement, 1885–1930*. Chicago: University of Chicago Press.

Cassirer, E. (1923) [1910]. *Substance and function*. Chicago: Open Court.

Chaves, M. (2006). "2005 H. Paul Douglass Lecture: All Creatures Great and Small: Megachurches in Context." *Review of Religious Research* 47 (4): 329–346.

Christerson, B., Edwards, K. L., & Emerson, M. O. (2005). *Against All Odds: The Struggle for Racial Integration in Religious Organizations*. New York: New York University Press.

"Christians for Comprehensive Immigration Reform: Statement of Principles." (2010). Retrieved from http://faithandimmigration.org/content/statement-principles

Claiborne, Shane. (2006). *The Irresistible Revolution: Living as an Ordinary Radical*. Grand Rapids, MI: Zondervan.

———. (2009, November 18). "What if Jesus Meant all that Stuff?" *Esquire*. Retrieved from http://www.esquire.com/features/best-and-brightest-2009/shane-claiborne-1209

———. (2010, April 13). "The Emerging Church Brand: The Good, the Bad, and the Messy." [*Sojourners* God's Politics weblog comment]. Retrieved from http://sojo.net/blogs/2010/04/13/emerging-church-brand-good-bad-and-messy

Claiborne, S., & Haw, C. (2008). *Jesus for President: Politics for Ordinary Radicals.* Grand Rapids, MI: Zondervan.

"Climate Change: An Evangelical Call to Action." (2006). The Evangelical Climate Initiative. Retrieved from http://www.npr.org/documents/2006/feb/evangelical/calltoaction.pdf

Clydesdale, T. T. (1999). "Toward Understanding the Role of Bible Beliefs and Higher Education in American Attitudes toward Eradicating Poverty, 1964–1996." *Journal for the Scientific Study of Religion 38* (1): 103–118.

Conger, K. H., & Green, J. C. (2002). "Spreading Out and Digging In: Christian Conservatives and State Republican Parties." *Campaigns and Elections 23* (1): 58–65.

Conger, K. H., & Racheter, D. (2006). "Iowa: In the Heart of Bush Country." In J. C. Green, M. J. Rozell, & C. Wilcox (Eds.), *The Values Campaign? The Christian Right and the 2004 Elections* (pp. 128–143). Washington, DC: Georgetown University Press.

Crouch, A. (2004). "The Emergent Mystique." *Christianity Today.* Retrieved from http://www.christianitytoday.com/ct/2004/november/12.36.html

Cutrer, C. (2000, August 1). "Clinton Visit Provokes Church Members." *Christianity Today Online.* Retrieved from http://www.ctlibrary.com/ct/2000/augustweb-only/54.0b.html

Davis, A. F. (1984). *Spearheads for Reform: The Social Settlements and the Progressive Movement 1890–1914.* New Brunswick, NJ: Rutgers University Press.

———. (2000). *American Heroine: The Life and Legend of Jane Addams.* Chicago: Ivan R. Dee.

Davis, N. J., & Robinson, R. V. (1996a). "Are the Rumors of War Exaggerated? Religious Orthodoxy and Moral Progressivism in America." *American Journal of Sociology 102* (3): 756–787.

———. (1996b). "Religious Orthodoxy in American Society: The Myth of a Monolithic Camp." *Journal for the Scientific Study of Religion 35* (3): 229–245.

———. (1999a). "Religious Cosmologies, Individualism and Politics in Italy." *Journal for the Scientific Study of Religion 38* (3): 339–353.

———. (1999b). "Their Brothers' Keepers? Orthodox Religionists, Modernists, and Economic Justice in Europe." *American Journal of Sociology 104* (6): 1631–1665.

———. (2001). "Theological Modernism, Cultural Libertarianism and Laissez-Faire Economics in Contemporary European Societies." *Sociology of Religion 62*: 23–50.

———. (2006). "The Egalitarian Face of Islamic Orthodoxy: Support for Islamic Law and Economic Justice in Seven Muslim-Majority Nations." *American Sociological Review 71* (April): 167–190.

———. (2012). *Claiming Society for God: Religious Movements & Social Welfare.* Bloomington: Indiana University Press.

Desmond, M. (2014). "Relational Ethnography." *Theory and Society* 43 (5):547–579.

DeYoung, C. P., Emerson, M. O., Yancey, G., & Kim, K. C. (2003). *United by Faith: The Multiracial Congregation as an Answer to the Problem of Race.* Oxford and New York: Oxford University Press.

DeYoung, K., & Kluck, T. (2008). *Why We're Not Emergent: By Two Guys Who Should Be.* Chicago: Moody.

Diamond, S. (1995). *Roads to Dominion: Right Wing Movements and Political Power in the United States.* New York and London: The Guilford Press.

———. (1998). *Not by Politics Alone: The Enduring Influence of the Christian Right.* New York and London: The Guilford Press.

DiMaggio, P., Evans, J., & Bryson, B. (1996). "Have Americans' Social Attitudes Become More Polarized?" *American Journal of Sociology* 102 (3): 690–755.

Dionne, E. J. (2008). *Souled Out: Reclaiming Faith and Politics after the Religious Right.* Princeton, NJ: Princeton University Press.

Dochuk, D. (2011). *From Bible Belt to Sunbelt: Plain-Folk Religion, Grassroots Politics, and the Rise of Evangelical Conservatism.* New York: W. W. Norton & Company.

Driscoll, M. (2006). *Confessions of a Reformation Rev.: Hard Lessons from an Emerging Missional Church.* Grand Rapids, MI: Zondervan.

———. (2011, September 19). "A Few Stories about Rick Warren." Retrieved from http://pastormark.tv/2011/09/19/a-few-stories-about-rick-warren?utm_source= feedburner&utm_medium=feed&utm_campaign=Feedpercent3A+pastormark +percent28PastorMark.tv percent29

Durkheim, É. (1995). *The Elementary Forms of Religious Life.* (K. E. Fields, Trans.). New York: Free Press. (Original work published 1912)

Eckholm, E. (2011, March 4). "Pastor Stirs Wrath with His Views on Old Questions." *New York Times.* Retrieved from http://www.nytimes.com/2011/03/05/ us/05bell.html?_r=1

"Election 2012 Post Mortem: White Evangelicals and Support for Romney" (2012). Retrieved from http://www.pewforum.org/2012/12/07/election-2012-post-mortem-white-evangelicals-and-support-for-romney/

Elisha, O. (2011). *Moral Ambition: Mobilization and Social Outreach in Evangelical Megachurches.* Berkeley and Los Angeles: University of California Press.

———. "All Catholics Now? Specters of Catholicism in Evangelical Social Engagement." In B. Steensland and P. Goff (pp. 73–93) *The New Evangelical Social Engagement.* Oxford and New York: Oxford University Press.

Ellingson, S. (2007). *The Megachurch and the Mainline.* Chicago: University of Chicago Press.

———. (2008). "The Rise of the Megachurches and Changes in Religious Culture: Review Article." *Sociology Compass* 2: 1–15.

Ellwood, R. (1973). *One Way.* Englewood Cliffs, NJ: Prentice Hall.

Elster, J. (1990). "Marxism, Functionalism and Game Theory." In S. Zukin & P. DiMaggio (Eds.), *Structures of Capital: The Social Organization of the Economy* (pp. 97–118). Cambridge: Cambridge University Press.

Emerson, M. O., & Woo, R. M. (2006). *People of the Dream: Multiracial Congregations in the United States.* Princeton, NJ: Princeton.

Emirbayer, M. (1997). "Manifesto for a Relational Sociology." *American Journal of Sociology 103* (2): 281–317.

———. (2004). "The Alexander School of Cultural Sociology." *Thesis Eleven 79* (5): 5–15.

Emirbayer, M., & Schneiderhan, E. (2013). "Dewey and Bourdieu on Democracy." In P. S. Gorski (Ed.), *Bourdieu and Historical Analysis* (pp. 131–157). Durham, NC: Duke University Press.

Emirbayer, M., & Williams, E. M. (2005). "Bourdieu and Social Work." *Social Service Review 79* (4): 689–724.

Engelke, M., & Tomlinson, M. (2007). *The Limits of Meaning: Case Studies in the Anthropology of Christianity.* New York: Berghahn Books.

Engle, L. (2009, December 31). "Evening Session." One Thing Conference [video blog]. Retrieved from http://ihop.org/onething09

Eskridge, L. (2013). *God's Forever Family: The Jesus People Movement in America.* Oxford and New York: Oxford University Press.

Falwell, J. (1980). *Listen, America! The Conservative Blueprint for America's Moral Rebirth.* New York: Bantam Books.

———. (2001). September 13). "700 Club." [Event Transcript]. Retrieved from http://www.beliefnet.com/Faiths/Christianity/2001/09/You-Helped-This-Happen.aspx

Farrell, J. (2011). "The Young and the Restless? The Liberalization of Young Evangelicals." *Journal for the Scientific Study of Religion 50* (3): 517–532.

Felson, J., & Kindell, H. (2007). "The Elusive Link between Conservative Protestantism and Conservative Economics." *Social Science Research 36*: 673–687.

Findlay, J. F., Jr. (1969). *Dwight L. Moody: American Evangelist 1837–1899.* Chicago and London: University of Chicago Press.

Finke, R., & Stark, R. (1988). "Religious Economies and Sacred Canopies: Religious Mobilization in American Cities, 1906." *American Sociological Review 53*: 41–49.

Fiske, A. P. (1991). *Structure of Social Life: The Four Elementary Forms of Human Relations.* New York: Free Press.

Flory, R. W., & Miller, D. E. (2008). *Finding Faith: The Spiritual Quest of the Post-Boomer Generation.* New Brunswick, NJ: Rutgers University Press.

"For the Health of the Nation: An Evangelical Call to Civic Responsibility." (2004). Retrieved from http://www.nae.net/images/content/For_The_Health_Of_The_Nation.pdf

Fowler, M. (2008, April 11). "Obama: No Surprise that Hard-Pressed Pennsylvanians Turn Bitter." *The Huffington Post.* Retrieved from http://www.huffingtonpost.com/mayhill-fowler/obama-no-surprise-that-ha_b_96188.html

Frank, T. (2004). *What's the Matter with Kansas?: How Conservatives Won the Heart of America.* New York: Henry Holt.

Freeman, A. (2008) "Who Am I?" [web log comment]. Retrieved from http://www.isthisbiblical.com/?page_id20%=20%12

Freeman, A., & Greig, P. (2007). *Punk Monk: New Monasticism and the Ancient Art of Breathing*. Ventura, CA: Regal Books.

Friedman, M. (1953). *Essays in Positive Economics*. Chicago: University of Chicago Press.

Galli, M. (2009, April). "How to Shrink a Church." *Christianity Today*. Retrieved from http://www.christianitytoday.com/ct/2009/aprilweb-only/116-41.0.html?start=2

———. (2011). "Heaven, Hell, and Rob Bell." *Christianity Today* [web log comment]. Retrieved from http://www.christianitytoday.com/ct/article_print.html?id=91120

Garriott, W., & O'Neill, K. L. (2008). "Who Is a Christian? Toward a Dialogic Approach in the Anthropology of Christianity." *Anthropological Theory 8*: 381–398.

Gasaway, B. W. (2014). *Progressive Evangelicals and the Pursuit of Social Justice*. Chapel Hill, NC: The University of North Carolina Press.

Gibbs, E., & Bolger, R. K. (2005). *Emerging Churches: Creating Christian Community in Postmodern Cultures*. Grand Rapids, MI: Baker Academic.

Gilgoff, D. (2007). *The Jesus Machine: How James Dobson, Focus on the Family, and Evangelical America are Winning the Culture War*. New York: St. Martin's Press.

Glaser, B. G., & Strauss, A. L. (1967). *The Discovery of Grounded Theory*. Hawthorne, NY: Aldine de Gruyter.

Glendon, M.-A. (1991). *Rights Talk: The Impoverishment of Political Discourse*. New York: Free Press.

Gold, H. J., & Russell, G. E. (2007). "The Rising Influence of Evangelicalism in American Political Behavior, 1980–2004." *Social Science Journal 44*: 554–562.

Goldman, M. S. (1995). "Continuity in Collapse: Departures from Shiloh." *Journal for the Scientific Study of Religion 34* (3): 342–353.

Goodstein, L. (2006, February 8). "Evangelical Leaders Join Global Warming Initiative." *New York Times*. Retrieved from http://www.nytimes.com/2006/02/08/national/08warm.html?scp=1&sq =evangelicals percent 20join percent20global percent20warming percent20initiative&st=cse

———. (2006, October 6). "Evangelicals Fear the Loss of their Teenagers." Retrieved from http://www.nytimes.com/2006/10/06/us/06evangelical.html?_r=1&pagewanted=all

Gordon, D. F. (1984). "The Role of the Local Social Context in Social Movement Accommodation: A Case Study of Two Jesus People Groups." *Journal for the Scientific Study of Religion 23* (4): 381–383.

Gorski, P. S. (2003). *The Disciplinary Revolution: Calvinism and the Rise of the State in Early Modern Europe*. Chicago: University of Chicago Press.

———. (2004). "The Poverty of Deductivism: A Constructive Realist Model of Sociological Explanation." *Sociological Methodology 34*: 1–33.

———. (2009). "Conservative Protestantism in the United States? Toward a Comparative and Historical Perspective." In S. G. Brint & J. R. Schroedel (Eds.), *Evangelicals and Democracy in America*, Volume 1: *Religion and Society* (pp. 74–114). New York: Russell Sage Foundation.

———. (2013a). "Bourdieusian Theory and Historical Analysis: Maps, Mechanisms, and Methods." In P. S. Gorski (Ed.), *Bourdieu and Historical Analysis* (pp. 327–366). Durham, NC: Duke University Press.

———. (Ed.) (2013b). *Bourdieu and Historical Analysis*. Durham, NC: Duke University Press.

Graham, B. (1971). *The Jesus Generation*. Grand Rapids, MI: Zondervan.

Greeley, A., & Hout, M. (2006). *The Truth about Conservative Christians: What They Think and What They Believe*. Chicago and London: University of Chicago Press.

Green, J. C. (2008, June 5). "Assessing a More Prominent 'Religious Left.'" [Event Transcript]. Retrieved from http://www.pewforum.org/2008/06/05/assessing-a-more-prominent-religious-left/

———. (2009). "Exploring the Traditionalist Alliance: Evangelical Protestants, Religious Voters, and the Republican Presidential Vote." In S. G. Brint & J. R. Schroedel (Eds.), *Evangelicals and Democracy in America*, Volume 1: *Religion and Society* (pp. 117–158). New York: Russell Sage Foundation.

———. (2014). "New and Old Evangelical Public Engagement: A View from the Polls." In B. Steensland & P. Goff (Eds.), *The New Evangelical Social Engagement* (pp. 129–156). Oxford and New York: Oxford University Press.

Green, J.C. and Clement, S. (2010). "Much Hope, Modest Change for Democrats." Retrieved from http://www.pewforum.org/2010/08/11/much-hope-modest-change-for-democrats-religion-in-the-2008-presidential-election/

Green, J. C., Conger, K. H., & Guth, J. L. (2006). "Agents of Value: Christian Right Activists in 2004." In J. C. Green, M. Rozell, & C. Wilcox (Eds.), *The Values Campaign? The Christian Right in the 2004 Election* (pp. 22–55). Washington, DC: Georgetown University Press.

Green, J. C., & Jackson, J. S. (2007). "Faithful Divides: Party Elites and Religion." In D. E. Campbell (Ed.), *A Matter of Faith? Religion in the 2004 Presidential Election* (pp. 37–64). Washington, DC: The Brookings Institution.

Green, J. C., Rozell, M. J., & Wilcox, C. (Eds.). (2000). *Prayers in the Precincts: The Christian Right in the 1998 Elections*. Washington, DC: Georgetown University Press.

———. (2003). *The Christian Right in American Politics*. Washington, DC: Georgetown University Press.

———. (2006). *The Values Campaign? The Christian Right and the 2004 Elections*. Washington, DC: Georgetown University Press.

Gushee, D. P. (2008). *The Future of Faith in American Politics: The Public Witness of the Evangelical Center*. Waco, TX: Baylor University Press.

Guth, J. L. (1983). "The New Christian Right." In R. Liebman & R. Wuthow (Eds.), *The New Christian Right* (pp. 31–45). Hawthorne, NY: Aldine Publishing.

Guth, J. L., Beail, L., Crow, G., Gaddy, B., Montreal, S., Nelsen, B., & Walz, J. (2003). "The Political Activity of Evangelical Clergy in the Election of 2000: A Case Study of Five Denominations." *Journal for the Scientific Study of Religion 42* (4): 501–514.

Hall, D. (Ed.). (1997). *Lived Religion in America: Toward a History of Practice.* Princeton, NJ: Princeton University Press.

Hankins, B. (2010). *Jesus and Gin: Evangelicalism, the Roaring Twenties and Today's Culture Wars.* New York and Basingstoke: Palgrave Macmillan.

Harding, S. F. (2000). *The Book of Jerry Falwell: Fundamentalist Language and Politics.* Princeton, NJ: Princeton University Press.

Harding, C. (2009, August 7). "Three New Nations Pray 24–7!" [Web log comment]. Retrieved from http://www.24-7prayer.com/blog/1065

Harper, Lisa S. (2008). *Evangelical Does Not Equal Republican . . . or Democrat.* New York: The New Press.

Hart, S. (1992). *What Does the Lord Require? How American Christians Think about Economic Justice.* Oxford and New York: Oxford University Press.

Hatch, N. O. (1989). *The Democratization of American Christianity.* New Haven, CT: Yale.

Hedstrom, P., & Bearman, P. (2009). "What is Analytical Sociology All About? An Introductory Essay." In P. Hedstrom & P. Bearman (Eds.) *The Oxford Handbook of Analytical Sociology* (pp. 3–24). Oxford and New York: Oxford University Press.

Henry, C. F. H. (1947). *The Uneasy Conscience of Modern Fundamentalism.* Grand Rapids, MI: Wm. B. Eerdmans Publishing Company.

Himmelstein, J. L. (1983). "The New Right." In R. Liebman & R. Wuthow (Eds.), *The New Christian Right* (pp. 15–30). Hawthorne, NY: Aldine Publishing.

Hitlin, S. and Vaisey, S. (2013). "The New Sociology of Morality." *Annual Review of Sociology 39*:51–68.

Hofstadter, R. (1963). *Anti-Intellectualism in American Life.* New York: Alfred A. Knopf.

———. (1965). *The Paranoid Style in American Politics.* New York: Alfred A. Knopf.

Hollinger, D. (1983). *Individualism and Social Ethics.* Lanham, MD: University Press of America.

"How the Faithful Voted." (2008). Retrieved from http://pewforum.org/Politics-and Elections/How-the-Faithful-Voted.aspx

"How the Faithful Voted: 2014 Preliminary Analysis." (2014). Retrieved from http://www.pewforum.org/2014/11/05/how-the-faithful-voted-2014-preliminary-analysis/

———. (1987). *Evangelicalism: The Coming Generation.* Chicago: University of Chicago Press.

———. (1991). *Culture Wars: The Struggle to Define America.* New York: Basic Books.

———. (1994). *Before the Shooting Begins: Searching for Democracy in America's Culture War*. New York: Free Press.

———. (2010). *To Change the World: The Irony, Tragedy, and Possibility of Christianity in the Late Modern World*. Oxford and New York: Oxford University Press.

Hunter, J. D., & Wolfe, A. (2006). *Is There a Culture War? A Dialogue on Values and American Public Life*. Washington, DC: Brookings Institution Press.

Hybels, B. (1998). *Making Life Work: Putting God's Wisdom into Action*. Downers Grove, IL: InterVarsity Press.

Hybels, L., & Hybels, B. (1997). *Rediscovering Church: The Story and Vision of Willow Creek Community Church*. Grand Rapids, MI: Zondervan.

Hybels, B., & Mittelberg, M. (1994). *Becoming a Contagious Christian*. Grand Rapids, MI: Zondervan.

Jerolmack, C., & Khan, S. (2014). "Talk Is Cheap: Ethnography and the Attitudinal Fallacy." *Sociological Methods and Research 43* (2): 178–209.

Kane, A. E. (1997). "Theorizing Meaning Construction in Social Movements: Symbolic Structures and Interpretation during the Irish Land War, 1879–1882." *Sociological Theory 15* (3): 249–276.

Karnes, K., McIntosh, W., Morris, I. L., & Pearson-Merkowitz, S. (2007). "Mighty Fortresses: Explaining the Spatial Distribution of American Megachurches." *Journal for the Scientific Study of Religion 46* (2): 261–268.

Kazin, M. (2006). *A Godly Hero: The Life of William Jennings Bryan*. New York: Random House.

Keeter, S. (2007). "Evangelicals and Moral Values." In D. E. Campbell (Ed.), *A Matter of Faith? Religion in the 2004 Presidential Election* (pp. 80–94). Washington, DC: The Brookings Institution.

Kellstedt, L. A., & Green, J. C. (2003). "The Politics of the Willow Creek Association Pastors." *Journal for the Scientific Study of Religion 42* (4): 547–561.

Kellstedt, L., Green, J. C., Guth, J., & Smidt, C. (1994). "Religious Voting Blocs in the 1992 Election." *Sociology of Religion 55*: 307–326.

Kennedy, D. J., & Newcombe, J. (2008). *How Would Jesus Vote?: A Christian Perspective on the Issues*. Colorado Springs, CO: Waterbrook Press.

Kimball, D. (2003). *The Emerging Church: Vintage Christianity For New Generations*. Grand Rapids, MI: Zondervan.

Kirkpatrick, D. D. (2007, October 28). "The Evangelical Crackup." *New York Times Magazine*. Retrieved from http://www.nytimes.com/2007/10/28/magazine/28Evangelicalst.html?_r=1&scp=1&sq=thepercent20evangelicalpercent20crackup&st=cse

Kristof, N. D. (2008, February 3). "Evangelicals a Liberal Can Love." *New York Times*. Retrieved from http://www.nytimes.com/2008/02/03/opinion/03kristof.html?scp=1&sq=Evangelicals percent20a percent20Liberal percent20Can percent20 Love&st=cse

Lakatos, I. (1980). *The Methodology of Scientific Research Programmes*, Volume 1: *Philosophical Papers*. Cambridge and New York: Cambridge University Press.

Land, R. (2002). "The So-called 'Land Letter.'" Retrieved from http://erlc.com/article/the-so-called-land-letter/

Land, R., & Perry, J. (2002). *For Faith and Family: Changing America by Changing the Family*. Nashville, TN: B & H Publishing Group.

Lawson, T. (1997a). "What Has Realism Got to Do with It?" *Economics and Philosophy* 15: 269–282.

———. (1997b). *Economics and Reality*. New York and Oxford: Routledge.

Layman, G. C., & Hussey, L. S. (2007). "George W. Bush and the Evangelicals: Religious Commitment and Partisan Change among Evangelical Protestants, 1960–2004." In D. E. Campbell (Ed.), *A Matter of Faith? Religion in the 2004 Presidential Election* (pp. 180–198). Washington, DC: The Brookings Institution.

Lichterman, P. (2005). *Elusive Togetherness: Church Groups Trying to Bridge America's Divisions*. Princeton, NJ: Princeton University Press.

Lichterman, P., Carter, P. L., & Lamont, M. (2009). "Race Bridging for Christ? Conservative Christians and Black–White Relations in Community Life." In S. G. Brint & J. R. Schroedel (Eds.), *Evangelicals and Democracy in America*, Volume 1: *Religion and Society* (pp. 187–220). New York: Russell Sage Foundation.

Lichterman, P., & Eliasoph, N. (2003). "Culture in Interaction." *American Journal of Sociology* 108 (4): 735–794.

Lichtman, A. (2008). *White Protestant Nation: The Rise of the American Conservative Movement*. New York: Atlantic Monthly Press.

Liebman, R., & Wuthow, R. (Eds.). (1983). *The New Christian Right: Mobilization and Legitimation*. Hawthorne, NY: Aldine Publishing.

Lindsay, D. M. (2007). *Faith in the Halls of Power: How Evangelicals Joined the American Elite*. Oxford and New York: Oxford University Press.

———. (2008). "Evangelicals in the Power Elite: Elite Cohesion Advancing a Movement." *American Sociological Review* 73: 60–82.

Lorentzen, L. J. (1980). "Evangelical Life-Style Concerns Expressed in Political Action." *Sociological Analysis* 41: 144–154.

Luhr, E. (2009). *Witnessing Suburbia: Conservatives and Christian Youth Culture*. Berkeley: University of California Press.

Luo, M., & Goodstein, L. (2007, May 21). "Emphasis Shifts for New Breed of Evangelicals." *New York Times*. Retrieved from http://www.nytimes.com/2007/05/21/us/21evangelical.html?scp=1&sq=Emphasis percent20Shifts percent20for percent20New percent20Breed percent20of percent20Evangelicals&st=cse

Malley, B. (2004). *How the Bible Works: An Anthropological Study of Evangelical Biblicism*. Walnut Creek, CA: Alta Mira Press.

Marsden, G. M. (1987). *Reforming Fundamentalism: Fuller Seminary and the New Evangelicalism*. Grand Rapids, MI: Wm. B. Eerdmans Publishing Company.

———. (2006). *Fundamentalism and American Culture* (2nd ed.). Oxford and New York: Oxford University Press.

Marsh, C. (1997). *God's Long Summer: Stories of Faith and Civil Rights*. Princeton, NJ: Princeton.

———. (2005). *The Beloved Community: How Faith Shapes Social Justice from the Civil Rights Movement to Today*. New York: Basic Books.

Marti, G. (2005). *A Mosaic of Believers: Diversity and Innovation in a Multiethnic Church*. Bloomington: Indiana University Press.

Marti, G., & Ganiel, G. (2014). *The Deconstructed Church: Understanding Emerging Christianity*. Oxford and New York: Oxford University Press.

Martin, J. L. (2011). *The Explanation of Social Action*. Oxford and New York: Oxford University Press.

McAdam, D. (1999). *Political Process and the Development of Black Insurgency*. Chicago: University of Chicago Press. (Original work published 1982)

McConkey, D. (2001). "Whither Hunter's Culture War? Shifts in Evangelical Morality, 1988–1998." *Sociology of Religion* 62 (2): 149–174.

McDannell, C. (1995). *Material Christianity: Religion and Popular Culture in America*. New Haven and London: Yale University Press.

McGrath, A. (1997). *The Genesis of Doctrine: A Study in the Foundation of Doctrinal Criticism*. Grand Rapids, MI: Wm. B. Eerdmans Publishing Company.

McGuire, M. B. (2008). *Lived Religion: Faith and Practice in Everyday Life*. Oxford and New York: Oxford University Press.

McKnight, S. (2007). "Five Streams of the Emerging Church." *Christianity Today*. Retrieved from http://www.christianitytoday.com/ct/2007/february/11.35.html

McLaren, B. D. (2001). *A New Kind of Christian: A Tale of Two Friends on a Spiritual Journey*. San Francisco: Jossey-Bass.

———. (2004). *A Generous Orthodoxy: Why I am a Missional, Evangelical, Post/Protestant, Liberal/Conservative, Mystical/Poetic, Biblical, Charismatic/Contemplative, Fundamentalist/Calvinist, Anabaptist/Anglican, Methodist, Catholic, Green, Incarnational, Depressed-Yet-Hopeful, Emergent, Unfinished Christian*. Grand Rapids, MI: Zondervan.

———. (2006). *The Secret Message of Jesus: Uncovering the Truth that Could Change Everything*. Nashville, TN: Thomas Nelson.

———. (2007). *Everything Must Change: Jesus, Global Crises, and a Revolution of Hope*. Nashville, TN: Thomas Nelson.

McLaren, B. D., & Campolo, A. (2003). *Adventures in Missing the Point: How the Culture-Controlled Church Neutered the Gospel*. Grand Rapids, MI: Zondervan.

McLaren, B. D., Rah, S., Mach, J., Blue, D., & Clawson, J. (2010, May). "Is the Emerging Church for Whites Only?" *Sojourners*.

McLaren, B. D., & Tickle, P. (2008). *Finding Our Way Again: The Return of the Ancient Practices*. Nashville, TN: Thomas Nelson.

McManus, E. (2001). *An Unstoppable Force: Daring to Become the Church God Had in Mind*. Grand Rapids, MI: Zondervan.

McRoberts, O. M. (2003). *Streets of Glory: Church and Community in a Black Urban Neighborhood*. Chicago: University of Chicago Press.

McVeigh, R., & Sobolewski, J. M. (2007). "Red Counties, Blue Counties, and Occupational Segregation by Sex and Race." *American Journal of Sociology 113* (2): 446–506.

Miles, M. B., & Huberman, A. M. (1994). *Qualitative Data Analysis: An Expanded Sourcebook*. Thousand Oaks, CA: SAGE Publications.

Mische, A. (2011). "Relational Sociology, Culture, and Agency." In J. Scott & P. Carrington (Eds.), *Sage Handbook of Social Network Analysis* (pp. 80–97). London: Sage Publications.

Mittelberg, M. (2001). *Building a Contagious Church: Revolutionizing the Way We View and Do Evangelism*. Grand Rapids, MI: Zondervan.

Mohler, A., Jr. (2005, June 20). "'A Generous Orthodoxy'—Is It Orthodox?" [web log comment]. Retrieved from http://www.albertmohler.com/2005/06/20/a-generous-orthodoxy-is-it-orthodox/

Moll, R. (2005, September 2). "The New Monasticism." *Christianity Today*. Retrieved from http://www.christianity today.com/ct/2005/september/16.38.html?start=2

———. (2007, May 17). "The New Monasticism Continues." *Christianity Today*. Retrieved from http://www.christianitytoday.com/gleanings/2007/may/new-monasticism-continues.html

Morris, A. D. (1984). *The Origins of the Civil Rights Movement*. New York: Free Press.

Myrdal, G. (1944). *An American Dilemma: The Negro Problem and Modern Democracy*. New York: Harper & Row.

"National Pastors Convention 2009 Speakers Announced!" (2008, April 24). [Web log comment]. Retrieved from http://zondervan.typepad.com/zondervan/2008/04/national-pastor.html

Niebuhr, H. R. (1929). *The Social Sources of Denominationalism*. New York: Meridian.

Nietzsche, F.W. (1989). *On the Genealogy of Morals*. (W. Kaufman & R. J. Hollingdale, Trans.). New York: Random House. (Original work published 1967)

Noll, M. (1988). *One Nation under God? Christian Faith and Political Action in America*. San Francisco: Harper and Row Publishers.

———. (1995). *The Scandal of the Evangelical Mind*. Grand Rapids, MI: Wm. B. Eerdmans Publishing.

———. (2001). *The Old Religion in the New World: The History of North American Christianity*. Grand Rapids, MI: Wm. B. Eerdmans Publishing.

Numbers, R.L. (1998). *Darwinism Comes to America*. Cambridge, MA: Harvard University Press.

Orsi, R. (1997). "Everyday Miracles: The Study of Lived Religion." In D. Hall (Ed.), *Lived Religion in America: Toward a History of Practice* (pp. 3–21). Princeton, NJ: Princeton University Press.

Packard, J. (2012). *The Emerging Church: Religion at the Margins.* Boulder, CO: First Forum Press.

Pagitt, D. (2005). *Church Re-Imagined: The Spiritual Formation of People in Communities of Faith.* Grand Rapids, MI: Zondervan.

———. (2007). "The Emerging Church and Embodied Theology." In R. Webber (Ed.) *Listening to the Beliefs of Emerging Churches: Five Perspectives* (pp. 117–143). Grand Rapids, MI: Zondervan.

Pally, M. (2011). *The New Evangelicals: Expanding the Vision of the Common Good.* Grand Rapids, MI: Wm. B. Eerdmans Publishing.

Park, J. Z., & Reimer, S. H. (2002). "Revisiting the Social Sources of American Christianity 1972–1998." *Journal for the Scientific Study of Religion 41* (4): 733–746.

Pattillo-McCoy, M. (1998). "Church Culture as a Strategy of Action in the Black Community." *American Sociological Review 63:* 767–784.

Perkins, J. (2007). *With Justice for All: A Strategy for Community Development.* Ventura, CA: Regal. (Original work published 1982)

Piper, J. and Grudem, W. (1991). *Recovering Biblical Manhood and Womanhood: A Response to Evangelical Feminism.* Wheaton, IL: Crossway Books.

Pohl, C. D. (1999). *Making Room: Recovering Hospitality as a Christian Tradition.* Grand Rapids, MI: Wm. B. Eerdmans Publishing Company.

Postone, M., LiPuma, E., & Calhoun, C. (Eds.). (1993). *Bourdieu: Critical Perspectives.* Chicago: University of Chicago Press.

Rah, S. (2009). *The Next Evangelicalism: Freeing the Church from Western Cultural Captivity.* Downers Grove, IL: InterVarsity Press.

Regnerus, M. D., & Smith, C. (1998). "Selective Deprivatization among American Religious Traditions: The Reversal of the Great Reversal." *Social Forces 76* (4): 1347–1372.

Rice, C. (2005). "Mark 4: Lament for Racial Divisions within the Church and our Communities Combined with the Active Pursuit of a Just Reconciliation." In The Rutba House (Ed.), *School(s) for Conversion: 12 Marks of a New Monasticism* (pp. 55–67). Eugene, OR: Cascade Books.

Richardson, J. T. (1982). "Financing the New Religions: Comparative and Theoretical Considerations." *Journal for the Scientific Study of Religion 21* (3): 255–268.

Richardson, T., & Davis, R. (1983). "Experiential Fundamentalism." *Journal of the American Academy of Religion 51:* 397–425.

Ricoeur, P. (1974). *The Conflict of Interpretations.* D. Ihde (Ed.). Evanston, IL: Northwest University Press.

———. (1976). *Interpretation Theory: Discourse and the Surplus of Meaning.* Fort Worth, TX: Texas Christian University Press.

Robertson, P. (2004). *The Ten Offenses.* Brentwood, TN: Integrity Publishers.

Rutba House (Eds.). (2005). *School(s) for Conversion: 12 Marks of a New Monasticism.* Eugene, OR: Cascade Books.

Samson, W. (2014). "The New Monasticism." In B. Steensland & P. Goff (Eds.), *The New Evangelical Social Engagement* (pp. 94–108). Oxford and New York: Oxford University Press.

Sandeen, E. R. (1970). *The Roots of Fundamentalism: British and American Millenarianism 1800–1930*. Chicago and London: University of Chicago Press.

Sargeant, K. H. (2000). *Seeker Churches: Promoting Traditional Religion in a Nontraditional Way*. New Brunswick, NJ: Rutgers University Press.

Schaeffer, F. (1982). *A Christian Manifesto*. Wheaton, IL: Crossway Books.

Schneiderhan, E. (2009). *Help for Help's Sake: Jane Addams and the Rise and Fall of Pragmatist Social Provision at Hull-House, 1889–1908*. (Doctoral Dissertation). Retrieved from Proquest Dissertations and Theses.

Schusterman, R. (Ed.). (1999). *Bourdieu, A Critical Reader*. Oxford: Blackwell.

Sewell, W. H., Jr. (1985). "Ideologies and Social Revolutions: Reflections on the French Case." *Journal of Modern History* 57 (1): 57–85.

———. (1999). "The Concept(s) of Culture." In V. Bonnell & L. Hunt (Eds.), *Beyond the Cultural Turn: New Directions in the Study of Society and Culture* (pp. 35–61). Berkeley: University of California Press.

Shea, W. (2004). *The Lion and the Lamb: Evangelicals and Catholics in America*. New York: Oxford University Press.

Sherkat, D. (2007). Review of the book *The Truth about Conservative Christians: What They Think and What They Believe*. *Journal for the Scientific Study of Religion* 46 (1): 137–139.

Sider, R. J. (2005). *The Scandal of the Evangelical Conscience: Why Are Christians Living Just Like the Rest of the World?* Grand Rapids, MI: Baker.

———. (2008). *I Am Not a Social Activist: Making Jesus the Agenda*. Scottsdale, PA: Herald Press.

Sider, R. J.Perkins, J.M., Gordon, W. L.Tizon, F. A. (2008). *Linking Arms, Linking Lives: How Urban-Suburban Partnerships Can Transform Communities*. Grand Rapids, MI: Baker Books.

Skocpol, T. (1985). "Cultural Idioms and Political Ideologies in the Revolutionary Reconstruction of State Power: A Rejoinder to Sewell." *Journal of Modern History* 57 (1): 86–96.

Smidt, C., & Kellstedt, P. (1992). "Evangelicals in the Post-Reagan Era: An Analysis of Evangelical Voters in the 1988 Election." *Journal for the Scientific Study of Religion* 31 (3): 330–338.

Smith, C. (2000). *Christian America? What Evangelicals Really Want*. Berkeley and Los Angeles: University of California Press.

———. (2003). *Moral, Believing Animals: Human Personhood and Culture*. Oxford and New York: Oxford University Press.

———. (2009). *Souls in Transition: The Religious and Spiritual Lives of Emerging Adults*. Oxford and New York: Oxford University Press.

Smith, C., & Emerson, M. O. (2000). *Divided by Faith: Evangelical Religion and the Problem\of Race in America*. New York: Oxford University Press.

Smith, C., with Emerson, M., Gallagher, S., Kennedy, P., & Sikkink, D.. (1998). *American Evangelicalism: Embattled and Thriving*. Chicago: University of Chicago Press.

Smith, D. E. (1987). *The Everyday World As Problematic*. Boston: Northeastern University Press.

"Sojourners Annual Report." (2007). Retrieved from http://www.sojo.net/about_us/2007_Annual_Report.pdf

"Sojourners Annual Report." (2008). Retrieved from http://sojo.net/sites/default/files/2008_Annual_Report.pdf

"Sojourners Annual Report." (2009). Retrieved from http://www.sojo.net/about_us/2009_Annual_Report.pdf

Steensland, B., & Goff, P. (2014a). "Introduction: The New Evangelical Social Engagement." In B. Steensland & P. Goff (Eds.), *The New Evangelical Social Engagement* (pp. 1–30). Oxford and New York: Oxford University Press.

———. (Eds.). (2014b). *The New Evangelical Social Engagement*. Oxford and New York: Oxford University Press.

Steensland, B., Park, J. Z., Regnerus, M., Robinson, L., Wilcox, W. B., & Woodberry, R. D. (2000). "The measure of American Religion: Improving the State of the Art." *Social Forces* 79: 291–318.

Steinmetz, G. (2004). "Odious Comparisons: Incommensurability, the Case Study, and 'Small N's' in Sociology." *Sociological Theory* (22) 3: 371–400.

Stetzer, E. (2006, January 10). "First Person: Understanding the Emerging Church." Retrieved from http://www.crosswalk.com/church/pastors-or-leadership/first-person-understanding-the-emerging-church-1372534.html

Stewart, D. T., & Richardson, J. T. (1999). "Mundane Materialism: How Tax Policies and Other Governmental Regulation Affected Beliefs and Practices of Jesus Movement Organizations." *Journal of the American Academy of Religion* 67 (4): 825–847.

Strauss, A. (1987). *Qualitative Analysis for Social Scientists*. New York: Cambridge University.

Streiker, L. (1971). *The Jesus Trip*. Nashville, TN: Abingdon.

Swartz, D. (2012). *The Moral Minority: The Evangelical Left in an Age of Conservatism*. Philadelphia: University of Pennsylvania Press.

Swidler, A. (1986). "Culture in Action: Symbols and Strategies." *American Sociological Review* 51 (2): 273–286.

———. (2001). *Talk of Love: How Culture Matters*. Chicago: University of Chicago Press.

Teles, S. M. (2008). *The Rise of the Conservative Legal Movement:The Battle for Control of the Law*. Princeton, NJ: Princeton University Press.

"The Chicago Declaration of Evangelical Concern." (1973). Retrieved from http://www.cpjustice.org/stories/storyReader$928

The Holy Bible, New International Version. (1973, 1978, 1984). Grand Rapids, MI: Zondervan.

"The Institute for Communitarian Policy Studies: About Us." (n.d.). Retrieved from http://www.gwu.edu/~ccps/about_us.html

"The New Evangelical Partnership for the Common Good: Initiatives." (n.d.). Retrieved from http://www.newevangelicalpartnership.org/?q=node/1

Thumma, S., & Travis, D. (2007). *Beyond the Megachurch Myths.* San Francisco: Jossey Bass.

Tickle, P. (2008). *The Great Emergence: How Christianity is Changing and Why.* Grand Rapids, MI: Baker.

Vaisey, S. (2007). "Structure, Culture, and Community: The Search for Belonging in 50 Urban Communes." *American Sociological Review 72* (6): 851–873

———. (2009). "Motivation and Justification: A Dual-Process Model of Culture in Action." *American Journal of Sociology 114* (6): 1675–1715.

Vaisey, S. and Lizardo, O. (2010). "Can Cultural Worldviews Influence Network Composition?" *Social Forces 88* (4): 1595–1618.

Wald, K. D., Owen, D. E., & Hill, S. S., Jr. (1989). "Evangelical Politics and Status Issues." *Journal for the Scientific Study of Religion 28* (1): 1–16.

Wald, K., & Scher, K. (1997). "Losing by Winning." In M. J. Rozell & C. Wilcox (Eds.), *God at the Grass Roots, 1996: The Christian Right in American Elections* (pp. 79–98). Lanham, MD: Rowman & Littlefield.

Wallis J. (2005). *God's Politics: Why the Right Gets it Wrong and the Left Doesn't Get It.* San Francisco: Harpers.

Wacquant, L. J. D. (1993). "From Ruling Class to Field of Power: An Interview with Pierre Bourdieu on *La Noblesse d'État.*" *Theory, Culture, and Society 10* (3): 19–44.

———. (1998). "Pierre Bourdieu." In R. Stones (Ed.), *Key Sociological Thinkers* (pp. 215–229). New York: New York University Press.

Warner, R. S. (1993). "Work in Progress Toward a New Paradigm for the Sociological Study of Religion in the United States." *American Journal of Sociology 98* (5): 1044–1093.

———. (2005). *A Church of Our Own: Disestablishment and Diversity in American Religion.* Piscataway, NJ: Rutgers.

———. (2014). "Evangelicals of the 1970s and 2000s: What's the Same, What's Different, and What's Urgent." In B. Steensland & P. Goff (Eds.), *The New Evangelical Social Engagement* (pp. 280–291). Oxford and New York: Oxford University Press.

Warren, R. (1995). *The Purpose-Driven Church: Growth Without Compromising Your Message or Mission.* Grand Rapids, MI: Zondervan.

———. (2002). *The Purpose-Driven Life: What On Earth Am I Here For?* Grand Rapids, MI: Zondervan.

———. (2008, August 16). "Saddleback Civil Forum on the Presidency" [Event Transcript]. Retrieved from http://transcripts.cnn. com/TRANSCRIPTS/0808/16/se.02.html

Webber, R. (2007). *Listening to the Beliefs of Emerging Churches: Five Perspectives.* Grand Rapids, MI: Zondervan.

Weber, M. (1958). *The Protestant Ethic and the Spirit of Capitalism.* (T. Parsons, Trans.). New York: Charles Scribners. (Original work published 1905)

———. (1993). *The Sociology of Religion.* (E. Fischoff, Trans.). Boston, MA: Beacon Press. (Original work published 1922)

———. (2004). *The Essential Weber: A Reader.* S. Whimster (Ed.). New York: Routledge.

Wilcox, C., Merolla, L. M., & Beer, D. (2006). "Saving Marriage by Banning Marriage." In J. C. Green, M. J. Rozell, & C. Wilcox (Eds.), *The Values Campaign? The Christian Right and the 2004 Elections* (pp. 56–75). Washington, DC: Georgetown University Press.

Wilford, J. (2012). *Sacred Subdivisions: The Postsuburban Transformation of American Evangelicalism.* New York: New York University Press.

Williams, D. K. (2014). "Prolifers of the Left: Progressive Evangelicals' Campaign against Abortion." In B. Steensland & P. Goff (Eds.), *The New Evangelical Social Engagement* (pp. 200–220). Oxford and New York: Oxford University Press.

Wolfe, A. (1998). *One Nation, After All: What Middle Class Americans Really Think about God, Country, Family, Racism, Welfare, Immigration, Homosexuality, Work, the Right, the Left, and Each Other.* New York: Viking Penguin.

———. (2003). *The Transformation of American Religion: How We Actually Live our Faith.* New York: Free Press.

Wolpert, A. (2010). "Exploring the New Monasticism." *Relevant Magazine.* Retrieved from http://www.relevantmagazine.com/god/church/features/21029-the-new-monastics

Wood, F.G. (1991). *The Arrogance of Faith: Christianity and Race in America from the Colonial Era to the Twentieth Century.* Boston, MA: Northeastern University Press.

Wood, M., & Hughes, M. (1984). "The Moral Basis of Moral Reform: Status Discontent vs. Culture and Socialization as Explanations of Anti-Pornography Social Movement Adherence." *American Sociological Review* 49: 86–99.

Worthen, M. (2008, February 3). "The Unexpected Monks." *The Boston Globe.* Retrieved from http://boston.com/bostonglobe/ideas/articles/2008/02/03/the_unexpected_monks/?page=1

———. (2013). *Apostles of Reason: The Crisis of Authority in American Evangelicalism.* Oxford and New York: Oxford University Press.

Wright, E. O. (2000). *Class Counts: Comparative Studies in Class Analysis.* Cambridge and New York: Cambridge University Press.

———. (2010). *Envisioning Real Utopias.* New York and London: Verso Books.

Wright, N. T. (1996). *Jesus and the Victory of God*. Minneapolis, MN: Fortress Press.

———. (1997). *What Saint Paul Really Said: Was Saul of Tarsus the Real Founder of Christianity?* Grand Rapids, MI: Wm. B. Eerdmans Publishing.

———. (2008). *Surprised by Hope: Rethinking Heaven, the Resurrection, and the Mission of the Church*. New York: HarperCollins.

Wuthnow, R. (1983). "The Political Rebirth of American Evangelicals." In R. Liebman & R. Wuthow (Eds.), *The New Christian Right* (pp. 167–185). Hawthorne, NY: Aldine Publishing.

———. (1988). *The Restructuring of American Religion*. Princeton, NJ: Princeton University Press.

———. (1989). *Communities of Discourse: Ideology and Social Structure in the Reformation, the Enlightenment, and European Socialism*. Cambridge, MA: Harvard University Press.

———. (1994). *Sharing the Journey: Support Groups and America's New Quest for Community*. New York: Free Press.

———. (2007). *After the Baby Boomers: How Twenty- and Thirty-Somethings Are Shaping the Future of American Religion*. Princeton, NJ: Princeton University Press.

Young, M. P. (2002). "The Religious Birth of U.S. National Social Movements." *American Sociological Review* 67 (5): 660–688.

Index

Addams, Jane, 67–69
abortion, evangelical views of, 9–10,
    22, 49–50, 61, 88, 99–104, 110,
    119–120, 144, 194–210, 214, 219,
    221–223, 286–287, 320n258,
    331n10, 331n11
anti-bureacratic rational organization,
    226, 253, 257, 269
arts, 7–8, 15, 68, 91, 93, 121, 167–169,
    173, 227, 233–240, 242–245,
    262–264, 273
Alexander, Jeffrey, 277, 322n319,
    329n52, 331n7, 334n52

Bellah, Robert, 222, 273–74, 336n97
Bielo, James, 17–18, 75–77, 299fn50,
    300n66, 301n89, 311n42, 311n44,
    312n55, 318n228, 319n236,
    319n239, 320n249
    and dialogic evangelicalism, 76–77,
    114–117
Bourdieu, Pierre, 19–21, 27, 29–30,
    72–81, 111–113, 126–130, 159,
    172, 238–240, 277–278, 299n57,
    318n230, 322n317, 323n321,
    323n328, 325n396, 337n13,
    337n24
    See also American evangelical field,
    capital, field theory

Bryan, William Jennings, 40–43
Bush, George W., 1, 9, 51, 103, 125, 153,
    198, 210, 219, 313n75

Campolo, Tony, 54, 85, 91, 99, 104,
    108, 142, 151, 154–156, 327n438
capital, 72–74, 81–87, 116, 122–123,
    126–127, 130, 152, 220–221,
    239–240, 281, 285
    cultural, 72, 74, 81, 83, 170
    economic, 72, 81, 83, 127, 239
    political, 81, 83–85
    specific (people), 82–87, 143, 147
    symbolic, 72–73, 82–83, 86–87,
    134–136, 145–148, 239
capitalism, evangelical views on, 34,
    44–46, 51, 64, 67, 105, 119, 214,
    222
celebratory asceticism, 23, 160, 226,
    249, 252–253, 269, 283
Chicago Declaration of Evangelical
    Social Concern, 54–56, 85,
    303n30, 307n156
Christian America, 10, 17, 41–42, 51,
    87, 95–98, 110, 119, 206, 212
Christian Right
    origins and identity, 8–11, 48–51,
    306n125, 306n122, 312n47,
    313n76,

Christian Right (*cont.*)
  position in evangelical field, 82–85,
    118–125
  position-takings, religious and
    political, 87–88, 95–98,
    99–100, 102–105, 118–122,
    125–126, 153, 190, 194–195,
    197–200, 203–204,
    208–212, 241–242, 285–297,
    298n42, 299n55, 331n110,
    337n27
Claiborne, Shane, 87, 91–92, 98,
  106–108, 113, 131, 141–144,
  148–151, 153–154, 164
Collectives, Urban Monastery, 168,
  227, 235, 244, 250–251, 257–258,
  262–263
conflation, downwards and upwards,
  19, 37, 39–40, 280, 300n59,
  327fn443
contradictory cultural location, 22, 104,
  143–144, 151, 155–156, 159–160,
  199–203, 217–219, 222–224, 286,
  331n7
consistent ethic of life, 103, 144, 219,
  223, 317n188, 332n50
culture war, 8–13, 47, 79, 96, 139, 144,
  199, 202, 298n20

D-Groups, Urban Monastery, 186,
  249–251, 257–261, 264, 272
Durkheim, Emile, 241, 245
Dobson, James, 9, 50, 84, 101

Elisha, Omri, 18, 312n47, 312n53,
  317n188
emerging church
  critiques of, 124–125, 145–148, 287,
    325n394
  Emergent, 137, 145–148
  internal conflict, 145–148

and megachurch evangelicalism,
    91–93, 95, 120–122, 130–133,
    136–138, 320n267, 321n277
  origins and identity, 76–77, 86,
    145–146, 311n44, 314n85,
    314n88, 333n6
  position in evangelical field, 82–83,
    86, 118–125
  position-takings, religious and
    political, 92–95, 110, 114–115,
    120–121, 136–138, 142–143,
    279, 286–287, 310n29, 312n47,
    312n54, 315n117, 319n236,
    325n384, 325n386
Emerson, Michael O., 63–65, 179,
  300n69
engaged orthodoxy, 135–141, 157–158,
  249
environmentalism, evangelical views
  of, 13, 18, 85, 88, 101, 103–104,
  106, 110, 150, 164, 199–200,
  214–215, 223, 275, 286, 314n84,
  328n38, 337n27
evangelical left
  origins and identity, 54–56, 219–221
  position in evangelical field, 83, 85,
    118–125
  position-takings, religious and
    political, 13–14, 110, 98–99,
    102–103, 107–108, 118–121,
    141–144, 154–155, 276,
    285–286, 303n36, 320n258
evangelicalism, defining, 79–80,
  112–118

Falwell, Jerry, 9, 48–49, 84, 104, 125,
  297n3, 312n47
field, American evangelical
  avant-garde positions, 21, 31, 115, 125,
    132–133, 142–145, 170–172, 176,
    220–221, 245

boundaries, 18, 20, 29, 40–43,
65–69, 82, 109–114, 116–117,
124, 142–152, 198, 219–221,
278–282, 299n58, 313n63,
318n228
challenger strategies, 73, 115,
123–126, 131–133, 136, 140, 143
classification schemes within, 29,
65, 69, 130, 146–155, 198,
241–244, 325n396
coalitions of the dominated,
142–145, 219–221
consecration, 122–124, 130–132, 141,
145–146, 221
conservation strategies, 73, 123–127,
136, 141, 321n272, 321n277
doxa, 20, 29, 38–39, 59, 65, 69,
109–111, 124–125, 134–141,
144–148, 157–159, 178, 182–185,
188–190, 195, 249, 264,
278–280, 282–283, 318n228
and ecumenism, 141–145, 154–155,
163–164, 220, 325n386, 333n6
evangelical book culture, 74–76,
82, 311n42, 311n45, 311n46,
326n421
founding points of view, 29, 39, 65,
69, 79, 92, 146, 311n44,
312n52
forms of capital, 81–87
heresy/heterodoxy, 124–126, 142,
144–148
and historical struggle, 20–21, 29,
32–33, 39–41, 43–44, 47, 51,
65–69, 111–114, 130, 152,
190–193, 284–288
permanent revolution, 133, 136–141,
288
politicization, 91–92, 152–158,
197–199, 215–221, 284–285,
327n438

relative autonomy, 39–40, 19–21, 72,
112–113, 127, 151–158, 198–199,
218–219, 284–285, 324n346,
field theory
artistic and religious field
homologies, 237–241
and habitus, 126, 325n396
as relational analysis, 21, 73–81, 108,
114–126, 156, 310n23, 312n55,
323n321
and relational ethnography, 301n81
and studying evangelicalism, 19–20,
72–81, 111–118
and textual analysis, 74–76, 78,
311n45, 319n236
See also American evangelical field,
capital, reductionism
figure 3.1, Neo-monasticism in the field
of American evangelicalism, 83
figure 4.1a, Evangelism priority to
holistic mission, 183
figure 4.1b, Individualism to
communiatarianism through
symbolic prioritization of the
Trinity, 184
figure 7.1a, Unified model of
evangelical position-takings, 280
figure 7.1b, Practical social
hermeneutic model of evangelical
meaning construction, 281
Finney, Charles, 36–37, 62, 303n36
fundamentalism / conservative
Protestantism, 40, 66–69
and the Bible, 34–39, 42, 44, 46–48,
and evangelism priority, 32, 35–41,
43–44, 46–47, 60–63
and race, 33, 35–37, 46, 50, 56, 62–64
and relationship to business sector,
32, 39, 44–46, 47–52
and religious nationalism, 8–11,
32–33, 41, 47, 56

fundamentalist-modernist struggle
  enduring effects on American
      evangelical field, 20, 29–30,
      32–33, 41, 47–48, 51, 65–69,
      190–191
  over evolutionary theory, 37–43
  racial roots, 35–37
  theological roots, 37–40
  and World War I, 40–42
Fuller, Charles, 43–45, 52, 304n72,
fuzzy logic of practice, 20, 258, 268,
      277–279, 283, 337n13

gay marriage. *See* homosexuality
God Story, 185–188, 264
Graham, Billy, 44–47, 58, 62–63, 101,
      157
Greig, Pete, 165–168

Henry, Carl F.H., 46
holistic communitarianism, 7–8, 16,
      21–22, 31, 33, 90–91, 109, 137,
      159–160, 172–175, 245–247,
      257–258, 281–283
  contradictions and limits,
      269–274
  and politics, 22, 99, 143–144,
      194–195, 202–204, 222–224
  as a strategy of action, 23, 178–181,
      225–226, 231, 257, 269
  as a theological meaning system,
      21–22, 178–184, 186–187,
      192–193, 277, 281–282
  and Trinitarian theology, 169,
      173–174, 182–184, 186–188,
      225, 257–258, 264–269,
      277–278, 282, 330fn60,
      333fn12
holistic mission, 23, 54, 90, 95, 121,
      138, 160, 172, 182–184, 225–226,
      257, 269, 283
  and the arts, 233–237

and deconstructing the sacred/
      secular divide, 226–227,
      241–246
  and hospitality, 228–233
homosexuality, evangelical views of,
      9–10, 18, 22, 49–50, 96, 99–103,
      119, 144–147, 194–197, 203–205,
      209–210, 215, 221, 286, 320n258,
      331n10
Hull House, 67–69
Hunter, James Davison, 10–12, 71–72,
      75, 139–141, 218, 297n13, 298n19,
      310n31, 319n236
Hybels, Bill, 14–15, 82–84, 100–101,
      120, 132–134, 275

innerworldly asceticism, 23, 128, 160,
      238, 248–253, 269
Iraq, war in, 14, 103, 149–150, 197,
      211–212

Jesus People
  and neo-monastic evangelicalism,
      67, 134, 167–168, 217–218, 247,
      272–273
  origins and identity, 57–60, 331n22

Kane, Anne, 179–182, 278, 330n67,
      337n13
Kennedy, D. James, 50, 84, 96–97,
      100, 105
Kimball, Dan, 92–93, 131, 138, 145,
      314n85

Lahaye, Beverly, 50, 84
Lahaye, Tim, 48, 50
Land, Richard, 9, 84, 96, 99–100, 105,
      313n75
leadership, gender egalitarian, 55, 100,
      105–106, 119, 205, 264–269, 287,
      338n41
Lindsay, D. Michael, 15, 47, 319n236

Marti, Gerardo, 298n40, 310n29, 312n47, 319n236, 325n384, 325n386, 333n6, 335n80

McLaren, Brian, 93–94, 124–125, 131, 142, 145, 148

meaning system, 21–23, 159–160, 174, 178–183, 186, 225, 246, 268–274, 277–283, 337n13

megachurch evangelicalism
  and business culture, 52, 71, 89–90, 95, 121, 123–124, 137, 240–241, 254–257, 279, 315n100
  critiques of, 77–78, 91–93, 95, 120–124, 130–133, 136–138, 143, 167–168, 174–177, 240–241, 254–257
  origins and identity, 51–53, 156,
  position in evangelical field, 82–84, 118–125
  position-takings, religious and political, 13–15, 78–79, 88–90, 100–101, 110, 120–124, 132–134, 136–137, 286, 312n47, 320n260, 323n339
  and theological individualism/ evangelism priority, 34, 52–54, 88–95, 100–101, 312n53
  and therapeutic personalism, 52, 71, 79, 137, 315n100

modernism / liberal Protestantism, 40, 66–69
  and the Bible, 38–41, 44
  See also social gospel

Moody, D.L., 34–35, 38–39, 43, 48, 52, 62–63, 101, 157, 302n19

moral cosmology theory, 17, 20, 22, 29–33, 60–67, 106, 144, 159–160, 174, 178–179, 202–203, 222–223, 270–273, 283–287
  and evangelical exceptionalism, 20, 22, 44, 61–62, 65–67, 284, 287

neo-monasticism
  origins and identity, 15–16, 67–68, 70, 161–165
  position in evangelical field, 81–83, 86–87, 118–125
  position-takings, religious and political, 20–23, 89–92, 97–98, 102, 105–109, 122, 130–131, 138–139, 141–144, 147–150, 159–160, 172–174, 193–199, 200–215, 221–224, 265–269, 286–287

New Friars, 6, 161–162

Obama, Barack, 1, 12, 14, 22, 85, 195–196, 199–204, 208, 210, 215, 221

Ockenga, Harold, 43–46, 304n72

Pagitt, Doug, 94–95, 145, 148, 151, 314n95

postmodern, 86, 92–95, 121, 123–125, 145–146, 246, 279, 320n267

poverty and inequality, evangelical views of, 2–5, 14, 33–34, 55, 67–68, 70, 91, 103–109, 119, 122, 150, 162, 191–194, 213–215, 223, 227–232, 250, 276–277, 286

practical social hermeneutic, 19–20, 23, 112, 276–283, 300n63, 318n225, 336n8

premillennial dispensationalism, 34, 38–41, 45, 48, 62–63, 217, 302n15, 332n25

privilege of youth, 133–136, 324n346

race, evangelical views of, 14–15, 32, 35–37, 46, 50, 54–56, 58, 62–64, 80, 87, 91, 98, 101, 103–104, 106, 110, 144, 150, 163, 179, 200, 214–215, 219–220, 227, 229, 231, 275, 286–287, 302n25, 303n30, 338n41, 313n58 reclaiming America for Christ, 11, 84, 88, 95, 99, 101, 120

Red Letter Christians, 142, 151, 154–156, 288, 326n421, 337n31

reductionism
and field theory, 19, 23, 74, 112, 126–128, 156–158, 280, 300n59, 319n234, 322n313, 322n319
and status resentment theory, 11–12, 19, 152, 156, 327fn430

reflexivity, 26–27, 301n94

religious consistency theory, 31, 153, 283–285, 297n13

religious economies theory, 113–114, 300fn2

religious nationalism, 8–11, 32–33, 41, 47, 56, 87, 97–99, 119, 122, 211–212, 275, 286

Robertson, Pat, 49–50, 84, 95–97, 100, 104–105, 306n125

sacred/secular divide, 8, 174–175, 236, 249, 260. *See also* holistic mission

secular humanism, 97–99, 115, 220, 241

Sider, Ron, 54–56, 85, 99, 104, 107–108, 142

Smith, Christian, 17, 26, 63–65, 75, 113–114, 179, 207–208, 226

single-issue voting, 22, 99–103, 119–122, 159, 194, 204, 286

social gospel, 37, 40, 43, 47, 66, 68–69, 173–174, 190–193

structural-hermeneutic, approach to cultural analysis, 180–182, 277–281

Swartz, David R., 17, 218, 299n58, 307n156, 328n38, 331n23

Swidler, Ann, 65, 129, 179–181, 225, 246, 277–278, 333n1, 336n97, 337n13

subcultural identity theory, 113–114

table 3.1, Textual analysis summary (approximated number of counts), 110

theological communitarianism, 17, 20, 22, 29, 32–33, 60–62, 64–66, 106–107, 179
See also holistic communitarianism

theological individualism, 16–17, 20–21, 32–33, 39, 60–66, 87, 101, 109, 120, 178–179, 182–184, 193, 212–213, 276, 281, 284, 287, 300n69, 318n219, 325n384, 329n45
and American individualism, 63, 90–91, 144, 222–223, 245, 272–274, 327n438
and evangelism priority, 34–35, 43–47, 62–63, 88–89, 157, 182–186, 193–194, 312n53
and racial inequality, 35–37, 62–64, 179

Wallis, Jim, 13, 54–56, 85, 98–99, 103–104, 108, 113, 119, 141–144, 148, 153–154, 276, 320n258

war and peace, evangelical views of, 14–15, 40–41, 90, 96–99, 102–103, 119, 149–150, 163, 196–197, 210–213, 215, 219–220, 313n75

Warren, Rick, 14–15, 52–53, 82–84, 88–90, 92, 120, 123–124, 131–134, 276, 286

Weber, Max, 23, 26, 80, 128–130, 160, 225, 237–239, 246–257, 269, 277, 322n313, 322n317, 337n22

Whitefield, George, 35–36

Wilson-Hargrove, Jonathon, 87, 163